MW00490628

Calling All Lightfoots

A LIGHTFOOT FAMILY HISTORY

Researched by
Edith Ellen Williams

Compiled by
Mary Edd Morton

HERITAGE BOOKS
2007

HERITAGE BOOKS
AN IMPRINT OF HERITAGE BOOKS, INC.

Books, CDs, and more—Worldwide

For our listing of thousands of titles see our website
at
www.HeritageBooks.com

Published 2007 by
HERITAGE BOOKS, INC.
Publishing Division
65 East Main Street
Westminster, Maryland 21157-5026

International Standard Book Number: 978-0-7884-2451-9

ANCESTORS

If you could see your ancestors
All standing in a row,
Would you be proud of them?
Or don't you really know?

Strange discoveries are sometimes made,
In climbing the family tree.
Occasionally one is found in line
Who shocks his progeny.

If you could see your ancestors
All standing in a row,
Perhaps there might be one or two
You wouldn't care to know.

Now turn the question right about,
And take another view.
When you shall meet your ancestors
Will they be proud of you?

FOREWORD

This compilation of the lineage of the Lightfoot family who are descended from John Lightfoot and his wife Ann Goodrich, has taken hundreds of hours of research, hundreds of dollars, and much persistence. It has been intriguing, greatly rewarding, and fun. In order that this work may not be lost, we are passing it along to our family.

To help you understand a little better your tremendous background of people that made history, here are a few explanations.

The ancestry as shown in this book is easily followed, as it is shown in America. The English ancestry may be explained when it is remembered that the families of both kings and barons intermarried only with royalty and nobility, so that if you are descended from one of the barons or kings, you are descended from many more.

As to the records, the ancients Druids kept most accurate records. The Roman Catholic Church also kept records of births, marriages, and deaths. It is said that the English never throw away anything, their records are stored mainly in Somerset House in London.

When you find Surety Barons it means that of the Barons of Runnymede, 25 were chosen to see that King John kept the laws of the Magna Charta to which he had agreed. They were called Sureties.

If you will turn to the page showing the generations from Saer de Quincey to Ann Goodrich, you will see new families added with each new marriage. Turning through the pages following, you will find the lineage of each of these new families. For instance John de Lacie, who married the granddaughter of Saer de Quincey, etc.

You will find your ancestors in every important development in the church and in the nation's government. May it inspire you to further the work of Christianity and also the enlightenment in your own day and age.

Edith Ellen Williams

iv

TABLE OF CONTENTS

Ancestors   iii
Foreword   iv
Acknowledgements   vii
I.   Early Lightfoots in England and America   1
II.   Lightfoot Family Chart
        Heraldry and Crests   13
III.   Richard Lightfoot, Reverend, 1562-1625
        Married Jane Jones   23
IV.   John Lightfoot, Esquire, 1598-1648
        Married Elizabeth Phillips   33
V.   John Lightfoot, 1622-1686
        Married Elizabeth Tailor   39
VI.   John Lightfoot, Colonel, 1646-1707
        Married Ann Goodrich   41
VII.   The Story of the White House   77
VIII.   Philip Lightfoot, 1648-1708
        Married Alice Corbin   89
IX.   Goodrich Lightfoot, Colonel, 1685-1738
        Married Mary Chew   105
X.   William Lightfoot, Major 1720-1805
        Married Elizabeth Barrow   125
XI.   John B. Lightfoot, Captain, 1752-1850
        Married Lavina Duncan   139
XII.   Hannah Lightfoot and George III   167
XIII.   The Chew, Duncan, Barrow, Stone, and Minor
        Line of Descent   173
XIV.   The Goodrich Line of Descent   189
XV.   A Priceless Heritage—MAGNA CHARTA   193
XVI.   The Surety Barons   199
XVII.   Saire de Quincey   217
XVIII. The Royal Ancestry of Margaret Bellemont, Wife of
        Saire de Quincey   231
XIX.   Lightfoot Tidbits   249
XX.   A Tribute to Edith Ellen Williams   265

v

Bibliography   ix
Index   xiii

ACKNOWLEDGMENTS

Edith Ellen Williams deserves first mention in this list of acknowledgments. She spent at least fifty years researching Lightfoots. She died at the age of 92 unable to finish her life long dream. And my aunt who is now deceased, Mrs. Blanche Tarpley, who sent me letters which helped so very much in locating many of the descendants.

Cathy Thompson from Duncanville was executor of Ellen's will and made sure I got all the material. Someone had disarranged her notes. As a little girl Cathy had known and loved Ellen Williams. As an adult she helped take care of Ellen and was with her when she died.

I wish to thank Lynda Davis for her typing of this book and Catherine White, my cousin in Tennessee who helped me to get the copyright for it.

John Lewis Beckham, a nephew of Ellen Williams, did the research and pictures of Stoke Bruerne, England.

My good friend Joe Ziegler from Cold Spring, Texas made the sketch of the "Lightfoot" shown on the cover. The sketch shows how the family got its name. He also gave me the boost I needed to finish this book.

To my cousin Leslie Oakes, from Virginia, for sending me all of the material for the chapter about the White House. We had many long telephone calls to keep me on track while putting Ellen's notes together. Laura Lightfoot Miller of Virginia, a Lightfoot descendant who contacted me of several mistakes that where being put on the Internet. Michael Shaver a Lightfoot descendant from Wisconsin who sent me some information and much encouragement.

And a special thanks to the many Lightfoot descendants who have helped with, furnished data or given me the encouragement I needed.

Mostly I thank my husband Elwyn Morton for proofreading and giving me all the love, patience and encouragement that I have needed while trying to put Ellen's notes back in order so that I could fulfill her wish to have this book published.

Mary Morton

CHAPTER I

EARLY LIGHTFOOTS IN ENGLAND and AMERICA

The name LIGHTFOOT was originally used as a nickname having reference to the light and springy tread or agility in running of the first bearer or messenger for the King. It is found in the ancient English records in the various forms of Lithefot, Lightefot, Lyghtfot, Lightefote, Litefoot, Lightefoot, Lightfoote, Lightfoot; and others, of which the last form mentioned is the most generally accepted in America today.

Families of this name were to be found at early dates in the English Shires of Kent, Cambridge, Oxford, Northampton, York and London and were, for the most part, of the landed Gentry or Yeomanry of Great Britain.

Among the earliest records of the name in England were those of William Lightfot of Cambridgeshire in 1273; Henry Lithfot of Oxfordshire about 1301; and Willelmus or William Lightfote of Yorkshire in 1379.

The will for a Robert Lightfoote, which reads as:

The 7th day of June 1693, I Robert Lightfoote of the Parish of St. Giles's, Cripplegate in co. Midd. gunner, do make my wife Anne Lightfoote, my lawful attorney, to receive all prize money, wages, etc., due to me, and I also make her my sole executrix.
Witness: John Boulton, John Aynge.
Proved at London 9 June 1703.

In the ADMINISTRATION ACT BOOKS were these various entries pertaining to the Lightfoot name.

On the 8th day of April 1695 a commission to Lucy Whitton alias Lightfoot (wife of Francis Whitton) sister of Francis Lightfoote who died lately in the Royal Ship the Nonshuch, bachelor, etc.,
On the 9th day of June 1707 a commission to Margaret Lightfoot relict of William Lightfoot late of the parish of St. Giles in the Fields in co. Midd. but who died in the merchant ship the Blessing of Liverpool (sic) etc.,

On the 20th day of June 1707 a commission to Sarah Lightfoot relict of John Lightfoot, late of the parish of St. Margarets, Westminster, in co. Midd. etc.,

On the 16th day of September 1713 a commission to John Lightfoot son of Edmund Lightfoot, late of the parish of St. Sepulchre's London, widower, etc.,

On the 5th day of April 1715, a commission to Joseph Stanwix, gent. attorney of Elizabeth Nicholson widow, sister and next of kin of Thomas Lightfoot late of the City of Carlisle in co. Cumberland, bachelor, to administer the goods, etc., of the said deceased, to the use of the said Elizabeth, now living in co. Cumberland.

John Lightfoot (1602-1675),[1] (who may or may not be related to our line) was an English Herbalist and Rabbinical Scholar. He was the Vice Chancellor of Cambridge University (1654); Prebendary of Ely (1668); assisted Brian Walton with the *Polyglot Bible*, and the author *of Harmonies of the Gospels and Old Testament*, and of *Horae Hebraicae et Talmudicae* (5 volumes, 1658-1674) his life work.

Our first documented Lightfoot ancestor began with Reverend Richard Lightfoot born in 1562. He was minister of Stoke Bruerne, Northamptonshire, England. He was installed 29 April 1601 by the Bishop of Canterbury and died 28 November 1625.

John Lightfoot, Esquire, Richard's eldest son was a Barrister at Law of Gray's Inn.

John Lightfoot, son of John Lightfoot, Esq. was captain of one of His Majesty Ships and died in 1686/87 at Surinam in the West Indies. He married Elizabeth Tailor.

John Lightfoot, eldest son of John Lightfoot, Captain, often called John the "Immigrant" by his descendants, came to Virginia in 1670 with his younger brother Philip. There will be more about the brothers later in the book.

The descendants of these and of other branches of the family in America have spread to all parts of the country and have aided as much in the development of the nation as their ancestors aided in its founding. They have been noted for their energy, industry, integrity, piety, perseverance, reckless courage, resourcefulness, initiative, and leadership.

The most popular male names of the family were William, John, Henry, Richard, Francis, Robert, George, Edward, Edmund, Thomas, Goodrich, and Philip.

---

[1] Webster's Biographical Dictionary, G&C Merrian County, p. 899.

The following were notes found in the Vestry and Register from Culpeper County, Virginia.

In 1757, the Vestry met at the Vestry House and the following gentlemen were present: Rev. Mr. Thompson, minister, Wm. Lightfoot, Robert Green, Goodrich Lightfoot, Wm. Green, Jas. Pendleton, Francis Slaughter, Robert Slaughter, Philip Clayton, Benj. Roberts and Henry Field[2].

In 1758, Wm. Lightfoot[3] removed out of the parish.

In 1761 Goodrich Lightfoot and Wm. Williams chosen churchwardens for the ensuing year and John Green, Collector.

In 1765 Goodrich Lightfoot and Wm. Williams chosen churchwardens for the ensuing year.

November 23, 1768 James Pendleton and Goodrich Lightfoot II, churchwardens for ensuing year and Cadwallader appointed vestryman in place of Robert Slaughter, deceased.

In 1770 leave is given to Samuel Henning to build a gallery in Buck Run Church at his own expense. The wardens are instructed to advertise the glebe for sale in the Virginia Gazette and to buy a more convenient site for a glebe. The glebe was sold to Samuel Henning for one hundred and ninety pounds current money. Goodrich Lightfoot and others report they had viewed several tracts of land and that Francis Slaughter's or George Catlett's was the most convenient for a glebe. The vestry adjourned to meet at Lawrence Catlett's and decided upon the site. John Green Vestryman in the room of William Green, deceased.

The following are tidbits found in several books and periodicals, which list or contain information about the Lightfoot.

Gentlemen of Long-tailed Families – William Lightfoot – 1788[4].

The following appeared in Purdie and Dixon's Gazette: March 14, 1771.

Yesterday was married in Henrico, Mr. William Carter, third son of John Carter, aged 23, to Mrs. Sarah Ellyson, relict of Mr. Gerard Ellyson, dead, aged 85 a sprightly old tit with three thousand pounds fortune.

Robert Ellyson, probably son of Robert Gerard Ellyson resided in New Kent County and was probably father of Robert Ellyson, who married Sarah, sister of John Clopton and had Anne Clopton Ellyson, who married first WILLIAM LIGHTFOOT, and second John Colgin of Charles City Co.

---

[2] Notes from Culpeper County, Virginia, by Slaughter (on Microfilm).
[3] This usually meant the person, persons or family moved.
[4] Gentlemen Freeholders, Chapel Hill, Gen. 975.5, by Chas. S. Sydnor.

In the St. Peter's Parish Vestry and Register of 1684 through 1786, in New Kent and James City County, Virginia were the following articles.

52 – *It is ordered that ye Churchwardens forthwith endeavor to find out some person that may take and keep Anne Chapman, now at Lightfoot's house, at as little charge to ye parish as they can.*

50-51 – *At a vestry held at the upper Church of St. Peters Parish in ye behalf of ye said parish this 16th day of November 1696.*

To Mr. John Lightfoot for keeping Anne Chapman 14 months and for salving and trouble with her. £450.

20 – *The severall Persons name in Companys that were ordered to procession and Re-mark ye bounds of Each Man's Land,*

Viz: William Harman, Mr. Lightfoot

336 – *Alice Lightfoot, daughter of John Lightfoot and Ann, his wife born 25 September 1698, and baptized the same day.*

Mary Lightfoot, daughter of Mr. Sherwood Lightfoot, born September 9, 1707.

Frances Lightfoot, daughter of Mr. Sherwood Lightfoot, born October 31, 1708.

John Lightfoot, son of Mr. Sherwood Lightfoot, born November 13, 1711.

Sherwood Lightfoot, son of Mr. Sherwood Lightfoot, born May 1, 17__.

Elizabeth Lightfoot, daughter of Mr. Sherwood Lightfoot, born February ye 23rd, 1716.

Anne Lightfoot, daughter of Mr. Goodrich Lightfoot, born February ye 22nd, 1708.

John Lightfoot, son of Mr. Goodrich Lightfoot, born February ye 7th, 1711.

Goodrich Lightfoot, Jr., son of Mr. Goodrich Lightfoot, baptized February 14, 171_.

Mary Lightfoot, daughter of Mr. Goodrich Lightfoot, born February ye 2nd, 1717.

Frances Lightfoot, daughter of Thomas Lightfoot, born February ye 3rd, 1717.

Frayzer Lightfoot, son of Thomas Lightfoot, born March 30, 1723.

Henry Lightfoot, son of Thomas Lightfoot, born March 30, 1723.

Mary Lightfoot, daughter of Thomas Lightfoot, born May 24, 1725.

536 – *Francis Lightfoot, son of John and Mary Lightfoot, born February 9, baptized March 20, 1736.*

519 – *Sherwood Lightfoot, son of John and Mary Lightfoot, born February 14, christened March 16, 1733.*

528 – *Frances Lightfoot, daughter of John and Mary Lightfoot, born July 30, christened September 2, 1737/38.*

359 – *Robert Harmon, son of Robert Harmon, baptized 20th day of June 1687.*

4

434 – *Colonel John Lightfoot, Esquire, obit XXVIII Die Maji circa Undecim Hor. & Anno Dmi. 1707.*

431 – *Will Harmon deceased, 4th day of January 1687/8.*

Jude Harmon, daughter of Robert Harmon (deceased) died ye 29 October 1687.

472 – *Frayzer Lightfoot, son of Thomas Lightfoot, died March 30, 1723 Frances Lightfoot died February 19, 1725/6.*

431 – *Martha, ye wife of Wm. Gardner, departed this life February 31, 1712.*

Major Sherwood Lightfoot dyed April 26, 1730.

Meeting of Vestry, New Kent County, October 25, 1707.

Ordered that Colonel Jos. Foster be elected vestryman in the place of Colonel Jno. Lightfoot, Esquire, deceased and to take ye oath of a vestryman as ye Law enjoyns.

From the Massachusetts Archives the PETITIONS AGAINST IMPOSTS, 1668[5] read:

Petitions against Imposts were called forth by an order, of the General Court at the October Session in 1668, to the effect that, after the first of the following March there should be "a custome imposed on all goods and merchandizes, in manner following, i.e., upon all goods, provisions, & merchandizes imported into this jurisdicion, two per cent; money, plate, bullion, gunpowder and salt excepted; and wine licquors &c., upon wch there is a custome already to be likewise exempted during the time for wch they ware farmed by order of the Court. And for cattle and corne imported into this jurisdicion, the allowance for same shall be as followeth, viz: Mares and neate cattle, of what age soeuer, five shillings a peece; wheate and all other graine, three pence for every bushell, provided alwaies all forreigne goods and merchandizes exported, upon certifficat that custome was paid for the importation thereof, they shall be paid the one half againe of what they paid and be freed from any further customs for the exportacon thereof; And all goods & merchandizes that doe pay custome shall be rate free in the public assessments of the county".

Petitions to repeal these duties signed by: ...William Lightfoot, along with 62 others.

The Historical Register of Virginians in the Revolution listed many Lightfoot and other kin.

LIGHTFOOT,

---

[5] New England-Genealogy-Periodicals, N.E. Hist. & Gen. Reg., v. 9, p. 82, copied by Wm. B. Trask, from Massachusetts Archives.

Daniel, 2nd Lieutenant Fluvanna Militia, Recruited February 1, 1781,
    Oath March 1, 1781
Edward, Enlisted
Frances, Enlisted
John, Lieutenant, appears on lists in 1778, SP
John, A.C. of Hides, Albemarle Barracks, August 1781
John, referred to as Captain in a rejected claim, Enlisted
John, 1st, CL
Philip, Lieutenant, 1st Continental Artillery, 1778, Resigned January
    1, 1781, Died 1786
Philip, Private, WD, 2 CL, 6 CL
Philip, Corporal, 1st Virginia State Regiment
Tarpley, Corporal, Infantry, NBLL
Thomas, Lieutenant, 1777-8, Enlisted
William, Lieutenant of James City Company, 1776-7, Enlisted
William, Culpeper Militia, Enlisted
William, 1st Light Dragoons

COLVIN

Benjamin of Boone Company, Mo., Born in Culpeper, dmp
Daniel, Clark's II Regiment, NBLL, Culpeper BW
Elkin, BW
George, Rappahannock, 71mpl
Henry, Infantry, NBLL
James, 9 CL, 13 CL
Jeremiah, Sergeant, 10 CL
Mason, Clark's II Regiment, NBLL, Culpeper BW
William, Sergeant, Ensign Colvin's Commanded Militia, Stationed in
    Redstone in January 1778

DUNCAN

Archibald, Clark's III Regiment
Benjamin, Clark's III Regiment
Charles, Clark's III Regiment
Charles, 7 CL, 11 CL, 11 & 15 CL
Christopher, 11 CL
Christopher, Morgan's Riflemen
Claiborne, IP
David, Lieutenant of a State Regiment, Taken Prisoner at Long Island
    August 17, 1776
David, Assistant Quarter Master at Fort Pitt in 1781, T-CV 2 P 959
David, Corporal, 6 CL

David, Clark's III Regiment
Edward, Enlisted
Gabriel, KY pens
George, Captain, Fluvanna Company Militia, Recruited August 7
    1777, Oath September 4, 1777
George, Captain, Robert Barnes's Company
George, &&, Orange Company Ind., mpl
James, Captain, Benjamin Harrison's Company
James (Joseph), Sergeant, 7 CL, 12 CL
James, Fort Pitts, Orange pet
John, Captain, Washington Militia
John, Sergeant, 1st Virginia State Regiment, 3 and 4 CL, 4 CL, 4,8
    and 12 CL, 7 CL, 8 CL, and 13 CL
John, Wounded in expedition under Colonel Clark against Indians,
    Northwest Territory Expense Account
John, Frederick Company, Aid given widow, Mary, in 1780
John, Monongalia Militia, Enlisted
Jonah, Enlisted
Joseph, of Fauquier, Armorer, Clark's III Regiment in 1781, T-CV1-
    P 301
Joseph, Armorer, Clark's Ii Regiment T-KV2 P 479
Joseph, Armorer at Falls of the Ohio in 1781, T DV1 P 335
Joseph, Sergeant, 7 CL
Joseph, Clark's II Regiment
Luke, Enlisted
Nimrod, Clark's II Regiment
Robert, Enlisted
Samuel, Clark's II Regiment
Samuel, Frederick Company, Widow sought aid in 1779

BECKHAM

Griffis, W. Northumberland, Enlisted
James, 2 CL
Robert, WD
William, 6 CL, Pensioned in Amherst, Enlisted
William, Lieutenant, 1781
William, 10 CL, 6 CL

TUCK

Edward, Halifax pens.
John, 8 CL, Enlisted
Thomas, Halifax, 71 mpl

Thomas, Halifax, 71 mpl

FRY

Benjamin, Sergeant, 14 Cl
Gabriel, 1 and 10 CL, 2nd
George, Corporal, 1 and 10 CL, 10 CL, 14 CL
Jacob, Fort Pitts
John, Lieutenant, Henry Bowyer's Troops, 1ˢᵗ Light Dragoons
John, killed at Bryan's Station in 1782, T-FV1 P 11
Joseph, 14 CL
Joshua, Garrard Company, Ky mpl
Nathan, Henrico pens
Samuel, Corporal, WD
Thomas, Seaman, Navy
William, Shenandoah Militia, Recruited as Ensign, May 31, 1782

William Byrd, II was the son of William Byrd, who inherited from an uncle, lands on the James River where he became wealthy and influential in early Virginia. William Bryd, II has a place in this book because of his close associations with the Lightfoot families, and his diaries of these associations.

Byrd was elected to the House of Burgesses in 1692, and became a member of the Council of State in 1709. He made several trips to England, where he served as Agent for Virginia. He was one of the commissioners who surveyed the dividing line between Virginia and North Carolina in 1728.

He built a beautiful home at Westover, where he entertained the social leaders of the Virginia Aristocracy.

Bryd's private diary gives a good picture of the life of the aristocracy of Colonial Virginia.

The following is entitled *The Secret Diary of William Byrd of Westover, 1709-1713:*

November 11, 1711. *I rose about 7 o'clock and read nothing because I prepared to go home. However, I said my prayers and ate some cranberry tart for breakfast. Mr. Graeme came to go home with me and I gave him some Virginia wine. About 10 o'clock we got on our horses and called at Green Springs, where we drank tea and then took our leave and proceeded to* FRANK LIGHTFOOT's[6] *and were conducted there by a dog which we found at the ferry. We designed to take Frank with us home but he was obliged to go to court next day, but promised to dine with us on Tuesday. I*

---

[6] Francis Lightfoot of James City County later made naval officer of the Upper District of the James River.

ate boiled beef for dinner. In the afternoon we sent to Major Harrison to come to us and then took a walk and met a pretty girl and kissed her and so returned. About 6 o'clock Major Harrison came to us but we could not persuade him to go with us to Westover. We sat up and were merry until 11 o'clock and then went to bed. I neglected to say my prayers but had good health, good humor, and good thoughts, thank God Almighty.

November 13, 1711. *I rose about 7 o'clock and read nothing because of my company. However, I said a short prayer and drank chocolate for breakfast and ate some cake. Then Mr. Graeme and I went out with bows and arrows and shot at partridge and squirrel which gave us abundance of diversion but we lost some of our arrows. We returned about one o'clock but found that* FRANK LIGHTFOOT *had broken his word by not coming to us. About 2 o'clock we went to dinner and I ate some venison pasty and were very merry. In the afternoon we played at billiards and I by accident had almost lost some of my fore teeth by putting the stick in my mouth. Then we went and took a walk with the women and Mr. Graeme diverted himself with Mrs. Dunn.[7] In the evening came Mr. Mumford who told me all was well again at Appomattox.[8] We played at cards and drank some pressed wine and were merry until 10 o'clock. I neglected to say my prayers___ ___, and had good health, good thoughts, good humor, thank God Almighty.*

March 5, 1712. *I rose about 7 o'clock but read nothing. However I said my prayers and danced my dance before I went out of my chamber, I drank chocolate for breakfast. We were merry again this morning, but poor Colonel Hill had the headache very much. Nothing happened very remarkable. Colonel Epps came about 11 o'clock from the (...) and let me know that there was some difficulty in persuading the people to range as they had promised to do. About 1 o'clock we went to dinner and I ate some boiled beef for dinner. We took a walk to the ship and about 3 o'clock took leave of the company and went home in the coach but our horses balked at the hills on the way and my wife was out of humor because we came away. We got home about 5 o'clock and found all pretty well. Thank God. Captain H-n had been there and left some spice and some fruit for a present.* FRANK LIGHTFOOT, *Tom Randolph, and Captain H-n came to visit me and stayed and ate some roast beef and Captain B-n-d-f-r came with them. The two first tarried all night. I neglected to say my prayers but had good health, good thoughts and good humor, thank God Almighty.*

March 6, 1712. *I rose about 7 o'clock and read nothing because of the company. However I said a short prayer and drank chocolate for breakfast. Then we walked bout the garden, because it was good weather and then we played at billiards and I won three shillings. About 12 o'clock*

---

[7] Mrs. Dunn was Mrs. Byrd's sister.

[8] Appomattox was one of Bryd's plantations.

9

and I ate some pigeon and bacon for dinner. In the afternoon we played again at billiards and then Colonel Hill went away and we took a walk about the plantation until the evening and then MR. LIGHTFOOT *and Mr. Jimmy Roscow took their leave and went to Mrs. Harrison's one to make love to the mother and the other the daughter. But Tom Randolph stayed and I let him understand that I agreed he should be my general overseer. We discoursed of several things concerning the subject until about 9 o'clock. I neglected to say my prayers but had good health, good thoughts, and good humor, thank God Almighty. John G-r-l was a little out of order.*

March 7, 1712. *I rose about 7 o'clock and read nothing. However I said my prayers and drank chocolate for breakfast. I danced my dance. About 10 o'clock Tom Randolph went away and notwithstanding the weather threatened rain I walked to Mrs. Harrison's to visit the two gallants and their mistresses, but* FRANK LIGHTFOOT *was gone before I got there, but the rest were there. Poor Jimmy Roscow was melancholy though I did all I could to make him merry. I went into the study and chose some books and about 2 o'clock we went to dinner and I ate some boiled pork. In the afternoon it rained very hard which kept me there till night and then my wife sent a horse for me. It thundered and rained very hard. I found all my people well but I quarreled with John about his work and with the overseer for working the ox in the rain. I wrote in my journal and read nothing. I said my prayers and had good health, good thoughts and good humor, thank God Almighty. John G-r-l was still out of order.*

August 6, 1712. *I rose about 5 o'clock and read a chapter in Hebrew and two chapters in Greek. I said my prayers and had warm milk from the cow. I danced my dance. The weather was cloudy and hot but did not rain. My wife was indisposed. I read a little law but was interrupted by company. About 9 o'clock came Mr. Rogers with two persons from Chickahominy and soon after came Colonel Hill and Mr. Anderson and dined with me. I ate some boiled goose for dinner. In the afternoon came Mrs. Harrison and stayed about half an hour. She made so much haste because* FRANK LIGHTFOOT *and Major Harrison came over the river to visit her. About 6 o'clock my company went away, and I took a walk about the plantation. The weather cleared up in the afternoon and was very hot. I said my prayers and had good health, good thoughts and good humor, thank God Almighty.*

September 4, 1712. *I rose about 5 o'clock and read a chapter in Hebrew and some Greek in Herodian. I said my prayers and had warm milk from the cow for breakfast. The weather continued cool but my wife and the overseer were indisposed again. My wife had the headache and a little fever. I read some English. Colonel Ludwell's man called here and told me that Colonel Harrison and Colonel Ludwell were sick. About 12 o'clock came* FRANK LIGHTFOOT *and his brother[9] and dined with us, and I ate some roast beef. In the afternoon we went and played billiards and I won most games. Then we took a walk to see the granary; then we returned to the house and they took leave and went to Mrs. Harrison's from whence they came. At night I read the Tatler. I said my prayers and had good health, good thoughts, and good humor, thank God Almighty.*

September 22, 1712. *I rose about 6 o'clock and read a little Hebrew and nothing in Greek because I prepared to go to* MR. LIGHTFOOT's *on the Pamunkey River in order to meet the Governor next day at the Pamunkey Indian Town. I said my prayers and ate some boiled milk for breakfast. About 11 o'clock I left my orders with Bannister concerning the sloop and everything else and took leave of my wife and with Mr. Catesby rode to Drury Stith's where we drank some persico and then proceeded to* MR. SHERWOOD LIGHTFOOT's[10] *where we arrived about 5 o'clock. He received us very courteously and gave us some boiled beef for supper of which I ate heartily. He lives in a good plantation and seems to be very industrious. About 9 o'clock we retired to bed. I said a short prayer and had good health, good thoughts, and good humor, thank God Almighty. Riding cured my cold, thank God.*

September 23, 1712. *I rose about 7 o'clock and shaved myself. I said a short prayer and about 9 ate some roast beef for breakfast. The weather was cloudy and threatened rain, however about 10 o'clock we rode to* MR. GOODRICH LIGHTFOOT's[11] *who lives about a mile from thence. It rained as soon as we got on our horses. There we stayed until the governor and all the company came in by the man-of-war boat. About 12 o'clock they came by and then notwithstanding the rain was violent we went over the river where the Governor received me very kindly and so did all the rest of the company, except Mrs. Russell. It rained violently all day so that the company could see nothing and the Governor's cook could scarcely get dinner. However he did get one about 2 o'clock and I ate some boiled mutton. We were merry but were forced to stay in one of the Indian cabins all day and about 5 o'clock the company were forced to return in the rain to Captain Littlepage's but Mr. Catesby and I returned to* MR. LIGHTFOOT's. *Abundance of people came to the Indian town to see the Governor but were very wet and indeed the rain disappointed us all. There is an Indian called P-t W-l who has now his 20 wives. There was also an Indian who was ill of a bite of a rattlesnake but was on the recovery having taken some sankeroot. About 9 o'clock we ate some blue wing and then*

---

[9] Note says Philip Lightfoot of James City County.

[10] Son of John Lightfoot, who died in 1707; a large landowner of New Kent County, and cousin of Francis Lightfoot of James City County mentioned earlier in the diary.

[11] Another son of John Lightfoot.

retired to bed. I neglected to say my prayers but had good health, good thoughts, and good humor, thank God Almighty.
September 24, 1712. *I rose about 7 o'clock and we prepared to go to the election of burgesses in New Kent. I said my prayers and ate some beef for breakfast. About 10 o'clock we took leave and* MR. LIGHTFOOT *went with us to the courthouse where abundance of people were assembled and about 12 o'clock they chose Mr. Merriweather and Captain Stanhope their burgesses without opposition. Captain Littlepage told me the Governor resolved to reach home this night. However I resolved to go to Colonel Bassett's because I had promised to meet the Governor there. Accordingly we rode there and arrived about 5 o'clock. The Colonel had been sick but was better but his son was sick. We had some fish for supper. The Colonel and his wife received us kindly. About 9 o'clock we went to bed. I said a short prayer and had good health, good thoughts and good humor, thank God Almighty.*

References in old records to *Martin with the light foot* have been found and special mention is given in the life of Hereward, the Saxon. The synonymous Dutch name is *Lightvoet.*

The Lightfoot family in America has been since the earliest times a very distinguished one. The Virginians of this name are descendants of Reverend Richard Lightfoot of Northamptonshire, England. He was born in 1563. He is the first of the family of whom there is authentic record.

Colonel John and Philip were the first of our line of Lightfoot's in America.

12

CHAPTER II

LIGHTFOOT FAMILY CHART
HERALDRY and CRESTS

In ancient times, direct communication between a ruler and his people was often impossible. The rulers used special officials, called heralds, to deliver messages and orders, and to announce important events to the people. During the Middle Ages, they were considered personal agents for the kings, somewhat like modern ambassadors and enjoyed great honors as the king's representatives. It was a crime to interfere with their work as they went from one country to another.

Medieval heralds became authorities on Coats of Arms, the emblems used on the shields and clothing during battle, supervising the selection and new designs to prevent duplication.

The name of Lightfoot derived from old Sagas and chronicles, purporting the great accomplishment of agility in running, endurance and speed. The name Lightfoot is found as early as 1273 in the person of William Lightfoot, and from that date down to present day the Lightfoot family has been distinguished in England and America for religious, social and statesmanlike qualities. The family of the present interest was of the famous Virginia Lightfoots. They were of English origins, coming mostly from County Kent, and later Northampton, England.

Heraldry is used to distinguish individual families, to authenticate official documents, and refers to the art of reproducing these designs in picture form. A heraldic design is called a coat of arms, and a knight wore it over his armor. It was an emblem embroidered and customarily placed on his surcoat.

Richard Lightfoot Lineage Chart

Richard Lightfoot of the Parish of Stoke Breuern, Co. Northampton, Clerk in Holy Orders. Formerly Curate of the Parish of St. Lawrence Pountney, London (1598). Installed as Rector of Stoke Breuern, 27 April 1601 and buried there 28 November 1625, aet. 63 years, M.I. there. Held freehold lands and other property in Stoke Breuern as by his Will dated 5 May and proved 6 December 1625. (Archd: Ct. Northampton).

Jane Jones mentioned in and appointed sole-extrix of her husband's Will, 1625 and mentioned in that of her son John, 1647. Will dated 20 December 1649, proved in Archd: Ct. of Northampton, afsd.

Ann Baptised 27 December 1546 at St. Lawrence Pountney, afsd.

John of Gray's Inn, afsd. Barrister-at-Law and a Fellow of Gray's Inn. Eldest son, baptised 9 April 1598 at St. Lawrence, Pountney, afsd. Matric: 15 May 1615 as of Lincoln College, Oxford University, aged 17 years and Admitted to Gray's Inn 30 June 1617. Mentioned in the Will of his father, 1625 and mother, 1649. Held lands, etc in Stoke Breuern, afsd. and an estate in Gray's Inn with chamber lodging as by his Will dated 1 January 1647, proved 24 March 1648/9 (P.C.C.)

Elizabeth dau of Francis Phillips, Esq., one of the Auditors of H.M. Exchequer. Mentioned in and proved her husband's Will, 1647/9. Held household goods at Ickenham, Co. Middlesex as by her Will dated 1 May 1679 and with a Codicil, 2 2 November 1681, proved 24 December 1686 (P.C.C.). (Bequest to poor of the Parish of St. Sepulchres, London).

Rose Mentioned in her father's Will, 1625 as having had her marriage portion and as deceased in that of her brother, John Lightfoot, 1647.

John Lightfoot a Captain of one of H.M. Ships, died at Sea: Anno. 1682. (Vide: Herald's Visitation of London, 1687). Aeti: Circa 55 years, 1682. Admitted 18 February 1641 to Gray's Inn, afsd. as eldest son of John Lightfoot, one of the Fellows. Mentioned in the Wills of his father, 1647, paternal grandmother, 1649 and in that of his mother, 1679 and to have £40 yearly for life.

Died a Widower at Surinam in the West Indies and Admōn: granted 7 March 1686/7. (P.C.C.).

Elizabeth, dau. of John Tailor of Maidstone, Co. Kent, Deceased before 1687.

John Lightfoot of New Kent County Virginia. Died 1707.

John Lightfoot mentioned in the Will of his paternal grandmother, 1679, to have £10 yearly and after his father's death, £40 yearly for life, or up to £500 for him to be settled in any office or employment. Mentioned in his father's Administration, 1687.

Philip Lightfoot Mentioned in his father's Administration, 1687.

(This chart was compiled by Conrad Swan, Esquire, M.V.O., Ph.D.,)

14

Thomas Jones mentioned as my dearly beloved brother in Will of his brother-in-law, Richard Lightfoot, 1625 and a witness thereto.

John Jones mentioned in the Will of his cousin, John Lightfoot, 1647 and a Life in an estate in Gray's Inn, Co. Middlesex.

Mr. Thomas Jones mentioned in the Will of John Lightfoot, 1647, as my loving cousin.

Sarah baptised 8 February 1600 at St. Lawrence Pountney, afsd. Mentioned in her father's Will, 1625 as having had her marriage portion. Married 16 January 1622/3 at Stoke Breuern, afsd. to Robert Kingston. He mentioned in the Will of his mother-in-law, 1649

Richard of the Parish of Chadwell, Co. Essex. (1603-1649) Clerk in Holy Orders. Matric: 27 January 1624/5 as of Lincoln College, afsd. aged 17 years. B.A. 26 July 1628. Installed as Rector of Kennardington, Co. Kent, 1623. Of Wilmington, Co. Norfolk, 1647 and Chadwell, 1603. Mentioned in the Will of his father, 1625 and to have lands and houses in Stoke Breuern, afsd. In that of his mother, 1647 and brother John, 1647. Died circa 1649.

... Mentioned, but not named in the Will of her brother-in-law, John Lightfoot, 1647.

Jane mentioned in her father's Will, 1625, then unmarried portion as with either of her sisters. Mentioned in the Will of her brother, John Lightfoot, 1647 and then married and sole-extrix; and residuary legatee of her mother's Will, 1649, whereon she is mentioned as wife of William Asbie (Ashbie) of Hanslop, Co. Bucks.

William Lightfoot, sometime of London, Gent, one of the Attorneys in the Lord Mayor's Court and Register of Sutton's Hospital; aet. 53 in 1687, and afterwards of the Parish of Hackney, Co. Middlesex. Admitted 29 October 1653 to Gray's Inn, afsd. as son of John Lightfoot, late of Gray's Inn, Esq. deceased, Admoner and paternal uncle to John and Philip, sons of John Lightfoot late of Surinam, afsd deceased, March 1686/7. Will dated 28 August 1695, proved 23 January 1699/1700. (P.C.C.). Bequest to poor of the parishes of St Michael Bassisham, London, St John at Hackney and of Teddington, Co. Middlesex).

Catherine, dau. of Robert Abbott. Mentioned as deceased in her husband's Will, 1695 and buried in Guildhall Chapel, London.

Philip Mentioned in the Wills of his father, 1647, and mother 1679.

Other Issue

Philip Lightfoot of "Tedington" Charles City County, died 1708. M.I. there, on which is inscribed his descent from Stoke Bruen in Northamptonshire.

(M.A., F.S.A.; York Herald of Arms at the College of Arms)

Each individual selected a symbol to use that represented an incident in their lives or their quality of life. Then there was great confusion because of duplication of coats of arms. This eventually led to the need for heralds, who supervised the selection of colors and symbols.

A complete coat of arms consists of a shield, crest, and motto. The basic element is the shield or escutcheon and the helmet or supporters may be added. Accessories included the wreath, mantling or scroll. The device used to cover the point where the crest was attached to the knight's helmet was the wreath. The knight was protected from direct sunlight by the mantling, which also kept back stains and rust.

The Richard Lightfoot crest (as seen on page 17) is a human heart pierced with a passion nail in bend. The Arms were a "Barry of six." The last coat of arms created by John and Philip Lightfoot (page 18) was a Griffins head with three escallops placed diagonally on a shield.

A blazon is the technical description of coats of arms. All terms used in heraldry have an exact meaning to avoid confusion when giving a verbal description.

The right side of the shield from the wearer's viewpoint is called the dexter side, and the left is the sinister side. The colors are called Tincture and represent two metals, seven colors, and various furs. Each tincture uses a French term and has a special heraldic name, such as *or* for gold, *argent* for silver, *gules* for red, *azure* for blue, *sanguine* for blood color, and *sable* for black. The most frequently used furs are ermine and vair. The shield contains the field, or surface, on which is placed the charge, or figures that form the design.

Some countries use additional devices on the shield to indicate the exact family relationship. In Great Britain, marks of cadency serve this purpose. These devices are necessary because more than one individual often claims the same coat of arms. The file or label is the mark of cadency of the oldest son.

The Lightfoot Line is Arms: Barry of six or and gules, on a bend of sable, three escallops argent. The three escallops represent the Holy Trinity adopted by Richard Lightfoot from an ancient coat of arms, (as seen on page 20) origin unknown, to be used on his Coat of Arms and are still in use today. The ancient motto: *"Noblesse Oblige"* which means the obligation of honorable, generous and responsible behavior associated with high rank or birth.

The custom of bearing symbols on shields, helmets and standards existed in ancient times. The Old Testament refers to the separate symbols of each of the twelve tribes of Israel – for example, the lion of the tribes of Judah or the wolf of the tribe of Benjamin.

Heraldic symbols, as we know them today developed with the use of armor in the Middle Ages. The suit of armor made it difficult to distinguish friend from foe during violent hand-to-hand combat, and

Lightfoot

(This was the Coat of Arms of Richard Lightfoot. The crest is a human heart pierced with a passion nail in bend. The Arms were a "Barry of six".)

17

Lightfoot

(John and Philip Lightfoot adopted the Coat of Arms of a Barry of six or and gules, on a bend sable three escallops argent. The crest was a Griffins head erased proper, collared sable charged with three escallops argent.)

knights developed heraldic symbols so they could identify each other. Symbolism was a vital force in the thought and action of medieval times, and knights naturally chose symbols as their marks of identification. The symbols usually commemorated an event in the knight's life, or some outstanding quality. One set of symbols was developed during the Crusades. Knightly feats in tournaments or pageants brought about the development of others.

During this period, heraldic symbols were also used in everyday life. Most persons did not know how to write, so they had to develop some way of proving the authenticity of various documents. It became common practice to use a seal with a person's heraldic design as a signature.

The introduction of gunpowder into warfare made armor obsolete. As a result, heraldic symbols were no longer needed as a means of recognition on the battlefield. These symbols became more useful as an emblem distinguishing a particular family than as the mark of an individual knight.

Heraldic symbols do no necessarily denote aristocracy or an exclusive class. These emblems of distinction were the reward of personal merit and could be secured to the humble as well as the upper classes. Today they testify to the bravery, heroism and meritorious deeds of our ancestors and are proudly displayed by the informed descendants of these noteworthy families, as the valiant acts and self-sacrifice of contemporary persons would appeal to the pride of their posterity.

(This Coat of Arms is ancient and there is no information as to its origin.
Noblesse Oblige means the obligation of honorable, generous and
responsible behavior associated with high rank or birth.)

(A rubbing of the brass plate at Richard's Memorial done by John Lewis Beckham during his trip to England in 1964.)

22

CHAPTER III

RICHARD LIGHTFOOT, REVEREND, 1562-1625
MARRIED JANE JONES

Richard Lightfoot, a minister of Stoke Bruerne, Northamptonshire, England was born in 1562 and died in 1625. Berry's History of Northamptonshire states that he was installed 27 April 1601 and was buried there 28 November 1625. There is in the church a brass plate (12'x16') having the figure of a priest kneeling before an altar with the Lightfoot arms, and this inscription:

Memoriae

*Richard Lightfoot, Hujus Essliae per XXIIII
Annos Rectoris, Evangelii Praeconis,
J.L. Filius et Haeres Suus Posuit
Pascentem Exemplo Populos Vergoq. Ciboq.
Mors Suggressa Levi Est Non Inopina Pede
Vita Brevis, Nam Longa Fuit Meditatio Mortis.
Sic Alios Docuit Vivere Sep. Mori.
Dni. 1625
Obiit An
Aet. Suae 63*

This may be rendered as follows: *This tomb was placed here to the memory of Richard Lightfoot, minister of the gospel and rector of this church for twenty-four years by J.L., his son and heir. Death quietly and unexpectedly overtook him while feeding his flock by work and deed. His life was short, for it was a long meditation on death. Thus he taught others* to live and himself to die. *He died in the year of our Lord 1625, aged 63 years.*

The will of Richard Lightfoot is recorded in the District Registry attached to the Probate Division of Her Majesty's High Court of Justice at Northampton:

In the name of God Amen, I Richard Lighfoot Clerke, Parson of Stoke Brewen in the County of Northton being in helth of bodie but of pafitt memory praised by God Doe make and declare this my last Will and testament first I bequeath my soule into the hands of Almightie God assuredlie trusting through the infinite meritts & mediacon of Jesu Christ my saviour & redeemr to have everlasting salvacon And my bodie to be interred in the chancell of the chancell (sic) of the parish church of Stoke aforesaid My Estate thus I dispose of first of my lands & tenements by me purchased I give unto my eldest sonne John Lightfoote my house at Northton & all other things hereunto appertayninge purchased of Thomas Gutteridge Cordwiner and the gate house adionyinge purchases of Tobie Coldwell and all those lands and meadowe grounds with there appurtenances in the psh of Stoke aforesaid wch I purchased of Richard Wickens, William Wickens and William Kingston and every or ainey of them and all writings and evidences concernynge the same to have & to hold unto my sonne John and his heirs for ever Item I give unto my sonne Richard Lightfoote and his heirs for ever all those lands arable meadowe and pasture with their appurtenances wch I have bought or contracted for of Robt Wickens of Northton but if the bargaine goe not forwarde then I give unto my said sonne Richard Lightfoot so much as I should have given for the said lands Item I give unto my said sonne Richard & his assignes my house in the occupation of William Yorke and all the lands ground and other hereditaments which I bought of John Jackson together with the newe house latlie erected upon part thereof Item I give my twoe houses with all the lands thereunto belonging wth there appurtenances wch I purchased of John Walke Esq and John Smith unto my well beloved wife Jane Lightfoote for and duringe the terme of her naturall life and her decease unto my said sonne John Lightfoote & his assignes And my Will is that when my said sonne shall have possession of the last two mencened houses or either of them he shall pay unto his two sisters Sarah and Rose if they be then living five pounds apice And I give all my bookes unto my said two sons equally to be divided between them And my Will is that the porcon of my daughter Jane shall be so much as the best procon given in marriage with either of her sisters to be pd unto her at those daies and tymes upon and after her marriage as the porcon of her sister Rose was paid and touchinge anye wise those poore people at Stoke I doe for divers respects me inducinge forbeare to mencon any by leave the same to the

24

discretion of my wife and sonne John to do therein hereafter (as the carriage of the parish to themward considered) they shall thincke meete And my Will is in respecte to the guifte hereby to my said wife that she release her dower and third in all my free lands & not doubting but that such love will rest in her towards her children and such dutie in them to herward that they would have made as equall if not more perfitt & indifferent distribucon of my estate than I have done hereby

The rest of all my good debts and estate not bequeathed I give to my well beloved wife, Jane Lightfoote whome I make sole Executrix of this my last Will and I desire my dearly beloved brother Thomas Jones Esqr to be overseer hereof to see the same pformed in all things accordinge to my true meaninge hereby requestinge all the parties legatees beforenamed to make him judge, and decidr of all controversies which shall arise between them or anie of them

In witness whereof I have hereunto put my hand and seale the 5th daie of May Anno Dni 1625 And in the first yeare of the raigne of our Soveraigne Lord King Charles &c

Richard Lightfoote

Sealed published and declared by the said Richard Lightfoote as and for his last Will & Testamt in the presence of us Thomas Jones, John Winterborne, Thomas Marshe
Proved 6 December 1625.

The will of Jane (Jones) Lightfoot, the widow of Richard Lightfoot, is recorded in the same District Registry:

In the Name of God Amen I Jane Lightfoote of Stoake Bruen in the County of Northon Gentlewoman being weake in body yet in pfect minde & memory (thankes be to God) doe make this my last Will & Testament in manner & forme following First I bequeath my soule into the hands of Almightie God my Creator & of Jesus Christ, my only Savior and Redeemer & of the holy ghose my Sanctifier & pserver And my body I will be decently brought to the ground & buried in the Chancell of the says Stoake Bruen in sure & certaine hope of resurrection to eternall life As for my worldly goods and Chattels first I give to my sonne Richard Lightfoot one little cottage pott with one little brasse pan half my pewter in the pewter chest and the feather bed at Stoake Bruen to be delivered within one month after my decease being lawfully demanded Item I give to my grandchild John Lightfoot the sonne of John Lightfoot the bigger silver bole to be delivered as before Item I give to my sonne-law Robert Kingstone my other ---silver bole & my little silver spoone to be delivered as before Item I give to my grandchild Sarah Kingstone one little feather bed with bedstead & all the other furniture belonging to it to be delivered

25

as before Item I give to Mr. Macham of the said Stoake Bruen one gold ring & one silver thimble to be delivered as before The rest of my goods & chattels unbequeathed I give to my well beloved daughter Jane of Hanslop in the County of Buckon the now wife of William Asbie whom I make the true and full executrix of this my last Will & Testament in writing Robert Wickens Gentln & Richard Plowman yeoman of the said pish of Stoake Bruen my loving neighbors to be the overseers of this my last Will & Testament And in witness hereof I have to these pents sett to my hand & seale this twentieth day of December in the year of our Lord God (cy computar of or Church of England) one thousand six hundred fortie nine

the mark of
Jane X Lightfoot

Sealed & acknowledge in
   the psence of
      Joseph Dayes
      the mark of
   Elizabeth X. Dunkley

Richard Lightfoot, who was Rector of Stoke Bruerne in Northamptonshire, heads a pedigree of four generations of his family registered during the Heralds' Visitation of London made in 1687. The registration is signed by William Lightfoot, of London, grandson of the Reverend Richard, one of the Attorneys in the Lord Mayors Court and Register of Sutton's Hospital.

Robert Lightfoot, brother to the William who filed the Lightfoot pedigree, was Apothecary to the Queen Dowager, Queen Catherine of Braganza, wife of Charles II of England.

Pedigree of the Phillips Family:

"William Phillips of London gent, mentioned in the Visitation of London made 1568 being then one of the Queene's Customers for the wool married Joane, daughter of Thomas Houghton. Their 5th son, Francis Phillips, Esquire, one of his Maties Auditors of the Exchequer licensing 1633 married Olive, daughter of George Sawyer of Cawson Com. Norff. gent., sister to Sir Edmund Sawyer Knight, one of his Maties Auditors. Their first daughter, Elizabeth, wife to John Lightfoot of Grayes Inn Vtter Barrester."

[1]"In regard to the Reverend Richard Lightfoot, may I add a few items from Henry I. Longden, Northamptonshire and Rutland Clergy, volume 8, page 261, 263. It is stated that he was probably of the City of London, was

---

[1] Quote from letter from J.F. Dorman, dated 10 March 1979.

instituted rector of Stoke Bruerne, 27 April 1601 and buried there 28 November 1625, aged 63, and that his children by Jane were:

JOHN, *was the son and heir, born 9 April 1598, marticulated Lincoln College, Oxford, 5 May 1615, aged 17; student of Gray's Inn, 1617; barrister at law.* He married ELIZABETH PHILLIPS.

MARTHA *was christened 18 January 1602/3 at Stoke Bruerne.*

ROSE *was christened 15 April 1604 at Stoke Bruerne. She married* LEONARD DARE *and had issue.*

RICHARD *was christened 31 July 1608 at Stoke Bruerne and took the Holy orders.*

SAMUEL *was buried 15 November 1626 at Stokes Bruerne. He was a young man when he died.*

JANE *was christened 25 January 1612/13 at Stokes Bruerne. She married 15 February 1636/37 to* WILLIAM ASHBY *of Hanslope, Bucks, at St. Sepulchre's, Northampton.*

SARA *was married 16 January 1622/23 at Stokes Bruerne to* ROBERTSON KINGSTON *of Stokes Bruerne by whom she had issue.*

"In an addenda in volume 16, page 88, it is further shown that Richard Lightfoot was ordered deacon and priest 14 March 1582 by John, Bishop of Gloucester, and was licensed as a preacher 11 December 1589 by John Archbishop of Canterbury.

I do not know enough about ecclesiastical practices in Elizabethan England to put this forward with any certainty, but it would seem likely that Richard Lightfoot, having been ordained by the Bishop of Gloucester, would have served cures in Gloucestershire for a time. Some investigations of Gloucestershire records reveal Richard, and perhaps even the baptism of his son John which occurred prior to his removal to Stoke Bruerne, although a pre-1600 date would be early for many surviving registers."

[2] *"I spent almost all of today in Stoke Bruerne, I doubt that I really accomplished much but at least I tried. The plaque (12X16) Memorial to Richard Lightfoot is a small bronze one. It was once gold plated, and traces of the gold still remain. Because it is polished, it reflects light terribly, and my photographs may not be much better than those of my predecessors...will make a rubbing from it, which I may do tomorrow, if I can find the paper, etc. But where are the two graves? I never could find them but I think I know where they are. They are either under the organ or under the choir stalls. In 1901, someone...redecorated the church, with awful consequences...A huge, very bad organ, now unplayable, was*

---

[2] Excerpts from a letter dated 29 September 1964 from John Lewis Beckham (Nephew of Mrs. Stanley A. Williams) to his Mother.

(The Normans (1066) began the Church on the hill above the Village: And one of their small windows is in the West Wall of the splendid tower, which was completed, with Battlements in the 15th century, when the richly carved Stone Cross was set above the east wall of the chancel. The Nave Arcades with four Circular Clerestory Windows above them are 14th century. The Church that Richard Lightfoot was the rector at until 1625 is still standing and in use. The Octagonal Font is Medieval, all over the Church we come upon the beautifully lettered gravestones under which lie the Arundels, the Sheppards, the Lightfoots, the Jones and other families who lived in Stoke Park. The choir stalls are modern, and on the walls behind them are wooden panels with 15th century tracery. There are similar panels in the much restored Medieval pulpit, and a few old ones at the base of the chancel screen, the upper part of which is an excellent copy of the 14th century panel.)

(The Parsonage-Home of Richard and Jane (Jones) Lightfoot. The House is still standing like the church.)

(The top of the Lightfoot Memorial.)

installed in what had formerly been the entrance to the baptistery, and tiny edges of tombstones are visible at the front. The plaque is right next to the organ. The new choir seats are over a bunch of other tombs, and these are right under the monument. In all other cases I could find, monuments on the walls announced people whose tombs were immediately below, which would mean that the choir seats are over the tomb, or the organ is. Both weigh many "tons", and could not be moved for easy inspection. Then, too, a new tile floor was put in up the center aisle in 1901, and the tomb may have been covered by this. Anyway, it isn't visible. The rector did not know where it was, and the sexton was away—the sexton is supposed to have a map which shows.

"I asked the elderly lady who was cleaning the churchyard if the old rectory had been destroyed. "Oh, no," she said, "It is down the drive past the post office." I looked, and lo, a gothic house, seemingly as old as the church. It had been sold three years ago to a London family who had lived there twelve years. I went to the door and knocked, but got no response. Then the heating system repairman came, and the dogs began to bark, and Mrs. Taylor emerged. She took me all through the house, and let me make pictures in the yard. I let her read the wills (of Reverend Richard Lightfoot and his wife Jane (Jones) Lightfoot) and she asked if she might have copies of them. I assured her and her husband you would send them. This is the oldest record of the house the Taylor's could find and they were more anxious for help.

The house is gigantic. I am not sure of the exact number of rooms. It was added to time and time again, but none of the additions seem later than 1600. The hall fireplace, which was doubtless the stove when the house was young, is almost 8 feet wide and head high. The hearth is flat with the floor. The floor is red and black tiles, definitely medieval, in a large diamond pattern. The other floors were beautiful stone, but the present owners don't like stone and are taking them up to put down asphalt tile. The upstairs has at least six bedrooms. Some of the oak beams are as thick as your body, and then some.

Several years ago the rector of Stoke Bruerne took all the records to the Northampton County Records Office, Delapre Abbey, 1508 Rd., Northampton, England.

The marriage date of John Lightfoot, Esq., and Elizabeth Phillips, daughter of Francis Phillips is given as 16 January 1626/27 at St. Andrews Undershaft, London.

In the parish record for Saint Lawrence Pountney, London, I find:

LIGHTFOOT, John, father Richard Lightfoot, christened 9 April 1598.
LIGHTFOOT, Sarah, father Richard Lightfoot, christened 8 February 1600.
I also found:

LIGHTFOOT, *Anna, father Richard Lightfoot, christened 27 December 1596. Anna may have been the first child of Richard and Jane Lightfoot, but there is no other information about her."*

The will of Richard Lightfoot May 5, 1625 speaks of *"my dearly beloved brother, Thomas Jones, Esq."* Richard's wife Jane was sister of Thomas Jones.

The following was taken from the book Monumental Inscriptions of St. Mary Lewisham.

"Near the former (on ye north wall of ye chancel Bishop Kennett) is another mural monument of alabaster and black marble, with the inscription in gilt Roman capitals – 'To the memory of Thomas Jones, Esq., Common Sargent-at-Law of the Citie of London for the space of 12 years, beloved and bemoaned by all, departed this life at the age of 54 years, October 1 1625, and of Priscilla, his loyall wife, daughter of Robert Aske, Esq., of the Aske of Aughton in the County of Yorke (England), who died the 25th of November in the same yeare, and, according to their mutuall desires, are here together interred neare the bodie of the said Robert Aske and others of that blood and familie, having issue three sonnes – Thomas, Francis and William – and one daughter Martha – 'Sir Richard Yonge, Knight, and Baronet; William Boswell, Thomas Jones, and John Lightfoot, Esq., have erected this monument that the just might be had in everlasting remembrance.'"

CHAPTER IV

JOHN LIGHTFOOT, ESQUIRE 1598-1648
MARRIED ELIZABETH PHILLIPS

Richard Lightfoot followed his father in the ministry. *Richard[1] Lightfoot, son of Richard, of Stoke Bruerne, Northants, sacred. (i.e. priest) Lincoln College, matriculated 27 January 1625-6, aged 27; B.A. 26 July 1628, rector of Kennarding, Kent, 1632, of Whinbergh, Norfolk, 1647, and of Chadwell, Essex, 1663.*

JOHN LIGHTFOOT, the eldest son of Richard and Jane (Jones) Lightfoot was born 9 April 1598, at St. Lawrence Parish, London, England, before his father became rector of the parish of Stoke Bruerne. He died in 1648 in Middlesex County, England.

He is undoubtedly the John who was a student at Oxford: *John Lightfoot, of London (City), cler. fil. Lincoln Coll., matric. 5 May 1615, aged 17.* The editor of this register of students added a note that he was probably the John Lightfoot who was a student at Gray's Inn.

Foster's Gray's Inn Admissions contains this entry: *June 30, 1617, John Lightfoot, son and heir of Richard Lightfoot, Co. Northampton, clerk.*

Gray's Inn was one of the Courts of Law; John Lightfoot therefore received legal training. After he completed his training we find that he was admitted as a Fellow of Gray's Inn.

---

[1] Alumni Oxonienses: the Members of the University of Oxford, 1500-1714, edited by Joseph Foster (Oxford and London: 1892), V. 1, p. 914.

He married ELIZABETH the daughter of FRANCIS PHILLIPS, ESQUIRE, one of His Majesty's Auditors of the Exchequer, 16 January 1621. Elizabeth died 24 December 1686. They had thirteen children:

JOHN LIGHTFOOT *married* ELIZABETH TAILOR.
  JOHN LIGHTFOOT
  PHILIP LIGHTFOOT
FRANCIS LIGHTFOOT
  CHARLES LIGHTFOOT
GEORGE LIGHTFOOT
EDMUND LIGHTFOOT
JOHN LIGHTFOOT
WILLIAM LIGHTFOOT
  WILLIAM LIGHTFOOT
ROBERT LIGHTFOOT
  JOHN LIGHTFOOT
MARY LIGHTFOOT
PHILIP LIGHTFOOT
ANNE LIGHTFOOT
JANE LIGHTFOOT
RICHARD LIGHTFOOT
  JOHN LIGHTFOOT
REBECCA LIGHTFOOT
ELIZABETH LIGHTFOOT *married* JOHN TURNER.

The pedigree of the Phillips[2] family begins with William Phillips of London, Gent. who was mentioned in the visitation of London made in 1568 as then one of the Queen's Customers for the Wool. No coat of arms is appended to this pedigree and it is probable that the Phillips were one of those mercantile families who rose to prominence in the Tudor period. William Phillips married Joane, daughter of Thomas Houghton, and left eight sons and five daughters.

The fifth son of William was Francis Phillips, Esq., of London, one of his Majesty's Auditors of the Exchequer. He married Olive, daughter of George Sawyer of Cawson, Norfolk, Gentleman, and sister of Sir Edmund Sawyer who was also one of His Majesty's Auditors.

Sir Edmund Sawyer of Dunston, Norfolk, and of London was granted arms.[3] His youngest son was Sir Robert Sawyer of the Inner Temple who

---

[2] The Visitation of London, Anno Domini, 1633, 1634, and 1635, edited by Joseph Jackson Howard (Harleian Society, Publications, V. 16-17; London: 1883, V. 2, p. 161.
[3] LeNeve's Pedigrees of the Knights, edited by George W. Marshall (Harleian Society, Publications, V. 8; London: 1873, p. 321.

was knighted at Whitehall 17 October 1677. He was Attorney General, Speaker of the House of Commons in the reign of Charles II, Attorney General in the reign of James II, and was Burgess for Cambridge in the first Parliament of William and Mary. He died 5 July 1692 at High Chere, Southampton, where he lived. His only child and heir was Margaret Sawyer who became the wife of Thomas Herbert, Earl of Pembroke and Montgomery.

Francis and Olive (Sawyer) Phillips were the parents of four sons and five daughters: Francis (of the Inner Temple, Barrister, eldest son, age about 25 years in 1633), John, Stephen, George, Elizabeth (who married John Lightfoot), Anne (who married Leonard Dare of Inner Temple, Esq.), Jane, Mary and Philip.

John Lightfoot's will[4] is recorded in the Prerogative Court of Canterbury, in book Fairfax 32 (Somerset House, London):

1 January 1647, John Lightfoote of Grayes Inn, Middx, Esq. Desires no mourning espense but to be kept 25 hours from the grave. To the poor of the parish of Stoke Brewen, Northon, 20 s. and so much to the poor of the parish where I shall be buried. To my dear mother, Mrs. Jane Lightfoot rents & profits of lands I am possessed of in Stoke Brewerne for 20 years and £10 as also £5 yearly during her life to be paid quarterly. To my dearly beloved wife, household staff, the old gold & jewels in her possession, £150 and such books as she shall choose. To Jane Ashbie my sister 5 marks & remittance of a debt owing by her husband to testator. To the children of my late sister Rose 40 s. each and 40 s. to their mother-in-law. To my loving father & mother, Francis Phelps, Esq. & his wife, to Sr. Edmond Sawyer, Knt. & his lady, Sr Thos Allen, Knt, Robert Harrington, Esq. and to my godmother, his wife, Mr. Augustine Phillips, my brother Frances Phelips, Esq., Mr. Wm Paylton, Wm Allafrye, Esq., Mr Francis Ridley, my brother Leonard Dare, Esq. & my sister, his wife, Mr. Henry Riley, to my brother Mr. Richard Lightfoote & his wife, to Mr. John, Mrs Mary and Mr Phillip Phelips, my loving brother & sisters, to Mr John Cockstint, Mr Edward Taylor, the elder, & my said dear Mother, rings to each -- Printed books, MSS. goods & estate not hereby disposed of to be sold to the best advantage. My friend Edward Bing, Esq: to have chamber lodging at Gray's Inne, wherein testator has an estate for life, & the life of his cousin, Mr. John Jones, at such reasonable price as shall be agreed upon. To my eldest son various books, Cambden's Britannica &c., also books "to my said brother Richard" & to each of his children 20 s. To my loving cousin, Mr Thomas Jones 5 marks. To Robert Kingston 20 s. out of

---

[4] Tyler Quarterly, William and Mary College, V.2, p. 90.

money he owes to testator & 20 s to each of his children. To each of my servants 20 s. "I leave a wife and many children, God bless them."
(In margin: 1. John. 2. Francis. 3. George. 4. William. 5. Richard. 6. Edmond. 7. Phillip. 8. Robert. 9. Mary. 10. Anne. 11. Jane. 12. Elizabeth. 13. Rebecca.)

Remainder of estate to be divided amongst testator's children -- appoints that the profit of all the estate be "wholly payed to my wife for the maintenance of herself & children" make further provision concerning this. I remit unto my said Father Phelips all money & "demands" between us. Ordains said wife, Elizabeth Lightfoote full & sole executrix. Desires Mr Harrington & Mr Riley to be overseers & gives them £5 each, desiring they will on all occasions proceed with the advice of said loving brother, Francis Phelips to whom testator gives 4 law books. "To each of my elder sonnes I give a Ringe or seale."

(No witnesses)

Proved at London 24 March 1648/9, by oath of Elizabeth Lightfoote, relict.

The will of Elizabeth (Phillips) Lightfoot shows that she survived her husband by thirty-five years. It is recorded in the Prerogative Court of Canterbury, 167 Lloyd.

I Elizabeth Lightfoot of London, widow. My body to be buried as near to my husband as conveniently may be. The poor of the parish of St Sepulchres, London, £5. To my son John Lightfoot £40 a year for life. Whereas my son Francis borrowed £50 of my son John: I now direct that the said sum be paid by my executors. To my daughter Webb and to my daughter Crosyer £10 each. To my daughter Elizabeth £200. I forgive my son Francis £150 which he owes me. To my sons William, Edward and Philip £100 each. To my son Robert £10, having respect to the £100 I gave him with my grandson John as his apprentice. To my Godsons Charles son of my son Francis, William son of my son William, John son of my son Richard deceased and John son of my son Robert £10 each. To my Godson Charles Lightfoot £40. To John Lightfoot son of my son Edmund £50. To my brother and sisters John Phillips Esq., Anne Dare the wife of Leonard Dare, Esq., and Philippa wife of William Rosewell, Esq., 40 s each. I will that my executor pay to my grandson, John Lightfoot, son of my said son John during his father's life £10 a year, and after his father's death £40 a year. And if my said executor with the advice of my son in law John Crosyer shall think fit to advance any sum of money (not exceeding £500) for the settling of my said grandson John: then the said yearly payments of £10 & £40 to cease. To my son in law Edward Leigh Esq. £10. I ordain my son William Lightfoot my executor.

Witnesses: George Aldrich, Mary Walker, William Vincent.
Codicil dated 22 November 1681.
Whereas by my will I have given to my daughter Eliz. £200: now forasmuch as since that time she has married Mr. John Turner to whom I have paid £500: I hereby revoke the said bequest.

To my daughter Scott late wife of my son Richard £10. To my daughter Turner's daughter one of my silver plates. My household goods at Ickenham I give to my daughter Crosyer.

Witnesses: George Day, Judith George, Elizabeth Haids.
Proved at London 24 December 1686.

CHAPTER V

JOHN LIGHTFOOT 1622-1686
MARRIED ELIZABETH TAILOR

John Lightfoot, the eldest son of John and Elizabeth (Phillips) Lightfoot, was born about 1622/23.

Foster's Gray's Inn Admissions contains the entry:

February 18, 1641/2, John Lightfoot, eldest son of John L., one of the fellowes of this Inn.

He was admitted 18 February 1641 into Gray's Inn, aforesaid as the eldest son of John Lightfoot, one of the Fellows. We may assume that he was about nineteen years old at the time since that was the age at which his father was admitted to Gray's Inn. His brother William Lightfoot was admitted on 24 October 1653 and his brother Richard Lightfoot on 14 November 1653, both as sons of John Lightfoot, deceased.

John is mentioned in the wills of his father in 1647, his paternal grandmother in 1649 and in that of his mother in 1679. He was to receive £40 yearly for life.

He married ELIZABETH TAILOR the daughter of JOHN TAILOR of Maidstone, co. Kent. She died before him since he is listed as a widower who died at Surinam in the West Indies.

We know that Captain John Lightfoot was in Virginia waters in 1666 when he lost his ship. We also think it very likely he was the Captain Lightfoot who commanded a merchant ship, The Convertine of London, which had just returned from a voyage to Virginia in June 1670.

He was known as the "Honorable" Captain John Lightfoot of Middlesex County, England and he died before 7 March 1687 in Surinam, West Indies as War Captain of His Majesty's Ship. The following notation was found in Herald's Visitation of London, 1687.

John Lightfoot a Captain of one of the H.M. Ships, died at Sea: Anno. 1682. Aet: Circa 55 years, 1682.

William & Mary Quarterly, Administration Act Books. *"On the 7th day of March 1687 here issued a commission to William Lightfoote 'Patruo" of John & Philip Lightfoot in parts beyond the seas, sons of John Lightfoote, widower, who lately died at Surinam in the West Indies, to administer the goods, etc. of the said deceased, during the absence & for the use of the said children."* The will names sons, JOHN and Philip, living outside of England.

Both John and Philip Lightfoot immigrated to Virginia prior to 1670.

His son Philip Lightfoot was mentioned in his father's administration in 1687. Philip Lightfoot of "Tedington", Charles City County, Virginia, died in 1708.

"I am not at all sure we are warranted in saying that John of New Kent and Philip Lightfoot of Sandy Point are brothers. Dr. Tyler begins his article by saying they were styled "brothers" in a General Court record, but does not give the date. Now which John and which Philip is he speaking of? If the captain in the Royal Navy was the father of John of New Kent (as I believe), his presence in Virginia could well have resulted in a General Court record saying he was Philip's brother (since we know that John Lightfoot and Elizabeth Phillips had sons named John and Philip) and this would make Philip of Sandy Point the uncle of John of New Kent. This, of course, we know to be incorrect. John and Philip were the only sons of John and Elizabeth (Tailor) Lightfoot.

Unfortunately the information about John and Elizabeth (Tailor) Lightfoot is almost nonexistent. What we have in this chapter is all we could locate that was authentic.

CHAPTER VI

JOHN LIGHTFOOT, COLONEL 1646-1707
MARRIED ANN GOODRICH

John and Phillip Lightfoot[1], sons of Captain John Lightfoot and his wife Elizabeth Tailor came to settle in Virginia about 1670. John, the eldest of these brothers, made his home in Gloucester County. It is probable that John Lightfoot was not permanently settled in Virginia until the time of his marriage to ANN GOODRICH. Ann Goodrich, daughter of LIEUTENANT COLONEL THOMAS GOODRICH and his wife ANNE SHERWOOD, was born in England and died in New Kent County, Virginia. Thomas and Anne Goodrich immigrated to Virginia in 1653 from England and settled in Rappahannock County. Anne Sherwood was the daughter of PHILIP SHERWOOD and you may have noticed the name Sherwood was a popular given name of the Lightfoots. Thomas served as Major of Militia of Rappahannock County, Virginia. He was the son of JOHN GOODRICH. Thomas Goodrich was a Lieutenant General with the forces of Nathaniel Bacon during Bacon's Rebellion in 1676. After Bacon's death when the rebellion was put down, many participants were punished. Thomas and Benjamin Goodrich (his brother) were among those who were required to come into court with halters around their necks and appeal, on bent knee, for forgiveness for having taken part in the rebellion. It is said that the Council was so strongly on the side of the rebels against the governor that the men only wore tapes around their necks. July of 1676, Bacon's forces clashed with supporters of Governor Berkeley at Piscataway (now called Dunbrooke).

---

[1] Americana, v. 19, p.215.

Thomas Goodrich made his will 15 March 1679 and it was proved just twenty days later on 3 April 1679 at Rappahannock County Court. He named his sons Benjamin, Joseph, Charles and Peter and bequeathed:

To daughter Ann 900 acres of land with the profits it being one Moyetie of a Devident of 1800 Acres called Matapony as abovesaid and to the heirs forever, Also to daughter Ane four Negroes Betty Watts Tho: Evans Fuller and her now Sucking child to be delivered to my said daughter upon her Marriage Day or at the age of one and twenty years which shall first come.[2]

Anne[3], the widow of Thomas Goodrich, later married Colonel Edward Hill.

John[4] and Ann were married 3 December 1681 in Rappahannock County, Virginia. He may not have moved into the New Kent County area until 1685. On 25 November 1686 the Vestry Book of Saint Peter's Parish carried this order:

It is ordered that Mr John Lightfoots family be added to y Surveyer of ye highway of ye Lower Road between the Lower Church and Black Creek Mill[5].

He was appointed by the King on 10 June 1670 Auditor-General of Virginia but it was found that the reversion of the office had been granted to Edward Digges and the grant to Lightfoot was withdrawn. This grant seems to have aroused considerable controversy. "A Memorial Concerning the Auditor's Place of Virginia", written by Francis Moryson, opposed John Lightfoot[6]. Moryson stated, in part:

That Captaine Lightfoote is in all respects most improper for that place, being noe Councellor nor Inhabitant, And (as I am informed) having many great debt uppon him (one noe less than a statute for seven hundred pounds) soe that if he hath the place, he must be forced to execute it by Deputy (w'ch as I conceave it contrary to lawe) it being an office of trust.

[2] Rappahannock Co., Va., Wills No. 2, 1677-1682, p. 118. Cited in William Montgomery Sweeney, Wills of Rappahannock County, Virginia, 1656-1692. Lynchburg, Va.: 1947. P.77.

[3] Rappahannock Co. Deeds 1676-1682, v.1, p. 167.

[4] William & Mary Quarterly, v.2, p.204.

[5] Virginia State Library, The Vestry Book and Register of St. Peter's Parish, New Kent and James City Counties, Virginia, 1684-1786. Edited by C.G. Chamberlayne. Richmond: 1937. p.9.

[6] Virginia Magazine of History and Biography, v. 19, p. 363.

He also stated that John Lightfoot was in Virginia, he believed, at the time the grant to Edward Digges was made. This would place the time of his arrival in the colony some time earlier than 1670.

There is on record in Essex a deed dated 1703, from Benjamin Goodrich of James City County, to William Aylett of King and Queen County, for part of a tract of land granted to Colonel Thomas Goodrich in 1689. By his will dated, March 16, 1678-9, he left it to his son Joseph Goodrich, who after possessing said land for some time, by his will bequeathed it to his son, Danby Goodrich, who, died in his minority. The said land passed to said Benjamin Goodrich, (son of Colonel Thomas Goodrich). The said whole tract was divided in 1681 between the said Joseph Goodrich, and John Lightfoot, gent. who had married Joseph's sister. Joseph Goodrich evidently had another son, Thomas, who died a minor.

In Rappahannock County Deeds 1676-1682, V. 1, p. 167, Deed. John Lightfoot to Philip Lightfoot – 1681.

I, John Lightfoot, of the Parish of Piscataway in the County of Rappahannock --- for a Competent Subsistence --- or dower for Ann my now wife, one of the daughters of Tho: Goodridge, decd. in case she shall survive me, --- have sold --- unto Philip Lightfoot of the Pish of Petso. in the County of Gloucester --- all which were the proper goods and estate of my said wife before out Inter-marriage --- bequeathed by her father --- 3 December 1681.

/s/ *John Lightfoot*

Witnessed and delivered to Edward Hill of Charles City County who recorded it in behalf of Lt. Coll. Philip Lightfoot.
Wit: John Bannister, John Stith and Paul Williams.
Rec: Rappa: 5th July 1682
Edmo: Craske: Cl Cur

In 1687, the birth of a Negro belonging to Mr. John Lightfoot was entered in the register of St. Peter's Parish, New Kent Co.

He apparently visited England, since in 1692 it is said that John Lightfoot, "lately come into the county," was councilor.

The Vestry was a political as well as an ecclesiastical body and was charged with the upkeep of the roads. This order directed the surveyor (or overseer) of the road to call upon John Lightfoot's slaves to assist in keeping the road clear and passable.

The records of New Kent County were burned in several fires at the courthouse and the records of James City County are also destroyed. (The home of his brother Philip Lightfoot at "Tedington," Charles City County, remained in the possession of his descendants until 1831, and the house itself stood until destroyed by a fire in the early years of the Twentieth Century.)

There are few references to John Lightfoot in the remaining records until 1695. After that date we again have considerable information about his stormy career. It must be remembered in reading the following extracts from the Virginia records that men were not so reserved in their words as now and that unsubstantiated charges were frequently and rather loudly made. Political jealousy was as rife then as now.

On 25 September 1696 the Minutes of the Council of Virginia show that John Lightfoot produced the King's Letter for his admission to that body, but in view of his general ill reputation and known misbehavior the Council decided that he be not sworn. The Council again considered his admission on 26 September and 22 October, but both times deferred action for further consideration. Finally, on 30 October it was ordered that he be summoned to attend the next Council.[7]

His associates on the Council then were Ralph Wormeley, Richard Lee, William Byrd, Christopher Wormeley, Edward Hill, Edmund Jenings, Henry Hartwell (removed to England), James Blair and Daniel Parke (both "intended for England"), Richard Johnson, Charles Scarburgh, all leading men of the Colony.[8]

On 10 May 1699 the Council Journals recorded:

Whereas John Lightfoot Esqr. hath Complained to His Excellency and the Honble. Councill that he peruseing the Councill Booke conceives two Orders therein contained doe tend much to his disreputacon, one on the twenty fifth of September 1696; the other of the first of March 1696-7 Since both which he was admitted and Sworne One of His Majts. Councill of this Colony.

Therefore he earnestly move's that His Excellency and the Honourable Councill, would cause an Order of Councill to be Entered either in haec verba, or to this Effect, (vizt)

That upon Consideration of the Said Complaint this Board are obliedged in Respect to truth to declare that from the time, the Complainant was Sworne of the Councill, which is above two yeares, he hath given his Constant Attendance, and behaved himself without Offence, nor hath in the least deserved, an ill Character Since, therefore

Ordered, that the same be entered accordingly...[9]

---

[7] Great Britain, Public Record Office, Calendar of State Papers. Colonial Series. America and West Indies. V. 1696-97 (London 1904), p. 145, 184, 186.

[8] Ibid. p. 458.

[9] Virginia Council Executive Journals. V. 1, p. 433.

On 3 June 1699 John Lightfoot, Esq., was appointed by the Council, colonel and commander in chief of the New Kent County militia and escheator of lands between James York rivers in place of Thomas Stegge.[10]

Sometime before 1700 Colonel John Lightfoot as a new Councilor of State had a mansion erected in keeping with his official position, which stood in the Government next to the Royal Governor, himself. The White House Mansion was a commodious one, with adequate room for entertainment of a large gathering and guests such as could be provided for by a large Colonial Plantation with servants a plenty and provisions of all kinds.

It was from this White House on the Pamunkey that the White House in Washington got its name.

On 13 July 1703 Governor Francis Nicholson took his oath of office and John Lightfoot was one of the three members of the Council to administer it.[11] He seems to have been very much a favorite of Governor Nicholson during the early years of his administration and Nicholson apparently was the person who was responsible for John Lightfoot's original appointment to the Council. At a later date, 9 February 1704/05, when their friendship was strained, the Council Journal records that Governor Nicholson

...*was also pleased to tell the sd. Coll. Lightfoot that it was through his Excellcy's means that he the sd. Coll. Lightfoot was of the councill, & admitted afterwards when Sir Edmd. Andros denied him and that if it had been left to the councill here to name him, he would never have been named in that station. And Coll. Lightfoot owned that his Excellcy. did recomment him to Sr. Edmd. Andros, from my Lord Pembroke.*[12]

On 2 December 1701 Governor Nicholson had written to the Council of Trade and Plantations in London about his difficulties in summoning a sufficient number of Councilors to carry on business, but listed those who could easily attend:

...*The honourable Coll. Jennings lives but 7 miles off, and Coll. Lightfoot about 40 miles (but very good road, and he hath never a creek to pass)*...[13]

The full details of the controversies in which Governor Nicholson became involved cannot be discussed here, but the government of the colony became very much divided in opinion. John Lightfoot aligned himself with the faction opposing the Governor.

On 20 May 1703 Robert Carter, James Blair, Philip Ludwell, John Lightfoot, Matthew Page and Benjamin Harrison prepared a memorial on

---

[10] Ibid. pp. 444-45.

[11] Ibid. V. 2, p. 328.

[12] Ibid. V. 2, p. 422.

[13] Great Britain. Public Record Office, <u>Calendar of State Papers. Colonial Series, America and West Indies.</u> V. 1701, p. 642.

Governor Nicholson's maladministration and also addressed a petition to the Queen. The petition stated, in part:

Nothing but a true regard to your Majesty's service, the peace and happiness of this Colony, and to that trust your Majesty has been pleased to repose in us, should have at present induced us to this unusual way of addressing your sacred Majesty for relief of ourselves and other your Majesty's good and loyal subjects of this country from the many great grievances and pressures we lye under by reason of the unusuall insolent and arbitrary methods of Government, as well as wicked and scandalous examples of life, which have been now for divers years past put in practice by H.E. Governor Nicholson, which we have hitherto in vain endeavoured, by more soft and gentle applications to himself, to remedy and prevent; but to our unspeakable grief, we have reaped no other fruit of our more private representations, but that thereby we have so highly exasperated the revengefull mind of the said Governor to the highth of implacable malice and enmity against ourselves and the better part of your Majesty's good and loyall subjects of this Colony, who are of the same sentiments, that without your Majesty's seasonable interposition, we cannot but apprehend the dangerous consequences of such practices, not only in kindling and fomenting of lasting feuds and animosities, but in endangering the publick peace and tranquility of this country. The particular instances of his maladministrations are so many that we have chosen rather to transmitt them in Memorials to some noted friends of this Country to be by them laid before such persons as your Majesty shall think fit to appoint to examine them...[14]

That the memorial was an extended one is evident from the fact that five pages of the <u>Calendar</u> were required to enter its contents. It appears that all of the charges made in it were not based on facts, since Governor Nicholson was able to refute some of them by citing the official records, but many of them were just grievances.

Nicholson's statement regarding Carter and Lightfoot contains these references:

Lightfoot is made a meer toole by them only to make up the number six, yt. they might there be ye major part of the Council...

This Coll. Lightfoot is a person generally of an ill reputation, &c, as will appear by ye annexed paper (which was not printed here) concerning him & he is so far from being amended, that of late he has grown worse, the

---

[14] Ibid. V. 1704-05, p.86.

five others that signed with him knowe all this to be true & formerly gave him such character as is not proper to be named here.[15]

Two letters written by John Lightfoot appear to be preserved in the English records. One was a note stating he could not be present at a meeting of the Council. The other was a letter that he wrote from Williamsburg on 21 October 1703 to the Rev. James Blair. Stating that the Governor abused me for siding with that d—d Scotch Parson, Blair, and said that there is a d—d Scotch conspiracy afoot against him, and that he had not a Councilor but was a rogue and a coward, etc., etc.[16]

John Lightfoot became a vestryman of Saint Peter's Parish on 1 June 1704 after that parish had been divided and some of the previous vestrymen had fallen into Saint Paul's Parish.[17]

We were able to obtain these various records:

The Colonial Virginia Register by Standard – Page 42.
The Council (Date is time of appointment or first appearance in the records which are extant) – Also Twelve Virginia Counties by Gwathney:
Members of Council from New Kent:

William Claiborne	*1623*
John Lightfoot	*1692*
William Bassett of Eltham	*1702*

Page 47 – *Among scattered records of New Kent County in 1699 may be found reference to John Lightfoot, Colonel, Joseph Foster, Lieutenant Colonel, and William Basset, Major, in 1699. George Keeling was the sheriff in 1708. Captain Charles Crump, who commanded a company of New Kent Militia in 1758. Captain John Lacey, who was an officer in the New Kent Militia of 1777.*

John's death is recorded in the parish register as:

Collo John Lightfoot Esqr. Obijt xxviii Die Maji circa Undecim Hor. & anno Dmi 1707.[18]

That is, he died on 29 May 1707 about eleven o'clock in the morning.

John Lightfoot and his wife, Ann Goodrich, had four children whose names are recorded:

---

[15] Virginia Magazine, v. 8, pp. 55-56.
[16] Calendar of State Papers. Colonial Series. America and West Indies, V. 1704-05, p. 104.
[17] The Vestry Book and Register of St. Peter's Parish, p. 99.
[18] Ibid. p. 434.

COLONEL GOODRICH LIGHTFOOT *and* MARY CHEW *are located in Chapter IX.*

MAJOR SHERWOOD LIGHTFOOT *was born around 1684 in New Kent County, Virginia and died 26 April 1730 in New Kent County, Virginia.*

The Parish Register shows that Major Sherwood Lightfoot owned many slaves since the baptisms of twenty-seven and the deaths of sixteen are there recorded.

The diary of William Byrd gives us a description of Sherwood Lightfoot on 22 September 1712: "...then proceeded to Mr. Sherwood Lightfoot's where we arrived about 5 o'clock. He received us very courteously and gave us some boiled beef for supper of which I ate heartily. He lives in a good plantation and seems to be very industrious. About 9 o'clock we retired to bed."[19]

JOHN LIGHTFOOT *was born 13 November 1711 in New Kent County, Virginia and died in 1782. He married* MARY MUNFORD *the daughter of* WILLIAM GREEN *and* ANN STANHOPE MUNFORD *of Charles City County, Virginia.*

FRANCIS "FRANK" LIGHTFOOT *was born 9 February 1736 in New Kent County, Virginia and was baptized 20 March 1736. He married* MARY ? *and died in 1804 in Edgefield County, South Carolina. He lived in Virginia, Antigua and the Abbeville District of South Carolina. His will was signed 8 August 1803 and probated 23 May 1804 in Edgefield, South Carolina.*

HENRY BENSKIN LIGHTFOOT, JR. *died a bachelor in 1823 in Edgefield County, South Carolina. His estate was probated 6 October 1823 (#17-594) by his brother John Lee Lightfoot leaving his brothers and sister as his heirs. Bond was signed by Larkin Griffin and George Munn. The estate was appraised by William Bullock, Wesley Brooks and David Cunningham.*

MARTHA "PATSY" LIGHTFOOT *was the administrator of John Lee Lightfoot's estate 26 February 1827 and died in 1845 in Edgefield County, South Carolina. Her will was signed 18 February 1841 and probated 9 January 1846.*

   BRUENTTA JOHNES

ELIZABETH "BETH" LIGHTFOOT *married* GEORGE JOHNSON.

FRANCES "FANNIE" LIGHTFOOT *married* NATHANIEL SAMUELS.

MARY "POLLY" LIGHTFOOT *married* JOHN McCALLISTER.

SUSANNAH "SUKEY" LIGHTFOOT *married* JOHN JOHNSON. *They had three children:* FRANKEY, SUSANNAH M. *and* ANTHONY LIGHTFOOT.

---

[19] Louis B. Wright and Marion Tinling, ed. The Secret Diary of William Byrd of Westover, 1709-1712, p. 587.

NANCY LIGHTFOOT *died in 1819. Her estate was administered December 1819 by her brother Henry Benskin Lightfoot, II and his bond signed by John Lee Lightfoot and Robert Burns. Citation was read at Fellowship Meeting House and at the house of Captain Bullock...her heirs were brothers and sisters and children of Susannah (Lightfoot) Johnson, deceased.*

JOHN LEE LIGHTFOOT *died unmarried sometime before 26 February 1827. His heirs were his brothers and sisters, except for Henry Benskin Lightfoot who was already deceased.*

HENRY BENSKIN *was born around 1747 in New Kent County, Virginia and lived n Antigua. He never married and died 1 November 1805 in Richmond, Virginia, leaving his estate to his nieces and nephews and brother Nicholas.*

PHILIP LIGHTFOOT

JOHN LIGHTFOOT *married twice. The first wife was Catherine Norvell the daughter of WILLIAM NORVELL who died in 1802, but the second wife's name is unknown. During the French and Indian War (1756-1763) there were two regiments of soldiers of Virginia men. One was headed by Colonel George Washington and the other under William Byrd. On June 3, 1758 there were in Winchester headquarters of Byrd three men seeking commissions as captains: Mr. Cocke, Mr. John Lightfoot and Mr. Munford. Their commissions were temporarily turned down. They were first made lieutenants and then later given commissions as captains. The Byrd regiment fought under the British General Forbes at Fort Duquesne. Captain John Lightfoot was on the Committee of Defense in 1774. In 1773 Virginia had trouble with counterfeit money. The chief officer who "apprehended and guarded the persons accused" was Captain John Lightfoot with his brother Sherwood. Captain John was paid £200 for his service. He was paid for recruiting in 1770. They also show he was given a large warrant for £2000 for the use of Continental troops on Hicks Creek March 27, 1781. This means he was fighting under Nathaniel Greene. Virginia troops fighting with Greene in South and North Carolina divided the forces of Cornwallis on Hicks Creek. The Tax Assessors books note that Captain John Lightfoot whose name in the first assessment after the Revolution in 1781, had already died. He died sometime before 1781.*

WILLIAM MARSTON LIGHTFOOT *was born around 1758 and in 1794 he married LUCY ARMISTEAD DIGGES the daughter of COLE and MARTHA WALKER DIGGES. In 1783 he listed 150 acres in his name. William was appointed 2nd Lieutenant 21 March 1777. William won a seat in the Virginia Assembly in 1795, he was elected to this service several times. On 10 March 1809 he died while still a member of the Virginia Assembly. At the time of his death his title was "Major". The title probably came from heading a local militia in the years just preceding the War of 1812.*

After William's death, Lucy married Joseph Repiton of Williamsburg. He was the editor of the "Phoenix Gazette and the Williamsburg Intelligence". The LIGHTFOOT home was Hill Pleasant, about one-half mile from the present village, LIGHTFOOT.

ARMISTEAD NORVELL LIGHTFOOT *died about 1834.*

    LUCY A. LIGHTFOOT

    WILLIAM LIGHTFOOT

    JOHN LIGHTFOOT

CATHERINE NORVELL LIGHTFOOT *was born 12 March 1796. On 18 November 1812 she married* ? HENLEY *and died 8 December 1882 in James City County, Virginia. She is buried next to her husband in the LIGHTFOOT family graveyard on the farm of Hill Pleasant.*

ELIZABETH DIGGES LIGHTFOOT *married* WILLIAM B. TAYLOR.

    LIGHTFOOT TAYLOR *inherited property from Uncle George Benskin Lightfoot.*

GEORGE BENSKIN LIGHTFOOT *married* MARY ANN VAUGHN.

SUSAN LIGHTFOOT *married* JAMES FARTHING *who took the name* LIGHTFOOT.

MARY C. LIGHTFOOT *married* DAVID P. HANKINS.

ARMISTEAD LIGHTFOOT *died about 1875.*

JOHN L. LIGHTFOOT *was born in 1805 in Brunswick County, Virginia. He married* LOUISA F. ?*and died in his home 23 May 1845 in Madison County, Alabama. His will was signed 20 May 1845.*

HARRISON LIGHTFOOT *was born in 1797 in Brunswick County, Virginia and married* MARY ? *who was born around 1804 in Virginia. They made their home in Madison County, Alabama.*

    MARY LIGHTFOOT *was born in 1829 in Virginia.*

    JOHN LIGHTFOOT *was born in 1832 in Virginia.*

    JAMES LIGHTFOOT *was born in 1832 also.*

WILLIAM CLAXTON LIGHTFOOT *was born around 1834 in Alabama. In 1860 he married* MARGARET WILSON BRAGG *in Hope, Hempstead County, Arkansas and died in 1891 in Lauderdale County, Tennessee. Margaret, a schoolteacher in Hope, Arkansas was born around 1840 in Rialto County, Tennessee and died in Lauderdale County, Tennessee.*

Lightfoot, Tennessee was once Union. A Mr. Wilson gave a plot of land on which to build a church. It was called Union Church. The church was for all denominations but became predominantly

Methodist. The family settled there in the early 1800's and the community was named after the family.

WILLIAM LIGHTFOOT *was born around 1863 in Arkansas and married* RHETTA WHITSON.

FREDERICK LIGHTFOOT *was born in 1864 in Lauderdale County, Tennessee. He married* MARY LEE CARNEY *who was born in 1868 in Somerville, Tennessee. Both of them died in Somerville, Tennessee.*

ARCHIBALD LIGHTFOOT *was born around 1868 in Lauderdale County, Tennessee and married* NORA ALSTON.

MARY BELLE LIGHTFOOT *was born about 1870 in Lauderdale County, Tennessee and married* RICHARD FORTNER.

FRANCES ANN LIGHTFOOT *was born about 1874 in Lauderdale County, Tennessee.*

LILLIAN LIGHTFOOT *was born around 1876 in Lauderdale County, Tennessee and married* WYATH LUNCEFORD.

CHARLES LIGHTFOOT *was born in September of 1879 in Lauderdale County, Tennessee and married* ADA WOODARD.

VADER T. LIGHTFOOT *was born in 1883 in Lauderdale County, Tennessee and married* IDELL TURNER *who was born in 1889 in Lauderdale County, Tennessee.*

DAISY LIGHTFOOT *was born after 1880 in Lauderdale County, Tennessee and married* HARRY LOUDER.

HENRIETTA LIGHTFOOT *was born around 1838 in Alabama.*

THOMAS M. LIGHTFOOT *was born in May of 1840 in Alabama and was a grocer.*

BEE R. LIGHTFOOT *was born in November of 1871 in Texas and married* EDNA P.C. ?.

MORGAN C. LIGHTFOOT *was born in January 1882 in Texas and married* VIOLA ARMITTA "MITTY" LANDES. *Mitty was born 15 December 1889 in Dublin, Erath County, Texas. After Morgan's death in Fort Worth, Texas she married* JEFF BURNETT. *She died in Wilbarger County, Texas.*

VIRGIL IRA LIGHTFOOT *was born in Big Spring, Texas. He married* MILDRED McGILL *in Tucumcari, New Mexico and died in Amarillo, Texas. Mildred was the daughter of* ERNEST H. *and* CORA ALICE TOWNSEND McGILL *of Des Moines, Iowa.*

AUDREY ALICE LIGHFOOT *married* BASIL PIPPIN *in Vernon, Texas.*

BILLY MAC LIGHTFOOT *married* BEVERLEY ANN ?.

RICHARD EARL LIGHTFOOT *was born in Hartley County, Texas and married* LORETTA SUE TYLER *in Clovis, New Mexico.*

PAMELA ANN LIGHTFOOT *was born in Corpus Christi, Texas and married* LAURENCE JAMES KENNON, JR. *in Amarillo, Texas.*

JAMES EARL LIGHTFOOT *was born in Amarillo, Texas.*

AUDREY NAOMI LIGHTFOOT *was born in Big Spring, Texas and died in Dumas, Texas. She married* ALBERT HARMON.

BYTHEL J. LIGHTFOOT *was born in Big Spring, Texas and married* ERMA DOBBS.

ELTON LIGHTFOOT *was born in Big Spring, Texas.*

WALTER LIGHTFOOT *was born about 1842 in Alabama.*

MILBURN LIGHTFOOT *was born around 184? in Alabama.*

MAJOR GUSTAVOS LIGHTFOOT *was born in 1847 in Alabama and died 22 May 1863 in Vicksburg, Mississippi. He died while serving the United States Calvary in the War Between the States. He was in the Missouri 12th Infantry and Sergeant Major for the 3rd Infantry, a Captain and a Major at the time of his death.*

SARAH LIGHTFOOT *was born about 1849 in Alabama.*

CLACKSTON LIGHTFOOT *was born 6 March 1790 in Brunswick County, Virginia. On 6 January 1819 he married* CLARA P. WINN *in Brunswick County, Virginia and died in June of 1846 of dropsy of the heart of which he had had a severe attack some four years before. The family had moved to Madison County, Alabama in 1823. Claxton left a considerable estate when he died. His widow made her will on the 21 of August in 1865.*

PHILIP C. LIGHTFOOT *was born 10 August 1802 in Brunswick County, Virginia. On 4 January 1826 he married* MARTHA D. SNEED *in Madison County, Alabama and died 10 August 1864 in Grant County, Alabama.*

REBECCA LIGHTFOOT *was born in Brunswick County, Virginia and on 27 May 1819 she married* HARRISON HARTWELL *in Brunswick County, Virginia.*

SARAH LIGHTFOOT *married ?* VAUGHN *and died in Alabama.*

MARY LIGHTFOOT *married ?* WESTMORELAND *and died in Alabama.*

EDWARD LIGHTFOOT

ALLEN A. LIGHTFOOT *was born 18 August 1796 in Georgia and in 1829 married* MARY WILLIAMS *in Pensacola, Florida. He died 13 May 1859 in Alabama. Mary was born 25 August 1811 in*

Georgia and died a couple of months before Allen on 25 March 1859.

PRUSILLA LIGHTFOOT *was born in 1830 and married* J.L. NICHOLS.

LUCINDA LIGHTFOOT *was born in 1831 and married* ? PEACOCK.

ALEXANDER LIGHTFOOT *was born in 1833 and married* MATILDA COSTON.

    MINNIE C. LIGHTFOOT *married* NEWELL STEPHENS *on 18 December 1890.*

ALLEN B. LIGHTFOOT *was born in 1836 and died in 1897.*

    MAJOR LIGHTFOOT *left Coffee County, Alabama for Texas in 1896.*

IRVIN LIGHTFOOT *was born in 1838 and died in 1859.*

JOSEPH GREENBERRY LIGHTFOOT *was born in 1841 and married twice. His first wife was* MARY STONE. *His second wife was* SALINA WESLEY CREW *who was born in 1841.*

MARY AN RIO LIGHTFOOT *was born in 1844 and married* JAMES KNIGHT.

DAVID LIGHTFOOT *was born in 1847.*

JULIA ANN AMINDA LIGHTFOOT *was born in 1849.*

WILLIAM ESTR. LIGHTFOOT *was born in 1852 and married twice. His first wife was* SARA JANE GUTHRIE. *His second wife* SALLIE STUART *was born in 1854.*

JOHN W. "JESSE" LIGHTFOOT *was born in 1805 in Georgia and in 1834 married* SUSAN M. LOWE *who was born about 1820 in Georgia, the daughter of* WILLIAM LOWE. *Jesse and Susan are found in the 1830 and 1840 census for Dale County, Alabama. He joined the Confederate army and died in 1862.*

    WILLIAM T. LIGHTFOOT *was born approximately 1840 and on 29 March 1860 married* ELIZABETH A. JOHNSON *in Jones County, Georgia. William died 31 October 1861 in Jones County, Georgia of Typhoid Fever.*

    BENJAMIN LIGHTFOOT *was born about 1838.*

    HENRY WESLEY LIGHTFOOT *was born 5 December 1842 in Georgia and died in Atlanta, Georgia. Henry worked a cotton mill and made dyes. He married twice. He married his first wife* LOUVESTER JEFFERSON "JEFFREY" WEAVER *on 20 September 1883 in Georgia. Jeffrey was born 28 June 1864 and died in Hapeville, Georgia.*

        JAMES WESLEY LIGHTFOOT *was born 15 May 1884 and died in Birmingham, Alabama. He married* MITTIE VASHTIE HATLEY *in Hapeville, Georgia.*

CHARLES HENRY LIGHTFOOT *was born 1 July 1887. He was a World War I veteran and died in Augusta, Georgia a bachelor.*

BERTHA BARTHENA LIGHTFOOT *was born 21 January 1891 and died when she was nine years old.*

JOHN WILLIAM LIGHTFOOT *was born 9 January 1894 in Stonewall, Mississippi and died in Atlanta, Georgia. He married twice. His first wife was* EUNICE THAMES.

FRANK W. LIGHTFOOT

His second wife was SARA ELIZABETH ADAMS. *Sarah married* ? VENABLE *after John's death.*

CHARLES EARL LIGHTFOOT *was still a child when he died.*

FLORENCE LIGHTFOOT *married* J.E. OSMENT *in Houston, Texas.*

SHIRLEY ANN LIGHTFOOT

JESSE LIGHTFOOT *died in Chattanooga, Tennessee.*

DOROTHY LIGHTFOOT *married* E.M. VARNON *in Birmingham, Alabama.*

MINNIE ESTHA LIGHTFOOT *was born 10 April 1896 and died in Houston, Texas. She married* ROWAN THOMAS HINSON.

BESSIE MAY LIGHTFOOT *was born 4 July 1899 and died exactly one year and one day later.*

GRACIE IRENE LIGHTFOOT *married* ERNEST A. TUCKER *and died in Haywood, California.*

His second wife SARA ELIZABETH BARROW *was a widow who was born 9 February 1876 in New Hope, Mississippi and died in Atlanta, Georgia.*

BEULAH BARROW *was Sara's daughter from her first marriage and was born 25 July 1899 in Stonewall, Mississippi.*

TOMMIS LIGHTFOOT *was stillborn.*

FRANCES KATHRYN LIGHTFOOT *married* JOHN W. WILCOX.

MURRAY WESLEY WILCOX

JOHN W. WILCOX, JR. *was an attorney in Atlanta, Georgia.*

EDWARD BARROW LIGHTFOOT *married twice and died in Georgia. His first wife was* WILLIE PEARL RICHARDSON.

JAMES EDWARD LIGHTFOOT

His second wife was JULIA HARDIN.

PRESCILLA LIGHTFOOT *was born about 1844.*

LAVINIA LIGHTFOOT *was born about 1846.*

MALISSA LIGHTFOOT *was born around 1848.*

WESLEY LIGHTFOOT *was born in 1811 in Georgia and died in 1859 in Little Oak, Alabama. On 2 August 1832 he married* MARY MAYBERRY.

On 11 July 1833 he married SARAH SNIDER *in Pike County, Alabama. He died in 1859 in Little Oak, Alabama. Sarah was born in 1815 and died in 1873.*

JOSHUA LIGHTFOOT *was born in 1834 and married* SOPHRONIA JENNY MIMS SNIDER

JOHN LIGHTFOOT *was born in 1836.*

MARTHA LIGHTFOOT *was born in 1837 and married* JAMES WARD.

ALLEN LIGHTFOOT *was born in 1838.*

JAMES HENRY LIGHTFOOT *was born in 1842 and married twice. His first wife was* EDITH L. HUTCHINSON *who was born in 1843 and died in 1887. His second wife was* ELIZABETH WILSON *who was born in 1840.*

JESSE LIGHTFOOT *was born in 1847 and married* JULIA OPHELIA WILSON.

MATTHIAS LIGHTFOOT *was born in 1855 and married* MARY ELLA SNIDER *who was born in 1860.*

JACQUELINE LIGHTFOOT *died in 1818.*

NICHOLAS LIGHTFOOT *died in 1818 also.*

TABITHA LIGHTFOOT *married* JOHN WALKER.

SHERWOOD LIGHTFOOT *was born 14 February 1733 in New Kent County, Virginia. He was baptized 16 March 1733. He owned a tavern called Fleur de Hundred and was the ferry keeper.*

FRANCES LIGHTFOOT *was born 30 July 1738 and was baptized 2 September 1738. On 17 July 1760 she married* GEORGE BENSKIN POINDEXTER *in New Kent County, Virginia. George was born 26 August 1739 in New Kent County, Virginia and was baptized 23 September 1739. He was the son of* GEORGE *and* SUSANNA MARSTON. *Frances died around 1776 and George married* SARAH PARKE *20 March 1777.*

EDWIN POINDEXTER *was born 10 January 1762 in New Kent County, Virginia.*

ROBERT POINDEXTER *was born 23 February 1765 in New Kent County, Virginia.*

GEORGE POINDEXTER *was born 29 March 1767 in New Kent County, Virginia.*

JAMES POINDEXTER *was born 7 January 1770 in New Kent County, Virginia.*

LIGHTFOOT POINDEXTER *was born 20 October 1772 in New Kent County, Virginia.*

ARMISTEAD POINDEXTER *was born 14 May 1775 in New Kent County, Virginia.*

SUSANNAH POINDEXTER *was born 3 May 1778 in New Kent County, Virginia. She was from George's second marriage.*

PARKE POINDEXTER *was born 12 March 1779 in New Kent County, Virginia.*

FRANCES POINDEXTER *was born 10 September 1781 and died 17 September 1785 in New Kent County, Virginia.*

NICHOLAS LIGHTFOOT *was born in James City County, Virginia and died unmarried in 1806.*

SHERWOOD LIGHTFOOT, JR. *was born 1 May 1714 in New Kent County, Virginia and appears in the Virginia records for the last time in 1741. There is a strong possibility that he went to the West Indies. It is noted a Sherred Lightfoot had a draw in the 1805 land lottery as a resident of Burke County. Sherwood died in Burke County, Georgia.*

PHILIP LIGHTFOOT *settled in Antigua and then Georgia in 1764. He petitioned for 200 acres of land 30 October 1767 in Burke County, Georgia next to John Taylor.*

RICHARD LIGHTFOOT *was born 25 February 1768 in Burke County, Georgia and died 9 June 1825 in Washington County, Georgia. He married* MARTHA *? who was born 18 June 1783 in Burke County, Georgia and died 7 April 1859 in Washington County, Georgia.*

CAPTAIN PHILIP LIGHTFOOT *was born 21 February 1810 in Washington County, Georgia and died 29 March 1898 in Shorter, Alabama. On 28 December 1837 he married* CAROLINE WOLFE *in Autauga County, Alabama. Caroline was born 30 September 1821 in Orangeburg, South Carolina to* JACOB *and* MARGARITE STOUDTENMIRE WOLFE. *She died 25 August 1889 in Shorter, Alabama. Philip served as 2nd Lieutenant Washington County, Georgia from 13 April 1830 through 27 July 1830 and Captain Washington County, Georgia from 16 January 1832 through 1 April 1834.*

ROBERT WALTON LIGHTFOOT *was born 19 December 1838 in Shorter, Alabama.*

MARTHA ANN "MATTIE" LIGHTFOOT *was born 16 February 1841 in Shorter, Alabama and died 21 September 188?.*

JOHN STEELE LIGHTFOOT *was born 31 May 1844 in Shorter, Alabama and on 15 December 1869 he married* REBECCA ELLEN CARMICHAEL *in Fitzpatrick, Alabama. Rebecca was born 24 September 1850 in Macon County, Alabama and died 28 July 1889 in Shorter, Alabama. She was the daughter of* MALCOLM M. *and* NANCY OSWALT CARMICHAEL.

MINNIE E. LIGHTFOOT *was born 3 March 1871 in Shorter, Alabama and died 17 June 1872.*

CAROLINE REBECCA LIGHTFOOT *was born 17 May 1872 in Shorter, Alabama*

NANNIE TALLULAH LIGHTFOOT *was born 12 November 1874 in Shorter, Alabama. Nannie was a twin. Her twin died at birth.*

PHILIP MALCOLM LIGHTFOOT, M.D. *was born 17 December 1876 in Shorter, Alabama and married* MAMIE ROSE PINKSTON. *Mamie was born 7 March 1884 in Macon County, Alabama the daughter of* WILLIAM F. *and* CAPITOLA HADEN PINKSTON.

  PHILIP MALCOLM LIGHTFOOT, JR.

  JOHN PINKSTON LIGHTFOOT

  MARTHA "MATTIE" STEELE LIGHTFOOT

  ROBERT MALCOLM LIGHTFOOT, M.D. *married* ALICE JEAN BAHR *the daughter of* WILLIAM AUGUSTUS *and* ALICE RAY DICKSON BAHR *in Marion County, California.*

MARTHA "MATTIE" STEELE LIGHTFOOT *was born 12 August 1880.*

JULIA STEELE LIGHTFOOT *was born 29 March 1887.*

WILLIAM TALLEY LIGHTFOOT *was born 19 April 1847 in Shorter, Alabama and died 20 April 1848; he was one year and one day old.*

MARY JANE LIGHTFOOT *was born 17 June 1849 in Shorter, Alabama.*

JAMES PHILIP LIGHTFOOT *was born 26 May 1852 in Shorter, Alabama and died a young child 23 May 1854.*

RICHARD NEAL LIGHTFOOT *was born 7 March 1855 in Shorter, Alabama.*

EMMA CAROLINE LIGHTFOOT *was born 26 August 1859 in Shorter, Alabama.*

SALLIE LIGHTFOOT *was born in Shorter, Alabama.*

NANCY LIGHTFOOT *was born 1 January 1819 in Washington County, Georgia and died 8 October 1878 in Washington County, Georgia. She married* WILLIAM WEBSTER, *who was born in 1806 in Washington County, Georgia and died 16 September 1881.*

MARTHA WEBSTER *was born in 1838 and married* WILLIAM WALLER.

MARY WEBSTER *was born 30 January 1840 and died 3 July 1871. She married* WILLIAM DOOLITTLE.

SARAH ELIZABETH WEBSTER *was born in 1844 and married* HOWELL JONES *who was killed in the Civil War.*

ANN WEBSTER *was born in 1846 and married* WILLIAM FROST.

JAMES WEBSTER *was born 1847 and was married twice. His first wife was* LOU JONES. *His second wife was* MARY JONES.

ROBERT WEBSTER *was born in 1849 and married* VIENNA TAPLEY.

SUSAN WEBSTER *was born in 1851 and married* GEORGE DOOLITTLE.

CHRISTIANNA WEBSTER *was born in 1852 and married* ? YATES.

VIOLA YATES

JOHN WEBSTER *was born in 1853 and married twice. He married first* HANNAH FORBES. *His second wife was* DELIA WOOD.

RICHARD DANIEL WEBSTER *was born 8 August 1854 and on 15 October 1882 he married* SALLY DUKE.

AMANDA WEBSTER *was born 1857 and died unmarried in 1878.*

SMYTHE MARDISSA WEBSTER *was born 24 January 1859 and married* JOHN JAMES DUNN *in Augusta, Georgia.*

MARGARET WEBSTER *was born 24 January 1859 and married* WALTER DUKE.

SALLY WEBSTER *was born after 1860 and married* BEN JONES.

RICHARD LIGHTFOOT, JR. *was born 24 December 1824 in Sandersville, Georgia and died 27 November 1887 in Alabama. He was married twice. His first wife was* MARY E. HURST.

REVEREND PHILIP H. LIGHTFOOT *was born 23 April 1846 in Washington County, Georgia. Jesse Wood found Philip in his father's blacksmith shop and said he had remarkable spiritual appearance. He took him to the parsonage at Cotton Valley where he attended school under Captain J.W. McNeely. Philip was converted and joined the church in his 14th year and in his 20th year, while still in school was licensed to preach. He was received into the Alabama Conference in December of 1872. He was a Methodist Preacher and died 26 November 1879 in Dallas County, Alabama.*

His second wife was ANN E. NUCKOLLS.

RICHARD WILLIAM LIGHTFOOT *was born 16 September 1870 in Shorter, Macon County, Alabama and died in Tuskegee, Alabama. He married* MARGARET THOMAS McGOWAN *the daughter of* THOMAS F. *and* MARY LOUISA CUNNINGHAM McGOWAN *of Tuskegee, Alabama.*

TEMPERANCE LIGHTFOOT *was born 12 March 1816 in Washington County, Georgia and died in Columbia County, Florida. She married* DAVID SHEPPARD *in Washington County, Georgia. David was born in 1811 in Georgia and died 16 September 1864.*

WILLIAM F. SHEPPARD *was born in 1836 in Washington County, Georgia and married* SOPHRONIA V.R. WHITE.

MARTHA ANN ELIZABETH SHEPPARD *was born 23 December 1837 and died 22 May 1887. On 6 May 1856 she married* JOHN JOSEPH KELLY.

NANCY ANN SHEPPARD *was born 17 April 1839 and on 11 December 1860 she married* GEORGE F. TOMPKINS.

MELISSA TEMPERANCE SHEPPARD *was born 20 March 1842 and died as a child 7 December 1845.*

MARY JANE SHEPPARD *was born 6 December 1844 in Washington County, Georgia and on 9 December 1869 married* WILLIAM F. WILLIAMS.

LOUISA CORNELIA SHEPPARD *was born 11 April 1847 in Washington County, Georgia and on 2 April 1868 she married* DANIEL L. HANCOCK.

CHARLES RICHARD WILTON SHEPPARD *was born 22 May 1850 in Washington County, Georgia.*

DAVID WINGFIELD JACKSON SHEPPARD *was born 4 October 1852 in Washington County, Georgia and on 1 March 1877 he married* SARAH JANE EDGE.

WILEY PARKS SHEPPARD *was born 1 March 1854 in Washington County, Georgia and on 21 March 1875 he married* LOVEY R. EDGE.

PHILIP HUTSON SHEPPARD *was born 4 December 1858 in Washington County, Georgia and died as a child 6 February 1862.*

ROBERT D. LIGHTFOOT *was born in 1808 in Washington County, Georgia and died in 1890 in Holmes County, Mississippi. He married* ELIZABETH PERRY.

SARAH FRANCES "FANNY S." LIGHTFOOT *was born 15 March 1845 and on 1 January 1867 she married* JAMES A GRAY. *James was born 22 March 1841 and died 1 January 1867.*

JESSE LIGHTFOOT GRAY *was born 7 November 1883 and married* EMMA DUNN.

VIRGINIA FRANCES GRAY *married* S. HASSEL FORD.

VIRGINIA "GINGER" FRANCES FORD

JESSE LIGHFOOT GRAY, JR.

LOU ELLA GRAY *was born 15 November 1867 and married* R.F. HICKERSON *26 April 1891. Mr. Hickerson died 16 January 1898.*

LUELLA FRANCIS HICKERSON *was born 4 September 1895 and died 22 May 1896.*

Her second husband was WILLIAM MEAD CAMPBELL.

LILLIAN ELIZABETH GRAY *was born 2 December 1871 and died a child 16 August 1876.*

CLARA NELLA GRAY *was born 2 October 1875.*

VIRGINIA GRAY *was born 2 November 1880 and married* J. OSCAR HEIDELBERG *in Monteagle, Tennessee.*

PHILIP LIGHTFOOT *died of "Camp Fever" in the Civil War.*

LOUISA WINFORD LIGHTFOOT *was born around 1834 and married* DR. BENJAMIN WICKHAM MOORE.

ELIZABETH LIGHTFOOT *married* JOHN CRAWFORD.

SUSAN CORNELIA LIGHTFOOT *was born in 1850 and married* DONALD GRAY *a Bible student.*

WILLIAM LIGHTFOOT *married* HANNAH GORNTO *on 8 August 1847 and was last heard of in 1891 in Columbus, Georgia. Hannah was born in 1830 in Irwin County, Georgia the daughter of* DAVID GORNTO *who was born 1 November 1805 in Bullock County, Georgia and married on 20 November 1827* ELIZA ALLEN *who was born in 1811 in North Carolina. Eliza's father was the first sheriff of Irwin County, Georgia.*

WILLIAM D. LIGHTFOOT *was an Ensign for Washington County, Georgia from 18 June 1834 to 17 July 1835. In 1834 he joined the Mineral Springs Baptist Church.*

MARGARET SUSANNAH LIGHTFOOT *was born in 1764 in Virginia and died 11 April 1847 in Alabama. She married* HENRY COOK *in 1780 in South Carolina. Henry was kidnapped in Germany and brought to fight the colonists. George Washington captured him in 1776, in Trenton, New Jersey. He enlisted in General Washington's army. Margaret fell in love with Henry while visiting in South Carolina. They moved to Orangeburg District, South Carolina in 1790 and later to Abbeville District, South Carolina on Hard Labor Creek. Henry was associated with the Swamp Meeting House. By trade he was a tanner and trader. He died in April of 1801 and his will was probated the same year.*

ELIZABETH COOK *was born in August of 1781 in Abbeville District, South Carolina and died in August of 1865 in St. Claire County, Alabama. On 29 November 1820 she married* DAVID SIBERT *the son of* REVEREND JOHN DAVID *and* ? WILMORE SIBERT *in Abbeville District, South Carolina.*

PHILIP COOK *was born in 1782 in Abbeville District, South Carolina and died in 1844 in Mississippi at the home of his son JOHN COOK. Philip was married three times. His second wife's name is unknown but his first wife was* MARY IRWIN *who he married in 1800 and his third wife was* PEGGY RUSH.

JOHN COOK *was born in Abbeville District, South Carolina and moved to Mississippi.*

SUSANNA COOK *was born in the Abbeville District, South Carolina and died in Pickens County, Alabama. Her first husband was* JACOB MOUCHETTE *of St. Claire County, Alabama.*

MARY COOK *was born in Abbeville District, South Carolina and died in Pickens County, Alabama. She married* ? PEEPLES *in St. Claire County, Alabama.*

RACHEL COOK *was born in Abbeville District, South Carolina and died in Alabama. She married* ? IRWIN.

After his death she married HENRY CLARK *about 1804 in South Carolina and died around 1820. Margaret died in the home of her son-in-law C.G. Beeson.*

MARTHA CLARK *was born 31 March 1805 in Abbeville District, South Carolina and died 12 August 1863. On 29 July 1822 she married* CURTIS GRUBB BEESON *in St. Claire County, Alabama.*

JAMES H. BEESON *was born in 1830 in Alabama.*

JOHN F.M. BEESON *was born in 1832 in Alabama.*

MARTHA A. BEESON *was born in 1836 in Alabama.*

LOUISA J. BEESON *was born in 1839 in Alabama.*

CURTIS G. BEESON *was born in 1843 in Alabama.*

JASPER N. BEESON *was born in 1845 in Alabama.*

LAURA M. BEESON *was born in 1846 in Alabama.*

SENIA S. BEESON *was born in 1848 in Alabama.*

PHILIP LIGHTFOOT, JR. *was born in 1765 and died in Lee County, Georgia. He married* BATHSHEBA ELTON. *Bathsheba was born 9 March 1792 she was the daughter of* ANTHONY MALCOLM ELTON *a soldier of the Revolutionary War was born 2 December 1753 in County Down, Ireland and died in 1836 in Jackson County, Georgia. He married* ELEANOR McELVANY *in 1791 in South Carolina. Eleanor was born 5 March 1759 in South Carolina and died in 1809 in Jackson County, Georgia.*

PHILIP LIGHTFOOT III, *married* RACHEL ATKINSON.

JAMES ARCHIBALD LIGHTFOOT *was born 5 June 1807 and died 22 May 1871 in Burke County, Georgia. James married* PENELOPE HOLTON *on 17 December 1835.*

ELISHA LIGHTFOOT *was born 24 March 1837.*

THOMAS JAMES LIGHTFOOT *was born 10 May 1838 and died in Jenkins County, Georgia. On 10 June 1860 he married* GEORGIA ANN WALLACE. *Georgia was born 22 March 1846.*

EMILY LIGHTFOOT *was born 8 November 1839 and on 13 August 1854 she married* JAMES GRAY.

LOUIS BERRIEN LIGHTFOOT *was born 11 March 1843 and on 6 November 1862 he married* SARAH E. HARSHBERGER.

SARAH E. LIGHTFOOT *was born 26 May 1844 and married* ? MANOR.

GEORGIA V. LIGHTFOOT *was born 9 March 1848 and on 10 December 1865 she married* DAVID H. LEWIS. *David was born 8 September 1845.*

After her death he married MARY ATKINSON *on 17 November 1857. Mary was born 18 August 1831.*

MARY D. LIGHTFOOT *was born 4 October 1860.*

MARY JANE LIGHTFOOT *was born 15 November 1862 and on 22 November 1888 she married* H.D. GODBEE.

JAMES ARCHIBALD LIGHTFOOT, JR. *was born 27 December 1863 and married* MAXIE J. ?.

HARRIET RACHEL LIGHTFOOT *was born 16 October 1866.*

PHILIP BENJAMIN LIGHTFOOT *was born 27 August 1868 and on 8 November 1888 he married* MARTHA "MARIETTA" WIGGINS. *Marietta was born 25 December 1866 and died 3 December 1894.*

CAROLUS LIGHTFOOT *married* DRUSCILLA CARPENTER.

WILLIAM LIGHTFOOT

ELIZABETH LIGHTFOOT

RICHARD LIGHTFOOT

SHERWOOD LIGHTFOOT

JESSE LIGHTFOOT

JOHN ELTON LIGHTFOOT

WILLIAM "BILLY" PHILIP LIGHTFOOT *was born 8 April 1856 in Lee County, Georgia and married* LACIE ROSETTIE BASS. *Lacie was born 20 February 1865.*

ELIZA AMMANDY LIGHTFOOT *was born 22 December 1885 and married* ? PHELPS.

WILLIAM EVERETT LIGHTFOOT *was born 26 July 1894.*

BERL LIGHTFOOT

MARY LOU LIGHTFOOT *was born 27 March 1897 and married* ? HUFF.

ANNIE BELLE LIGHTFOOT *married* ? McKELLAR.

JIM GARRETT LIGHTFOOT

JOHN B. LIGHTFOOT

JOSEPHINE "JOSIE" LIGHTFOOT *married* ? JONES.

GUSSIE ELTON LIGHTFOOT *died in Tipton, Georgia.*

ROY LIGHTFOOT

GREEN JACKSON, LIGHTFOOT SR. *was born in 1863 in Lee County, Georgia and died in Tift County, Georgia. On 14 July 1886 he married* ANNIE ELIZA BRYAN. *Annie was born in 1871 and was the daughter of* JOSEPH *and* SARAH ? BRYAN.

JESSE FAULTON LIGHTFOOT *was born in Worth County, Georgia and died in Albany, Georgia. He married* MARY LOU HOBBY *in Crisp County, Georgia.*

JESSE HOBBYE LIGHTFOOT *married* MARY NELL BAILEY *in Blakely, Early County, Georgia.*

ROY FAULTON LIGHTFOOT *was born in Baker County, Georgia and married twice. His first wife was* EDNA GERTRUDE GORE *from Albany, Dougherty County, Georgia. Edna was the daughter of* DEAN FRANKLIN *and* EDNA BELL GORE. *His second wife was* JO ANN WILSON.

MARILYN VIRGINIA LIGHTFOOT *was born in Albany, Georgia.*

CAROLYN EUGENIA LIGHTFOOT *was Marilyn's twin and she married* FREDERICK MISAJON *in New London, Connecticut.*

JASMINE KALANI MISAJON

DON PHILLIP LIGHTFOOT *was born in Albany, Georgia.*

JAMES A. "TONY" HALLIGAN LIGHTFOOT *was born in Albany, Georgia.*

WILLIAM PHILIP LIGHTFOOT *was born 22 June 1896 and died in Miami, Florida. He married* VIOLETTE McBRYDE.

EMMIE ELESIFF LIGHTFOOT *married* FRANCIS STEGER McCOY *in Charleston, South Carolina.*

TIMOTHY CHARLES McCOY

FRANCES ANN McCOY

MARY LIGHTFOOT *was born in 1888 and married twice. Her first husband was* RUFUS BURGE.

Her first daughter married L.J. JUDGE *in Cordele, Georgia.*

Her second husband was CHARLIE WILLIAMSON.

JOHNNIE WILLIAMSON *moved to Canada.*

ELLEN WILLIAMSON

GRACE WILLIAMSON *married* ? KNOTT.

GREEN JACKSON LIGHTFOOT, JR. *was born in October of 1893 and died in Winter Haven, Florida. He married* MARIETTA DANIELS *in Worth County, Georgia.*

DANIEL JACKSON LIGHTFOOT

WILLIAM LIGHTFOOT

WARREN LIGHTFOOT

MOSES EDWARD LIGHTFOOT *died in Lafayette, Indiana and married* BERNICE ? *in McAllen, Texas.*

SHERWOOD LIGHTFOOT *in 1884 was married to* MARY "MOLLIE" McDANIEL.

ROY LIGHTFOOT

EARNEST LIGHTFOOT

E.D. "EDDIE" LIGHTFOOT

THOMAS BENJAMIN LIGHTFOOT *married* ADDIE BELL WHITTINGTON *in Quincey, Florida.*

LEE ROY "BILL" LIGHTFOOT *was born in Worth County, Georgia and married* NOMIE ELLENDER STEPHENS *the daughter of* WILLIAM MARCUS JASPER *and* ZENOMIE BROWN STEPHENS *in Worth County, Georgia.*

VIVIAN RUTH LIGHTFOOT *was born in Worth County, Georgia and married* ARTHUR RAY DEAL.

ARTHUR DAVID DEAL

VIVIAN RENEE DEAL

MARGARET JERALDINE LIGHTFOOT *was born in Worth County, Georgia and died in Hensley, Arkansas. He married* ARLIE LOUIS SISCO *in Worth County, Georgia.*

STEPHEN DALE SISCO

CAROLYN ANN SISCO

MERLIN LEE ROY LIGHTFOOT *only lived for a few days.*

VERNON ROY LIGHTFOOT *was born in Worth County, Georgia and married twice. His first wife was* PATRICIA ALENE HAGIN.

REED NORVEL LIGHTFOOT

CALVIN TOM LIGHTFOOT

His second wife was JUNE CUMBUS.

ELIZABETH ANNETTE LIGHTFOOT *died as an infant.*

JANICE LEONA LIGHTFOOT *married* LARRY WAYNE McGEE.

JANICE MICHELE McGEE

KI ALANE McGEE

WANDE BERNEICE LIGHTFOOT *married* STEVEN MANCY HAIRE *the son of* AARON MANCY *and* EUNICE NADINE CHAPMAN HAIRE *in Worth County, Georgia.*

JEFFREY STEVEN HAIRE

LERON MANCY HAIRE

LEON LAMAR LIGHTFOOT *married* LYDIA ANN REYNOLDS *the daughter of* J.F. *and* BERNEICE SANDERSON REYNOLDS *in Colquitt County, Georgia.*

    ANGELA LEANN LIGHTFOOT
    MARSHALL LYNN LIGHTFOOT
  JIM FRANK LIGHTFOOT
  MARY LIGHTFOOT
  SUE LIGHTFOOT
  EMMA LIGHTFOOT
  FLORENCE LIGHTFOOT
  EDNA LIGHTFOOT
  KATE LIGHTFOOT
ED LIGHTFOOT
SUE LIGHTFOOT
FLORENCE S. LIGHTFOOT
EDNA LIGHTFOOT
JOHN LIGHTFOOT
SHEROD LIGHTFOOT

THOMAS A. LIGHTFOOT *was born in 1768 in Brunswick County, Virginia and died in 1830 in Lawrence County, Alabama. Thomas was listed as a Soldier from 1784 to 1797. He served the State of Georgia in the Indian Wars. On 10 April 1801 he married* SARAH ALLEN *in Davidson County, Tennessee. Sallie was born in 1781 in Surry County, North Carolina to* DAVID ALLEN *a Revolutionary War soldier and* NANCY McCONNELL. *She died in 1846.*

HENRY COLE LIGHTFOOT *was born in 1802 in Davidson County, Tennessee and died in 1834 in Green County, Alabama. In 1826 he married* ELIZABETH C. SIMMONS *in Lawrence County, Alabama. Elizabeth was born in 1810 in Georgia and married* JOHN T. HART *8 December 1835 in Perry County, Alabama after Henry's death.*

DR. WILLIAM M. LIGHTFOOT *was born in 1827 in Alabama and died 21 February 1856 in Bonham, Fannin County, Texas. The doctor never married and made his will in Greensbuff, Alabama, but it was probated in Texas.*

SARAH ANN LIGHTFOOT *was born in 1830 in Alabama and died in September of 1870 in Fannin County, Texas. In 1846 she married* DR. JAMES M. REID *in Sumter County, Alabama. The doctor was born in 1815 in North Carolina to* B. *and* T. REID.

  S. EMMA REID *was born in 1847 in Alabama and married* SYLVANUS REED *in 1866 in Fannin County, Texas. Sylvanus was born in 1834 in Missouri.*

    MARY REED *was born in 1867 in Fannin County, Texas.*
    FRANK REED *was born in 1869 in Fannin County, Texas.*

KATE REED *was born in 1873 in Fannin County, Texas and died in May of 1880 in Fannin County, Texas.*

SYLVANUS REED *was born in 1875 in Fannin County, Texas.*

HENRY REED *was born in 1877 in Fannin County, Texas.*

RUTH REID *was born in 1851 in Alabama.*

WILLIAM S. REID *was born in 1855 in Alabama.*

ANN REID *was born in 1859 in Texas.*

WILLIE REID *married* EUGENE V. AGNEW *in Fannin County, Texas.*

HENRY COLE LIGHTFOOT, JR. *was born in 1833 in Alabama and died in September 1870 in Fannin County, Texas. On 17 July 1856 he married* SARAH ANN JOUETT *in Red River County, Texas. Sarah was born in 1839 in Arkansas to* THOMAS *and* NARCISSA ? JOUETT/JEWETT.

LUCY H. LIGHTFOOT *was born about 1857 in Fannin County, Texas and died in September of 1870.*

JAMES R. LIGHTFOOT *was born around 1859 and was dead by 1879.*

SALLIE B. LIGHTFOOT *was born approximately 1860 and died before September of 1870.*

ROBERT W. LIGHTFOOT *was born in 1815 in Davidson County, Tennessee and died in 1878 in Lawrence County, Alabama. In 1842 he married* CATHERINE DELIA REED, *the daughter of* JAMES *and* JANE NORVELL READ.

HENRIETTA LIGHTFOOT

SUSAN M. LIGHTFOOT

JOHN FRAZIER LIGHTFOOT *was born 1 December 1805 in Davidson County, Tennessee and on 8 October 1833 he married* MALEANA JONES McKISSACK, *the daughter of* ARCHIBALD *and* SUSAN HARRISON McKISSACK.

THOMAS LIGHTFOOT *was born 20 July 1834 in Pulaski, Tennessee and died 15 February 1895 in Fannin County, Texas. He served in the Confederate Army as an officer under General Sterling Price and moved to Fannin County, Texas at the close of the war. His first wife* MATTIE TWEEDY *he married in Lawrence County, Alabama.*

THOMAS ELDRIDGE LIGHTFOOT *was born in 1861 and died in 1877.*

JOHN McKISSACK LIGHTFOOT *was born in 1869 and died in 1875.*

ROBERT DUNCAN LIGHTFOOT *was born 30 November 1864 in Arkansas and died in Temple, Texas. He married* MATTIE CLAIRE GANO *in Dallas, Texas.*

LEE GANO LIGHTFOOT

His second wife MARY MAXEY *he married in 1879 in Savoy, Texas.*

HENRY WILLIAM LIGHTFOOT *was born 6 May 1880 and died unmarried.*

MATTIE LIGHTFOOT *was born 4 July 188? and married* G.W. MORGAN *in Fannin County, Texas.*

DORA LIGHTFOOT *was born 22 February 1886 and died unmarried.*

MARY LIGHTFOOT *was born 10 October 1888 and died unmarried.*

SARAH ANN LIGHTFOOT *married* JOHN O. EWING *in Alabama.*

ARCHIBALD McKISSACK LIGHTFOOT *was born in 1837 and died in 1852.*

SUSAN LIGHTFOOT *was born in 1839 and died in 1845.*

JOHN FRAZIER LIGHTFOOT, JR.

MALEANA LIGHTFOOT *was born in 1843 and died in 1849.*

JAMES M. LIGHTFOOT

HENRY WILLIAM LIGHTFOOT *was born 29 December 1846 in Lawrence County, Alabama and married twice. When he was sixteen, he joined the Confederate Army in the Volunteers Eleventh Alabama Cavalry. After the war he moved his family to Texas. His first wife was* DORA BELL MAXEY *the daughter of* GENERAL S.B. MAXEY.

MAXEY BELL LIGHTFOOT *was born in 1875 and died the next year.*

SALLIE LEE LIGHTFOOT *was born in 1878 and never married.*

THOMAS CHENOWETH LIGHTFOOT *was born in 1880 and never married.*

His second wife was ETTA WOOTEN *the daughter of* DR. THOMAS *and* HENRIETTA GOODALL WOOTEN.

WOOTEN LIGHTFOOT *was born in 1890 and married* MORTON SMITH *in Galveston, Texas.*

WILLIAM HENRY LIGHTFOOT *was born in 1892 and married* HATTIE BELL MALLORY *in 1819. She was born in 1893 in Paris, Texas.*

HENRIETTA LIGHTFOOT *was born in 1896 in Dallas, Texas and married* MELVIN BINNEY *in Wilkes Barre, Pennsylvania.*

MARCUS ORVILLE LIGHTFOOT *was born in Lawrence County, Alabama.*

LUCY LIGHTFOOT *was born in Lawrence County, Alabama.*

NARCISSA W. LIGHTFOOT *was born in 1810 in Davidson County, Tennessee and died in 1845. On 8 April 1827 she married* JOHN MILLER.

NANCY ANN LIGHTFOOT *was born in 1812 in Davidson County, Tennessee and died in 1882. In 1835 she married* ASA MESSENGER.

JESSE LIGHTFOOT *was a Judge of Inferior Court of Tattnall County, Georgia around 1800. He was located in Readsville, Georgia from 1805-1810. He deeded land in 1816 to Mathew Jones. He was in Mobile, Alabama 2 February 1822 and on 1 April 1822 he was in Pensacola, Florida.*

JOHN LIGHTFOOT *was born in 1776.*

FRANCES LIGHTFOOT *was born 31 October 1708 in New Kent County, Virginia.*

MARY LIGHTFOOT *was born 9 September 1707 in New Kent County, Virginia. In 1733 she married* WADE NETHERLAND. *Wade was born in 1705 to* JOHN *and* SARAH ? NETHERLAND, SR. *He signed his will 28 June 1764, died in 1769 and his will was probated 24 April 1769 in Cumberland County, Virginia.*

WADE NETHERLAND, II *was born in 1734 and married* ANNE WILLIAMSON.

FRANCES NETHERLAND *was born in 1735.*

MARY LIGHTFOOT *married* TUCKER WOODSON *22 February 1762 and died in December of 1775.*

WADE WOODSON

SARAH "SALLIE" WOODSON *was born 22 September 1764 and married* WILLIAM MACON.

SALLIE WOODSON MACON *was born 1790 in Cumberland County, Virginia and married* THOMAS THOMPSON SWANN *in 1806. Thomas was born in 1785 in Easton, Pennsylvania and was the great-grandson of George Taylor "Signer".*

FLEMING LIGHTFOOT SWANN *was born 14 November 1816 in Cumberland, Virginia and died 15 April 1870. In 1860 he married* NANCY NEILL WISELY *in Bates County, Missouri.*

TARLETON WOODSON

ELIZABETH LIGHTFOOT *was born 23 September 1716 in New Kent County, Virginia.*

THOMAS LIGHTFOOT *was born about 1691 in Gloucester County, Virginia. He married* ELIZABETH STONE *and died about 1750. Elizabeth was born around 1704 and died 2 April 1759.*

FRANCES LIGHTFOOT *was born 8 August 1717 in New Kent County, Virginia and died 19 February 1725.*

ANNE LIGHTFOOT *was born 7 August 1720 in New Kent County, Virginia.*

FRAYSER LIGHTFOOT *was born 30 March 1723 in New Kent County, Virginia and died the same day.*

HENRY LIGHTFOOT *was born 30 March 1723 in New Kent County, Virginia the twin of Frayser. Henry married* MARY ?_ *and died 17 November 1781 in New Kent County, Virginia. Mary died 14 May 1783 in New Kent County, Virginia. When Henry died his estate was worth £78,389.*

MARY LIGHTFOOT *married* ? CLARK *sometime before 1780.*

SUSANNAH "SUKEY" LIGHFOOT *was born about 1765 in Brunswick County, Virginia and died in September of 1840. She married* JESSE STONE *the son of* THOMAS *and* PHEBE PRICE STONE. *Jesse was born 8 August 1734 in Brunswick County, Virginia and died 9 September 1840 in Edgeville County, South Carolina.*

THOMAS STONE *was born around 1779 and died in September of 1842 in Edgefield County, South Carolina. He married three times. His first wife was* MARTHA JOHNSON, *his second wife was* FRANCES FOWLER *and his third wife was* EMILY MOORE HILL.

HENRY STONE *was born around 1785 and died 3 April 1849 in Edgefield County, South Carolina. He married* HARRIETT ? *who was born about 1793.*

MARTHA "PATSEY" FRAZIER STONE *was born approximately 1787 and never married.*

NANCY STONE *married* ROBERT WALLACE.

ELIZABETH STONE *married* ABNER "ABRAHAM" CLARK *who died in 1834 in Edgefield County, South Carolina. Elizabeth died 5 June 1848 in Edgefield County, South Carolina.*

ABNER STONE *was born 5 April 1791 in Edgefield County, South Carolina and died 29 July 1861 in Sardis, Alabama. He married* ABIGAIL JORDAN *who died around 1861 in Sardis, Alabama.*

JINCY STONE *married twice. Her first husband was* LAWRENCE RAMBO. *The second husband was* PETER PUTNELL. *Jincy died in September of 1852 in Sumter County, Alabama.*

SARAH "SALLY" STONE *married* LEVI JORDAN *and died in Texas.*

JESSE STONE, JR.

DAVID STONE *married* SARAH WALLACE.

DAVID STONE

SUSANNAH STONE

MARTHA "PATTY" LIGHTFOOT *was born around 1770 and 16 May 1791 married* CHARLES JOHNSON *in Brunswick County, Virginia.*

ELMIRA "ELLY" LIGHTFOOT

PHILIP "PHILL" LIGHTFOOT *was born in Brunswick County, Virginia and died 1 November 1841 in Edgefield County, South*

Carolina. He never married and lived in Virginia and North and South Carolina.

NANCY LIGHTFOOT *married* WILLIAM HAMMOND *around 1780.*

WILLIAM LIGHTFOOT *was born in Brunswick County, Virginia. He married twice. On 4 March 1822 in Northampton County, North Carolina he married* PATSY RHODES.

JOHN A. LIGHTFOOT *was born 27 September 1780 in North Carolina and died 7 March 1855 in Taliaferro County, Georgia. He married twice. His first wife* ELIZABETH RHODES *he married on 4 September 1802 in Berty County, North Carolina. The records also list John A. as a Justice of the Peace of Talliaferro County, Georgia, who married James S and Anna. John is listed in the Tax Returns of 1825.*

THOMAS H. LIGHTFOOT *was born 26 September 1803 in Virginia and died 8 October 1846. On 1 January 1834 he married* JANE CAROLINE SIMONTON *in Newton County, Georgia. He joined the White Plains Baptist Church, Hancock County, Georgia on the 20th of August 1832. He was a teacher of the poor school of Greene County, 142 District, Georgia. He was teaching there 1 April 1830.*

DR. WILLIAM S. LIGHTFOOT *was born 4 February 1805 in Virginia and died 4 August 1864 in Macon, Georgia. He married* MARY ANN JONES *1 April 1834. Mary was born 25 November 1815 in Warren County, Georgia and died 4 June 1882 in Macon, Georgia. She was the daughter of* HENDLEY *and* MARY BAKER JONES. *William joined the White Plains Baptist Church 14 August 1835. They lived in Jones County, Georgia, and moved to Macon about 1849. They lived in Gray when he was Justice of the Inferior Court in 1845. He practiced medicine from 1839-1849. William was appointed guardian to his niece Catharine Elizabeth Lightfoot, minor child of John W. Lightfoot, 17 March 1851. After the Doctor's death Mary married* EDWIN C. THOMAS *in Bibb County, Georgia.*

MARY J. LIGHTFOOT *was born around 1839.*

SARAH M. LIGHTFOOT *was born about 1844.*

JOHNNIE LIGHTFOOT *was born 27 November 1851 and died 28 August 1854.*

WILLIAM "WILLIE" T. LIGHTFOOT *was born about 1856 and died 18 March 1878.*

ALLEN LIGHTFOOT *was born 13 November 1808.*

PETERSON B. LIGHTFOOT *was born 23 October 1814 and died 20 June 1837.*

EDWIN B. LIGHTFOOT *was born 12 November 1810 and died 25 September 1884. He married* CATHERINE DONALDSON CODY *the daughter of* BARNET *and* SINAI McCORMICK CODY, *4 November 1833. Edwin was a hotelkeeper and an assistant Marshall.*

JAMES NEWELL LIGHTFOOT *was born 1 August 1839 and died 18 September 1885 in Henry County, Alabama. On 4 November 1862 he married* MARY GORDON McALISTER. *Mary was the daughter of* GENERAL A.C. *and* EVELYN HUDSPETH GORDON. *He joined the Confederate Army. After the war he was a farmer from 1871-1877 of cotton. He later had a cotton business in Savannah, Georgia. An interesting little news item about the James Newell Lightfoot family: Colonel J.N. Lightfoot and family of Savannah have been visiting in Abbeville and will not return home till Jack Frost has conquered yellow fever.*

DAISY LIGHTFOOT *was born 27 May 1865 and married* A.S. STEGALL.

LILLIE GORDON LIGHTFOOT *was born in 1866 and married* STERLING PRICE BRADLEY *who was born in 1863.*

LAWRENCE GORDON LIGHTFOOT *was born 9 April 1868.*

SARAH LIGHTFOOT *was born 20 October 1841 and died 7 June 1884 in Greensboro, Georgia. On 15 October 1863 she married* FELIX CALLOWAY REID *in Greene County, Alabama. Felix was the son of* NANCY JARRELL *of Talliaferro County, Georgia. He was born 5 November 1840 and died 18 April 1875 in Greensboro, Georgia.*

FELIX CALLOWAY REID, JR. *was born 19 August 1876 and married* MARY BELLE KING *whom was born 8 December 1879.*

MARY KATHERINE REID *was born 16 April 1867 and died 24 August 1887 in Greensboro, Georgia.*

THOMAS REESE LIGHTFOOT *was born about 1848 and died 27 October 1896 in Fort Garner, Georgia. During the Civil War he joined Ewell's Brigade.*

WILLIAM EDWIN LIGHTFOOT *was born in Blakely, Georgia. He married* BETTY FARMER *in 1836 and fought for the Confederate Army in the 6th Alabama Regiment.*

CAROLINE DONALDSON LIGHTFOOT *married* DR. R.L. REEVES *26 November 1868 in Auburn, Alabama.*

EDWIN LIGHTFOOT REEVES
FRANK CLYDE REEVES
MARGARET CAROLINE REEVES
JOHN RICHARD REEVES

CATHARINE S. LIGHTFOOT *was born 30 July 1812 and died 30 October 1847. She married* ELISHA P. JARRELL *22 January 1829 in Taliaferro County, Georgia.*

ANDERSON J. LIGHTFOOT *was born 31 August 1818 and died in 1855.*

JULIA LIGHTFOOT

COLONEL COLLEN "CULLEN" A. LIGHTFOOT *was born 11 September 1821 and died 13 November 1853 in Warrenton, Georgia. He married on 31 December 1850 but his wife's name is unknown.*

JULIA LIGHTFOOT

JOHN W. LIGHTFOOT *was born 5 October 1806 and died 10 July 1836. On 8 December 1835 he married* CAROLINE A. HILL *in Baldwin County, Georgia. After John's death Caroline married* THEODORE A. GOODWIN.

CATHERINE ELIZABETH LIGHTFOOT

He married his second wife ASENATH REYNOLDS *26 May 1850 in Taliaferro County, Georgia. Asenath was born 12 November 1811.*

ELIZABETH LIGHTFOOT *was born 6 November 1782 in North Carolina and married* NATHANIEL SMITH.

MARY LIGHTFOOT *was born 20 March 1785 in North Carolina.*

WILLIAM C. LIGHTFOOT *was born 6 March 1790 in North Carolina.*

JAMES SHARP "T" LIGHTFOOT *was born 14 December 1792 in North Carolina and on 8 February 1820 he married* ANNA LANCASTER *in Hancock County, North Carolina.*

His second wife was CATHERINE BRYAN *on 18 January 1831 in Northampton County, North Carolina.*

SARAH "SALLIE" LIGHTFOOT *was born in 1766 in Virginia and died in 1793 in Virginia. She married* HENRY JONES *16 December 1786 in Brunswick County, Virginia. Henry Jones was born 9 February 1762 in Dinwiddie County, Virginia to* HENRY *and* WINNIE ELDER JONES *and died 15 May 1851 in Barbour County, Alabama. He married twice after Sallie's death. His second wife was* MARY HOGAN *and his third wife was* NELLIE PAYNE.

WILLIAM JONES *was born 26 March 1789 and died as a child.*

HENRY LIGHTFOOT JONES *was born 16 September 1791 in Virginia and died around 1860 in Bienville Parish, Louisiana. He married* MARY ELIZABETH MARCUS *in 1815 in Jones County, Georgia. Mary was born in 1803 in South Carolina or Georgia to* DANIEL *and* MARY MARCUS *and died around 1865.*

LOUISA DANIEL JONES *was born in Georgia and married* THOMAS WILLIAMS.

WILLIAM HENRY JONES *was born in Georgia and married* REBECCA WESTBROOK. *He served the Confederate Army and died in Federal Prison Camp Chase in Ohio.*

SARAH LIGHTFOOT JONES *was born 22 February 1822 in Meriwether County, Georgia and died in Barbour County, Alabama. On 7 November 1842 she married* WILLIAM USHER WILKES *in Barbour County, Alabama.*

MARTHA ANN JONES *was born in 1824 in Meriwether County, Georgia and died in Bienville Parish, Louisiana. In December of 1847 she married* JOHN G. McDOWELL *in Barbour County, Alabama.*

JOHN HOLLINGER JONES *was born 28 December 1826 and died 3 October 1873 in Covington County, Alabama. On 30 March 1852 he married* LURANA STEWART *in Pike County, Alabama.*

MARY ELIZABETH JONES *was born 3 March 1831 in Meriwether County, Georgia and died 20 September 1893 in Red River Parish, Louisiana. She had married twice. Her first husband was* WILLIAM BARNETT WATTS *and her second husband was* JOHN PORTER McFARLAND *from Coushatta, Louisiana.*

EMILY JANE JONES *was born 16 December 1832 in Meriwether County, Georgia and died in Bullock County, Alabama. She married twice. Her first husband was* BUNYAN YOUNG *from Alabama and her second husband was* CRADDOCK RILEY *also from Alabama.*

THOMAS JONES *was born 8 March 1793 and died as a child.*

REBECCA "BECKY" LIGHTFOOT *was born about 1768 in Brunswick County, Virginia and died after 1823 in Brunswick County, Virginia. She married* ALEXANDER DAMERON *9 September 1788 in Brunswick County, Virginia.*

JOHN H. DAMERON

WILLIAM HENRY DAMERON *married* JULIA MANGUM.

ANNE MOREHEAD DAMERON *was born in 1794 and died after 1860. On 21 July 1818 she married* THOMAS H. BARROW.

ANGELINA DAMERON *married* JOHN BROWDER *8 March 1834.*

MARTHA DAMERON *married* GRIFFIN SHORT.

JAMES DAMERON *moved to Mississippi.*

SARAH M. DAMERON *married* LEWIS BARROW *and died in Madison County, Mississippi.*

DR. THOMAS LIGHTFOOT *was born about 1760 in Brunswick County, Virginia and died around 1830 in Alabama. He was a soldier from 1784-1797 and fought for the State of Georgia in the Indian War and also served in the Revolutionary War. In 1793 he was located in*

Wilkes and Warren Counties, Georgia and in 1808 he was in Hancock County. He married LUCRETIA "RENNIE" ?.

DR. WILLIAM THOMAS LIGHTFOOT *was born in 1814 and died in 1870 in Macon, Georgia. On 19 May 1836 he married* EMILY HILL MITCHELL *in Thomasville, Georgia. Emily was the daughter of* NATHANIEL RAINES *and* TEMPERANCE JORDAN MITCHELL *and died 6 October 1857 in Bibb County, Georgia. After her death William married* HARRIET COLLINS *11 November 1858 in Bibb County, Georgia.*

ROBERT JAMES LIGHTFOOT *was born about 1842 in Georgia and died 23 July 1878 in Macon, Georgia. He married* ELLEN ROSS. *He enlisted 9 June 1861 in the Central City Blues as Company H 12th Regiment of the Georgia Volunteer Infantry Army of North Virginia as a private and was appointed as quartermaster 6 July 1861. This was an article was in the paper: We learn that Mr. Robert Lightfoot, well known in Macon and a former resident of this city, was very seriously injured at his place in Monroe County by an explosion of a blast in a well. Whether it was from a premature or a delayed explosion, we could not learn. One of his lower limbs was very badly lacerated and he received other injuries. A messenger came to the city yesterday for medical and surgical aid for the wounded man.*

THOMAS JEFFERSON LIGHTFOOT *was born about 1824 in Georgia. On 25 March 1845 he married* MINERVA TUBERVILLE *in Jones County, Georgia. Thomas had many professions: Doctor, Dentist and Merchant. On 5 April 1848 he married* TEMPERANCE JORDAN McKINNON *in Thomas County, Georgia. Tempy was born 11 January 1832 in Thomas County, Georgia and died 2 June 1899 in Pelham, Georgia. She was the daughter of* NEILL *and* SARAH RAINES MITCHELL McKINNON.

CORNELIUS LIGHTFOOT *was born in 1850 in Thomas County, Georgia.*

WILLIAM J. LIGHTFOOT *was born in 1854 in Thomas County, Georgia and on 28 November 1878 he married* NELLIE HAMILTON.

ROSA LEE LIGHTFOOT *was born in 1857 in Thomas County, Georgia and married* ? TUCKER *before 1880.*

FRANCES "FANNIE" H. LIGHTFOOT *was born in 1859 in Thomas County, Georgia and on 21 October 1881 she married* EVERETT GORNTO.

WALLACE LUCIUS LIGHTFOOT *was born 23 September 1861 in Thomas County, Georgia and died in Brooklyn, New York. On 20 July 1892 he married* MARIE PAULINE RYAN *in Savannah,*

Georgia. Marie was born 22 December 1867 in Charleston, South Carolina and died in Amityville, New York.

WILLIAM O. LIGHTFOOT

TALULA LIGHTFOOT *was born about 1862 in Thomas County, Georgia and married* EVERETT GORNTO.

ROBERT L. LIGHTFOOT *was born in 1864 in Thomas County, Georgia.*

MINNIE "PINKIE" LIGHTFOOT *was born about 1867 in Thomas County, Georgia.*

HENRY McKINNON LIGHTFOOT *was born in June of 1870 in Thomas County, Georgia and in 1895 he married* LILLIE MADORA SHELTON. *Lillie was born in December of 1868 to* MATTIE A. SHELTON *of Tennessee.*

HENRY C. LIGHTFOOT *was born in July 1896 in Texas.*

JOHN C. LIGHTFOOT *was born in September of 1897 in Texas.*

THOMAS O. LIGHTFOOT *was born in November of 1898 in Texas.*

CLARIA B. LIGHTFOOT *was born in Texas.*

KATE LIGHTFOOT

ELLA E. LIGHTFOOT *was born in 1873 in Thomas County, Georgia and on 14 January 1892 she married* ? SENTERFIT.

CLARENCE LIGHTFOOT *was born in Thomas County, Georgia.*

MARY "MAMIE" LIGHTFOOT *was born in 1875 in Thomas County, Georgia and married* LEROY NAPIER.

MARY LIGHTFOOT *was born 24 May 1725 in New Kent County, Virginia.*

ALICE LIGHTFOOT *was born 25 December 1698 in New Kent County, Virginia.*

CHAPTER VII

THE STORY OF THE WHITE HOUSE

There have been few plantations in Virginia or America that have been so intimately related to the history of the United States as the White House Plantation on the Pamunkey River.

After the Indian Massacre in 1644, the General Assembly set up on the rivers several forts for the safety and protection of outlying settlers. At Rickahock there was stationed a small body of men under Captain Roger Marshall. This small garrison became the personal responsibility of Captain Marshall on the condition that he maintain ten men at the place for a period of three years, and in settlement he should have in return Fort Royal, otherwise called Rickahock, and six hundred acres of land.

Whereas by Act of Assembly dated at James City the 5th day of October 1646, Fort Royal als, Rickahock with Six Hundred Acres of Land joyning upon the same with all Houses and Edifices belonging to the same was granted unto Capt. Roger Marshall upon condition that he the said Capt. Marshall should Mayntayne ten men upon the Same dureing the tyme of three yeares which said condition being performed &c.[1]

Captain Roger Marshall was granted a patent to the six hundred acres and the houses erected at the Fort on March 14, 1649. This tract was sold to Manwarring Hammond on the same day, and it became the nucleus of the large tract which was granted to General Hammond and incorporated in his Patent to 3760 acres of land lying on the south side of York River.

The description of this land conforms to the natural boundaries, which are recognizable to this day.

Manwarring Hammond Esq: 3760 acres in York County, 15 March 1649, lying up York River on the south side thereof commonly called Fort Royal bounded North East, North West, South West, North East and North upon the River; South southwest by South upon the mountains, and

---

[1] Hening, Book No. 2, p. 195.

northwest by North upon Black Creek & South East upon the Bay, including on the other side the said Bay one neck of land containing 350 acres. Six hundred acres purchased of Capt. Roger Marshall to whom it was granted 14th of this instant March & 3160 acres for the transportation of 63 persons.[2]

On March 14, 1649, Colonel Philip Honeywood Esq: was granted 3050 acres of land next to Warrannucock Island (which is the Pamunkey Indian Reservation of today), 1550 acres above the Island and 1500 acres on the south side of the York River near the said Island. Bounded southeast along marked trees of Mr. Jernew, south west by south and west by south along the mountains, including two tongues of land running to the river containing 14 acres.[3]

These two large tracts covered more than six square miles of land. The two gentlemen who received the patents to these tracts were Royalist Officers who had escaped England to find safety in Virginia away from Cromwell. As soon as the Restoration came they hied it back for home, but for some years held title to these properties in Virginia. Fortunately the deeds of transfer have been preserved conveying this land to Captain William Bassett of Eltham, which deeds were dated January 23, 1670.

The deeds of transfer from William Bassett to Colonel John Lightfoot have been lost in the fires that consumed the colonial records of New Kent County. It is believed that John Lightfoot purchased the lands from William Bassett's Estate at the time he came to New Kent County which was about 1686 when he was listed in the procession records of St. Peter's Parish. He was charged with 3000 acres of land in 1704 and subsequent facts establish the fact that he was living here in 1707 when he died.

Colonel John Lightfoot had been appointed to the Council in 1692 and was Collector for the Counties between the York River and James River and Commander-in-Chief of King and Queen County.

During his residence there are frequent mention of his difficulties with the Indians, who lived across the Pamunkey, opposite to his Estate.

It must be remembered that the members of the Council were in Colonial Virginia next to the Governor in status and their position required personal wealth, social standing and the Councilor enjoyed a mansion of dimensions in keeping with his position. The findings at White House indicate that the base of the first house erected here was larger than the two, which were built later on the same foundations. The masonry indicates that the house was erected during the residency of Colonel John Lightfoot prior to 1707 when his death was recorded in the Register of St. Peter's Parish.

In 1670 William Bassett wrote to Colonel Henry Norwood asking about the lands of Colonel Philip Honeywood in Virginia. And stated that

---

[2] Patent Book No. 2, p. 195.
[3] Patent Book No. 2, p. 194.

Colonel Hammond, *"'ad it from Sir Philip for seating it, if soe I jud S' Philip hath forgot that I had his consent in y' room at White Hall."*

Colonel Henry replied that he sent a conveyance of the lands in question and reassured William Bassett that he would *"in case there is yet any formality wanting from these parts to make it more firm unto you."*

The letter of Bassett to Norwood and Norwood's reply to Bassett in January 1670 are conclusive as to the transfer of the land to Captain Bassett.[4]

When Colonel John Lightfoot died in 1707, he left his large landed Estate to his sons, Goodrich, Sherwood and Thomas. As was the custom, the eldest son received the home place and the other sons, lesser estates depending on the father's will. There was also one daughter, Alice Lightfoot.

The scant records of St. Peter's Parish indicate that the sons of Colonel John Lightfoot resided in the parish. In 1712, Colonel William Byrd in his diary gives very definite information of the residence of two of the Lightfoot sons: Mr. Sherwood Lightfoot who was seated at Rickahock and his brother, Goodrich Lightfoot, at the White House.

Colonel Goodrich Lightfoot moved to Spotsylvania County in 1727 and then to Orange County where he died in 1738. His brother, Major Sherwood Lightfoot died in New Kent County on April 20, 1730. The deeds of conveyance from the Lightfoots to Colonel John Custis have been lost with the early records of New Kent, but in 1735 Colonel John Custis owned Old Quarter and the land upon the river.[5]

At the Petition of Wm Paisley an Overseer of the High Road from the Old Church to Mr. Chamberlayne's Ordinary, That we have Wm Atkinsons Titheables, Stephen Brooker, Lodwick Alford, Goodrich Alford, and Julius Alford, Mich. Harfield's Tithe Richd Ross Majr Dandridge's, John Lightfoots, & Col. Custis's at the Old Quarter and upon the river.

In time Colonel John Custis had acquired the large tract which Colonel John Lightfoot had owned during his lifetime and which had been the estates of his sons, who conveyed the lands to the Custises.

There are many ties that bind Martha Dandridge to the Parish of St. Peter's and the County of New Kent. She was born at Chestnut Grove and was reared in the Parish.

Martha Dandridge had grown up in the Parish and had known Daniel Parke Custis all her life for they attended St. Peter's and Daniel was a Vestryman. At eighteen she attracted the attention of Daniel Parke Custis, who was then thirty-seven and unmarried. The unhappy marital relations

---

[4] I V 453 et seq.

[5] Vestry Book of St. Peter's Parish, p. 246.

of his father and mother, and the unfortunate marriage of his sister, Fanny, and the known eccentricities of his father, had contributed to his being a bachelor.

The mother of Daniel was Frances, daughter of Colonel Daniel Parke, the younger, and his wife, Jane Ludlow, of Greensprings.

This lady, Frances Parke, became the wife of Colonel John Custis of Arlington on the Eastern Shore of Virginia. Her married life was one of unhappiness and fraught with discord. The stories of the disagreements and Colonel Custis heartless behavior are commonplace.

After the death of Colonel Parke in Antigua, his Estate in Virginia fell to his two daughters, Frances Custis and Lucy Byrd. A settlement was finally reached between Colonel Custis and Colonel Byrd as to the Parke lands in Virginia.

A short time after this Colonel John Custis and Fanny, his wife, signed Articles of Agreement pending their separation, but death intervened, on March 14, 1714/5. Fanny Custis was buried in the graveyard on Queens Creek belonging to the Parke family, where later two children of Daniel Parke Custis and he, himself, is buried.

There was a tombstone placed over her grave which in recent years with the tombstones of the two Custis children have been removed to Bruton Churchyard in Williamsburg.

> *Here lied the Body of*
> *Frances Custis, daughter of Daniel Parke Esq:*
> *Who departed this Life March the*
> *14th 1714/5 in the 29th Years*
> *of Her Age*

Withal Frances Custis must have been a woman of courage.

Daniel Parke Custis served his father as Overseer at the White House Plantation until his father's death.

Colonel John Custis made his last will and testament on 14th November 1749 and unexpectedly died eight days later on the 22nd November 1749. He left his son; his large landed Estate, numerous Negroes, and other property, all in fee simple.

Daniel and Martha's wedding was held at Chestnut Grove, the Dandridge home, on May 10, 1750, when the Reverend Mister Chichley Corbin Thacker, Minister of Blisland Parish, performed the ceremony.

It devolved upon Daniel the settlement of his Father's Estate. The most difficult duty imposed upon him was the monument that Colonel Custis ordered to be placed over his grave at Arlington, in which he directed that on penalty of forfeiture, the inscription should be exactly as he had written it.

UNDER THIS MARBLE TOMB LIED THE BODY
OF THE HONORABLE JOHN CUSTIS ESQ:
OF THE CITY OF WILLIAMSBURG
AND PARISH OF BRUTON
FORMERLY OF HUNGAR'S PARISH ON THE
EASTERN SHORE
OF VIRGINIA, AND COUNTY OF NORTHAMPTON
AGED 71 YEARS, AND YET LIVED BUT SEVEN YEARS
WHICH WAS THE SPACE OF TIME HE KEPT
A BATCHELOR'S HOME AT ARLINGTON
ON THE EASTERN SHORE OF VIRGINIA.

Daniel Parke Custis obeyed the order and had engraved on the back of the stone:

THIS INSCRIPTION PUT ON HIS TOMB WAS AT
HIS OWN POSITIVE ORDERS.

Mr. Custis and his bride established themselves at the White House, and there were few planters in Tidewater, Virginia who had more lands and resources. They lived here happily and prospered.

In the course of seven years, Martha bore her husband, four children, all born at the White House.

Col. Daniel Parke Custis was married to Martha Dandridge on 15th of May 1750 by Rev. Mr. Thacker.
Daniel Parke Custis was born 19th November 1751.
 Mr. James Power and his daughter, Molly, Col. John Dandridge and Mrs. Dandridge, Godfather and Godmothers.
Fanny Parke Custis was born the 17th of April 1753
 Miss Nancy Dandridge, Daniel Parke Custis & Martha Custis stood for her.
John Parke Custis born 1754
Martha Custis born 1755.[6]

Mr. Custis was added to the quorum in the New Commission of Justices for New Kent County, issued on September 30, 1734, by the Council. It is probable that he served on the Court in the years that followed for in 1752 he was named in the second place in the Commission, which showed that he had moved up.[7]

---

[6] Data furnished by the Courtesy of Mr. George H.S. King.

[7] Executive Journals of the Council of Colonial Virginia, V. 4, p. 333 and V. 5, p. 393.

On July 8, 1757, Daniel Parke Custis died suddenly at his plantation, the White House, when he was 46 years. The details of his burial are few but it is known that Charles Crump made a black walnut casket and his body was placed in it and taken to the Custis-Parke burying ground on Queens Creek for burial beside two of his children who had died a few years before.[8]

The sudden death of Colonel Custis without a will, left the young widow, Martha, twenty-six, the entire burden of the management of the large Estate and the guardianship of her two surviving children: John Parke and Patsy.

One of the certainties of colonial life in Virginia was that an attractive widow with an ample fortune would marry in a short time. The period of mourning was short by custom and the urgent need of a husband to take over the management of an Estate was a necessity.

Mrs. Custis, was a widow for eight months and eight days when Colonel George Washington crossed the Pamunkey River on the 16th of March 1758 by Williams Ferry and met her for the first time! He came ashore at Poplar Grove, the home of Colonel Chamberlayne who pressed him to dismount and dine. On that day Mrs. Martha Custis was paying a neighborly visit at the Chamberlayne home and was presented to Colonel Washington. He then hastened on to Williamsburg to attend to his business.

The simple facts are given that Colonel Washington enroute to Williamsburg, crossed the Pamunkey and came ashore at the Chamberlayne residence, dined with the family while Bishop held his horse. He met Mrs. Custis and then hastened on to Williamsburg to attend to his business.[9]

He was in Williamsburg on the 18th of March 1758 and returned to see Mrs. Custis at the White House in a few days. He returned to Williamsburg to conclude his reports with the Governor and had arrived in Fredericksburg by March 30th, and was at Mount Vernon on April 1, 1758.

This was a rapid pace, for in two weeks the young Colonel had conferred with the Authorities in Williamsburg and deviated from his military duties to court Martha Custis with success, before he returned to the frontier with dispatches. He served in the Army until the latter part of December when he resigned from the Army and returned home to happier days at Mount Vernon. In this brief space of time, the plans for the marriage had been going forward.

---

[8] Statement of Dr. Earl G. Swem. These Tombstones have been since placed in Bruton Churchyard.
[9] Personal Recollections of Washington, Geor. W.P. Custis, p. 11.

The 6th day of January, the date set for the marriage came at last. The bridegroom arrived, the neighbors and friends came, and the Minister, the Reverend Mister David Mossom, was on hand to perform the ceremony.

Colonel John Lightfoot had built the White House Mansion sometime before 1700 and as Councilor of State, he erected a mansion in keeping with his official position, which stood in the Government next to the Royal Governor, himself. The house was a commodious one, with adequate room for entertainment of a large gathering and guests such as could be provided for by a large Colonial Plantation which had servants a plenty and provisions of all kinds.

At the appointed hour, the nuptial vows were said and the Reverend Mister Mossom pronounced George Washington and Martha Custis, man and wife

Among the neighbors who were present that day at the wedding were the Macons from "the Island" and the Atkinsons from Lilly Point. Both families left accounts of the wedding and the feast at the White House.

There has been much discussion as to the place of the wedding in recent years. As a matter of fact, in 1759 there were very few weddings in the rural churches of Virginia. It was not the custom for widows to marry in church. And besides on Wednesday, January 6, 1759, to go three miles through mire and mud to a cold church would not have been in keeping with the good sense demonstrated by the principals, the contracting parties, in all else they did.

It was many years later when George Washington Parke Custis, who was reared at Mount Vernon and lived on most intimate terms with his grandmother, Martha Washington, wrote his recollections of George Washington, and in this account he stated:

"The wedding took place about 1760 at the White House in the County of New Kent."[10]

While there is no doubt in the mind of many persons that the marriage did take place at the White House, there is no record known to prove it.

The Washington family moved to Mount Vernon in the spring of 1759, having spent some time in Williamsburg where Colonel Washington attended, as Burgess, the General Assembly.

Washington assumed the responsibility of the vast Custis Estate. In behalf of his wife's interest and that of her two children, he employed a steward to manage the property, which for many years was operated as a

---

[10] Recollections and Private Memoirs of Washington by G.W. Parke Custis of Arlington, Compiled from files of the National Intelligencer, Washington, 1859.

"Quarter," along with other plantations belonging to the Custis Estate on the Pamunkey River.

The White House Mansion, in the course of time, was removed to make way for the structure, which stood on the same site and burned on June 27, 1862. Joel Cooke reported that the house standing in 1862 had replaced a much larger White House on the same site.

The Custis Estates in New Kent were operated as Quarters and when Jackie Custis arrived at his majority, they were turned over to him.

After his untimely death in 1781, his son and heir, George Washington Parke Custis, fell heir to the New Kent Plantations, which during his infancy had been in the charge of numerous stewards and for many years under the oversight of George Washington.

In 1798 George Washington Parke Custis received from General Washington and his Grandmother, Martha Washington, the large White House and Rickahock Plantations. He continued the management under stewards and the numerous slaves and their increase did the farming down through the years.

George Washington Parke Custis died at Arlington in 1857. He made a will in which he gave to his grandsons his plantations in New Kent and King William. He appointed Colonel Robert E. Lee, who had married his only daughter, to see that the provisions of the will were carried out.

The four years of Civil War left the White House and Rickahock Plantations in a depleted state. Mrs. Mary Custis Lee, seeking refuge in Richmond before the movement of McClellan's Army up the Pamunkey, left at the White House a note written by her stuck on the door:

"Northern Soldiers who profess to revere Washington forbear to desecrate the home of his first married life – The property of his wife, now owned by her descendants. A Granddaughter of Mrs. Washington."

Federal Armies had camped in the broad fields and left a path of destruction; the Negroes had for the most part moved away with the Armies; the dwelling house had been burned, and devastation was complete.

In 1865 General William H.F. Lee, as soon as he was out of the Confederate Army, moved into the Rickahock house, which was probably an overseer's house, and immediately set to work to farm the great fields. After a few years, General Lee employed a manager. Mr. Willie Winston Jones for many years was the manager and lived in the Rickahock house. He operated the farm for Gen. Lee, who had moved to Ravensworth in Fairfax County.

General William H.F. Lee died in 1891 and by a will made in August 1891 and proved in November 1891, he left to his wife his entire estate for

(This is the second "White House" which was built on the same foundation as John Lightfoot's original mansion. The original house was much larger.)

her lifetime and at her death it was passed to his two sons: Robert E. Lee and George Bolling Lee.[11]

The Estate was not divided at Mrs. Lee's death. When Col. Robert E. Lee made his will in 1922, he too devised to his wife, for her lifetime, his interest in the landed estate in New Kent County and at her death it was to go to Dr. George Bolling Lee, his brother. Col. Robert E. Lee died at Ravensworth prior to December 22, 1926 when his will was probated at Fairfax.[12]

---

[11] New Kent Records W.B. No. 2, page 263.
[12] New Kent Records W.B. No. 2, page 270.

(The owner, Robert Runions, believes this springhouse is the original from the Lightfoot days.)

The death of Mrs. Robert E. Lee brought the whole of the White House property into the sole ownership to Dr. George Bolling Lee, who sold the entire holdings to C. L. Woodward and Mr. Martin in 1946. These two gentlemen divided the land. Mr. Martin's Estate owned the lower tract. And Mr. Woodward's heirs owned the upper tract. Mr. Robert Runions bought it from Woodward and Martin in the 70's.

After the Civil War another house was erected at White House on the same foundations with some alterations, this house burned in 1880.

The private residence in New Kent County in earlier days called "the White House" is what the present home of presidents in Washington was named after.

(Some of the old original foundation can still be seen here amongst all the weeds.)

CHAPTER VIII

PHILIP LIGHTFOOT, 1648-1708
MARRIED ALICE CORBIN

The HONORABLE PHILIP LIGHTFOOT of Gloucester County, Virginia, was born in England in 1648 and died in 1708 in Gloucester County, Virginia. Not much is known about the elder Philip Lightfoot, who was the father of the Philip Lightfoot of Yorktown, but there is enough to identify him as active in local colonial affairs. Born in England, he came to Virginia with his brother John before 1670. He held many titles and political positions during his lifetime. In 1677 he was called "Mr.", in 1680 his title was Lieutenant Colonel and in 1690 he was referred to as Captain. He served as the Surveyor-General in 1676.[1] In 1680 he was listed as Lieutenant Colonel of Gloucester and Justice of the Peace.[2] From 1684 through 1685 he was Administrator of Captain Frances Leigh, he resigned his position as Vestryman and Captain John Smith succeeded him in 1690.[3] Apparently Lightfoot either moved from the York River to the James River, or maintained more than one residence, for in 1699 along with John Grice, Samuel Pond and John Marrable, he became Justice of James City County, and Collector from the Upper District of the James River. His will was probated in 1709.[4]
Official reports mention that during Nathaniel Bacon's rebellion in 1676,

"Mr. Philip Lightfoot was a great Looser and suffered both in Estate and person being both Plundered and Imprisoned by the Rebells."

Philip married ALICE CORBIN, daughter of the HONORABLE HENRY and ALICE (ELTONHEAD) CORBIN of "Buckingham House",

---

[1] Conway Robinson Council Journal Notes.
[2] Virginia Magazine of History and Biographies, January 1893.
[3] Petsworth Parish, Gloucester County, Vestry Book.
[4] Hennings Stat. V.P. III.

Middlesex County on 28th September 1679. *"Major Philip Lightfoot and Alice Corbin was married p. Lycence 23 September 1679."*[5]
Both of their tombs at "Sandy Point" bear the Lightfoot arms (a griffin's head) impaling the Corbin arms. They had two sons, Francis and Philip.

Philip Lightfoot was the Philip of Charles City County, Virginia. He based his identification upon the inscription on the gravestone of Philip Lightfoot at "Tedington," Charles City County, which bears the Lightfoot coat of arms and these words:

> *Philip Lightfoot*
> *Son of John Lightfoot*
> *Barrister at Law son of John*
> *Lightfoot Minister of Stoke*
> *Bruan in Northampton Shire.*

Dr. Tyler believed that the name of the grandfather of Philip Lightfoot was incorrectly inscribed on the gravestone, since there was no John Lightfoot who was a minister of the parish of Stoke Bruerne, but Richard Lightfoot was established by many records to have been the minister there.

If we accept this assumption, however, we must admit that John Lightfoot of New Kent County, Virginia, who died in 1707, was active in civil and military affairs at the age of eighty-three, a most unusual situation in colonial America.

It is equally logical to assume that the gravestone is correct in stating that John Lightfoot was the father of Philip Lightfoot, that another John Lightfoot was his grandfather, but in error in referring to the grandfather as a priest of the Church of England (the great-grandfather being the minister).

Furthermore, the will of Elizabeth (Phillips) Lightfoot mentions her grandson John Lightfoot, son of her son John, and settles upon him a considerable estate – at a time when John Lightfoot of New Kent County, Virginia, was not yet married.

John Lightfoot, son of John and Elizabeth (Phillips) Lightfoot, was born about 1622-23, married Elizabeth Tailer, had two sons John and Philip, and died at Surinam in 1686. The two sons were the John and Philip Lightfoot, brothers, who were in Virginia.

The Lightfoot House[6], related to other two-story brick structures in Williamsburg, the George Wythe and Ludwell-Paradise houses, the Brafferton, and the President's House of the College of William and Mary, was distinctive among local buildings. Built in the early eighteenth century

---

[5] Parish Register of Christ Church, Middlesex County, VA., for 1653-1812, p. 18.
[6] "18th Century Houses of Williamsburg", by Marcus Whiffen.

as a monument, reflected alterations sometime before 1750. Of any original residence in town it was setback from the street line the deepest,[7] which gave it an aura of remoteness surpassed only by Bassett Hall.

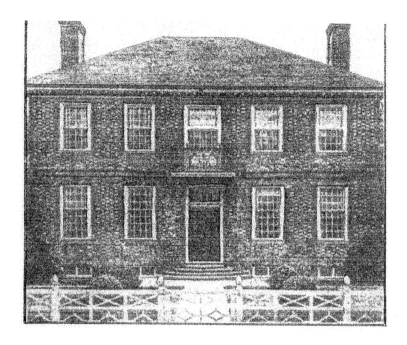

(THE LIGHTFOOT HOUSE. The home of Philip Lightfoot and his descendants in Williamsburg. It was built sometime in the early 18th century. The earliest history of the house has been lost, although research confirms its post-Revolutionary War ownership by the Lightfoot's.)

---

[7] Williamsburg's 1699 and 1705 building acts stipulated a uniform 6-foot building setback for Duke of Gloucester, the main street, where the houses all had "to front alike," but such restrictions on the town's back streets were left to the discretion of the directors appointed to supervise the laws. The Palace and John Custis and Nicholas-Tyler houses had deep setbacks similar to that of the Lightfoot House, while among original structures, the Nelson-Galt and Chiswell houses were situated farther than 6 feet from the street lines yet closer than the other dwellings cited.

Although research confirmed some facts of its post-Revolutionary ownership the earliest history is lost of the Lightfoot Property. Many have speculated that the Lightfoot ownership of this site on Francis Street, along with other Williamsburg properties including the nearby William Lightfoot House, dated from the early years of the town's establishment. It has been hinted that the building might have been used for commercial as well as residential purposes during its tenement era. It was acquired by the Lightfoot family around mid-century and converted into a townhouse.

The earliest specific reference to Lightfoot family ownership of the property occurred in 1783 when Philip Lightfoot III of Bowling Green, Carolina County, advertised the house for sale. In 1786 his nephew and heir, William Lightfoot of Tedington in Charles City County, sold the house and a parcel of six lots.

A British traveler gave an indication of the Lightfoot family's wealth in 1736 when he described their Yorktown residence as *"equal in Magnificence to many of our superb ones at St. James."*[8] York County records show that in 1747 Philip Lightfoot I, a prosperous merchant owned widespread Virginia plantations. He served as clerk of York County until appointed to the Governor's Council in 1733, willed to his son John all his *"Lots and Houses in the City of Williamsburg"* including *"the furniture in the House in Williamsburg."*[9]

Philip Lightfoot's will, dated 1708, left three tracts of land at "Sandy Point" to his son Francis. The will stipulated that if Francis died without issue, the land would go to his brother Philip. Frances had two children, a son who died in childhood, and a daughter, Elizabeth ("Betty"), who on December 22, 1737, married Beverley Randolph, one of the King's councilors in the colony. She was described by the Virginia Gazette as "an agreeable young lady with a fortune of upwards of £5000." According to her grandfather's will, "Sandy Point" would be hers. But her father left it to Philip, who paid Elizabeth £2,500 for compensation. This was later officially settled by an act of the legislature in 1740, and Philip became legal owner of the land.[10]

The younger Philip Lightfoot established the family name and its social and economic standing in Yorktown. He was born in 1689, and died May 30, 1748. Known as the "Merchant Prince," Philip Lightfoot amassed an immense fortune. He owned large estates in York, Surry, Charles City,

---

[8] "Observations in Several Voyages and Travels in America in the year 1736," WMQ 1st Ser., XV (April 1907), p. 222.

[9] York Co. Recs., Wills and Inventories, XX, pp. 104-106.

[10] Ibid; William Waller Hening, comp., Statutes at Large: Being a Collection of all the Laws of Virginia from the First Session of the Legislature in the Year 1619 (Richmond, 1809-1823), V. 112-114; Virginia Gazette (Parks), December 30, 1737.

Brunswick, Goochland, New Kent, Prince George, and Hanover counties; houses, storehouses, and lots in Yorktown, Williamsburg, and Blandford; and had a fortune in slaves, silver, cattle, etc.[11]

In 1707 Lightfoot was appointed clerk of York County and moved to town shortly after. He bought one of the two town lots sold in 1709, Thomas Nelson buying the other. Both lots had been taken up under the Port Act of 1706 and deserted. Lightfoot purchased his Lot from the town trustees for 180 pounds of tobacco, with the stipulation that within twelve months he would build and furnish *one good house to contain at least twenty foot wherein if he fail then his present grant to be void.*[12] Apparently Lightfoot built a house on the lot, for he kept title to the land.

Between 1709 and 1742, Lightfoot bought many lots in Yorktown and much plantation land in various Virginia counties. In 1717 he acquired the Washington lease on the upper side of Martins Creek in York County. In 1723 land in James City County was purchased from David Morce.[13]

Lightfoot's second townhouse, and probably the one occupied by the family, was built after he purchased the Lot from Warren Cary for £150 of English currency in 1724. It was a large brick mansion on a high bluff overlooking the harbor of Yorktown. Later Lightfoot purchased adjoining lots for gardens and other purposes. He owned enough land in the immediate area for his house and grounds to be considered pretentious and befitting a wealthy merchant and planter. Needless to say this house was one of the most elegant in Yorktown. In a description of the town by Edward Kimber in 1736, we read these words:

You perceive a great Air of Opulence amongst the Inhabitants, who have some of them built themselves Houses, equal in Magnificence to many of our superb ones at St. James's; as those of Mr. Lightfoot, Nelson, &c. Almost every considerable Man Keeps an Equipage...The most considerable Houses are of Brick; some handsome ones of Wood, all built in the modern Taste.

Lightfoot also had use of an area in the town "Commons" of Yorktown, the area along the waterfront below the cliffs. This region, omitted by Benjamin Read, original surveyor, who instead placed the fifty acres for

---

[11] York County, Wills and Inventories, No. 20 (1746-1759), pp. 103-106.
[12] Edward M. Riley, "The History of the Founding and Development of Yorktown, Virginia, 1691-1781" (a typed manuscript in the library of Colonial National Historical Park, Yorktown, Virginia), p. 75; York County, Deeds and Bonds, No. 2 (1701-1713) m pp. 334-335.
[13] York County, Deeds and Bonds, No. 3 (1713-1729), pp. 130-131, 255, 273, 395.

the town on high ground, continued in an ambiguous relationship to the town for years. After Read's death, his son Gwyn laid claim to the waterfront. A number of abutting owners, and others, used this area, by one arrangement or another, for wharves, warehouses, shops, storehouses, and related purposes. Many leading merchants were granted squares on the waterfront prior to 1738. Charles Carter was granted as much of the beach as lay between his lot (Lot 10) and the river, but was warned not to interfere with the land of Philip Lightfoot. Lightfoot probably used all, or part, of the ground fronting which was the location of "Colonel Lightfoot's Landing".

Philip Lightfoot was a leading citizen of the colony. In addition to serving as clerk of York County for twenty-six years (1707-1733), in 1715 he was agent for the public storehouse at Yorktown. His tenure as county clerk ended only when he was appointed to the Council of Colonial Virginia, in 1733. He served on the Council until 1747, the year before his death.

Apparently Lightfoot and Nelson controlled a large part of the commercial interests of Yorktown. In 1739 Richard Chapman wrote to Edward Athawes:

Since my being in Virginia Col. Lightfoot was Clerk of York Court and one of our most Considerable Merchants at one and the same time, and every man, who has sense enough to judge right, is convinced that near to that Gentlemans own Genius, and the Friends which that merited and procured him on your side of the water, the Business of the Office concurred to the Increase and Establishment of the other; of which he was so sensible, that he would never give it up till the King, by his Letter, called him up to the Council.

Francis Jerdone, who came to Virginia in 1746 as part owner of a cargo of goods, and as the representative of some London merchants, wrote home that both Lightfoot and Nelson preferred Bristol and Liverpool to London for many staple articles. His advice to the London merchants after Lightfoot's death was indicative of Lightfoot's proficiency in commercial matters:

Col. Philip Lightfoot is now dead, so that you can never have so fair a way open'd to you for establishing a store, as at this present time; his great riches while he continued in health deterred everybody from settling here, none being of ability to vie with him but Mr. Nelson, who always had an equal share of trade with him.

Mary Lightfoot died in 1775, apparently occupying the large town house until then, and outliving all of her children. In her will she mentioned two of her daughters-in-law—Mildred (William's wife) and Anne (Armistead's wife), grandsons William and Philip Lightfoot, and James Burwell (and his daughter Anne). There was reference, too, to granddaughters Mary Allen, Anne Lightfoot, Elizabeth Hewitt, and Mildred and Elizabeth Coles, as well as to Lewis Burwell, William Allen and Richard Hewitt. Also, she remembered the poor people of Yorktown.

Armistead's family inherited the town house in Yorktown. It became the residence of the Griffins, for Armistead's daughter Mary had married into that family. In 1814, after the fire, the ladies of the town, families whose property were destroyed, were cared for "under the spacious and hospitable roof of Major Griffin's house." At the time of Lafayette's visit in 1824 "Major Griffin's romantic house" served as headquarters for the invited guests.

The tenure of the Lightfoot influence in Yorktown lasted only from 1707, when Philip Lightfoot was appointed county clerk and moved to the town, to 1775 when his widow died, all four children having previously died. During this period the family established itself prominently in the life of Yorktown—as civic and political leaders, as controllers of commerce, and surely in the social activities. Their town house occupied one of the most beautiful spots in town, on a high bluff overlooking the York River. Perhaps second only to the Nelsons, the Lightfoots were the most noted Yorktown family of the eighteenth century.

Philip Lightfoot was described as "descended from an ancient family in England, who came over to Virginia in a genteel and honorable character."

The following, by Mrs. William Reynolds, gives some details of much interest regarding the portraits and plate once at Sandy Point or Tedington:

"There is preserved a portrait of William Lightfoot, with date 1750, full length, life size, in blue court dress; a portrait of his brother Philip, same size and style, in red court dress. These portraits were pronounced very fine by Volkmar, the best authority in this line. He said the only ones he had ever seen like them were some sent him to be cleaned by General Robert E. Lee, and identified them positively as the work of Hudson, the master of Sir Joshua Reynolds. Portrait of Mrs. Howell, with infant daughter, Mildred (afterwards the wife of William Lightfoot), on her knee. The mother's figure is life size, and in white court dress. This is also a very fine picture, and Volkmar thought it must be a Copley. Portrait of "Sir John Howell, London, 1680' (name and date on back of canvas), full length, in grey court dress, leaning on sword. He was, presumably, the grandfather of Mildred. Portrait of half-grown youth and landscape, pronounced in Philadelphia to be the work of Sir Peter Lely—a Howell picture.

The lineage of Philip and Alice (Corbin) Lightfoot is a long, outstanding and heroic one.

FRANCIS LIGHTFOOT *was born in 1687 in Gloucester County, Virginia and died 7 January 1727 in James City County, Virginia. He married* ELIZABETH ?, *who was born in 1693 and died in 1727. He served as Justice of James City County and as Naval Collector.*

FRANCIS LIGHTFOOT *was born in 1722 and died in 1730 in James City County, Virginia.*

ELIZABETH LIGHTFOOT *was born in 1725 in James City County, Virginia and on 30 December 1737 she married the* HONORABLE BEVERLY RANDOLPH *of "Turkey Island", Henrico County, Virginia in Williamsburg, Virginia. He was the son of* COLONEL WILLIAM *and* ELIZABETH (BEVERLEY) RANDOLPH *of "Turkey Island". There were no children by this couple.*

HONORABLE PHILIP LIGHTFOOT *was born in 1689 in Gloucester County, Virginia and died 30 May 1748 in "Sandy Point", Charles City County, Virginia. He married* MARY (ARMISTEAD) BURWELL *the widow of Honorable James Burwell, of King's Creek and daughter of the* HONORABLE WILLIAM *and* ANN (LEE) ARMISTEAD *in 1720. He was known as the "Merchant Prince," and owned large estates in York, Surry, Charles City, Brunswick, Goochland, New Kent and Hanover Counties. He owned houses, storehouses and lots in Yorktown, Williamsburg and Blandford and slaves, silver and the immense Lightfoot fortune. He served as the Clerk of York County from 1707 through 1733, Agent for the Public Storehouse in 1715, on the King's Council in 1733, and was a liberal supporter of the Established Church. He left to the Yorktown church a flagon and chalice, with his arms engraved thereon and £40 in goods to be given to the poor, and to William and Mary College £500 for the education of two young men for the ministry of the Church of England. The two recipients of this foundation were William Stith and Ed Wilcox from 25 March 1753 to 25 March 1755.*

HONORABLE WILLIAM LIGHTFOOT *was born in 1722 and died prior to 1771. He married* MILDRED HOWELL *in 1746. He served as High Sheriff of York County, Virginia in 1746 and is known as the Honorable William of Tedington.*

WILLIAM LIGHTFOOT *of Tedington was born in 1750 in Virginia and died in 1809. His first wife was* ANNE COCKE.

WILLIAM HOWELL LIGHTFOOT *of "Cabin Point" was born in 1779 and died in 1810. He married* SARAH SHORT STEWARD. *After William's death Sarah married John Minge of Charles City County, Virginia. John's first wife Sarah Harrison was the youngest daughter of Benjamin Harrison, signer and sister of*

William H. Harrison, President of the United States. John and Sarah had a daughter, Sarah Melville who married Robert Bolling of Petersburg.

WILLIAM LIGHTFOOT *was born in 1806 and died unmarried in 1831.*

FRANCIS LIGHTFOOT *was born in 1780 in Sandy Point, Virginia and died 3 November 1813 in Sandy Point, Virginia. He married* ELIZABETH VIRGINIA NICHOLAS, *daughter of* COLONEL JOHN *and* LOUISA (CARTER) NICHOLAS *in 1802. Elizabeth was born in Carter's Grove, Virginia and died in October of 1814.*

WILLIAM ALLEN LIGHTFOOT *was born 8 April 1806 in Tedington, Virginia and died 22 September 1881 in Tedington, Virginia. He married* CAROLINE MATILDA GUERRANT *1 June 1826.*

William's parents died when he was very young, so an uncle took him to Avonia, in Buckingham County, Virginia. He lived on his own estate of several hundred acres near the Slate River in Virginia. When he became ill, he and his Caroline were taken to the home of his youngest son, James Anderson Lightfoot. He died at night and Caroline died the next morning. She was well; out in the yard picking flowers, when told her husband was dead, the doctor said she died of a broken heart.

GEORGE A. LIGHTFOOT *was born 31 August 1830 and married* MARY BALLOU.

JOHN FRANCIS LIGHTFOOT *was born 16 July 1828 and died in 1866. He married* SALLY BALLOU.

ELLA LIGHTFOOT *died unmarried.*

JOHN LIGHTFOOT *died unmarried.*

LUTHER FRANCIS LIGHTFOOT *was born 13 September 1863 and married* JUDITH M. HANES *22 May 1889. Judith was born 29 July 1866.*

MAUDE MAE LIGHTFOOT *was born 13 October 1898 and married* ROBERT WESLEY LEBER.

SALLIE BLANCHE LIGHTFOOT *was born 2 August 1890 and married* JULIAN ELDRIDGE SMITH.

MARY ELLA LIGHTFOOT *was born 16 January 1892 and died a child on the 28th of December 1896.*

ANNIE GARLAND LIGHTFOOT *was born 11 August 1895 and married* FRANK SELF.

JOHN LUTHER LIGHTFOOT *married* FANNIE PYLE.

JAMES COSBY LIGHTFOOT *married* DeLORES ABSHER.

CLYDE AUBREY LIGHTFOOT *married first* NANNIE SNODDY *and secondly* ALICE HURT.

PHILIP W. LIGHTFOOT *was born 23 March 1837 and married* NANCY GUERRANT.

VIRGINIA NICHOLAS LIGHTFOOT *was born 16 March 1827 and married* CHARLES ROBERTS.

HENRIETTA FRANCES LIGHTFOOT *was born 30 November 1841 and married* LITTLEBERRY LESEUER.

JAMES ANDERSON LIGHTFOOT *was born 5 May 1847 and died in Norfolk, Virginia. He married* JANE ELIZA MITCHELL *15 December 1867. Jane was born 11 July 1844 in Buckingham County, Virginia.*

ALMIRA CAROLINE LIGHTFOOT *was born 9 March 1872 in Buckingham County, Virginia and married* JOSEPH P. JORDAN *22 December 1892. Joseph was born 9 October 1867 in Sangersville, Virginia and died in Baltimore, Maryland.*

MARJORIE JORDAN *married* L. GALE BROCE *and lived in Beaumont, Texas.*

GRACE LIGHTFOOT *married* WILBUR McLAUREN EVERETT *and lived in Norfolk, Virginia.*

MARY E. LIGHTFOOT *was born 28 March 1833 and married* PROFESSOR ? LANE.

LOUISA C. LIGHTFOOT *was born 31 July 1844 and died a child on the 4ᵗʰ of October 1856.*

JOHN FRANCIS LIGHTFOOT, M.D. *was born 28 July 1809 in Tedington, Sandy Point, Virginia and died unmarried.*

VIRGINIA CARTER NICHOLAS LIGHTFOOT *was born 8 May 1811 in Tedington, Sandy Point, Virginia and married* ? SCRUGGS.

CARTER LIGHTFOOT *was born in Tedington, Sandy Point, Virginia and died unmarried.*

PHILIP JOHN LIGHTFOOT *was born about 1782 and married* MARY ANN VAUGHN. *Philip made his will on the 11ᵗʰ of June 1819 and it was probated 15 July 1819.*

MARY ELIZABETH BOLLING LIGHTFOOT *was born around 1785 in Charles City County, Virginia and married* GEORGE BLAKELEY.

ANNE COCKE LIGHTFOOT *was born approximately 1787 in Charles City County, Virginia and married* WILLIAM LEWIS. WILLIAM *married* ANNE CLOPTON ELLYSON *after Anne's death. He made his will 27 April 1809 and it was probated 17 August 1809. After William's death Anne married John Colgin.*

ROBERT ARMISTEAD LIGHTFOOT *was born around 1790 in Charles City County, Virginia.*

SARAH LIGHTFOOT *was born sometime around 1795 in Charles City County, Virginia.*

PHILIP LIGHTFOOT *was born in 1752 in Yorktown, Virginia and died in 1786. He served with distinction as a Lieutenant in Harrison's Artillery on the Continental line for three years in the Revolutionary War He later worked in the Executive Department 11 July 1835. He received 2 land grants for his services. He married* MARY WARNER LEWIS, *the daughter of* COLONEL CHARLES *and* LUCY (TALIAFERRO) LEWIS *of Port Royal, Caroline County, Virginia. After the death of Philip, his widow, Mary married Dr. John Bankhead, a nephew of President Monroe. He was a graduate of Edinburg. They lived at "Spring Grove", Caroline County and had three sons: Charles, John and William Bankhead. The heirs of Philip Lightfoot were allowed Bounty of Land for his services.*

PHILIP LIGHTFOOT *was born 24 September 1784 in Port Royal, Caroline County, Virginia and died 22 July 1865. On 31 August 1804 he married* SARAH SAVIN BERNARD *the daughter of* WILLIAM *and* FANNY (HOPKINS) BERNARD *of Belle Grove, King George County, Virginia later of Mansfield, Spotsylvania County, Virginia. Sarah was born 7 March 1790 and died 22 August 1859. She was the granddaughter of the* HONORABLE WILLIAM *and* SARAH (SAVIN/SAVIGNE) BERNARD *of "Belle Grove" and of* JOHN *and* FANNY (PRATT) HOPKINS.

Philip took a prominent part in public affairs and was a Confederate Patriot. He appointed Efford B. Bently his attorney, "For me and my heirs to receive land bounty warrant that may be due for the services of my father, Philip Lightfoot, deceased, in the Revolutionary War", signed 11 June 1835. Monthly Court, Caroline County, 12 October 1831, Certified that Philip Lightfoot of East Royal, of the county is the only child and heir of Philip Lightfoot of Cedar Creek who was a Lieutenant in the Revolutionary War. Copy test, John L. Pendleton, Clerk of Caroline County, 3 November 18344. Warrant No. 8180 was issued to Philip Lightfoot.

PHILIP LEWIS LIGHTFOOT, M.D. *was born about 1805 in Port Royal, Caroline County, Virginia and died in 1884 in Eutaw, Greene County, Alabama. He is buried in Oak Hill Cemetery. He married* MARY VIRGINIA SMITH *in 1839 in Fredericksburg, Virginia. Mary was born 6 February 1818 in Dumfries, Virginia and died 17 March 1855 in Eutaw, Alabama. She was the daughter of* GEORGE *and* DELIA ? SMITH *of Dumfries, Virginia. They lived in Greene County, Alabama on a plantation between Boligee and Eutaw until her death.*

99

SALLIE SAVIGNE LIGHTFOOT *was born in 1846 in Alabama and married* GEORGE H. DUNLAP, JR. *in 1872.*
  GEORGE HAMILTON DUNLAP
  GEORGE HAMILTON DUNLAP
  PHILIP LEWIS LIGHTFOOT, JR.

Philip married ANN ISABELLE DRUMMOND *21 April 1857 in Harrison County, Mississippi. Ann was born 3 October 1827 in Brunswick County, Virginia and died 30 August 1861 in Eutaw, Greene County, Alabama. She was the daughter of* GREENE/GRIEVE *and* ELIZABETH (STONE) DRUMMOND.

  HARRIETT BROWN LIGHTFOOT *was born 13 July 1859.*

  BELLE DRUMMOND LIGHTFOOT *was born 7 August 1861.*

  EDWIN DRUMMOND LIGHTFOOT *was born 9 February 1858 in Eutaw, Greene County, Alabama and died 7 April 1898. He married* ELIZABETH "BESSIE" W. ANDERSON McALPINE *7 March 1889. Bessie was born 2 February 1866. Edwin graduated from the University of Alabama and was a merchant from 1879 through 1895.*

WILLIAM BERNARD LIGHTFOOT *was born 16 December 1811 in Port Royal, Caroline County, Virginia and died 5 February 1870 in Mobile, Alabama. He married* ROBERTA BEVERLY *of Essex County, Virginia, who died suddenly about eight months after their marriage. After her death he married* SARAH BEE ROSS *in 1835 in Greene County, Alabama. Sarah was born in 1817 in Mobile, Alabama. After their marriage they moved to Lowndes County, Mississippi and are in the 1840-50 Lowndes County census.*

  AMELIA ROSS LIGHTFOOT *was born around 1836 in Lowndes County, Mississippi and married* LEONARD EVANS LOCK, M.D.

  POLLY "SALLIE" BERNARD LIGHTFOOT *was born about 1838 in Mississippi and married* ROBERT TARLETON. *Sallie died in James River, Alabama.*

    MARGARET TARLETON *married* MARSHALL WINCHESTER *17 April 1895 in Maryland.*

    SARAH LIGHTFOOT TARLETON *was born in Greene County, Alabama and married* ALEXANDER ROBERT COLVIN, M.D.

  PHILIP LIGHTFOOT *was born approximately 1842 in Mississippi.*

  ROSALIE B. LIGHTFOOT *was born in 1844 in Mississippi.*

  CENORIA "NORA" LIGHTFOOT *was born in 1847 in Lowndes County, Mississippi and married* WILLIAM REYNOLDS.

<u>?</u> LIGHTFOOT *was born after 1850 in Mississippi.*

JOHN BERNARD LIGHTFOOT *was born in 1813 in Port Royal, Virginia and died in Caroline County, Virginia.* He married HARRIET FIELD *of Gloucester County, Virginia.*

JOHN BERNARD LIGHTFOOT, JR. *was born 29 March 1851 in Port Royal, Virginia and died in Westmoreland County, Virginia.* He married MARY "MOLLIE" WASHINGTON MINOR *8 February 1882. Mary was born in September of 1851. He founded the prominent tobacco firm that bore his name (J.B. Lightfoot & Co. Tobacco Firm) in Richmond, Virginia.*

WILLIAM B. LIGHTFOOT *married* EMMIE CRUMP *the daughter of* JUDGE *and* MRS. WILLIAM W. CRUMP *of Richmond, Virginia.*

LEWIS H. LIGHTFOOT

GEORGE LIGHTFOOT *is buried at St. Peters, Virginia.*

SARAH "SALLIE" LIGHTFOOT *is also buried at St. Peters, in Virginia.*

HOWARD LIGHTFOOT *is buried in Danville.*

HARRIETT LIGHTFOOT *married* FRANCIS E. BROOKE, M.D. *29 October 1867. Francis was born 16 August 1842 and died 30 March 1882.*

FRANCIS E. BROOKE, III *was born 12 September 1868.*

LIGHTFOOT BROOKE *was born 2 November 1876.*

PHILIP HOWELL BROOKE *was born 6 November 1861.*

EDGAR VIVIEN LIGHTFOOT *was born about 1815 in Port Royal, Virginia.*

FANNIE BERNARD LIGHTFOOT *was born approximately 1817 in Port Royal, Virginia and married* CAPTAIN ROBERT GILCHRIST ROBB. *Captain Robb was a captain in the U.S.N and later the C.S.N.*

ROBERT ROBB, SR. *married* AUGUSTA TURNER.

ROBERT ROBB, JR.

TURNER ROBB

He married ADA RANDOLPH *the daughter of* COLONEL RICHARD STUART *in King George County, Virginia.*

ELLEN BANKHEAD LIGHTFOOT *was born in 1819 in Port Royal, Virginia and married* DOCTOR CARTER WORMLEY *29 September 1836 in King William County, Virginia.*

MARY LEWIS LIGHTFOOT *was born approximately 1821 in Port Royal, Virginia and married* <u>?</u> VAIL *of England..*

ROSALIE VIRGINIA LIGHTFOOT *married* DOCTOR HUGH MASON *in Stafford County, Virginia.*

MARY LIGHTFOOT *was born 9 March 1750 in Charles City County, Virginia and died in 1789. She married* COLONEL WILLIAM ALLEN *the son of* JOSEPH ALLEN *of Surry County, Virginia 9 November 1765 in Surry County, Virginia. Colonel Allen was a graduate of William & Mary. He was the wealthiest landowner in Surry County and lived in Bacon's Castle. His first wife was Clara Walker. Colonel Allen died in 1793. Mary's portrait,*

painted by the renowned portrait painter John Wollaston when she was a young girl, is hanging in the DAR Museum.

COLONEL WILLIAM ALLEN *served in the War of 1812.*

PATSY ALLEN

ANN ALLEN *married* ? ARMISTEAD.

JOHN ALLEN

MARTHA ALLEN *married* ? BLAND.

MILDRED LIGHTFOOT *was born approximately 1758 in Yorktown, Virginia and married* WALTER COLES *in 1767 in Halifax County, Virginia.*

ELIZABETH LIGHTFOOT *was born 25 February 1747 in Westmoreland County, Virginia and died 27 July 1781. She married* ISAAC COLES *1 April 1771. Isaac the son of* JOHN *and* MARY

(WINSTON) COLES *was born 25 February 1747 and died 2 June 1813 in Pittsylvania, Virginia. Isaac was the Colonel of his County, a member of the First Congress of the United States and lived as an agriculturalist in Halifax and Pittsylvania. They lived at "Lightfoot Meadows" which is mentioned in George Washington's diary of 1791. He married his second wife* CATHERINE THOMPSON *on 2 January 1790.*

JOHN COLES *was born 20 October 1772 and died 17 May 1796.*
ISAAC COLES, II *was born 16 December 1777 and died 28 September 1820. He married* LIGHTFOOT CARRINGTON *7 February 1811. Lightfoot was born in Westmoreland County, Virginia and died 27 July 1781.*

JOHN COLES
JACOB T. COLES
LIGHTFOOT COLES *was born 12 June 1780 and died 4 December 1781.*

JOHN LIGHTFOOT *was born around 1725 in Gloucester County, Virginia and died 6 September 1751 in Brunswick County, Virginia. John's will is dated 30 April 1751 and was probated 6 November 1751. He married* MARY "MOLLY" CLACK, *the daughter of* JAMES *and* MARY (?) CLACK. *Mary was born in 1724 and married Robert Ruffin after John's death. She died in King William County, Virginia.*
PHILIP LIGHTFOOT, JR. *was born about 1728 in Yorktown, Virginia and died 23 October 1747 in Surry County, Virginia. His land belonged to Henry Lightfoot 30 March 1723. A bond was posted 18 March 1746 to collect levy laid on tithable persons in Surry County, Virginia. This same land was deeded to John Ingram 27 August 1792 of Brunswick County, Virginia. His estate was administered 14 May 1753. He married* SUSANNAH HURLEY.

FRANCIS LIGHTFOOT *was born sometime before 1747 and died sometime before 1771 because he isn't mentioned in his grandmother's will.*
ARMISTEAD LIGHTFOOT *was born in 1730 in Yorktown, Virginia and died in 1771. He married* ANNE "NANCY" BURWELL *28 September 1759. Nancy, the daughter of the* HONORABLE LEWIS *and* MARY (WILLIS) BURWELL *of White Marsh, was born in 1742 in White Marsh, Virginia and died before December 1777. She married the* HONORABLE CHARLES GRYMES *of Gloucester County, Virginia in 1773.*

MARY LIGHTFOOT *was born around 1750 in Yorktown, Virginia and married* JOHN TAYLOE GRIFFIN *in Yorktown, Virginia. In 1780 they were living in Goochland County, Virginia.*

CHAPTER IX

GOODRICH LIGHTFOOT, COLONEL, 1685-1738
MARRIED MARY CHEW

Goodrich Lightfoot, son of JOHN and ANN (GOODRICH) LIGHTFOOT, lived in New Kent County until at least 1722, when an Indian boy belonging to him (either as a slave or an indentured servant) is listed as dead in the Saint Peter's Parish register. By 10 September 1724 he had moved to Spotsylvania County where he witnessed the will of John Rogerts of Saint George's Parish.[1]

In 1726 he was sheriff, coroner and a justice of the peace of Spotsylvania County.[2] He was appointed Vestryman of St. George's Parish in 1727 and was appointed Mayor of Militia in 1729. His land was located in that part of Spotsylvania County that became Orange County in 1734 and Culpeper County in 1749. He was one of the first Justices of Orange County in 1734.

When the Parish of Saint Mark was formed in 1701, the freeholders and housekeepers of the parish met at Germanna on 1 January 1730/31 and elected vestrymen, including Goodrich Lightfoot.[3]

The diary of William Byrd records that he went from the home of Sherwood Lightfoot to that of Goodrich Lightfoot in New Kent County:

22 Sept. 1712. *"...I prepared to go to Mr. Lightfoot's on the Pamunkey River in order to meet the Governor next day at the Pamunkey Indian town."*
23 Sept. 1712. *"...about 10 o'clock we rode to Mr. Goodrich Lightfoot's who lives about a mile from thence. It rained as soon as we got on our horses. There we stayed till the Governor and all the company came in by the man-of-war boat...about 5 o'clock the company were forced to return*

---

[1] W.A.Crozier, Spotsylvania County, 1721-1800. Virginia County Records, V. 1; New York: 1905. p.1.
[2] Virginia in 1726. Virginia Magazine, V. 48. p. 150.
[3] Vestry Minutes, St. Mark's Parish, pp. 1-2. Manuscript.

in the rain to Captain Littlepage's but Mr. Catesby and I returned to Mr. Lightfoot's...About 9 o'clock we ate some blue wing and then retired to bed."

24 Sept. 1712. *"I rose about 7 o'clock and we prepared to go to the election of burgesses in New Kent. I said my prayers and ate some beef for breakfast. About 10 o'clock we took leave and Mr. Lightfoot went with us to the courthouse where abundance of people were assembled..."*[4]

Goodrich Lightfoot was also an officer of the Colonial Militia, being a colonel at the time of his death.

On 28 April 1738 Goodrich and his wife Mary deeded 500 acres of land to Thomas Jones, Jr., of Saint Stephen's Parish, King and Queen County.[5]

The Virginia Gazette of 14 July 1738 carried this notice of his death:

Williamsburg, July 14. We hear from Orange County, That Col. Goodrich Lightfoot died lately at his House in that County. He went to the Court-house in good Health, was taken ill there, carried home that Evening, and not withstanding all possible Care of him, he died the next morning.

Goodrich Lightfoot died intestate and the administration of his estate was granted on 22 March 1738 to his son Goodrich Lightfoot, with Philimon Kavanaugh and John Christophers as securities on a bond for £500.[6]

The inventory of his estate, valued at £208.11.10, was presented to the Court on 24 May 1739. Five Negro slaves and one indentured servant boy named William Barron were named in the inventory, as were 25 head of sheep, 42 head of cattle, several horses, farm implements, furniture and clothing.[7] Two additional inventories were presented on 28 February 1739 and 28 May 1741.[8]

GOODRICH was born about 1682 in New Kent County, Virginia and died 14 April 1738 in Orange County, Virginia. He married MARY CHEW on 9 June 1709. Mary was born in 1689 in Ann Arundel County, Maryland.

The Spotsylvania County, Virginia, Order Book 1724-30 had the following notation on page 122.

A list of the officers of the Colonial Militia who producing their commissions before the Court of His Majesty's Honorable Justices for the County aforesaid, took the Oaths as directed by law:

---

[4] The Secret Diary of William Byrd of Westover, 1709-1712, pp. 587-88.
[5] Orange Co., Va., Deed Book 2, pp. 317-21.
[6] Orange Co., Va. Will Book 1, pp. 79-80.
[7] Orange County, Va. Will Book 1, pp. 94-96.
[8] Will Book 1, pp. 116, 152.

Major Goodrich Lightfoot, Captain Robert Slaughter, and his officers, Francis Kirkly and William Payton; Captain John Scott and his officers Joseph Hawkins and John Lightfoot; Captain William Bledsor and his officers James Williams and George Home, took ye oath 2 September 1729.

The will of Goodrich Lightfoot, Jr., of St. Mark's Parish, Culpeper County, Virginia was dated 24 April 1778 and probated 15 June 1778.

Legatees: Wife Susanna Lightfoot
Daus: Elizabeth James, Ann Grasty, Mary Hubbard, Fanny Hackley, Susanna Brooks, Priscilla Lightfoot, Martha Lightfoot.
Sons: John Lightfoot, Philip Lightfoot (minor), Goodrich Lightfoot, Jr. (a minor)
Executor: Son John Lightfoot
Witt: Daniel Grinnan, John Grinnan, Jane J. Grinnan.

Concerning petition of the inhabitants of the North West Side of the Blue Ridge Mountains, praying that some person be appointed Magistrate.[9]
This order evidences the further advance of civilization in Virginia toward the West. The administration of justice had now become necessary, and Fredericksburg, to which place the county seat of Spotsylvania was removed in 1732, was at least 85 miles distant from the Opeguon settlement, with the Blue Ridge Mountains between them. The prayer of these petitioners was soon granted. In August 1734 the county of Orange was formed from Spotsylvania. East of the Blue Ridge it included territory embraced in present Orange, Culpeper, Rappahannock, Madison and Green Counties, while on the West it extended to "The utmost limits of Virginia".[10]
This was probably the greatest subdivision of territory ever created by legislative enactment in the Anglo-Saxon race. It included all that did then belong to Virginia west of the Blue Ridge, which comprised all of present West Virginia, and the states of Kentucky, Ohio, Indiana, and Illinois. Its jurisdiction was real as far as the white settlements then extended westward.
The first justices composing the County of Orange were:
Augustine Smith, Goodrich Lightfoot, John Talifero, Thomas Chew, Robert Slaughter, Abraham Field, Robert Green, James Barbour, John Finlason, Richard Mauldin, Samuel Ball, Francis Slaughter, Zachary Taylor, John Lightfoot, James Petlow, Robert Eastham, Benjamin Cave,

---

[9] Virginia Magazine. v. 13. p. 1.
[10] Hening vol. IV, pp. 450-51.

Charles Custis, Joist Hite, Charles Morgan, Benjamin Burden, John Smith, and Geo. Hobson. The five justices last named are the same persons mentioned in the Order, and all of them resided in the vicinity of present Winchester. No person living within the limits of present Augusta County

(Our Goodrich was one of the original founders of Little Fork Church in Culpeper County in 1731.)

appears in this list, which indicates that in 1734, nearly all of the inhabitants of the Virginia Valley resided in the present county of Frederick.

The westward movement of Virginia was now commencing in earnest, although it must be borne in mind that the country west of the Blue Ridge was still an almost unbroken wilderness.

In 1726 we find the name of Major Goodrich Lightfoot as a member of the vestry of St. George's Parish, Spotsylvania, when that parish and county embraced what was afterwards the parish of St. Mark's and County of Culpeper. He was one of the lay readers at the Germanna Church. He and Robert Slaughter were appointed to count all the tobacco plants from the mouth of the Rapidan to the mouth of Mountain Run, and up Mountain Run and across to the mouth of the Robinson River. This was done in obedience to an Act of the Assembly limiting the number of plants to be cultivated by each planter.

He was succeeded by his son, Captain Goodrich Lightfoot, II. He served as Vestryman and Churchwarden till he removed from the parish in 1771.

The lineage of Goodrich and Mary (Chew) Lightfoot:

ANNE LIGHTFOOT *was born 22 September 1708 in New Kent County, Virginia and died in 1765. On 3 June 1739 she married* COLONEL FRANCIS SLAUGHTER *in Spotsylvania County, Virginia. Francis was born in 1701 in Essex County, Virginia to* ROBERT *and* FRANCES ANNE JONES SLAUGHTER. *He served, as Captain in the Militia and in 1730 was Colonel Justice and Churchwarden. Francis died in 1766 in Culpeper County, Virginia.*

FRANCIS SLAUGHTER JR. *was born in 1730 and died in 1805 in Elizabethtown, Kentucky. He married* SARAH COLEMAN *the daughter of* ROBERT COLEMAN *of Culpeper County, Virginia on 18 December 1758 in Westmoreland County, Virginia. Francis served as Colonel of the Militia.*

COLONEL JOHN SLAUGHTER *was born in 1732 and married twice. His first wife was* MILDRED COLEMAN *was the daughter of* ROBERT COLEMAN *and was born in 1736 and died in 1758. Mildred was the sister of Sarah, wife of his brother Francis. His second wife was* ELIZABETH SUGGETT *the daughter of* EDGECOMB SUGGETT *who died in 1753 in Westmoreland County, Virginia. They were married 18 December 1758 in Richmond, Virginia.*

REUBEN SLAUGHTER *was born in 1733 in Culpeper County, Virginia and died in 1803 in Bedford County, Virginia. In 1760 he married* BETTY POINDEXTER *the daughter of* JOHN *and* CHRISTIAN POINDEXTER *in Louisa County, Virginia. Betty was born in 1739 and died in 1800. Reuben like his brother Francis was Captain of the Militia.*

CADWALLADER SLAUGHTER *was born in 1735 and died in 1798.*
He married twice. His first wife was MARGARET RANSDELL *in*
Fauquier County, Virginia. His second wife was LUCY SLAUGHTER
daughter of FRANCIS SLAUGHTER *of Jefferson County, Kentucky.*
FRANCES SLAUGHTER *was born in 1737 and married* CAPTAIN
WILLIAM BALL. *William was the son of* SAMUEL *and* ANNA
CATHERINE TAYLOE BALL. *Anna was the cousin of* MARY BALL
the mother of GEORGE WASHINGTON. *William was a vestryman of*
St. Mark's Parish.
ANNE SLAUGHTER *married* EDWARD THOMAS.
   EDWARD THOMAS, JR. *was born in Virginia and died in Kentucky.*
   He married SUSANNAH BEALL *the daughter of* WALTER BEALL
      LUCINDA THOMAS *married* DR. WILLIAM ELLIOTT *in New*
      Haven, Kentucky.
JOHN LIGHTFOOT *was born 7 February 1711 in New Kent County,*
Virginia and died in 1735 in Orange County, Virginia. He never married
and left a will that list his parents and siblings except Anne.
MAJOR GOODRICH LIGHTFOOT, JR. *was christened 14 February*
1713 in New Kent County, Virginia and died 26 April 1778 in Culpeper
County, Virginia. The Major was a man of great prominence in Culpeper
County. He served as a Vestryman and Churchwarden of St. Mark's
Parish. On 8 April 1736 he married SUSANNAH ELIZABETH
SLAUGHTER *in Culpeper County, Virginia. Susannah the daughter of*
ROBERT *and* MARY SMITH SLAUGHTER *was born in 1725 in*
Virginia and died in 1808 in Franklin County, Kentucky.
MARTHA LIGHTFOOT *was born 11 April 1766 in Culpeper County,*
Virginia and died 8 April 1842 in Kentucky. She married twice. Her
first husband was WILLIAM EDZARD *the son of* JAMES EDZARD.
William and Martha were married 30 December 1785 in Culpeper
County, Virginia. After William's death in 1795 Martha moved to
Franklin County, Kentucky, where the final settlement of her husband''
estate was made.
   SUSAN EDZARD *married* JAMES SUBLETTE *in Hickman County,*
   Kentucky. Susan and James both died in Clinton, Kentucky.
      JOHN C. SUBLETTE *was born in Clinton, Kentucky and married*
      ANN MARTHA RINGO *in Hickman County, Kentucky.*
         HARRY RINGO SUBLETTE *was born in Clinton, Kentucky and*
         married MARY LOU DAVIS *in Hickman, County, Kentucky.*
            MARTHA SUE SUBLETTE *was born in Clinton, Kentucky and*
            married CARL BIRK *in Hickman County, Kentucky.*
Martha married GEORGE JORDAN *a Revolutionary soldier before*
1803. George was born 26 January 1754 and died 1 March 1842. The
mantel from their old log home, which was demolished due to age, was
kept by a Mr. John Hawkins and given to Mrs. Carl Birk a descendant of

Martha's. George assisted establishing the American Independence while acting in the capacity of Private in Colonel Hugh Mercer's 3rd Virginia Regiment.

PRISCILLA MARGARET LIGHTFOOT *was born 2 October 1763 and died unmarried 20 December 1779.*

LIEUTENANT PHILIP LIGHTFOOT *was born 11 March 1761 in Virginia and died in 1820 in Adair County, Kentucky. He married* MARGARET MILDRED FRY *25 September 1780. Margaret was born 29 May 1765 in Albemarle, Virginia and died in 1809 in Mercer County, Kentucky. She was the daughter of* REVEREND HENRY *and* SUSAN WALKER FRY. *They moved from Culpeper County, Virginia to Adair County, Kentucky in 1799. They came under the influence of Methodist Revival back in Orange County, Virginia and established in Adair County. The land was given by Alexander Elliott a Presbyterian.*

MILDRED THORNTON LIGHTFOOT *was born 17 April 1782 and died in 1875 in Adair County, Kentucky. She married twice. She married first* LINCEFIELD GRADY *on 2 December 1796 in Madison County, Virginia.*

MARGARET "PEGGY" THORNTON GRADY *was born 4 April 1799 in Virginia and died 20 May 1868. She married twice. In 1813 she married* GEORGE HUGHES.

MILDRED HUGHES *married* JAMES DIDDLE.
She married GEORGE CAMPBELL ELLIOTT *in 1852.*
BETSY ANN GRADY *married* CHARLES LEE COX.
WILLIAM FRY GRADY *died in 1852.*
SUSAN PEACHY GRADY *married* JOSEPH CRAIG *in 1821.*
LINCEFIELD GRADY, JR. *was born in 1811.*

Her second husband was ROBERT CRAIG *who she married 22 August 1811.*

SUSANNAH "SUKEY" FRY LIGHTFOOT *was born 25 December 1784 in Virginia and died in 1823. She married* JOSEPH O'BANNION NELSON *23 June 1799. Joseph died in 1852.*

WADE NELSON
HENRY NELSON
JAMES JOSIAH NELSON
SUSAN NELSON *was born 12 October 1817 and died 6 May 1884. On 5 March 1836 she married* WILLIAM ELLIOTT.
PHILIP NELSON *married* PAMELIA T. CREEL *in 1824 and died in 1833.*

HENRY FRY LIGHTFOOT *was born 22 February 1787 in Madison County, Virginia and died 10 February 1846 in Boyle County, Kentucky. On 21 February 1811 he married* MARY TURNER JONES *in Adair County, Kentucky. Mary was born 6 January 1792.*

JOHN ASHBY LIGHTFOOT *was born 3 September 1814 in Adair County, Kentucky and died 23 September 1891. John married twice. His first wife was* SUSAN J. JONES. *They were married 24 September 1838 and she died 5 September 1844. John worked in the U.S. Custom House in New Orleans.*

    HENRY F. LIGHTFOOT *was born 1 September 1840 and in 1864 he married* FANNIE F. KELLY.

      HENRY W. LIGHTFOOT

After her death he married MARGARET CORNELIA SIGLER.

    CHARLES W. LIGHTFOOT

    MARY A. LIGHTFOOT

    SUSAN M. LIGHTFOOT

GOODRICH E. LIGHTFOOT *was born 19 April 1817 and on the 1st of December of 1842 he married* NANCY B. CALLARMAN. *Nancy was born 3 March 1826.*

    MARY E. LIGHTFOOT *was born 18 September 1847 and married* JOHN F. FAGAN.

    ELIZABETH J. LIGHTFOOT *was born 22 June 1849 and on 6 September 1870 she married* RICHARD T. LEWIS. *Richard was born 18 April 1838 and served in the Company G 16th Illinois Cavalry in the Civil War.*

    JAMES R. LIGHTFOOT *was born 17 April 1852 and on 24 December 1873 he married* JULIA R. PLUNKETT.

    SUSAN M LIGHTFOOT *married* JOHN L. CALLERMAN, JR. *8 January 1874.*

    JOHN L. LIGHTFOOT

    JUDITH L. LIGHTFOOT

    ALICE B. LIGHTFOOT

    JULIA ANN LIGHTFOOT

DOLLY ASHBY LIGHTFOOT *was born 9 February 1820 in Adair County, Kentucky and on 6 December 1839 she married* PETER LANTERMAN *in Sangamon County, Illinois. Peter was born 4 September 1817 in Fleming County, Kentucky and died 9 October 1876 in Elkhart, Illinois.*

MARGARET S. LIGHTFOOT *was born 16 November 1822 in Warren County, Kentucky and died 15 December 1847 in Alabama while visiting. She married* PHILIP F. LIGHTFOOT *in Sangamon County, Illinois.*

    REUBEN LIGHTFOOT *enlisted in 1862 in Company A 38th Illinois Infantry. He was wounded in the battle of Stone's River and died 4 January 1863.*

    GABRIEL LIGHTFOOT

ROBERT SLAUGHTER LIGHTFOOT *was born 13 March 1825 in Warren County, Kentucky and died in the California Gold Rush in 1849.*

ELIZABETH M. LIGHTFOOT *was born about 1827 in Warren County, Kentucky and died in Sangamon County, Illinois. She married* HENRY SHUCK *in Sangamon County, Illinois.*

  ANNIE LIGHTFOOT SHUCK

PHILIP H. LIGHTFOOT *was born 24 August 1829 in Kentucky and died in 1835 in Sangamon County, Illinois.*

GABRIEL M. LIGHTFOOT *was born 8 August 1832 in Springfield, Illinois and died 12 March 1846.*

GOODRICH LIGHTFOOT *was born 6 June 1788 in Adair County, Kentucky and in 1818 he married* LOUISIANA ? *in Adair County, Kentucky. He fought in the War of 1812.*

MARTHA "PATSY" FRY LIGHTFOOT *was born 16 August 1790 and died in 1867. On 22 December 1807 she married* JOHN BOHON *in Mercer County, Kentucky.*

MARGARET FRY BOHON *was born 1 May 1809 and died in 1867. On 5 June 1828 she married* THOMAS DEAN.

WILLIAM FRY BOHON *was born 10 November 1810 and died in 1873. On 30 January 1840 he married* VERLINDA HUTCHINSON.

REUBEN L. BOHON *was born 25 November 1812 and died in 1894. He married* MARY ANN THRELKELD *22 December 1835.*

JUDY FRY BOHON *was born 9 October 1814 and died in 1841. She married* HARVEY MITCHELL *in 1834.*

MARTHA DIVERS BOHON *was born 16 September 1818 and died in 1864. In 1841 she married* JOHN FINNELL.

JOHN L. BOHON *was born 29 December 1820 and married* SARAH HEDRICK.

LUCY L. BOHON *was born 1 October 1822 and on 27 October 1842 she married* MERRILL WILLIAMS.

MILDRED GRADY BOHON *was born 26 January 1827 and in 1847 she married* WILLIAM C. McAFEE.

RICHARD HENRY BOHON *was born 26 February 1829 and on 24 October 1849 he married* MARY VANARSDELL.

MARY HANNAH BOHON *was born 24 May 1834 and died 24 June 1849. In 1848 she married* JAMES T. ROWLAND.

JOHN JONES LIGHTFOOT *was born in 1792 and on 3 June 1822 he married* MARTHA A. BARNET.

LUCY GILMORE LIGHTFOOT *was born about 1795 and married* ELIJAH BOHON *22 November 1812 in Mercer County, Kentucky.*

REUBEN LIGHTFOOT *was born 11 January 1799 and died 31 May 1882. On 24 February 1820 he married* SUSAN M. ELLIOTT *in Adair County, Kentucky. Susan was born around 1800. Her parents were* MIDSHIPMAN ALEXANDER *and* ANN "NANCY" CAMPBELL ELLIOTT. *Alexander was born in 1763 and died in 1852. Nancy was born in Lancaster County, Pennsylvania.*

WILLIAM FRY LIGHTFOOT *was born 20 August 1801 and died in Warren County, Kentucky.*

TILITHA (MATILDA OR DELITHA) *married* JAMES H. RICHEY *17 April 1844 in Warren County, Kentucky.*

SID LIGHTFOOT

CHEAT LIGHTFOOT

ELIZABETH LIGHTFOOT *was born 14 June 1743 and died before 1823. She married* ? JAMES *before 1778.*

ANN LIGHTFOOT *was born 10 February 1748 and married* GEORGE GRASTY *before 1778.*

GOODRICH L. GRASTY *died in Breckenridge County, Kentucky.*

MARY LIGHTFOOT *was born 10 March 1750 and married twice. Her first husband was* EPHRAIM HUBBARD *before 1778. Her second husband was* JAMES BROOKS.

FRANCES LIGHTFOOT *was born 19 February 1753 and died 4 October 1825 in Lawrenceburg, Kentucky. She married* FRANCIS HACKLEY *of King George County, Virginia in 1768. Francis was born 16 May 1740 and died 17 July 1817.*

SUSANNAH LIGHTFOOT *was born 14 July 1755 and married* WILLIAM BROOKS *before 1778. William was a soldier in the Revolutionary War. He sold his pension and moved to North Carolina.*

SUSANNA BROOKS *was born around 1770 and married* STEPHEN CHEDESTER. *They moved to Green County, Tennessee in 1857.*

JAMES B. CHEDESTER *was born around 1812.*

CAPTAIN JOHN LIGHTFOOT *was born 19 March 1758 in Madison County, Virginia and died in 1809 in Nelson County, Kentucky. He married twice. His first wife was* TABITHA SLAUGHTER *who he married 20 August 1780. He served as Justice of Peace of Franklin County, Kentucky in 1795. His will was probated 15 November 1811 in Nelson County, Kentucky.*

NANCY LIGHTFOOT *was born 27 February 1795 and in May of 1812 she married* ROBERT HUDSON *in Woodford County, Kentucky.*

ELIZA JANE HUDSON *married* RICE W. OLIVER *in October 1833 in Mercer County, Kentucky. They lived at Forks of Elkhorn, Kentucky, near Frankfort.*

SUSANNAH H. LIGHTFOOT *was born 16 June 1782 and on 21 September 1816 she married* MARK LAMPTON *in Nelson County, Kentucky.*

ELIZABETH "BETSEY" LIGHTFOOT *was born 5 March 1786 and in 1800 she married* REVEREND EDMUND WALLER *in Franklin County, Kentucky. Edmund was born in 1747 and died in 1830. He was married to* ANN DURRETT *before he married Betsey. He taught at Salt River Church under John Penny and was granted credentials to celebrate rites of matrimony in Franklin in 1802.*

REVEREND JOHN LIGHTFOOT *was born in 1809 and was a brilliant orator and writer. John was the editor of the "Baptist Banner" later changed to the "Western Recorder". John was ordained in 1840.*

JOHN GOODRICH LIGHTFOOT *was born 17 June 1790 and died 12 October 1818.*

PHILIP LIGHTFOOT *was born 28 November 1792 in Franklin County, Kentucky and died 26 October 1873 in Hardinsburg, Kentucky. He married* ADAH LANDER *27 November 1815 in Hardinsburg, Kentucky. Adah was born 8 December 1796 in Hardinsburg, Kentucky and died 11 March 1865 in Hardinsburg, Kentucky. She was the daughter of* NATHANIEL *and* MARY LANDER.

ROSINA LIGHTFOOT *was born 11 November 1816 in Breckenridge, Kentucky and died 30 March 1894 in Spencer County, Indiana. She married thrice. On 23 May 1833 she married* TRAVIS DANIEL. *Travis was born in 1813 in Clark County, Kentucky and died 10 October 1837. He was the son of* PETER *and* NANCY HUNT DANIEL. *Peter was born in 1761 and died in 1821 in Breckenridge County, Kentucky. Nancy was born in 1770 in North Carolina and died in 1816 in Breckenridge County, Kentucky.*

PHILIP T. DANIEL *was born 27 September 1834 and died 18 February 1874. He married* MARIA ?. *Maria was born 15 April 1837 and died 9 November 1874. Philip was the Constable in Harrodsburg.*

NAT DANIEL *was born in 1863.*

ROSA DANIEL *was born in 1865.*

In March of 1841 she married JAMES HAMBLETON. *After 1870 she married* JAMES HAMMOND.

DELILA LIGHTFOOT *was born 29 January 1818 and died 17 August 1894 in Cloverport, Kentucky. On 27 August 1827 she married* EZEKIAL FISHER.

JOHN SLAUGHTER LIGHTFOOT *was born 24 December 1819 and died 6 August 1894 in Cloverport, Kentucky. He married* ANN T. NEWMAN *21 January 1841. Ann was born 16 September 1821 in Breckenridge County, Kentucky and died 9 January 1881 in Cloverport, Kentucky. She was the daughter of* THOMAS V. *and* MARY S. McQUIDDY NEWMAN. *After Ann's death John married* LUCY T. MARSHALL *30 September 1883 and 16 January 1887 he married* DEILA CLARK.

MARY ELLA "MOLLIE" LIGHTFOOT *was born 1 January 1842 and married* DR. C.W. GABBERT.

PHILIP T. LIGHTFOOT *was born 12 March 1843 and died 25 August 1850.*

JOHN FOSTER LIGHTFOOT *was born 25 September 1846 and died in Hawesville, Kentucky. On 27 May 1875 he married* REBECCA REYNOLDS *in Fordsville, Kentucky. Rebecca was the daughter of* JOHN *and* MARIAH BROOKS REYNOLDS.

FORREST LEE LIGHTFOOT *was born 7 May 1876 in Hawesville, Kentucky and died in Cloverport, Kentucky. In 1898 he married* MARY E. MILLER *in Breckenridge County, Kentucky. Mary was the daughter of* WILLIAM *and* NANCY JANE STILLMAN MILLER.

CHARLES ROSS LIGHTFOOT *was born in 1877 and died in Cloverport, Kentucky. He married* RESSIE SHREWSBURY.

SARAH JOHNNE LIGHTFOOT *married* JOHN CLYDE LEITCH *in Hawesville, Kentucky. Sarah died in Savannah, Georgia.*

ADELINE "ADDIE" LIGHTFOOT *was born 24 September 1847 in Breckenridge County, Kentucky and married* GEORGE DOWDEN.

ANNETTE VICTORIA LIGHTFOOT *was born 20 October 1849 and died 4 May 1884. She married* PETER S. MILLER.

CHARLES EDWARD LIGHTFOOT *married 17 October 1851 and married twice. He married* SOPHRONIA MILLER *first and after her death he married* CARRIE HAMILTON.

AMELIA JANE LIGHTFOOT *was born 14 July 1845 and died 11 October 1845 in Cloverton, Kentucky.*

MARY LIGHTFOOT *was born 23 October 1821 and married* THOMAS C. McGAVOCK. *Thomas was a farmer and was born in 1823 to* ROBERT *and* ANN McGAVOCK. *When Thomas and Mary died the children where left to Robert and Ann and to John S. Lightfoot.*

CLOYD McGAVOCK *was born in 1847.*

ROSINA McGAVOCK *was born in 1848.*

ANNA McGAVOCK *was born in 1852.*

LANDER McGAVOCK *was born in 1853.*

ADA McGAVOCK *was born in 1855.*

EMMA McGAVOCK *was born in 1857.*

GORDON McGAVOCK *was born in 1859.*

NATHANIEL LANDER LIGHTFOOT *was born 25 December 1823 in Hardinsburg, Kentucky and died in Henderson, Kentucky. Nathaniel was a Physician and a farmer. He served in the United States Cavalry as a Major in the 12th Kentucky Cavalry. He married twice. In 1856 he married* EMMA PATE. *Emma was born 18 September 1838 and died 11 September 1870 in Hancock County, Kentucky. She was the daughter of* MINOR E. PATE.

ELDRED WALKER LIGHTFOOT *was born 24 July 1857 and died 10 May 1868 in Hancock County, Kentucky.*

MARY BELLE LIGHTFOOT *was born 8 July 1861 and died 25 February 1868 in Hancock County, Kentucky.*

EWING LIGHTFOOT *was born in 1878.*

ROY LIGHTFOOT

EMMA LIGHTFOOT *was born in 1873.*

ALMA LIGHTFOOT *was born in 1864.*

LEONARD "LYNN" LIGHTFOOT *was born in 1867.*

FRANK LIGHTFOOT *was born in 1869.*
On 15 February 1872 he married SARAH E. PATE. *Sarah was born 27 December 1846 and died in Henderson, Kentucky.*

ELIZA LIGHTFOOT *was born 31 December 1826 and died 26 January 1853 in Hardinsburg, Kentucky. She married* ROBERT D. ALLEGREE.

DR. RICHARD P. LIGHTFOOT *was born 20 June 1828 and died 12 June 1889 in Jackson County, Illinois. On 30 September 1852 he married* MARGARET EVELINE NEWMAN. *Margaret was born 12 August 1830 and died in Jackson County, Illinois.*

EVA LIGHTFOOT

WALLER LIGHTFOOT

HENRY E. LIGHTFOOT *married* EMMA A. ?. *Emma was born in 29 June 1855 and died in Jackson County, Illinois.*

HOLLIE L. LIGHTFOOT *was born in October of 1881 in Jackson County, Illinois and died 2 June 1882 in Jackson County, Illinois.*

HARRY OWENS LIGHTFOOT *was born 16 January 1878 and died 23 December 1891 in Jackson County, Illinois.*

HENRY PENDLETON LIGHTFOOT *was born in 1873 and died in Jackson County, Illinois.*

HELEN P. LIGHTFOOT *was born in 1873 and died in Jackson County, Illinois.*

FRANK D. LIGHTFOOT *was born 7 December 1892 and died in Jackson County, Illinois.*

GEORGE P. LIGHTFOOT *was born 1 October 1884 and died 1 January 1898 in Jackson County, Illinois.*

RICHARD T. LIGHTFOOT *was an attorney and died in Paducah, Kentucky.*

WILLIAM PENDLETON LIGHTFOOT *was born in 1856 and died in Jackson County, Illinois. He married* LOUISA J. HAYES *who was born in 1854 and died in Jackson County, Illinois. They made their home in Carbondale, Illinois.*

ELLA I. LIGHTFOOT *died in Chicago, Illinois.*

RICHARD PENDLETON LIGHTFOOT *was born 7 December 1892 in Jackson County, Illinois.*

HENRY FAUSTER LIGHTFOOT *was born 13 June 1830 and died 8 April 1835.*

AMELIA JANE LIGHTFOOT *was born 13 August 1832 and died 5 April 1834.*

WILLIAM WALLIS LIGHTFOOT *was born 12 October 1835 and died 21 February 1838.*

ANNASTACIA LIGHTFOOT *was born 29 October 1836 and died 30 June 1898 in Cloverport, Kentucky. On 22 April 1856 she married* ROBERT LOUIS NEWSOM. *Robert was born 22 January 1832 in Springfield, Illinois.*

  MARY FRANCES NEWSOM *was born 13 March 1857 and died the same day.*

  WILLIAM WAVERLY NEWSOM *was born 17 March 1858.*

  LEILA MAY NEWSOM *was born 13 May 1860 and died 20 July 1860.*

  ALFRED LANDER NEWSOM *was born 13 April 1861.*

  INA BELLE NEWSOM *was born 17 July 1863.*

  PERCY LEE NEWSOM *was born 21 January 1865.*

  TRAVIS LIGHTFOOT NEWSOM *was born 13 March 1867 and died 15 March 1867.*

  LUELLA BRUCE NEWSOM *was born 13 December 1869 and married* FRANK LANDER BOYD *24 February 1892.*

  IRENE LIGHTFOOT *was born 13 July 1871.*

 TABITHA FRANCES LIGHTFOOT *was born 25 October 1839 and died after 1870. She married* ? SUTTON.

ROBERTA LIGHTFOOT *was born 22 September 1800 and married* DANIEL TRAVERS.

AMELIA LIGHTFOOT *was born 6 April 1788 and on 6 June 1808 she married* JOHN GARVEY *in Franklin County, Kentucky.*

 JOHN LIGHTFOOT GARVEY *was born 23 March 1813 in Kentucky and married* NANCY REED.

  SAMUEL THOMAS GARVEY

   DR. JOHN FREDERICK GARVEY

   MYRTLE GARVEY

  JOHN GARVEY

  JAMES GARVEY

  ROBERT A. GARVEY

  JANE THOMSY GARVEY

  ALICE GARVEY

  DR. PHILLIP LAWRENCE GARVEY

  AMELIA GARVEY

JAMES PENDLETON GARVEY *was born 6 June 1818 and died 21 March 1896 in Anderson, Indiana and is buried in Cincinnati, Ohio. He married twice. On 25 May 1852 he married* KATHERINE McBRAYER *in Warsaw, Kentucky. Katherine was born 24 February 1825 and died 29 April 1856.*

WILLIAM SANFORD GARVEY *was born in 1853 in Kentucky and married* ALLICE KAY BELLE *in 1887.*

CLIFFORD PENDLETON GARVEY was *born in 1856 in Kentucky and married* JANE DICKEY.

In 1856 he married MARY "MOLLIE" HAMILTON.

CLAYTON HAMILTON GARVEY *was born in 1859 in Kentucky and married* LUELLA RHODES.

WALLACE G. GARVEY *was born in Kentucky and married* VIRGINIA ?.

EDGAR LAWRENCE GARVEY *was born 27 August 1883 in Newport, Kentucky and married twice. He married* ROSA FRANKS *first and then he married* MARY LUTIE HAYS.

CLARENCE GARVEY *was born in Newport, Kentucky.*

JAMES STANLEY GARVEY *was born 8 March 1871 in Newport, Kentucky and died 11 March 1893. He married* KATHERINE "DILLIE" ?.

TABBY ELIZA GARVEY *was born 23 December 1810 and married* SAMUEL LAWRENCE.

PHILLIP G. GARVEY *was born 30 October 1815.*

WILLIAM S. GARVEY *was born 8 November 1820 and married* KATHERINE ?.

JOHN S. GARVEY
  WILL GARVEY
  ROY GARVEY
  RUBY GARVEY
  MARION GARVEY
JAMES RUSSELL GARVEY
  HARRY P. GARVEY
   HARRY P. GARVEY, JR.
   JAMES RUSSELL GARVEY
  BEN A. GARVEY
  HAZEL GARVEY
  CARY GARVEY
  VIRGINIA GARVEY
  KATHERINE GARVEY
BEN PENDLETON GARVEY
  BEN P. GARVEY
  NELL GARVEY
  RUTH GARVEY

EDGAR GARVEY

SUSANNAH GARVEY *was born 10 May 1823.*

FRANCES JANE GARVEY *was born 11 March 1828 and married* JOHN MADDOX.

ROBERT PIPER GARVEY *was born 12 August 18??. He was discharged at Camp Belknap after the Mexican War of 1846.*

GOODRICH LIGHTFOOT *was born 4 August 1784 and died 11 April 1785.*

MARY "POLLEY" LIGHTFOOT *was born 6 June 1797.*

His second wife was MARGARET "PEGGY" PENDLETON SLAUGHTER *who he married on 31 August 1809. Peggy was the widow of* ROBERT SLAUGHTER *who she had married in 1783. And after the death of John she married* REVEREND JOSHUA MORRIS.

PENDLETON GOODRICH LIGHTFOOT *was born 8 July 1810 and died before 1835 in Davis County, Kentucky. On 21 February 1831 he married* CAROLINE CROW, *the daughter of* JUDGE WARNER CROW, *in Ohio County, Kentucky.*

JOHN WARNER CROW LIGHTFOOT *was born 26 November 1832 and died 15 January 1896. On 9 October 1853 he married* ARRIA MOSELEY *in Ohio County, Kentucky.*

JOSHUA PENDLETON LIGHTFOOT *was born 26 December 1835 and died 5 November 1879 in Davis County, Kentucky. He married* MARY C. DAVIS, *a rich southern plantation lady from Bardstown, Kentucky. Mary was born 19 October 1835 in Bardstown, Kentucky and died 13 October 1874 in Davis County, Kentucky. She was the daughter of* TIM *and* B.B. DAVIS.

DORA ANN LIGHTFOOT

JOHN HENRY LIGHTFOOT *married* JEANNETTE LAIRD FINCH *2 April 1883 in Utah. John went to Texas at the age of fourteen and traveled from Texas to Salt Lake City, Utah on a cattle drive. He married Jeannette and setup a home in Goshen, Utah.*

HENRY WADSWORTH LIGHTFOOT

LLOYD H. LIGHTFOOT *married* OPAL L. ?.

CAROLINE CYNTHIA LIGHTFOOT

MARTHA FRANCES LIGHTFOOT

EVELINE ROBERTA LIGHTFOOT *married* FRANK KING.

JAMES PENDLETON LIGHTFOOT

MARSHALL LIGHTFOOT *lived in DeFuniak Springs, Florida.*

BAXTER DAVIS LIGHTFOOT.

WILLIAM GOODRICH LIGHTFOOT *was born 15 August 1774 in Culpeper County, Virginia and died in 1847 in Edgar County, Illinois. William lived in Illinois. He was a Private in Captain's Jacob Elliston's Company in the War of 1812. He taught school in Culpeper County, Virginia. In the early 1800's he moved to Adair County, Kentucky where appears in the tax records. He married* MARY HAWKINS, *the daughter of* MATTHEW *and* BETTY MAXWELL HAWKINS *of Culpeper County, Virginia.*

HENRY HARRISON LIGHTFOOT *was born in 1812 in Anderson County, Kentucky and died in 1885 at the home of his son Marquis in Linn County, Kansas. He had lands in Phillip County, Kansas. The family is in the 1850 Edgar County, Illinois census. On 23 February 1837 he married* ELIZABETH DYER. *Elizabeth was born in 1817 and died at the home of her son John in Unionville, Missouri.*

GEORGE JORDAN LIGHTFOOT *was born 1 December 1837 in Edgar County, Illinois and died in Louisburg, Kansas. In 1867 he married* CARRIE ?.

JOHN H. LIGHTFOOT *was born in Edgar County, Illinois and died in Unionville, Missouri. He married* FRANCES FUNNERLL.

IRVING WASHINGTON LIGHTFOOT *was born in Edgar County, Illinois and died in Tulsa, Oklahoma. He married* SUSAN ANN ?.

FRANCIS MARION LIGHTFOOT *was born 11 August 1848 in Edgar County, Illinois and died in Downs, Kansas. In 1888 He married* MARY A. NEVILL.

MAUD ETHEL LIGHTFOOT *was born 2 September 1889 and married* HAROLD HARRIS KENDALL.

FLOYD HENRY LIGHTFOOT *was born 18 January 1892 and married* FLORA BELLE MARIETTA *of Grand Junction, Colorado in Kirwin, Kansas. They made their home in Stockton, Kansas.*

ALICE LOUISE LIGHTFOOT *was born in Stockton, Kansas and married* ROBERT JAMES McCLAY

ANETA MARGUERITE LIGHTFOOT *was born in Stockton, Kansas and married* KENNETH IRWIN McCAULEY.

WILLIAM G. LIGHTFOOT *was born 11 April 1846 and died in Centerville, Iowa. He was married twice. He married* LAURA COFFRIN *and* RACHEL CENA PEARSON.

BENJAMIN FRANKLIN LIGHTFOOT *died a bachelor in Unionville, Missouri.*

MARQUIS de LA FAYETTE LIGHTFOOT *was born 14 April 1849 and died in Henryetta, Oklahoma. On 4 February 1878 he married* MARY FRASEE *in Belton, Missouri.*

ROBERT HARRISON LIGHTFOOT *was born 14 March 1852 in Edgar County, Illinois and died in Hobo, Oregon. On 14 January 1873 he married* DELILAH KORNS *in Missouri.*

FRANK KORNS, SR.

ANDREW JACKSON LIGHTFOOT *was born 12 February 1853 and married* JANE PHINNEY.

HARVEY MONROE LIGHTFOOT *was born 24 December 1855 in Edgar County, Illinois and married* MATILDA ELIZABETH VAN NUSS *2 April 1884 in Belton, Missouri.*

NANCY JANE LIGHTFOOT *was born in Unionville, Missouri and married* HENRY SPEERS. *She died in January of 1886.*

HUGH KYLE "JIM" LIGHTFOOT *was born in Unionville, Missouri and was a newspaperman in Phillips County, Kansas.*

JAMES MADISON LIGHTFOOT *was born in 1808 in Kentucky and died 13 March 1883 in Paris, Illinois. He married* MARY HEDGER.

WILLIAM LIGHTFOOT *married* MARGARET BODINE *21 January 1832.*

THORNTON LIGHTFOOT *was born about 1810 in Franklin County, Kentucky and married* MARGARET ?. *Margaret was born about 1808 in Nelson County, Kentucky.*

EMERINE LIGHTFOOT *was born about 1833 in Edgar County, Illinois.*

MARY A. LIGHTFOOT *was born around 1836 in Edgar County, Illinois.*

JAMES F. LIGHTFOOT *was born about 1838 in Edgar County, Illinois.*

NANCY E. LIGHTFOOT *was born around 1840 in Edgar County, Illinois.*

WILLIAM M. LIGHTFOOT *was born about 1842 in Edgar County, Illinois.*

ROBERT W. LIGHTFOOT *was born around 1846 in Edgar County, Illinois.*

JOHN GOODRICH LIGHTFOOT *was born 22 April 1822 in Kentucky and died in Holton, Kansas. John served in the War with Mexico in 1847 and served under an alias in the United States Cavalry during the Civil War. He married twice. He married* MARY FRANCES BARNES *in Boone County, Missouri.*

MARY ELLEN LIGHTFOOT *married* IRA MANN *in 1885 and after his death in 1897 she married* FRANK LOCKWOOD.

WALTER GOODRICH MANN *married* HANNAH TREMLIN.

RALPH EDWARD MANN *married* BEVERLY FAE WHIPPLE.

JUDY FAE MANN

GEORGE WALTER MANN

ALICE IRENE MANN

ALICE LUCILLE "DOLL" MANN *married* JOHN F. WILSON.

SARAH "SALLY" LIGHTFOOT *married* HARRISON H. MANN, *the brother of Ira.*

ARTHUR E. MANN

EARL E. MANN

WILLIAM HARRISON LIGHTFOOT *married* EVA PARKHURST.

JOHN B. LIGHTFOOT *married* ? CARLSON.
MARY LIGHTFOOT *married* W. VAUGHN EVANS.
   WILLIAM EVANS
   CLENICE EVANS
HAZEL LIGHTFOOT *married* WILBER BELKNAP.
LOLA LIGHTFOOT *married* DUNSTEN WINEBRENNER.
   TRULALEE WINEBRENNER
He married CLARA LYONS *after Mary's death.*
SUSANNAH LIGHTFOOT *was born 10 September 1807 and married*
JOHN GIST *around 1829.*
   JOHN GIST, JR.
   LUCILLE GIST *married* ? GOHAGAN
   SUSAN GIST *married* ? HURST.
     CLELL HURST
     HORASE HURST
ELIZA LIGHTFOOT *married* JOHN RAY.
EVALINA LIGHTFOOT *married* ? ELLIOTT.
ALMIRAH LIGHTFOOT *was born in 1813 and married* PATRICK
WHALEN.
ANN MARIAH LIGHTFOOT *married* BARTHOLOMEW WHALEN
18 September 1837.
MARY LIGHTFOOT *was born 2 September 1717 in New Kent County,
Virginia.*
WILLIAM LIGHTFOOT *was born in 1720 in New Kent County, Virginia
and married* ELIZABETH BARROW. *There is more on this family and
their offsprings in Chapter X.*
ELIZABETH LIGHTFOOT *was born in 1721 in New Kent County,
Virginia.*

CHAPTER X

WILLIAM LIGHTFOOT, MAJOR, 1720-1805
MARRIED ELIZABETH BARROW

MAJOR WILLIAM LIGHTFOOT, the son of GOODRICH and MARY (CHEW) LIGHTFOOT was born sometime around 1720 in St. Peter's Parish, New Kent County. Although no records have been found on which to base an estimate of his age.

He married ELIZABETH BARROW the daughter of EDWARD and ELIZABETH (MINOR) BARROW on 5 March 1746 in Westmoreland County, Virginia. Elizabeth was born about 1730 in North Farnham, Richmond County, Virginia and died in Culpeper County, Virginia or Jefferson County, Kentucky. Her father EDWARD BARROW was born in 1700 in Richmond County, Virginia and died in 1733 in Richmond County, Virginia. Her mother ELIZABETH MINOR was born in 1700 in Westmoreland County, Virginia and married a Mr. Whercett after the death of Edward. Elizabeth Minor was the daughter of NICHOLAS MINOR who died in 1744 in Westmoreland County, Virginia. Edward Barrow was the son of EDWARD and JANE (STONE) BARROW.

William was Vestryman of St. Martin's Parish between 1752-1758.[1] He served as a captain of the Virginia militia in 1758 and then as a major in the French and Indian War[2]. H.J. Eckenrode's List of the Revolutionary Soldiers of Virginia contains an entry that indicates that he also saw service by hauling supplies during the Revolutionary War.[3] William Lightfoot's beautiful sword, the ivory and brass hilt crowned with an eagle's head, is engraved "Major William Lightfoot" and is located at the DAR Building at Washington D.C.

The presence of the Culpeper Militia at Winchester in 1758 is shown in Governor Dinwiddie's letters. The William Lightfoot mentioned is none other than our William, son of Major Goodrich Lightfoot.

---

[1] William & Mary's Quarterly. Second series. V. 15. p. 428.
[2] Virginia Magazine. V. 7 p. 398.
[3] Virginia State Library. Report. 1911. Richmond: 1912.

--That in Obedience to this command your Petitioner raised upward of 300 men and marched with the Officers whose names are subjoined, to Winchester, where he was to receive the Orders of George Washington, Esq., then Commander of the Virginia Regiments and there being forces assembled there from other Counties, which in the whole were judged more than necessary, Colo. Washington, after holding a Council of War, determined to discharge part and save expenses, reserved part only from each county, that there might be no necessity to retain any of the Field Officers, under which regulations Two Companys of the men from Culpeper were kept there and employed during the summer.

That your Petitioner was not an Officer of the Militia at the time he received the said Commission, but accepted it for that service, and was afterwards employed in various services, such as recruiting men for the Royal American Regiment, and marching in a company of volunteers to the frontiers during the War.

That your Petitioner conceived himself and the Officers who marched under his Command as Aforesaid, intitled to Lands under his Majesty's Proclamant of Oct. 1783, and humbly prays for himself and them leave to Locate and Survey the same in order to obtain patents. And he will pray & C.

Tho's Slaughter, Colo.
Wm. Green, Major, dead & Wm. Green heir-at-law
Ambrose Powell, Capt. stayed all summer
John Field, Capt. stayed all summer, afterwards in the 2nd regiment.
Robert Green, Capt. discharged at Winchester
Benjamin Roberts, Capt. discharged at Winchester
Frances Kirkley, Capt. discharged at Winchester & Wm. Kirkley heir
Lt. Francis Slaughter
Lt. John Green
Ensigns: Geo. Weatherall, stayed the summer; James Barber; John Slaughter; Thos. Triplett; James Slaughter; Wm. Stanton; Francis Slaughter, Jr.; and Wm. Lightfoot

Endorsed Colo. Thomas Slaughter

This is the Petition by Colonel Thomas Slaughter written to Lord Dunmore.

That the Right Honorable John, Earl of Dunmore, his Majesty's Lieutenant and Governor General of Virginia, and the Honorable Council thereof:

The petitioner humbly sheweth:

That in the year 1758 he received a commission from the Honorable Robert Dinwiddy, Esquire, then Lieutenant Governor, to be Colonel of a

*body of forces from the County of Culpeper, with directions to raise 400
men to be marched on an expedition against the Indians above Winchester
under the command of your Petitioner, a Major, 5 Captains, 10
Lieutenants and proportionable Subaltern Officers.*

*The population in Virginia in the 17th Century contained about the same
proportion of families of gentle birth and those descended from merchants
and yeoman as England did.*

*We may take some instances of well-known families represented in
Council, Claiborne, Kemp, Thoroughgood, Wormeley, Bernard, Wyatt,
Ludlow, Digges, Bacon, Forsmander, Reade, Corbin, Moryson, Jennings,
Spencer, Page, Scarborough, Lightfoot, Robinson, Johnson, Burwell,
Randolph, Fairfax, and West were of Gentle Origin.*

It is known that on 19 October 1749, William Lightfoot, then a resident
of Richmond County, Virginia and his wife, Elizabeth, deeded to Thomas
Slaughter (the brother of his sister-in-law Susannah, wife of Goodrich
Lightfoot, Jr.) of Culpeper County, 300 acres in Orange County[4]. This is
the only record in Orange or Culpeper counties that has been found naming
his wife.

The Culpeper County Quitrent Roll for 1764 shows that Captain William
Lightfoot owned 200 acres.[5] The first land tax book under the
commonwealth, that of 1782, lists him with 300 acres, and in 1788 and
1789 he was taxed for 211 acres. In 1782 he paid personal taxes on 14
slaves, 7 horses and 33 head of cattle.

William moved with his sons John B. and Edward and his daughter
Frances in 1794 from Culpeper County, Virginia to Jefferson County,
Kentucky. His daughter Mildred (Lightfoot) Nabb also lived in Kentucky
as did the family of his eldest daughter Elizabeth. After that move he
became lost to Virginia Genealogy. His sons, Goodrich Lightfoot and
Philip Lightfoot remained in Virginia and many letters written to Philip
from relatives in Kentucky contain interesting data about the family.

There is an opinion of many that he may have married twice since his
children were born over a period of more than twenty-five years, but the
records do not give any proof of this speculation.

William Lightfoot paid money into the Virginia treasury and received the
warrants for a 4569-acre; parcel of land, which he then had surveyed and
received the grant. The survey paper shows the names of the men who did
the actual surveying --one being "Danl' Boone"! When Kentucky became
a commonwealth and separate from Virginia, they issued another
document from the Governor of the Commonwealth of Kentucky for the
same described land. We found that William paid taxes on this land for a

---

[4] Orange County, Deed Book 11, pp. 180-81.
[5] Photostat at Virginia State Library.

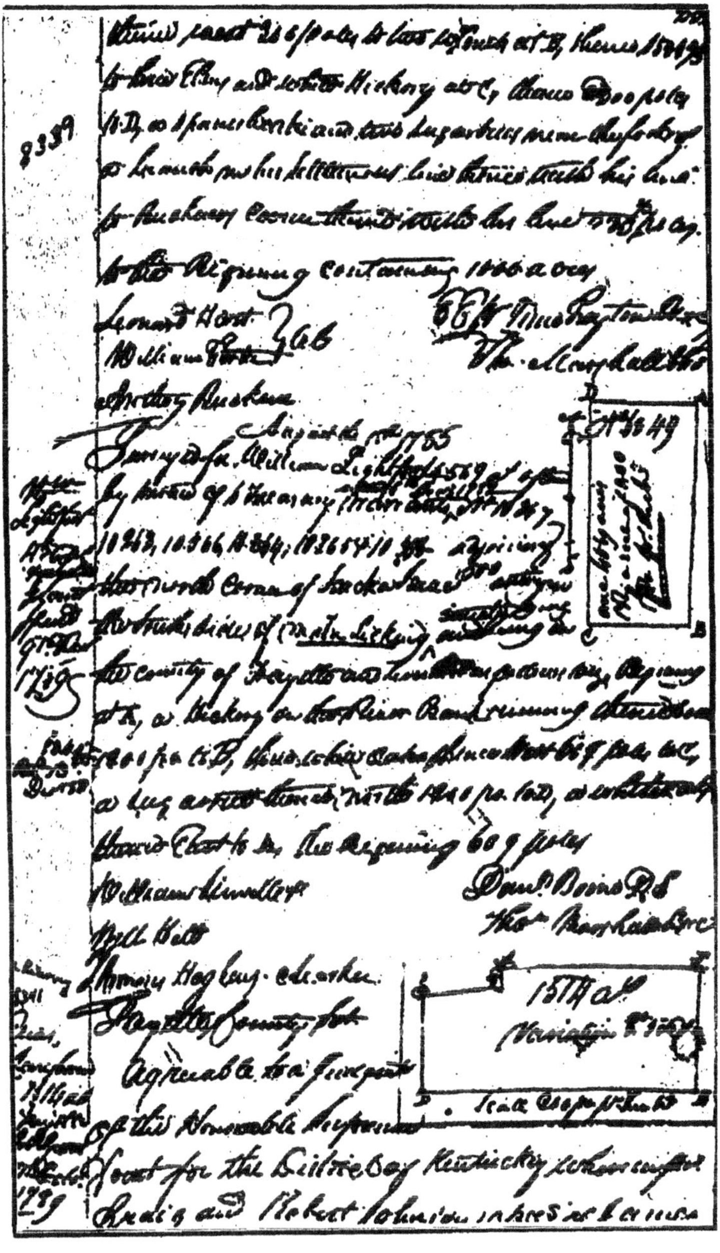

(The original survey done by Daniel Boone 18 August 1785.)

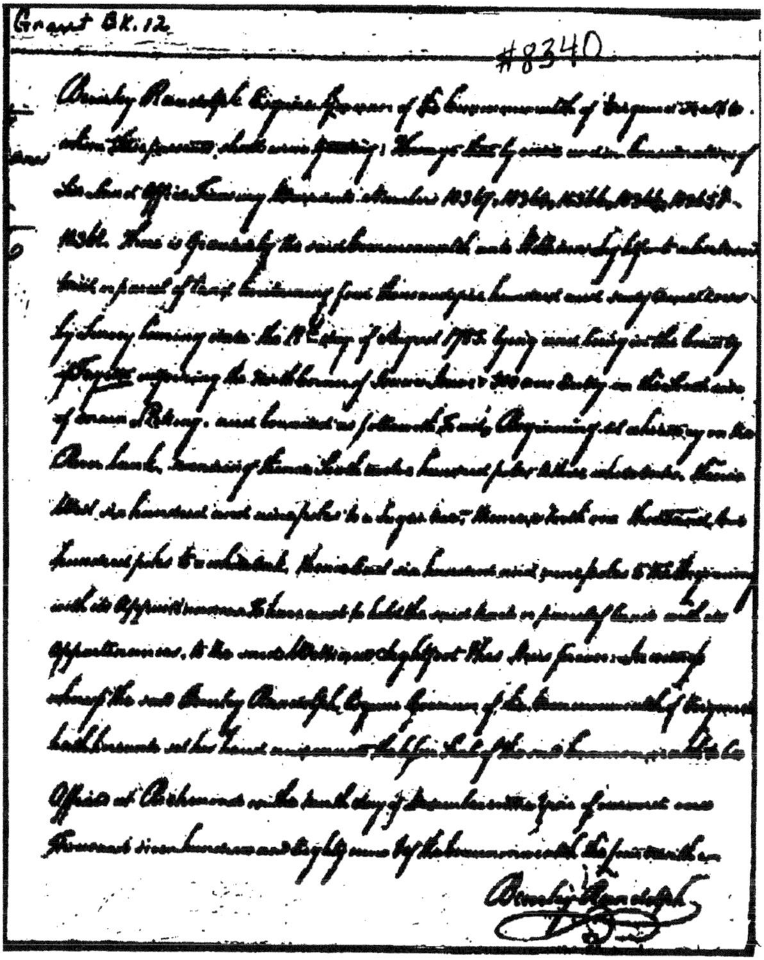

Grant Bk. 12

#8340

Beverley Randolph Esquire Governor of the Commonwealth of Virginia To all to whom these presents shall come greeting: Know ye that by virtue and in consideration of Land Office Treasury Warrants Numbers 10367, 10364, 10366, 10365, 10358, 10361. There is granted by the said Commonwealth unto William Lightfoot a certain tract or parcel of land containing four thousand five hundred and sixty nine acres by Survey bearing date the 18th day of August 1785 lying and being in the County of Fayette [illegible] the North branch of [illegible] 300 acres [illegible] on the [illegible] side of [illegible] and bounded as follows to wit, Beginning at a [illegible] on the River bank, running [illegible] South [illegible] hundred poles [illegible] thence West six hundred and ninety poles to a Sugar tree thence North [illegible] hundred poles to [illegible] thence East six hundred ninety poles to the Beginning with its Appurtenances To have and to hold the said tract or parcel of land with its Appurtenances, to the said William Lightfoot [illegible] In witness whereof the said Beverley Randolph Esquire Governor of the Commonwealth of Virginia hath hereunto set his hand and caused the lesser Seal of the said Commonwealth to be affixed at Richmond on the ninth day of December in the year of our Lord one thousand seven hundred and eighty nine and of the Commonwealth the fourteenth.

Beverley Randolph

(Original land grant of 4569 Acres in Fayette County, KY issued 9 December 1789 to William Lightfoot.)

few years. The subject of the early Kentucky land titles is a complicated one. There were so many conflicting and over-lapping surveys. We found a Suit of Ejectment in the court records of Pendleton County, Kentucky in regard, we believe, to such a conflicting claim. Apparently William's heirs had leased the land for 20 years in order to put someone else in possession and then brought suit to recover that land. A letter from John B. Lightfoot to his brother Philip concerns this matter. The original court document of the Ejectment Suit shows the judgment was for the defendants, they lost the 4569 acres.

William was the father of Goodrich, who married the daughter of the Reverend Henry Fry, who lived in the fork of Crooked Run and the Robinson River. Goodrich Lightfoot lived opposite to the present home of George Clark, Esq., on the Robinson River. He was the brother of the late Major Philip Lightfoot of the Culpeper bar, and of Walker Lightfoot (clerk). He was the father of Frank Lightfoot, clerk of Culpeper, who married Miss Fielder (father of Colonel Charles E. Lightfoot), and of Edward, of Madison, who married Miss Conner, and is the father of Virginia; and John, who married Miss Turner. Miss Turner was the granddaughter of Major John Roberts of the Revolution, whose wife was the daughter of the old vestryman Captain Robert Pollard.

William died 5 November 1805 in Jefferson County, Kentucky at the home of his daughter Mildred Lightfoot Nabb.[6] A letter from Robert Coleman at Jefferson County, Kentucky to Captain Philip Lightfoot, at Culpeper County, Virginia was written 3 December 1805, to let Philip know of the passing of his father.[7]

The will of William Lightfoot is recorded in Jefferson County, Kentucky on 22 August 1799. It names some of his children, not all of them in Kentucky.[8]

A Bible record for the children of William & Elizabeth (Barrow) Lightfoot, has never been submitted, the following has been researched from the names of the children. It is thought that there may be at least three other children but nothing is known of them at this time. The list below is all that we have.

ELIZABETH LIGHTFOOT *was born 2 December 1747 in New Kent County, Virginia and died 8 September 1822 in Pendleton County, Kentucky. She married twice. Her first husband was* DR. THOMAS HOWISON. *Dr. Howison was a wealthy Scottish physician and died in 1769 in Culpeper County, Virginia.*

---

[6] Kentucky Archives and DAR records.
[7] Lightfoot Papers. College of William and Mary Library.
[8] Bond and Power of Attorney Book No. 3. p. 31.

ELIZABETH HOWISON *was born before 1769 and on 15 February 1784 she married* JOHN THOMPSON. *John was born 2 October 1764 in Culpeper County, Virginia and died in 1808 in New Orleans, Louisiana.*

WILLIAM LIGHTFOOT THOMPSON *married* ELIZABETH MASSIE.

THOMAS HOWISON THOMPSON *married* ? THURSTON.

PHILIP ROOTES THOMPSON *was born 27 January 1799 and died 12 December 1872. On 13 November 1832 he married* ELIZABETH MARSHALL TOMPKINS.

ROBERT COLEMAN THOMPSON *married* SARAH WIGGLESWORTH.

FRANCES THORNTON THOMPSON

ELIZABETH THOMPSON

MALISSA THOMPSON *married* COLONEL BUIE.

FRANCIS THOMPSON

CAMILLA THOMPSON

MILDRED THOMPSON

CAROLINE THOMPSON *married* WILLIAM THOMPSON. *Her second husband was* ROBERT COLEMAN. *Robert was the son of* ROBERT *and* SARAH ANN SAUNDERS COLEMAN. *His father was the first of the name in Culpeper. The town of Fairfax was founded on 50 acres of his land in 1759. Robert died in 1817.*

JOHN BARROW LIGHTFOOT *who married* LAVINA DUNCAN *is located in Chapter XI.*

EDWARD LIGHTFOOT *was born in Culpeper County, Virginia and died in 1823 in Jefferson County, Kentucky. In 1793 he married* MARTHA ELDRIDGE *in Culpeper County, Virginia.*

WILLIAM ELDRIDGE LIGHTFOOT *was born in Jefferson County, Kentucky and died in May of 1833. On 10 March 1829 he married* AMELIA ELDRIDGE. *Amelia was born in Bourbon County, Kentucky and died in 1854 in Jefferson County, Kentucky. After William's death she married* JOHN B. WHITMAN.

THOMAS ELDRIDGE "EDWARD" LIGHTFOOT *was born in Jefferson County, Kentucky and died before 1880 in Jefferson County, Kentucky. His will was signed 10 May 1855 and probated 23 September 1880 in Jefferson County, Kentucky.*

CLARA ELDRIDGE WHITMAN *was Amelia's daughter from her second marriage.*

LAURA ALICE WHITMAN *was Amelia's daughter from her second marriage.*

GOODRICH E. LIGHTFOOT *was born in Jefferson County, Kentucky and on 4 June 1829 he married* JANE MARTIN *in Jefferson County,*

Kentucky. Jane was born around 1795 in Bourbon County, Kentucky to JOHN G. MARTIN.

QUINTELLA "FIDELIA" CINDERELLA LIGHTFOOT was born around 1834 in Indiana and married FRANCIS A. HILL in 1852. Francis died 6 April 1874. In 1855 they lived in Cumberland County, Illinois.

MARTHA ALICE HILL was born 4 November 1855 in Cumberland County, Illinois.

SARAH ANN REBECCA HILL was born 16 August 1858 in Cumberland County, Illinois.

MAY LUCY HILL was born in 1861 in Cumberland County, Illinois.

LYDIA ELIZABETH HILL was born 16 October 1864 in Cumberland County, Illinois.

CORA FIDELIA HILL was born 10 January 1871 in Cumberland County, Illinois and on 16 September 1888 she married CHARLES GARREN.

FRANCES LIGHTFOOT married ARTHUR FOX.

EDWARD TAYLOR LIGHTFOOT in the will of his cousin is listed as follows. "Edward Lightfoot Taylor, sort of an adopted child of his maternal aunt whose name successively was Frances Thompson Lightfoot, Frances Thompson Hasbrook, Frances Thompson Taylor (wife of Francis Henry Taylor). Edward Taylor Lightfoot sometimes known as Edward Lightfoot Taylor, having been received into the family of Francis Henry Taylor and his lawfully wedded wife, Frances Thompson Taylor, when quite young. The said Edward Taylor Lightfoot was, let it be plainly understood here, a lawful son and one of the lawfully begotten children of Goodrich Lightfoot who was the son and one of the lawfully begotten children of my paternal grandfather Edward Lightfoot and my paternal grandmother Martha Lightfoot."

MARTHA ANN LIGHTFOOT married ? TAYLOR and died before 1852.

FRANCES THOMPSON LIGHTFOOT in 1855 was the only surviving child of Edward's and Martha's. She married twice, ? HASBROOK and FRANCIS HENRY TAYLOR.

MAJOR PHILIP LIGHTFOOT was born around 1774 in Culpeper County, Virginia and died 17 April 1855 in Culpeper County, Virginia. He is buried at St. Stephen's Churchyard, Culpeper, Virginia. He remained in Culpeper as a lawyer, never to marry, active in Masonic work and was named Junior Warden in the charter issued to Fairfax Lodge on 9 December 1794. An address by George Dabney Gray delivered at the centennial of Fairfax Masonic Lodge at Culpeper on 27 December 1894 describes him. Major P. Lightfoot is well known to many of you: an old bachelor whose white cravat and linen bosom were always spotless – the only man ever known who could walk from his residence to the courthouse *without getting a stain on his shining shoes." His great love for his family was shown in many ways including his collection of their letters. These letters have been a tremendous help in establishing records of the Lightfoot history.*

FRANCES LIGHTFOOT *was born in Culpeper County, Virginia and died in Kentucky. It is not known if she ever married but she corresponded with her brother Philip on a regular basis telling him all about their life in Kentucky.*

GOODRICH LIGHTFOOT *was born about 1768 in Culpeper County, Virginia and died 17 October 1828 in Jefferson County, Kentucky. In 1786 he married* MARTHA FRY *in Culpeper County, Virginia. Martha was born 21 December 1767 in Culpeper County, Virginia and died 17 October 1828 in Madison County, Virginia. She was the daughter of* REVEREND HENRY *and* SUSANNAH WALKER FRY. *They resided at "Clifton", 150 acres deeded to Goodrich by Reverend Henry Fry. They are both buried at Fry Cemetery, "Elim", Culpeper County, Virginia.*

ELIZABETH LIGHTFOOT *married* JOSEPH HUME.

   ELLEN HUME

   EMMA HUME

SUSAN LIGHTFOOT *married* MATTHEW W. MAURY. *Matthew was the son of* BENJAMIN *and* E. GRANT MAURY. *Benjamin was the son of* REVEREND JAMES *and* MARY WALKER MAURY. *Mary was the niece of* DR. THOMAS WALKER *the Kentucky Explorer. Reverend James was the son of* MATTHEW *and* MARY ANN FONTAINE MAURY. *Mary Ann was born 12 April 1690 at Taunton, England and died 30 December 1755 in Virginia. She married Matthew 20 October 1716 in Dublin, Ireland. Matthew was of Castel Mauron, Gascony, who immigrated to Virginia in 1718 and died in 1752.*

   WILLIAM A. WIRT MAURY

   THOMAS WALKER MAURY *married* ? AMON. *He was a Mason and a Whig. Thomas died 12 March 1831 in Culpeper County, Virginia.*

   JOHN S. MAURY *married* ? BUCKERSTOWE.

   MARTHA MAURY *married* T. POTTER

   ELIZA M. MAURY *married* W. BALTHIS.

   REUBEN EDWARD MAURY

   SUSAN FRANCES MAURY

MARIA LIGHTFOOT *married* MR. SPENCE *of Wythe County, Virginia.*

CATHERINE W. LIGHTFOOT *married* JOHN MASE *of Botetourt on 28 April 1822. The wedding was proclaimed in the Central Gazette of Charlottesville, Virginia and preformed by her grandfather Reverend Fry just before his death.*

MARGARET F. LIGHTFOOT *was born 21 February 1799 in Madison County, Virginia and died 1 April 1840 in Madison County, Virginia. She married* DR. T. PATTERSON *in Fincastle.*

WILLIAM H.F. LIGHTFOOT *was born in Madison County, Virginia and died in Kentucky. On 5 May 1815 he married* CATHERINE "KITTY" MAURY. *Catherine was the daughter of* MATTHEW *and* MARY WALKER MAURY.

MARTHA ANNE LIGHTFOOT

WILLIAM HENRY F. LIGHTFOOT *was born about 1820 and married* NANCY W. HENDERSON *in 1846.*

MATILDA LIGHTFOOT *was born 28 March 1848 in Boyle County, Kentucky and died in Pettis County, Missouri. On 26 November 1868 she married* ALBION WOOD. *Albion was born 16 July 1844 in Pettis County, Missouri, the son of* CLIFTON *and* ELIZABETH SNELL WOOD.

STELLA MAY WOOD *was born 30 July 1869 in Missouri and died in Grady County, Oklahoma. On 30 July 1890 she married* WALTER PENQUITE. *Walter was born 4 November 1864 in Montgomery County, Ohio and died in Grady County, Oklahoma. His parents were* JOSEPH *and* MINERVA VANDERVORT PENQUITE.

ROBERT PENQUITE *was born 6 July 1897 in Pettis County, Missouri and died in Okmulgee County, Oklahoma. He married* HELEN MARIE HACK.

ELIZABETH WALKER LIGHTFOOT

JOHN JAMES LIGHTFOOT

MARIA FRANCES LIGHTFOOT

JOHN WESLEY LIGHTFOOT *was born 24 January 1792 in Madison County, Virginia and died 6 January 1822. He married* SUSAN ANN H.M. FRANKLIN *14 May 1812 in Amherst. Susan was born 31 July 1796 in Amherst.*

SUSANNAH H.M. LIGHTFOOT *was born 6 April 1813 and married* JOHN HENRY COOK.

JOHN HENRY COOK, JR.

FRANK COOK

VIRGINIA COOK

MARY COOK

JAMES COOK

JOEL FRANKLIN LIGHTFOOT *was born 16 October 1814 and died in 1872. He married* KATE GALLAGHER *in 1846. Kate was born in 1821 and died in 1882.*

JOHN WESLEY LIGHTFOOT, JR. *was born 8 January 18??.*

MARY M. C. LIGHTFOOT was *born 7 April 18??.*

CAROLINE E.B. LIGHTFOOT *was born 10 August 1820 and died in February of 1852. On 20 September 1842 she married* COLONEL RICHARD CARY ROYESTON *in Alabama. The Colonel was born 13 July 1805 in Greene County, Alabama and died in 1854 in Tippah County, Mississippi. His first wife was* MILDRED MARTIN.

MARY LIGHTFOOT "LITIE" ROYESTON *was born in 1843 in Alabama.*

FRANCIS "FRANK" THORNTON LIGHTFOOT *was born 1 November 1809 in Madison County, Virginia and died 6 April 1839 in Culpeper County, Virginia. On 25 August 1831 he married* GERALDINE GUIELMUS JACKSON FIELDER *in Culpeper County, Virginia. Geraldine was born 26 January 1812 in Madison County, Virginia and died 20 April 1896 in Culpeper County, Virginia.*

COLONEL CHARLES EDWARD LIGHTFOOT *was born 18 April 1834 in Culpeper County, Virginia and died 3 July 1887. He served in the Confederate Army during the Civil War. It is said that he was a gallant soldier in war and peace, a knightly courteous gentleman. On 5 December 1855 he married* GEORGIANA "GEORGIE" CHAPIN *in Lexington, Virginia. Georgie was born 28 March 1835 and died at the home of her son James Herndon Lightfoot in Takoma Park, Maryland.*

LAURA CATLETT LIGHTFOOT *was born 25 October 1856 in Lexington, Virginia and married* JOSEPH S. STRAYER *and after his death she married* JOSEPH FREDERICK BATCHELDER.

GEORGE CHAPIN LIGHTFOOT *was born 11 June 1864 in Lexington, Virginia and died in Culpeper County, Virginia.*

JAMES HERNDON LIGHTFOOT *was born 22 June 1867 in Culpeper County, Virginia and married* VIRGINIA DORSEY *in Takoma Park, Maryland. Virginia was born in 1880 to* REVEREND JAMES OWEN *and* CLARA VIRGINIA WYNKOOP DORSEY. *The Reverend was born 31 October 1848 and died 4 February 1895. He married Clara 18 April 1876.*

VIRGINIA DORSEY LIGHTFOOT, II *was born in Takoma Park, Maryland and married* FITZHUGH MacLEAN.

GEORGIA CHAPIN LIGHTFOOT

GERALDINE LIGHTFOOT *was born 25 April 1873 at Bethen Military Academy, Virginia and died 1 May 1896. On 26 November 1895 she married* JOSEPH C. PETTYJOHN *in Albany, New York.*

GEORGINA "GEORGIE" LIGHTFOOT *was born 25 March 1876 in Culpeper County, Virginia and on 26 March 1896 she married* JAMES ALEXANDER *in Culpeper County, Virginia.*

MARY CATLETT LIGHTFOOT *was born 20 November 1836 in Culpeper County, Virginia and on 1 February 1865 she married* JAMES CLOUD HERNDON, M.D. *in Culpeper County, Virginia. Dr.*

Herndon served as Assistant Medical Doctor of the staff of Robert E. Lee.

FRANCES THORNTON LIGHTFOOT *was born 13 November 1829 in Culpeper County, Virginia and on 23 November 1858 she married* COLONEL CHARLES T. CRITTENDEN *in Culpeper County, Virginia.*

REUBEN EDWARD LIGHTFOOT *was born 10 November 1800 in Culpeper County, Virginia and died 31 May 1882. His first wife was* ELIZABETH CONNER. *Elizabeth was born 13 August 1807 and died 21 May 1838.*

ANN VIRGINIA LIGHTFOOT *was born 21 May 1833 and married* ROBERT P. LAKE, M.D. *Robert was born 19 March 1822.*

JOHN LIGHTFOOT *was born 15 January 1836 and died 23 September 1880. He married* SUE M.E. TURNER *the granddaughter of* MAJOR JOHN ROBERTS *of the Revolutionary War and his wife was the daughter of the Old Vestryman,* CAPTAIN ROBERT POLLARD.

He married his second wife KEZIA ANN YANCEY *2 October 1837 in Culpeper County, Virginia. Kezia was born in 1816 in Culpeper County, Virginia to* THOMAS *and* SARAH MITCHELL YANCEY. *She died in 1881.*

SUSAN LIGHTFOOT *was born around 1838 in Culpeper County, Virginia.*

MILDRED LIGHTFOOT *was born in 1772 in Culpeper County, Virginia and died 15 February 1855 in Louisville, Kentucky. On 2 January 1797 she married* CHARLES NABB *in Jefferson County, Kentucky. Mr. Nabb died of a separation of the knee. He was a merchant and left Mildred three sons from a previous marriage and a daughter from their marriage. This is the letter Mildred wrote to her brother after her Mr. Nabb's death 1 July 1799. "My Dear Brother: How different are my prospects from when I last wrote you. Then were they pleasing but now gloomy indeed having lost the best the finest of men the first of July, my never to be forgotten Mr. Nabb, in death after a violent separation of his knee, left me with my dear little girl, six weeks old, and three sons by a former wife. Destitute of a home of our own though not I hope without a comfortable subsistence. The two oldest boys I've put out to school, the youngest and my daughter at with me at Mr. Coleman's where I expect to stay until I can purchase a home (?) which will take place this winter, then shall take my poor old infirm father to live with me."*

"I trouble you, my good brother, with a lock of highly prized hair to have me a locket made in the neatest manner with my deceased husband's name on the back of it (and) miniature for my girl. Have them done as soon as you can and you will much oblige your affectionate sister."

"All friends in this quarter fine and anxiously wish to see you."

A DAUGHTER *was born in May of 1799.*

She married JOHN PEAY *19 August 1802 in Jefferson County, Kentucky. John was born 19 September 1775 in Virginia and died 18 August 1838 in Bullitt County, Kentucky. He was the son of* AUSTIN *and* MILDRED TURNER PEAY.

AUSTIN LIGHTFOOT PEAY *was born 25 June 1803 in Jefferson County, Kentucky and died 24 June 1849 in Louisville, Kentucky. On 9 August 1832 he married* PEACHY WALKER SPEED.

ELIZA BARROW LIGHTFOOT *was born 16 August 1806 in Jefferson County, Kentucky and died 22 April 1841 in Louisville, Kentucky. On 13 April 1824 she married* JAMES MOORES CLENDININ *in Louisville, Kentucky. James was born 8 April 1796 in Hartford County, Maryland and died 27 March 1859 in St. Louis, Missouri. His parents were* JOHN E. *and* ELIZABETH GLASGOW CLENDENIN.

WILLIAM AUSTIN CLENDENIN *was born 28 February 1830 in Louisville, Kentucky and died 12 November 1894 in St. Louis, Missouri. On 28 February 1856 he married* ISABELLA RIPPEY KERR *in St. Louis, Missouri. Isabella was born 28 February 1832 in St. Louis, Missouri and died in Ferguson, Missouri.*

ELLEN CLENDENIN *was born 28 August 1859 in St. Louis, Missouri and died in St. Louis, Missouri. On 10 November 1886 she married* HENRY BRYAN MILTENBERGER.

GEORGE KERR MILTENBERGER *was born 10 August 1889 in St. Louis, Missouri and died in Webster Grove, Missouri. He married* DOROTHY ZELLE GORDON *in Bentonville, Arkansas. George was a veteran of World War I. Dorothy was born in St. Joseph, Missouri and died in Dallas, Texas. She was the daughter of* CHARLES HENRY ALLEN *and* ZELLA KATE PORTER GORDON.

GEORGE KERR GORDON MILTENBERGER *was born in St. Louis, Missouri and married* DELORES SHEPHERD *in Stephenville, Texas.*

CHARLES ELIOT MILTENBERGER *was born in St. Louis, Missouri and died in St. Louis, Missouri. He married* LYNN BARBARA KREUTER *in St. Louis.*

ANNE LIGHTFOOT *died in 1774 in Culpeper County, Virginia. On 20 May 1770 she married* LIEUTENANT HENRY FIELD *in Culpeper County, Virginia. Henry was born in Culpeper County, Virginia and was the son of* ABRAHAM FIELD, II. *Abraham served in the Revolutionary War and died during battle in 1778.*

ELIZABETH FIELD *died in 1796.*

JUDITH FIELD *was born 14 February 1774 and died 25 August 1852 in Ripley, Ohio. Judith lived with Field relatives after the death of her parents. They migrated to Kentucky about 1782. On 5 September 1795 she married* FRANCIS TAYLOR *in Jefferson County, Kentucky.*

Francis practiced law in Washington, Maco County, Kentucky and they moved to Ripley, Ohio in 1836. Francis died 22 August 1852 in Ripley, Ohio.

THOMAS WALKER LIGHTFOOT *was born in Culpeper County, Virginia. He remained unmarried and was the Clerk for Culpeper County.*

CHAPTER XI

JOHN B. LIGHTFOOT, CAPTAIN, 1752-1850
MARRIED LAVINA DUNCAN

JOHN BARROW LIGHTFOOT was the son of WILLIAM and ELIZABETH (BARROW) LIGHTFOOT. He was born about 1752 in St. Peter's Parish, New Kent County, Virginia and died after 1810 in Fleming County, Kentucky. In 1772 he married LAVINA DUNCAN in Culpeper County, Virginia. Lavina was born around 1753, the daughter of ROBERT and ANNE (GALLOP) DUNCAN and died approximately 1824 in Fleming County, Kentucky. Anne Gallop Duncan was the daughter of ROBERT GALLOP of Stafford Count, Virginia. Robert Duncan left a will, dated 7 June 1788 and proved 21 October 1793, which named his daughter Lavina and her husband John Lightfoot.

John Lightfoot did not purchase property in Culpeper County until 16 October 1786 when he bought from Charles Holloway and his wife Amey, for £100, 167 acres in Brumfield Parish, in the fork of Rappahannock River on the branches of Butler's Swamp.[1] He sold this land on 22 August 1794 to John Mason.

The tax list of 1782 shows that he owned four slaves, two horses and six head of cattle, but he disposed of much of his property before moving to Kentucky, where he settled in Pendleton County. A biography of his grandson, George Colvin Lightfoot, states that John B. Lightfoot taught at what may have been the first school conducted in Pendleton County.[2]

The death of John B. Lightfoot probably occurred between 1810 and 1820. His family in 1810 consisted of:

Males: under 10 - 1   Females: under 10 - 1
        26-45   - 1   26-45   - 1

---

[1] Culpeper Co., Va., Deed Book N, pp. 462-63.
[2] The Biographical Encyclopedia of Kentucky. Cincinnati: J.M. Armstrong, 1878. p. 305.

(Letter from John B. Lightfoot to his brother Philip Lightfoot of Culpeper Co., VA concerning the land grant of 4569 acres of land in KY of their father William Lightfoot.)

140

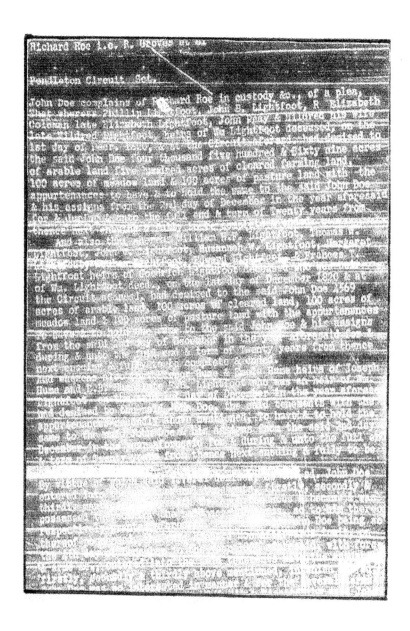

(The Declaration of Ejectment filed 16 April 1821 at the Pendleton Circuit Court of Kentucky that gave the Lightfoot land to Richard Roe.)

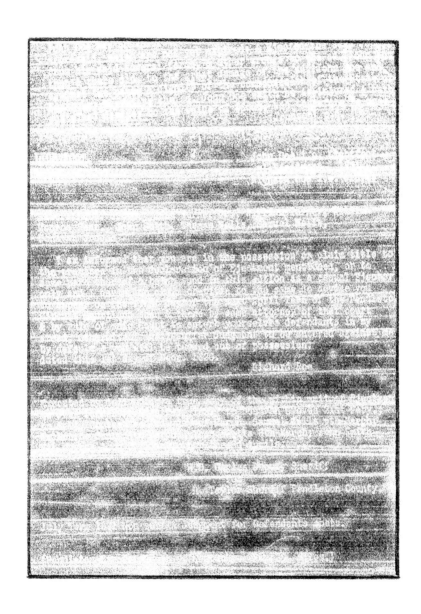

(The second page of the Declaration of Ejectment.)
142

```
over 45 -    1                         over 45 - 1
Slaves -     1³
```

He was undoubtedly the father of John Lightfoot, Jr., who paid taxes in Pendleton County in 1800. Almost certainly the father of DeEstang Lightfoot, Richard Lightfoot, Robert Lightfoot, Edward Lightfoot and others of the name who lived in Pendleton County before 1820, but a full list of his children has not been found.

John and Lavina Lightfoot had eleven children.

D'ESTAING LIGHTFOOT *was born around 1785 in Culpeper County, Virginia and died in Shelby County, Indiana. D'Estaing moved to Kentucky with his father and in 1793 he moved to Indiana. He was named after the French General of Revolutionary Fame. He married twice. On 9 November 1802 he married* JEAN STEELE *in Pendleton County, Kentucky.*

ELIZABETH LIGHTFOOT *was born in Pendleton County, Kentucky like the rest of D'Estaing and Jean's children.*

MARY LIGHTFOOT

JOHN LIGHTFOOT

JAMES STEELE LIGHTFOOT

ELEANOR ROSS LIGHTFOOT

JOEL LIGHTFOOT

On 14 July 1824 he married SARAH KENDALL *in Pendleton County, Kentucky. Sarah was born in 1802 in Virginia.*

MARGARET LIGHTFOOT *was born in 1834 in Indiana, as were all of Sarah's and D'Estaing's children.*

MONTGOMERY LIGHTFOOT *was born in 1836.*

EMILY LIGHTFOOT *was born in 1838.*

KATHERINE LIGHTFOOT *was born in 1840.*

McCALL LIGHTFOOT *was born in 1843.*

JOHN BARROW LIGHTFOOT, JR. *was born around 1780 in Culpeper County, Virginia and died in Pendleton County, Kentucky. It is noted that John paid taxes in Pendleton County, Kentucky in 1800.*

ROBERT LIGHTFOOT *was born about 1773 in Culpeper County, Virginia and in 1794 he married* JOANNA DULANY *in Pendleton County, Kentucky. Robert served in the War of 1812.*

WILLIAM LIGHTFOOT *was born 16 June 1796 in Culpeper County, Virginia. William came to Kentucky with his father in 1804. He married twice. In 1821 he married* ELIZABETH CALDWELL *in Fleming County, Kentucky. Elizabeth was born in Fleming County, Kentucky and*

---

³ Pendleton Co., Ky., 1810 census, p. 108.

died in 1849. She was the daughter of an Irish farmer ANDREW *and* ELIZABETH FARRIS CALDWELL.

DR. ROBERT ANDREW LIGHTFOOT *was born 19 April 1827 in Fleming County, Kentucky and on 26 May 1856 he married* SARAH E. STOCKWELL *in Fleming County, Kentucky. Sarah was born in Fleming County, Kentucky to* JOHN STOCKWELL *a merchant of Poplar Plains.*

Robert was reared on a farm, receiving his literary education at the common schools and at Richland Academy. He began the study of medicine in 1850 with Dr. John Shackelford, of Maysville, Kentucky and graduated from the University of Louisville in March of 1855. He located in Maysville in partnership with his former instructor, Dr. Shackelford. He went to Flemingsburg in August as a relief doctor during the cholera epidemic, where he was afterwards actively engaged. He served over three years in the Confederate Army, as surgeon of Colonel E.F. Clay's battalion. He was captured in 1864 at the battle of Half Mountain, eastern Kentucky, and was confined in Louisville, Fortress Monroe and in Fort Delaware about five months. He was exchanged for the celebrated Dr. Mary Walker, who was captured by the Confederates as a spy, near Dalton, Georgia. After his release Dr. Lightfoot was on Lieutenant-General Early's staff by recommendation of the medical director of Early's army. He participated in many battles and skirmishes, and returned home at the close of the war greatly impaired in health. Although a surgeon in the army, he was subject to most of the dangers and the hardships of the war. He was a member of the Methodist Episcopal Church South, a Mason, a K.T. Eminent Commander, and Past High Priest of the I.O.O.F.

DR. GROSS LIGHTFOOT *the eldest son, was a graduate of Jefferson Medical College, Philadelphia, Pennsylvania when only nineteen years old, and a physician of great promise. He died 30 October 1879 at the age of 22 of blood poisoning.*

MARY LIGHTFOOT
PEARCE LIGHTFOOT
IDA LIGHTFOOT
SALLIE LIGHTFOOT
GRACE LIGHTFOOT

JAMES EDWARD LIGHTFOOT *was born 28 September 1822 in Fleming County, Kentucky and died 14 May 1896 in Greene County, Iowa. On 15 September 1846 he married* MARTHA JANE HUTTON *in Fleming County, Kentucky. Martha was born 9 August 1822 in Fleming County, Kentucky and died 6 December 1889 in Greene County, Iowa. On 8 August 1838 she married* WILLIAM LIKES *and married James after William's death. She was the daughter of* JOHN *and* ELIZABETH McCULLOUGH HUTTON. *John was born in 1798 in Fleming County, Kentucky. Elizabeth was born in 1802 in Kentucky.*

JOHN WILLIAM BELL LIGHTFOOT *was born 3 September 1848 in Fleming County, Kentucky and died 14 May 1896 in Greene County, Iowa. On 22 February 1876 he married* JULIA WEBER *in LaSalle County, Illinois. Julia was born 7 October 1856 in Goodhue County, Minnesota and died in Greene County, Iowa. She was the daughter of* DANIEL *and* LAZETTA STRAUSENBACK WEBER.

WILLIAM HENRY LIGHTFOOT *was born 24 October 1877 in LaSalle County, Illinois and died in Boone County, Iowa. He married twice. He married* EMMA BATCHELLER *first and then he married* BESSIE A. RUNDBERG.

JOHN DANIEL LIGHTFOOT *was born 2 January 1880 in LaSalle County, Illinois and died in Webster County, Iowa. He married* SALLIE MARTENA JOHNSON *in Greene County, Iowa. Sallie was born 8 March 1880 in Greene County, Iowa and died in Webster County, Iowa. She was the daughter of* DANIEL *and* ANNA M. THOMPSON JOHNSON.

ROBERT RAY LIGHTFOOT *was born in Greene County, Iowa and married in Orange County, Texas.*

LOWELL DANIEL LIGHTFOOT *was born in Greene County, Iowa and died in Webster County, Iowa.*

HARRY JOHN LIGHTFOOT *married twice. His first wife was* KATHERINE ENDERS *in Cook County, Illinois. Katherine was born in Cook County, Illinois and died in Greene County, Iowa. His second wife was* BILLIE DZURIS.

MORT LIGHTFOOT *was born 27 March 1884 in Greene County, Iowa and died in Greene County, Iowa. He married* OLA MAE BATCHELLER *in Boone County, Iowa.*

LEMUEL ETHELBERT LIGHTFOOT *was born 14 October 1850 in Fleming County, Kentucky and died in Greene County, Iowa. He married* ALICE SPRINGER. *Alice was born in November of 1859 and died in Greene County, Iowa.*

JULIA C. LIGHTFOOT *was born in April of 1892 and married* GARLAND WADKINS. *Garland was the son of* JOHN WESLEY *and* SERENE "RENA" PRUITT WADKINS.

MARGARET JANE LIGHTFOOT *was born 8 December 1830 in Fleming County, Kentucky and died in Fleming County, Kentucky. On 27 March 1856 she married* ELIJAH HARN *in Fleming County, Kentucky.*

JOANNA MARIE LIGHTFOOT *was born around 1833 in Fleming County, Kentucky and died around 1858. On 17 October 1853 she married* REASON LOOMAN *in Fleming County, Kentucky.*

JOHN W. LIGHTFOOT *was born about 1837 in Fleming County, Kentucky and was last heard of in Iola, Clay County, Illinois.*

AMANDA F. LIGHTFOOT *was born around 1839 in Fleming County, Kentucky and married twice. On 10 September 1860 she married* GEORGE C. JACKSON *in Fleming County, Kentucky. They lived in Iola, Clay County, Illinois until George's death. After George's death she married* ? COGAN.

And on 9 January 1861 he married SUSAN D. HOPPER *in Lewis County, Kentucky. Susan is buried under the same marker as William at Mt. Carmel Cemetery in Fleming County, Kentucky.*

JAMES LIGHTFOOT *was born 13 February 1801 in Virginia and on 9 June 1825 he married* MARIA MATTHEWS *in Fleming County, Kentucky.*

ELIZABETH LIGHTFOOT *was born around 1800 and on 30 September 1819 she married* EDWARD FURR *in Fleming County, Kentucky.*

LEVINA LIGHTFOOT *was born around 1806 and on 6 July 1826 she married* EDWARD DEERING *in Fleming County, Kentucky.*

JOHN LIGHTFOOT *was born about 1810 and on 20 March 1828 he married* FRANCES LIGHTFOOT *in Fleming County, Kentucky. Frances was the daughter of* JAMES *and* MILDRED DELANY LIGHTFOOT.

SUSAN ANNE LIGHTFOOT *was born 27 February 1815 and on 11 September 1831 she married* CHARLES E. BAILEY *in Fleming County, Kentucky.*

WILLIAM L. LIGHTFOOT *was born 25 March 1774 in Culpeper County, Virginia and died 15 December 1864 in Wells County, Indiana. The biography of his son George Colvin Lightfoot states that he came to Kentucky as early as 1793, settling at Washington in Mason County, but shortly afterward moving to Pendleton County where he was a teacher. He was living in Pendleton County by 1800 when he was listed on the tax books. He moved to Rush County, Indiana in 1833. It is not known where he lived the last few years of his life. On 27 February 1798 he married* LEANNAH COLVIN *in Campbell County, Kentucky. Leannah was born 13 August 1779 in Culpeper County, Virginia and died 10 June 1855 in Decatur County, Indiana. She was the daughter of* JOHN COLVIN, *a veteran of the Revolutionary War.*

JOHN COLVIN LIGHTFOOT *was born 11 January 1799 in Pendleton County, Kentucky and died 2 September 1829. On 5 August 1824 he married* MARY "POLLY" SHAWAN *in Pendleton County, Kentucky.*

PAULINA ANN LIGHTFOOT *was born 18 November 1825 in Pendleton County, Kentucky.*

DAVID S. LIGHTFOOT *was born 19 September 1827 in Pendleton County, Kentucky.*

JOHN WILLIAM THOMAS LIGHTFOOT *was born 22 July 1829 in Pendleton County, Kentucky.*

WILLIAM BENNETT LIGHTFOOT *was born 29 March 1800 in Pendleton County, Kentucky and died 10 January 1831 in Rush County, Indiana. On 4 September 1823 he married* ELIZABETH COLVIN *in Pendleton County, Kentucky. Elizabeth was born 20 October 1801 in Kentucky and died 8 May 1874 in Rush County, Indiana. She was the daughter of* HENRY *and* CATHERINE WILLIAMS COLVIN. *William rode from Rush County, Indiana to Indianapolis in 1830 on a horse and entered an eighty-acre tract of wild land in Section 29, in Washington Township. He returned and started cutting logs for a cabin when he was stricken down with bilious fever and died.*

ALFRED C. LIGHTFOOT *was born 13 June 1824 in Pendleton County, Kentucky and died in 1894 in Rush County, Indiana. He married twice. His first wife was* ELIZABETH BENTON. *Elizabeth was born in 1825 in Kentucky.*

THOMAS BENTON LIGHTFOOT *was born in 1859 in Indiana. On 10 June 1874 he married his second wife* FLORA McCRADY *in Rush County, Indiana. Flora was born in 1850 in Franklin County, Indiana. She was the daughter of* JOHN *and* CATHERINE McCRADY *of Pennsylvania.*

ALFRED "FRED" W. LIGHTFOOT *was born 16 June 1875 in Rush County, Indiana and on 26 January 1896 he married* MARGARET ANN SMITH *in Rush County, Indiana. Alfred was a farmer, stock raiser and the President of Falmouth Bank in Indiana. He lived on three hundred acres he had inherited.*

FRANK ALFRED LIGHTFOOT *was born in Rush County, Indiana and was a student of engineering at Purdue University.*

DORIS JUNE LIGHTFOOT *was born in Rush County, Indiana.*

LUCINDA LEONA LIGHTFOOT *was born 24 October 1827 in Pendleton County, Kentucky and died unmarried 30 September 1855 in Rush County, Indiana.*

ARMISTEAD C. LIGHTFOOT *was born 4 January 1802 in Pendleton County, Kentucky and died 27 February 1804 in Pendleton County, Kentucky.*

GEORGE COLVIN LIGHTFOOT *was born 15 January 1804 in Pendleton County, Kentucky and died 11 January 1884. On 10 June 1830 he married* MALINDA B. HOLTON *in Pendleton County, Kentucky. Malinda was the daughter of* ELIJAH HOLTON. *George was a merchant, the owner of Jefferson House Hotel, a Mason for thirty years and an outstanding leader of the community.*

LAURA HOLTON LIGHTFOOT *was born in 1832 in Covington, Kentucky and on 30 October 1865 she married* JOHN HENRY BASS *in Fort Wayne, Indiana.*

GEORGE NICHOLAS LIGHTFOOT *was born in 1834 in Kentucky and fought at Chickamauga. He was disabled by disease but in August of 1864 he rejoined his company and fought at Jonesboro.*

MARGARET LIGHTFOOT *was born 18 March 1806 in Pendleton County, Kentucky and died in Tarrant County, Texas. On 24 July 1823 she married* BALDWIN COPPAGE. *Baldwin was born 3 March 1803 the son of* BALDWIN FIELDING *and* HANNAH WALLER COPPAGE. *Baldwin's father was* WILLIAM COPPEDGE *of Hamilton Parish, Fauquier County, Virginia who was the son of* JOHN COPPEDGE, JR. *the husband of* ELIZABETH DAMERON, *a cousin of George Washington.* JOHN COPPEDGE, SR., *the Surveyor married* ELIZABETH BASYE, *daughter of* EDMOND BASYE *and* ELIZABETH TAYLOR. *Elizabeth was the daughter of* JOHN TAYLOR *who came on the Ship "Amsterdam" in 1652 to the head of Fleet's Bay. In the 1830 Census they were located in Pendleton County, Kentucky and in the 1840 and 1850 Census they were located in Indiana. In the 1860 and 1870 Census they were back in Kentucky and in the 1880 Census they were in Tarrant County, Texas.*

WILLIAM FIELDING COPPAGE *was born 27 September 1829 in Pendleton County, Kentucky and on 9 September 1852 he married* CATHERINE MARIA KEITH. *Catherine was born 31 January 1827 in Pendleton County, Kentucky.*

GEORGIA A. COPPAGE *was born 12 August 1852 and married* ED ISHAM *who was born 18 January 1851.*

FRANK N. ISHAM *was born 8 November 1873 in Kentucky and died in Tarrant County, Texas.*

LENA C. ISHAM *was born 1 December 1878 in Kentucky and never married.*

ALBERT L. COPPAGE *was born 8 January 1856 and married* VIRGINIA BONDURANT.

B. LAWRENCE COPPAGE *married* ESTELLE HOWELL *of Willis Point, Texas and lived in Fort Worth, Texas.*

KEITH COPPAGE *married* FRED FRIES.

MARY E. COPPAGE *was born 24 April 1858 and married* EDWARD C. ORRICK.

EDNA ORRICK

GEORGIA ORRICK

HELEN ORRICK *married* CHESTER H. REAGAN.

THOMAS F. COPPAGE *was born 2 April 1860 and married* LELA PERRY.

FLORENCE COPPAGE

NINA COPPAGE

GEORGE ALLEN COPPAGE *married* ELEANOR O'FARRELL *in Kentucky.*

MARY COPPAGE

LAURA COPPAGE

SARAH COPPAGE

MARGARET COPPAGE *married* HUGH H. LEWIS.

CATHERINE COPPAGE

JAMES COPPAGE

MILTON COPPAGE

MARY COPPAGE

ELIZABETH COPPAGE

FERDINAND COPPAGE *was a farmer who was born in 1845 in Indiana and married* ELLA FLOWERS.

WILLIAM COPPAGE

JOHN COPPAGE *was a blacksmith who was born in 1850 in Indiana and married* SALLIE REED.

DORMAN COPPAGE

HOMER COPPAGE

FRANCIS ELKIN COPPAGE *was born 23 December 1837 and married* MARIA MADDEN.

EMILY LIGHTFOOT *was born 15 March 1808 in Pendleton County, Kentucky and died unmarried.*

FRANCIS DAY LIGHTFOOT *was born 14 September 1810 in Pendleton County, Kentucky and died in Pendleton County, Kentucky. On 30 March 1834 he married* LOUISA DUNCAN *in Pendleton County, Kentucky. Francis is the only one of his family that remained in Pendleton County, Kentucky.*

ELKIN D. LIGHTFOOT *was born 5 February 1836 in Pendleton County, Kentucky and died 28 November 1893 in Jackson County, Missouri. He married* SALLIE M. ? *in December of 1869.*

GEORGE ANN LIGHTFOOT *was born in 1839 in Pendleton County, Kentucky and on 10 January 1862 she married* M.L. BULGER.

JOHN E. LIGHTFOOT *was born in 1841 in Pendleton County, Kentucky and on 2 December 1869 he married* MARY LOUISA COLVIN.

THEODORE N. LIGHTFOOT *was born in 1850 in Pendleton County, Kentucky and on 1 November 1882 he married* ISABEL R. HITCH. *Theodore is the twin of Theodosia.*

THEODORE LIGHTFOOT

THEODOSIA LIGHTFOOT *was born 31 December 1885 in Kentucky and married twice. Her first husband was* E.W. OLDHAM. *Her second husband was* E.O. COOKENDORFER.

MARY LIGHTFOOT *married* ALF SHARP.

EMMA LIGHTFOOT *married* GEORGE ASHCRAFT.

THOMAS LIGHTFOOT

LAURA LIGHTFOOT *married* RUSSEL WILSON.

HILDA M. LIGHTFOOT *married* ARTHUR B. HUFFMAN.

THEODOSIA M. LIGHTFOOT *was born in 1850 in Pendleton County, Kentucky and on 21 November 1872 married* JAMES D. LOGAN.

ELKIN LIGHTFOOT *was born 7 June 1812 in Pendleton County, Kentucky and died 6 October 1898 in Tarrant County, Texas. He married twice. His first wife was* ANN L. WILLETT *whom he married 14 March 1829 in Pendleton County, Kentucky.*

MARTIN PERCIVAL LIGHTFOOT *was born 22 May 1840 in Pendleton County, Kentucky.*
On 24 December 1845 he married SARAH ANN HOBSON MATHEWS *in Pendleton County, Kentucky.*

CHARLES LESLIE LIGHTFOOT *was born 17 October 1846 in Pendleton County, Kentucky and died in Tarrant County, Texas. On 6 May 1869 he married* CYNTHIA ANNA WATSON. *Cynthia was born 10 October 1848 in Pendleton County, Kentucky and died 8 April 1894 in Tarrant County, Texas.*

ELKIN LIGHTFOOT *was born 20 February 1870 and died 3 March 1870.*

NORA EDITH LIGHTFOOT *was born 5 July 1872 in Kentucky and died the same day.*

EDWARD MORRIS LIGHTFOOT *was born 20 November 1872 and on 29 March 1894 he married* CORA EDWARD DONNELL *in Tarrant County, Texas. Cora was the daughter of* HARTWELL WEAVER *and* MARY PARALEE BASS DONNELL.

GLADYS PAULINE LIGHTFOOT *was born 5 September 1896 and married* JAMES DAVID FARMER, JR.

MARTHA CORA FARMER *married twice. Her first husband was* JOHNNY GRANT. *Her second husband was* LEO POYE.

BRENDA LEE POYE

PATRICIA ANN POYE

BILLYE POYE

QUANITA FARMER

JAMES DAVID FARMER, III *married* MAXINE ?.

JAMES DAVID FARMER, IV.

ALVIN MORRIS FARMER *married* JOYCE GRIFFITH.

CHARLES LARRY FARMER *married* JIMMY ?.

CHARLES HARTWELL LIGHTFOOT *was born 13 July 1898.*

ISOLA MAY LIGHTFOOT *married* LARRY THEODORE BROOKS.

BARBARA MAY BROOKS *married* WILLIAM H. SULLY.

CORA PARALEE PEARL ELLEN LIGHTFOOT

EDWARD MORRIS LIGHTFOOT, JR. *married* JANICE YOUNG.

JAMES AUGUSTUS LIGHTFOOT *was born 25 November 1874 in Kentucky.*

WILLIAM HOMER LIGHTFOOT *was born in September 1876 in Kentucky and resided in Tarrant County, Texas.*

CARRIE MAY LIGHTFOOT *was born 10 May 1879 in Kentucky.*

GUY DONALD LIGHTFOOT *was born 19 May 1882 in Texas and died in Tarrant County, Texas.*

FRANK LESLIE LIGHTFOOT *was born 19 February 1885 in Texas.*

P. AUGUSTUS LIGHTFOOT *was born 15 April 1848 in Bracken County, Kentucky.*

WILLIAM LIGHTFOOT *was born 31 October 1856 in Bracken County, Kentucky and in 1883 he married* ELIZABETH MORRELL. *Elizabeth was born in November of 1857 in Texas.*

LOUISE LIGHTFOOT *was born in November of 1883 in Texas and married* CHARLES FREELOVE *in Texas.*

ELKIN LIGHTFOOT *was born in April of 1887 in Texas and died in Nashville, Tennessee. She married twice. Her first husband was* DR. BASIL L. LOCKETT. *Dr. Lockett was a medical missionary to Oyo, Nigeria. He died from a disease he was exposed to while in Nigeria. Her second husband was* E.T. ALDREDGE.

WORTH LIGHTFOOT *married* MITTIEBELLE ROSS.

ROBERT HUNTER LIGHTFOOT

SALLIE LIGHTFOOT *was born 6 June 1860 in Bracken County, Kentucky and married* ? MOSBY.

PRESLEY G. LIGHTFOOT *was born 17 November 1814 in Pendleton County, Kentucky and died in Bates County, Missouri. He married* REBECCA HUNT *in Wayne County, Indiana. Rebecca was born 5 October 1822 in Kentucky and died in Bates County, Missouri. Presley founded the Burdette Baptist Church in Bates County, Missouri.*

T.W. LIGHTFOOT *was born in 1858 in Wells County, Indiana and married* ANNIE MUDD *in Bates County, Missouri. Annie was the daughter of* AUSTIN MUDD.

NIMROD C. LIGHTFOOT *was born 7 January 1817 in Pendleton County, Kentucky and married* JANET ? *in Hancock County, Indiana.*

MARTHA A. LIGHTFOOT *was born in Hancock County, Indiana, as were all of Nimrod and Janet's children.*

SAPHRONA E. LIGHTFOOT

FRANCES D. LIGHTFOOT

SUSAN L. LIGHTFOOT

MARY L. LIGHTFOOT *was born 10 March 1819 in Pendleton County, Kentucky and died 25 December 1888 in Butler County, Kansas. On 29 June 1843 she married* ELIJAH M.P. PARKS *in Rush County, Indiana. Elijah was born 23 February 1817 in Wilkes County, North Carolina and died 30 April 1882 in Butler County, Kansas. Mary had possession of the Family Bible.*

PAULINA LOUISA PARKS *was born 25 April 1844 in Hancock County, Indiana and died in Butler County, Kansas. On 6 August 1867 she married* DR. ADAM CLARK MIZENER *in Hancock County, Indiana. Adam was born 1 December 1817 in Union County, Pennsylvania and died in Butler County, Kansas. He was a pensioned Civil War veteran and served in Ohio.*

BELLPHENA ELLEN MIZENER *was born 12 November 1869 in Hancock County, Indiana and died in Cowley County, Kansas. On 24 December 1886 she married* JAMES ALVA BROWN *in Butler County, Kansas. James was born 10 January 1867 in Warren County, Ohio and died in Harvey County, Kansas.*

VIOLA MAE BROWN *was born 9 October 1887 in Butler County, Kansas and died in San Diego County, California. She married* ASA BLAINE BAKER. *Asa was born 27 August 1884 in Kiowa, Kansas and died in National City, California.*

ESTHER IRENE BAKER *was born in Lantham, Kansas and married twice. She married her first husband* EDWARD V. ROPER *in San Diego, California.*

LOUISE IRENE ROPER *was born in San Diego, California and married* ROBERT COX *in Chiula Vista, California.*

TERESA LYNN COX *was born in San Diego, California.*

GREGORY CHRISTOPHER COX

BRIAN CURTIS COX

Her second husband was LORENA J. BYRNE.

JO ANNE BYRNE *married* NORMAN RUFING.

JOHN JOSEPH RUFING *was born in San Diego, California.*

MARYLN JEAN BYRNE *married* JEROME TAPPAN *in San Diego, California.*

DAVID HOWARD TAPPAN *was born in Phoenix, Arizona.*

ORVILLE WAYNE BAKER *was born in Butler County, Kansas and married* LEONA JANE STIGALL *in Yuma, Arizona.*

BARBARA JEAN BAKER

STEVEN GALE BAKER

FOREST LEONARD BAKER *was born in Butler County, Kansas.*

INA ELEANOR BAKER *was born in Vinton, Kansas.*

JERALDEAN RUTH BAKER *was born in Butler County, Kansas.*

ORVILLE RAY BROWN *was born 13 August 1890 in Butler County, Kansas and died in Grainola, Oklahoma. He married* DAISY BENNET.

EARL LEON BROWN

ALICE EVALYN BROWN *was born 12 August 1893 in Butler County, Kansas and died in Kay County, Oklahoma. She married twice. She married her first husband* ALVIN STINSON *in Butler County, Kansas.*

VERA HELEN STINSON *married* ? BROWN.

JAMES MONROE STINSON *died in Maple City, Kansas.*

CLIFFORD ALVIN STINSON

EDWARD WARREN STINSON

Her second husband was ROY MILLER.

ETHEL HOPE BROWN *was born 29 April 1896 in Bodark, Kansas and married* EARL L. YOUNG.

DOYLE EARL YOUNG

MARCELLA JUANITA YOUNG

LOIS MILDRED YOUNG

EDNA GRACE BROWN *was born 20 February 1899 in Gordon, Kansas and died in Cowley, Kansas. She was married twice. She married her first husband* FRED BROWN *in Cowley, County, Kansas.*

LOWRENCE BROWN

WANDA GRACE BROWN

Her second husband was CLYDE CHARLES MOORE.

MAXINE LOUISE MOORE *was born in Kansas.*

KEITH MOORE *was born in Kansas.*

VIOLA NADINE MOORE *was born in Cowley, Kansas and married* DICKIE GENE WALKER *in Kansas.*

LARRY DEAN WALKER *was born in Arkansas City, Kansas and married* LYDIA KAY DONLAY.

EDDIE DEAN WALKER *was born in Arkansas City, Kansas.*

BRANDI LYNN WALKER *was born in Arkansas City, Kansas.*

CLINTON BRUCE WALKER *was born in Arkansas City, Kansas.*

DIXIE LEA WALKER *was born in Arkansas City, Kansas and married* DAVID ANDREW GIVINS.

LANCE DAVID GIVINS *was born in Arkansas City, Kansas.*

STACI LYNN GIVINS *was born in Arkansas City, Kansas.*

PAIGE LEA GIVINS *was born in Arkansas City, Kansas.*

MARCIA ADELL WALKER *was born in Arkansas City, Kansas and married* ROBERT LESTER CRANDALL.

ROBIN LEA ANN CRANDALL *was born in Bitburg, Germany.*

LYLE WAYNE CRANDALL *was born in Hastings, Nebraska.*

KIMBERLY IRENE CRANDALL *was born in Winfield, Kansas.*

CAROL ANN WALKER *was born in Arkansas City, Kansas and married* RONNIE LEWIS SHURTZ.

OLIVIA ANN SHURTZ

JARROD WAYNE SHURTZ

KENNETH MOORE

PEARL GLADYS BROWN *was born and died in Latham, Kansas. She married* JOE SPEER.

CECIL SPEER *was born in Hutchinson, Kansas.*

ROBERT EUGENE SPEER

WARREN ADAM WILSON BROWN *was born in Latham, Kansas and married* STELLA BARTLEY.

ROSALIE BROWN BARTLEY BROWN

His second wife was EDITH EDIMSTON.

AGNES AUDINE BROWN *was born in Latham, Kansas and married* DEAN GRAY.

RUBY GRAY

ROY DEAN GRAY

WILLIS GRAY

EDDIE GRAY

BENNY PAUL GRAY

BARBARA GRAY

PATRICIA SUE GRAY

ROSEMARY GRAY

ELBERT GRANET BROWN *was born in Vinton, Kansas and married* PEGGY BARTHOLEMEW.

CHARLES ELBERT BROWN

CARLTON LEROY BROWN

ELDON GEATHEN BROWN *was born in Vinton, Kansas and married* MARY ?.

GARY ELDON BROWN

SHIRLY JOAN BROWN

SARAH RUTH BROWN

VERNON HARLEY BROWN *was born in Vinton, Kansas and married twice. His first wife was* VERDA GRAVES. *His second wife was* DORIS SKATES.

BARBARA ANNE BROWN

BEVERLY JEAN BROWN

INFANT SON *was born 15 December 1871 in Hancock County, Indiana and died the next day.*

ALICE LEORA MIZENER *was born 17 January 1874 in Tipton County, Indiana and died in Butler County, Kansas. On 6 September 1894 she married* WILLIAM BURTON NICODEMUS *in Butler*

County, Kansas. William was born 13 February 1874 in Marion County, Kansas and died in Butler County, Kansas.

HAZEL ALBERTA NICODEMUS was born 4 May 1897 in Butler County, Kansas and died in Santa Barbara, California. She was married twice. Her first husband was ANDREW McCULLY. She married her second husband WALTER RAYMOND McCURDY in Oklahoma City, Oklahoma.

BILLY ROBERT McCURDY was born in Summer County, Kansas.

MARILEE McCURDY was born in Greenwood County, Kansas and married JAMES MANTON MEADOWS in St. Louis County, Missouri. James was born in Richland County, Illinois and died in Harris County, Texas.

JON MAC MEADOWS was born in Richland County, Illinois and married MARSHA MOSLEY in Caddo Parish, Louisiana.

JON PATRICK MEADOWS was born in Harris County, Texas.

ANN KATHRYN MEADOWS was born in Harris County, Texas.

SUSAN ELIZABETH MEADOWS was born in Harris County, Texas.

JEFFREY MANTON MEADOWS was born in Richland County, Illinois and married MYRNA RUTH PARNELL in Bossier Parish, Louisiana.

JACK RICHARD McCURDY was born in Greenwood County, Kansas and died in Harris County, Texas.

HARRY LEROY NICODEMUS was born 13 June 1899 in Butler County, Kansas and died 4 months later.

ALBERT "FRITZ" W. NICODEMUS was born in Butler County, Kansas and died in Neosho County, Kansas.

TABITHA ANN PARKS was born 4 November 1846 in Hancock County, Indiana and on 14 December 1864 she married GEORGE H. JACKSON.

LAURA BELL JACKSON was born 16 July 1869.

ALFRED BELL JACKSON was born 29 December 1871.

MARY L. JACKSON was born 7 May 1874 and died four months later.

ELI K. JACKSON was born 26 September 1875.

WILFORD T. PARKS was born 3 March 1851 in Hancock County, Indiana and died 10 days later.

WILLIAM ALFRED PARKS was born 27 May 1852 in Hancock County, Indiana and died in Butler County, Kansas. On 21 September 1873 he married SARAH JANE DOBBINS in Hancock County, Indiana. Sarah Jane was born 21 September 1853 in Fortville, Indiana and died in Butler County, Kansas. She was the daughter of LEVI and JANE DOBBINS.

IVA FLORENCE PARKS was born 15 August 1875 and died in Oklahoma. She married CHARLEY S. COX.

FRANCIS LEE PARKS was born 23 July 1880 in Hancock County, Indiana and died in Butler County, Kansas. He married MINNIE DUNGY who died in Cambridge, Kansas.

LAURETTA PARKS was born 19 February 1882 in Butler County, Kansas and died in Eldorado, Kansas. She married JAMES WESLEY CHARLES who was born 19 December 1875.

EDGEL OTIS PARKS was born 28 October 1883 in Butler County, Kansas and married IDA LOIS BROWN who was born 23 July 1887 in Leon, Kansas.

EVERT J. PARKS was born 31 July 1889 in Cook County, Texas and died in San Jose, California. He married ELVA LAUVENIA WILLIAMS. Elva was born 28 October 1895 in Jasper County, Missouri and died in San Jose, California. She was the daughter of JAMES LAZARUS and LULA MAUDE DONHAM WILLIAMS.

EVELYN IRENE PARKS was born in Butler County, Kansas and married IRA LeROY THARP in Boulder, Colorado.

ESTEL ARLENE PARKS was born in Butler County, Kansas and died in Santa Clara County, California. She married ELVIN DAVIS in Longmont, Colorado. She married her second husband PAUL REDDING in San Jose, California.

ERMA EILEEN PARKS was born in Butler County, Kansas and died in Yamhill County, Oregon. She married JOHN ANDREW ATTEBERRY in Reno, Nevada. John was born in Webster County, Missouri and died in Newberg, Oregon. He was the son of FERN and FRANCES LUVENA SNODGRASS ATTEBERRY.

FRANCES JEAN ATTEBERRY was born in Webster County, Missouri.

SHARON ANN ATTEBERRY was born in San Jose, California.

BONNIE LOU ATTEBERRY was born in Yamhill County, Oregon and married JERRY GRAY in Reno, Nevada.

LARRY DEAN ATTEBERRY was born in Yamhill County, Oregon.

IVAN EVERT PARKS was born in Butler County, Kansas and died in Santa Clara County, California. He married EVELYN MIRANDA.

LYLE ELBURN PARKS was born in Butler County, Kansas and married NORMADEAN MOODY.

DERALD DEAN PARKS was born in Butler County, Kansas and died in Carson City, Nevada. He married twice. The name of his *first wife is unknown but his second wife was* EVELYN MAE WALLING.

DONNA DARLENE PARKS *was born in Santa Clara County, California and married* ROBERT KOLSTAD.

MALINDA LIGHTFOOT *was born 7 March 1821 in Pendleton County, Kentucky and on 21 March 1841 she married* JOHN CAMPBELL *in Rush County, Indiana.*

WILFORD UNGLES LIGHTFOOT *was born 28 July 1823 in Pendleton County, Kentucky and died in Tarrant County, Texas. He married twice. In 1845 he married* MINERVA AUDREY *in Decatur County, Indiana. She died before September of 1857.*

MARY ELLEN LIGHTFOOT *was born 3 September 1849 in Decatur County, Indiana and married* CALVIN S. KEITH.

AMELIA EMILY LIGHTFOOT *was born 4 April 1852 and died 18 February 1897. She married* JACOB RUBRECHT. *After her death he married* JEANNETTA HAMILTON KIRK CASKEY. *This was Jeannetta's second marriage.*

ELIZABETH "LIZZIE" MINERVA LIGHTFOOT *was born 27 April 1858 and died 12 December 1884. She married* JAMES WALKER.

GEORGE ANNA LIGHTFOOT *was born 5 April 1861 and married* JOHN R. LEWIS.

JEANNETTE "NETTIE" KIRK LIGHTFOOT *was born 12 April 1864 and married* ED PARSLEY.

MARTHA "MATTIE" LEE LIGHTFOOT *was born 4 December 1866 and married* HELM HUNT. *She was the twin of Maggie who died when she was a day old.*

MARGARET "MAGGIE" LEANNA LIGHTFOOT *was born 4 December 1866 and died the same day.*

CLARA AUGUSTA LIGHTFOOT *was born 24 November 1869.*

LAURA MAY LIGHTFOOT *was born 24 November 1869 and was the twin of Clara. Laura married* ALONZO PARSLEY.

WILLIAM STOWERS LIGHTFOOT *was born 3 July 1872.*

SARAH KATHERINE LIGHTFOOT *was born 19 March 1876 and married* ? ALLEN.

EDWARD LIGHTFOOT *was born in Culpeper County, Virginia and died in 1823 in Jefferson County, Kentucky. On 18 September 1806 he married* SUSANNAH COLVIN *in Pendleton County, Kentucky.*

ANN "NANCY" M. LIGHTFOOT *was born in 1777 in Culpeper County, Virginia and died in June of 1857 in Pendleton County, Kentucky. On 25 July 1802 she married* ROBERT RIDDLE *in Pendleton County, Kentucky.*

GUTHRIE GOODRICH LIGHTFOOT *was born in 1779 in Culpeper County, Virginia and died in 1847 in Edgar County, Illinois. On 19 February 1801 he married* CATHERINE COLVIN *in Pendleton County, Kentucky. Catherine was born in 1792 in Culpeper County, Virginia and*

died before 1850 in Adams County, Illinois. She was the daughter of
JOHN *and* MARGARET COLVIN. *John was a shipbuilder in the Cheasepeake Bay. He was also a veteran of the Revolutionary War.*

FRANCIS DUNCAN LIGHTFOOT *was born in 1810 in Pendleton County, Kentucky. He married* NANCY ELIZABETH WOODSIDE *16 May 1841 in Des Moines County, Iowa. The family is located in Des Moines County, Iowa, Adams County, Illinois and in the 1850 Census of Eldorado County, California.*

SARAH CATHERINE LIGHTFOOT *was born around 1843 in Iowa.*

LOVE LIGHTFOOT *was born about 1848 in Illinois.*

LUCY ANN LIGHTFOOT *was born around 1849 in Iowa.*

ARMISTEAD C. LIGHTFOOT *was born in 1808 in Pendleton County, Kentucky and married* SARAH A. ?. *Sara was born in 1820 in Virginia. Armistead was a brick mason.*

ANN E. LIGHTFOOT *was born around 1841 in Illinois.*

TERESSA LIGHTFOOT *was born about 1845 in Illinois.*

JOHN SMITH LIGHTFOOT, SR. *was born in 1820 in Pendleton County, Kentucky and died in 1866 in Chattanooga, Tennessee. In 1846 he married* ELIZABETH RUSSELL *in Walker County, Georgia. Elizabeth was born in 1830 in Lafayette County, Georgia to* ETHELBERT *and* CYNTHIA JONES RUSSELL, *daughter of* NANCY MIDDLETON JONES *and died in Chattanooga, Tennessee. The family moved to Chattanooga, Tennessee in 1852. John was a millwright and built many of the mills along the Chickamauga Creek.*

WILLIAM LIGHTFOOT *was born 25 December 1846 in Walker County, Georgia and died in Chattanooga, Tennessee. In 1866 he married* LUCY McBRIDE *in Chattanooga, Tennessee. Lucy the daughter of* JOHN *and* MARY McCARTY McBRIDE *was born 20 December 1853. William and his sons shipped great quantities of strawberries from East Chattanooga around the turn of the century.*

WILLIAM LIGHTFOOT

LEE LIGHTFOOT *was born in Chattanooga, Tennessee and never married.*

JOHN LIGHTFOOT *was born in Chattanooga, Tennessee and married* LENA STERCHI.

JOHN LIGHTFOOT, JR. *died in Cleveland, Tennessee.*

ROSA LIGHTFOOT

VIOLA MAE LIGHTFOOT *attended Maryville College.*

HENRY DAVIS LIGHTFOOT *died in Birchwood, Tennessee.*

BERTHA BIRD LIGHTFOOT

HANNIBAL LIGHTFOOT *was born 15 March 1877 in Chattanooga, Tennessee and died in Lake County, Florida. He married* NELLIE SMITH *in Chattanooga, Tennessee. Nellie was born 12 December 1879 in Chattanooga, Tennessee and died in Lake*

County, Florida. *She was the daughter of* JOHN *and* SALLIE SMITH.

CLARENCE LIGHTFOOT *was born in Chattanooga, Tennessee and died in Lake County, Florida.*

BERTHA LIGHTFOOT *was born in Chattanooga, Tennessee and married* MARION GEER.

ROBERT L. LIGHTFOOT *married* AMALIE ?.

OLLIE LIGHTFOOT *was born in Chattanooga, Tennessee and married* CLIFTON WILLIAM COLLINS *in Altoona, Florida. Clifton was the son of* JAMES *and* MOLLIE GLASS COLLINS.

LOWELL CLIFFORD COLLINS *was born in Lake County, Florida and married* CATHERINE ELSIE RONCO *in Vancouver, British Columbia, Canada. Catherine was the daughter of* ATILLIO *and* MARY GAROFANI RONCO.

LESLIE CHRISTINE COLLINS *was born in Eustis, Florida and married* LARRY JAMES OAKES *in Lake County, Florida. Larry was the son of* JAMES *and* ARLENE HEITMAN OAKES.

DOUGLAS STEWART COLLINS *was born in Eustis, Florida.*

HENRY BYRD LIGHTFOOT *married* ANONA ? *and died in Palatka, Florida.*

HENRY LIGHTFOOT *was born in Chattanooga, Tennessee and died as a child.*

VIOLA LIGHTFOOT *was born in 1891 in Chattanooga, Tennessee and married* BOYD CHAPMAN. *Viola was a schoolteacher in Hamilton County, Tennessee.*

LAURA LIGHTFOOT *was born in 1896 in Chattanooga, Tennessee and married* ELWIN W. WYATT. *Laura like Viola was a schoolteacher in Hamilton County, Tennessee.*

CARRIE LIGHTFOOT *was born in Chattanooga, Tennessee and married* FRED STERCHI.

FRED S. STERCHI, JR.

ROY N. STERCHI *died in West Palm Beach, Florida.*

WILLARD STERCHI

ROBIN STERCHI

EUGENE STERCHI

JOSEPHINE STERCHI *married* ? CATE.

SARAH STERCHI *married* ? MORRIS.

ANNIE LIGHTFOOT *was born in Chattanooga, Tennessee and married* ARTHUR SMITH.

ALICE SMITH

WINIFRED SMITH

ROBBIE SMITH

CATHERINE LIGHTFOOT *was born in 1848.*

SAMUEL LIGHTFOOT *was born around 1863 and married* MOLLIE ?.

JOHN SMITH LIGHTFOOT, JR. *was born 10 September 1850 in Walker County, Georgia and died in Wichita County, Texas. In 1876 he married* MARY CATHERINE "KATIE" BIBLE *in Marion County, Tennessee. Katie was born 1 March 1853 in Marion County, Tennessee and died in Hardeman County, Texas. She was the daughter of* CHRISTOPHER COLUMBUS *and* ELIZABETH HALL BIBLE. *The family moved from Tennessee to Texas. They resided in Flagg and Whitney, Texas.*

CHRIS LIGHTFOOT *was born in 1877 in Marion County, Tennessee and married* KATIE ALVERSON.

HUGH H. LIGHTFOOT *was born in 1880 in Marion County, Tennessee and married* NANNIE ROSE *in Hill County, Texas.*

NEWT LIGHTFOOT *was born in 1897 in Hill County, Texas and married* RITA DANIEL.

BERTHA LIGHTFOOT *was born 9 September 1882 in Marion County, Tennessee and died in Hill County, Texas. She married* HENRY WATSON *in Hill County, Texas. Henry was born 20 September 1883 in Woodford County, Arkansas and died in Hill County, Texas. He was the son of* MADISON FRANKLIN *and* BRINTHE ELIZABETH THOMPSON WATSON.

LYMAN BAYARD WATSON *was born in Hill County, Texas and died during World War II at Luzon Island in the Philippines.*

WAYMAN RALEIGH WATSON *was born in Hill County, Texas and married* KAY WAINSCOTT *in Hill County, Texas.*

NEY FRANKLIN WATSON *was born and died in Hill County, Texas. He married* RUBY WALLER *in Hill County, Texas.*

HUGH AARON WATSON *was born in Hill County, Texas and died in Hill County, Texas. He married* WINNIE BESS CLARK *in Hill County, Texas.*

LORRAINE KATHRYN WATSON *was born in Hill County, Texas and died in Tarrant County, Texas. She married* ROBERT H. BLOOD *in Ohio.*

LARRY WATSON *was born in Hill County, Texas and married* PATSY HENSLEY *in Hill County, Texas.*

MARY EDD WATSON *was born in Hill County, Texas and married* ELWYN W. MORTON *in Wichita County, Texas.*

BELL LIGHTFOOT *was born in 1890 in Marion County, Tennessee and married* ARCH COX.

BLANCHE LIGHTFOOT *was born in 1885 in Marion County, Tennessee and died in Aztec, New Mexico. She married* JOE TARPLEY.

KATY MAE LIGHTFOOT *was born in 1894 in Hill County, Texas and died in Hereford County, Texas. She married* A.A. HARE.

JAMES/JOHN THOMAS LIGHTFOOT *was born 20 November 1856 in Chattanooga, Tennessee and died in Atlanta, Georgia. On 22 August 1889 he married* ELIZABETH BABCOCK POMEROY *in New York. Elizabeth was born 3 April 1870 in New York and died in Newport News, Virginia. She was the daughter of* WHITING GRISWOLD *and* OLIVE CELESTA BABCOCK POMEROY. *James/John was a Baptist Minister and wrote books on Prophecy and a book of poems. He named his first son after a Seminary Professor he really liked.*

JAMES TINDELL LIGHTFOOT *was born 12 May 1890 in Silver City, New Mexico and married* MARY ELIZABETH BENNETT *in Montour Falls, New York.*

WINIFRED LIGHTFOOT *was born 1 July 1891 and died two months later.*

OLIVE KILBURN LIGHTFOOT *was born 25 November 1893 in Chattanooga, Tennessee and married thrice. She married her first husband* HAROLD IRVING TABOR *in Oneonta, New York. She married her second husband* WILLIAM GORES GUSTAFSON *in Washington, D.C. She married her third husband* JAMES RALPH WATSON *in Couerd Alene, Idaho.*

WHITING POMEROY LIGHTFOOT *was born 12 December 1896 in Chattanooga, Tennessee and died in Waynesville, Missouri. He married* HELEN JOSEPHINE ROCKWELL *in Washington, D.C. Helen was born 21 March 1897 in New York and died in Waynesville, Missouri. Whiting was a Retired Colonel of the United States Air Force who saw action in World War II and was a member of the National Guard.*

WHITING ROCKWELL LIGHTFOOT *was born in Arlington, Virginia and married* TERRY ELLEN MYERS *in Des Moines, Iowa. Whiting adopted Terry's two children from a previous marriage.*

SHARON KAY MYERS LIGHTFOOT *married* JOSEPH TAYLOR.

DOROTHY FAY MYERS LIGHTFOOT *married* BASIL METROULAS.

LINDA LEE LIGHTFOOT *never married.*

HELEN ANN LIGHTFOOT *married* JACK FERRANTE *in Waynesville, Missouri.*

ALVAH HANEY LIGHTFOOT *was born in Bismarck, Missouri and died three days short of her first birthday.*

GERTRUDE BABCOCK LIGHTFOOT *was born in Bismarck, Missouri and died when she was five years old in Tarrant County, Texas.*

ROBERT SCOTT LIGHTFOOT *was born in Hill County, Texas and died in Newport News, Virginia.* He married ALBERTA TAYLOR *in Newport News, Virginia.*

MARY ABBY ROBERTA LIGHTFOOT *was born in Dexter, New Mexico and married thrice.* Her first husband was RICHARD M. WHITESIDE. *Her second husband was* ROY W. MALONE. *Her third husband was* EDDIE JOHN GENSENLUTER.

FRANCES "FANNIE" LIGHTFOOT *was born 10 July 1862 in Chattanooga, Tennessee and died in Chattanooga, Tennessee. On 22 August 1881 she married* ROBERT LaFAYETTE McELHANEY *in Chattanooga, Tennessee. Robert was born 14 November 1858 in Athens, Tennessee and died in Chattanooga, Tennessee.*

LEVINA LIGHTFOOT *was born 14 March 1821 in Pendleton County, Kentucky and died 11 June 1858 in Adair County, Missouri. On 17 October 1841 she married* BENJAMIN ARMISTEAD DUNHAM *in Des Moines County, Iowa. Benjamin was born 25 March 1821 in Montgomery County, Kentucky and died 30 September 1863 in Adair County, Missouri. He was the son of* AMOS *and* SARAH "SALLIE" COLLIVER DUNHAM. *After Levina's death Benjamin married* BARBARA ELLEN DYE. *He was a brick mason.*

GEORGE WASHINGTON DUNHAM *was born 29 June 1842 in Des Moines, Iowa and died in Adair County, Missouri. He married* M.J. CHANING *19 August 1861.*

WILLIAM HENRY DUNHAM *was born 5 December 1843 in Des Moines County, Iowa and died 31 July 1888. He married* LORETTA MARQUESS *14 January 1866. Loretta was born 2 December 1847 in West Virginia and died in Adair County, Missouri.*

ELIJAH COLLIVAR DUNHAM *was born 14 January 1845 in Des Moines County, Iowa and died in Grant County, Oklahoma.* He married MARY ANN MOORE *7 February 1867 in Adair County, Missouri. Mary was born 9 April 1848 in Osage, Missouri and died in Grant County, Oklahoma.*

QUINTIN PARKER DUNHAM *was born 28 December 1847 in Des Moines County, Iowa and died in Adair County, Missouri.*

JAMES GUILFORD DUNHAM *was born 17 September 1849 in Des Moines County, Iowa and married* ELWILDA PUGH *19 December 1869 in Adair County, Missouri. Elwilda was born 26 August 1852 in Indianapolis, Indiana.*

JOHN THOMPSON DUNHAM *was born 9 March 1851 in Des Moines County, Iowa and died in Adair County, Missouri. He married*

ELIZABETH JANE SWANK *in 1888. Elizabeth was born in 1853 in Ohio and died in Adair County, Missouri.*

JOSEPH ELDRIDGE DUNHAM *was born 28 January 1852 in Des Moines County, Iowa and married* ANNA E. BOLTON *14 October 1878 in Henderson County, Illinois. Anna was born 4 April 1856 in Kentucky.*

LEANDUS LOGAN DUNHAM *was born 3 April 1854 in Iowa and died 27 January 1858 in Missouri.*

SARAH CATHERINE DUNHAM *was born 2 March 1856 in Missouri and married* ZACHARY T. HENDREN. *Zachary was born 19 October 1852.*

SAMUEL ARTHUR DUNHAM *was born 1 March 1858 in Missouri and died in Adair County, Missouri.*

GEORGE WASHINGTON LIGHTFOOT *was born 8 September 1812 in Pendleton County, Kentucky and died 12 March 1895 in Fremont, Iowa. He married* MARGARET DUNHAM. *Margaret was born 9 December 1814 in Kentucky and died 3 July 1897 in Fremont, Iowa. She was the daughter of* AMOS *and* SARAH "SALLIE" COLLIVER DUNHAM.

WILLIAM LOGAN LIGHTFOOT *was born 3 October 1834 in Des Moines County, Iowa and died in Fremont, Iowa. In 1867 he married* ELIZABETH JONES *in Davis County, Iowa.*

NANCY JANE LIGHTFOOT *was born in 1837 in Des Moines County, Iowa.*

LIZZY ANN LIGHTFOOT *was born in 1839 in Des Moines County, Iowa.*

BENJAMIN LIGHTFOOT *was born in 1840 in Des Moines County, Iowa.*

AMOS LIGHTFOOT *was born in 1841 in Des Moines County, Iowa and married* MARY ?.

WASHINGTON MARION LIGHTFOOT *was born 15 February 1844 in Des Moines County, Iowa and died in Fremont, Iowa. On 25 April 1876 he married* ELIZABETH SMOOT *in Riverton, Iowa. Elizabeth was born 2 December 1847 in Adair County, Missouri.*

SARAH "SALLY" LIGHTFOOT *was born in 1845 in Des Moines County, Iowa and married* THOMAS WILLIKEN. *Thomas was born around 1843 in Indiana.*

SAMUEL ARTHUR LIGHTFOOT *was born in 1848 in Des Moines County, Iowa and died in Fremont County, Iowa.*

CATHARINE LIGHTFOOT *was born in 1850 in Iowa.*

MARGARET LIGHTFOOT *was born in 1853 in Iowa.*

PHILIP LIGHTFOOT *was born around 1782 in Culpeper County, Virginia and died before 1815. On 29 December 1803 he married* SUSANNAH SMITH *in Pendleton County, Kentucky. Philip died in the service of the United States of America. After Philip's death Susannah married* THOMAS WELLS *16 February 1815 in Pendleton County, Kentucky. Thomas was appointed as the guardian of Philip's and Susannah's children.*

WILLIAM S. LIGHTFOOT *was born 5 May 1806 in Pendleton County, Kentucky and died 14 October 1877 in Grant County, Indiana. On 5 October 1828 he married* PHOEBE BUTLER *in Rush County, Indiana. Phoebe was born in 1810 and died 11 April 1879 in Grant County, Indiana.*

CHRISTOPHER C. LIGHTFOOT *was born 15 July 1836 in Indiana and married* ELIZA J. BRIZEDINE *8 December 1872.*

WILLIAM S. LIGHTFOOT *was born 10 November 1873 in Rush County, Indiana and married* IVA THRAILKILL. *Iva was born 11 October 1880. She was the daughter of* DAVID *and* CHARITY ADAMS THRAILKILL.

LEO S. LIGHTFOOT *was born in Indiana and married* OSA T. SMITH. *Osa was born in Indiana.*

RICHARD LEE LIGHTFOOT *was born in Anderson, Indiana and married* ANNA M. FLATT *who was born in Tennessee.*

MARY JANE LIGHTFOOT *was born around 1829 and on 31 January 1850 she married* STEPHEN SMITH HENDRICKS *in Marion County, Indiana.*

PHILIP LIGHTFOOT *was born in 1832.*

ELI B. LIGHTFOOT *was born around 1834 and died in 1899.*

LEVI BUTLER LIGHTFOOT *was born in 1865.*

CLEON DEE LIGHTFOOT

EVELYN RAE LIGHTFOOT

SUSANNA LIGHTFOOT *was born around 1841.*

SYNATHIA LIGHTFOOT *was born about 1843.*

NANCY LIGHTFOOT *was born around 1845 and married* WILLIAM McKINLEY.

MARY JANE McKINLEY *was born 18 September 1863 in Grant County, Indiana and married* WILLIAM LEER.

GLADYS ANGELINE LEER *married* ? JOHNSON.

GWEN JOHNSON *married* HARVEY H. HOUSE.

ISABEL LIGHTFOOT *was born around 1849.*

NANCY LIGHTFOOT

JOHN LIGHTFOOT *was born in 1808 and married* LUCY ? *who was born in 1810. The family is located in the 1850 Census for Campbell County, Kentucky.*

MARY J. LIGHTFOOT *was born in 1832.*

WILLIAM LIGHTFOOT *was born in 1834.*

SARAH E. LIGHTFOOT *was born in 1836.*

JOHN LIGHTFOOT *was born in 1838.*

GEORGE W. LIGHTFOOT *was born in 1840.*

164

ELIZABETH LIGHTFOOT *was born in 1842.*

JOEL LIGHTFOOT *was born in 1845.*

THOMAS LIGHTFOOT *was born in 1850.*

DIANA LIGHTFOOT

LAVINA LIGHTFOOT

JAMES LIGHTFOOT

ELIZABETH LIGHTFOOT *was born in Culpeper County, Virginia and on 22 March 1834 she married* THOMAS TURNER *in Pendleton County, Kentucky.*

RICHARD LIGHTFOOT *was born in Culpeper County, Virginia.*

JAMES LIGHTFOOT *was born about 1790 in Culpeper County, Virginia and on 29 October 1810 he married* MILDRED "MILLY" DELANY *in Pendleton County, Kentucky.*

FRANCES LIGHTFOOT *was born 16 March 1828 and on 16 March 1828 she married* JOHN LIGHTFOOT *who was born in Fleming County, Kentucky.*

CHAPTER XII

HANNAH LIGHTFOOT AND GEORGE III

George III of England was born in June of 1738 and died in 1820. He was a kind, sweet child, but somewhat slow in learning. He succeeded George II, who was very critical and unkind to young George.

George III reigned during a very tempestuous period—that of the American Revolution, and also the French Revolution. He lost the American Colonies and the French Revolution affected England. He had become Prince of Wales at an early age. His ministers were Lord North and Younger William Pitt.

He married Charlotte of Mecklenburg-Stralitz after the royal family dissolved his marriage to Hannah Lightfoot. Later, Queen Charlotte, upon hearing about George's past life, insisted upon being privately re-wedded to the King. Unfortunately George was emotionally unbalanced, and became hopelessly insane in 1781.

One account concerning Hannah suggests that she had a cousin called Thomas who was a general. There was a Lieutenant General Thomas Lightfoot born 1775 and died November 1858 at Barbourne House, Worcestershire, and possibly a descendant of her half-brother Thomas Lightfoot. It is not known if Hannah Lightfoot is related to Reverend Richard Lightfoot's line or not. The following is a documented ancestry of Hannah Lightfoot.

[1]PEDIGREE OF HANNAH LIGHTFOOT 's FAMILY:

JOHN LIGHTFOOT *of Richmond, Yorkshire, England was from a Quaker stronghold.*
MATHEW LIGHTFOOT *was a shoemaker and cordwainer. He died the 6th of December at the age of 67 of "tissicks", in the parish of St. John's*

---

[1] Lightfoot Family Association Newsletter – V. 7, 1984, #1-4, Query 119-84.

Wapping, and was buried at Wapping Old Stairs. He married on 6 November 1683, RUTH NEWMAN, of Mile End who died 27 September 1744, "of age". She was 89 years of age and died in the parish of Spitalfields. She was buried at Wapping.

DOROTHY LIGHTFOOT was born 7 November 1686 and married DANIEL KILVENTON 20 November 1707.

MATTHEW LIGHTFOOT was born 28 October 1688 and died 27 February 1689.

MATTHEW LIGHTFOOT was born 1 February 1690 and died 1 February 1732 of asthma at St. John's Wapping. He married ELIZABETH CARTER 15 April 1713.

JAMES LIGHTFOOT was born 11 February 1713/14 in Wapping Street near King Edward's Stairs and died 3 January 1730/31.

MATTHEW LIGHTFOOT was born 19 September 1715 and died 19 October 1753.

JOHN LIGHTFOOT was born October 1716 and died 7 April 1717.

THOMAS LIGHTFOOT was born 19 September 1718.

SARAH LIGHTFOOT was born 10 December 1723.

MATTHEW LIGHTFOOT married MARY WHEELER, his second wife 13 August 1728, at the Savoy. She died 16 May 1760, at the age of 61, at St. James's. Issue by second wife:

HANNAH LIGHTFOOT was born 12 October 1730 in the parish of St. John's Wapping.

JOHN LIGHTFOOT was born 1 July 1732 and died 28 October 1733.

RUTH LIGHTFOOT was born 10 May 1692 and married JOSEPH HOLMES of Croydon 6 June 1721.

ELIZABETH LIGHTFOOT was born 28 November 1693 and married STEPHEN FOWLER of Spitalfields 8 September 1713.

SARAH LIGHTFOOT was born 11 August 1696 and died 9 September 1696.

JOHN LIGHTFOOT was born 3 October 1697 and died 5 April 1702.

SAMUEL LIGHTFOOT was born 8 February 1699/1700 at St. John's Wapping and died 5 December 1735 at St. Paul's Shadwell, of dropsy. He married SARAH ?. Issue:

SAMUEL LIGHTFOOT was born 26 November 1722.

SAMUEL LIGHTFOOT was born 24 July 1727 in the parish of St. Paul's, Shadwell and married CATALINA ?. He is buried at St. Mary's, Islington on 18 November 1799. Issue:

SAMUEL LIGHTFOOT was born 17 April 1760 and died 8 April 1798 at Islington. He married MARY ANNE ?. Issue:

ALFRED LIGHTFOOT married ANNE BENNETT.

MARY ANNE LIGHTFOOT was born 15 May 1788 and died 20 January 1797.

SAMUEL LIGHTFOOT *married his second wife LUCY BROWN 7 November 1789 at Islington. Issue:*

ELIZABETH LUCY LIGHTFOOT *was born 11 December 1790 and married* JAMES HENRY FRYE.

JANE JOSEPHA LIGHTFOOT *was born 6 January 1793 and married* EDWARD INNES.

SAMUEL LIGHTFOOT *was born 26 December 1794 and married* MISS COKE *of Bristol on 19 February 1821.*

ANNE LIGHTFOOT *married* HENRY MAY.

HENRY LIGHTFOOT

CATHERINE LIGHTFOOT

LEONORA LIGHTFOOT

SARAH LIGHTFOOT *was born 13 August 1729.*

ELIZABETH LIGHTFOOT *was born 12 July 1731.*

SARAH LIGHTFOOT *was born 9 June 1702 and died 19 December 1741.*

HANNAH LIGHTFOOT *was born 6 July 1706 and died 29 August 1722.*

Matthew Lightfoot was born 1 February 1690, in the Parish of St. John's Wapping. He was the third son of John Lightfoot of Richmond, England. His first marriage was to Elizabeth Carter, 15 April 1713. They had five children. Matthew married a second wife, Mary Wheeler, 13 August 1728, at the Savoy. They had Hannah Lightfoot born 12 October 1730 in Parish of St. John's Wapping. A son John was born 1 July 1732, shortly after his father Matthew died of asthma on 1 February 1732.

Mary Wheeler Lightfoot took her two small children and moved to live with her brother Henry Wheeler, who lived nearby and had a prosperous drapery business. Hannah's new home was much more luxurious than that of Matthew Lightfoot. The drapery shop was on the bottom floor of a building and the living quarters were upstairs.

Sometime later Henry Wheeler married and started his own family. Hannah and her mother helped the new wife with chores and with his children as they were born.

After her chores were finished Hannah spent many hours sitting in her window upstairs watching life go by on the busy street. Hannah being a Quakeress was not allowed going unescorted in public places. Her uncle hired a young woman to help with the housework, and she and Hannah became good friends. Hannah was allowed to go shopping and spend time away from home with her companion. They remained friends all through the years.

One day, as Hannah was sitting in her window watching the crowds go by, she saw the royal coach pass, and made eye contact with the Prince of Wales, George III. George fell in love with the exquisitely beautiful

Quaker maiden, Hannah Lightfoot. George passed by her window many times as he went through St. James Market to get another look at that wistful, haunting face; dark hair; and dark eyes.

Hannah's family had been close friends with the Axford family. Their son, Isaac Axford was a young assistant grocer at a grocery shop on Ludgate Hill. Some sources say her family arranged a marriage between Hannah and Isaac Axford. They were married at Keith's Chapel, Mayfair, 11 December 1753. One account stated that as the wedded pair left the chapel, the Prince of Wales mysteriously transported Hannah away from her husband. Later, George forced a Dr. Wilmot to marry them.

The following documents were printed in *The Appeal for Royalty*. It is not known for sure when the documents were first given to the world, but the date they were printed was 1858.

April 17th, 1759.

The marriage of these parties was this day duly solemnised at Kew Chapel, according to the rites and ceremonies of the Church of England, by myself

GEORGE P.	J. WILMOT
HANNAH	

Witnesses to this marriage—
W. Pitt.
Anne Taylor.

May 27th, 1759.

This is to certify that the marriage of these parties, George Prince of Wales to Hannah Lightfoot, was duly solemnised this day according to the rites and ceremonies of the Church of England, at their residence at Peckham, by myself,

GEORGE GUELPH	J. WILMOT
HANNAH LIGHTFOOT	

Witnesses to the marriage
of these parties-----
William Pitt.
Anne Taylor.

George R----. Whereas it is our Royal command that the birth of Olive, the Duke of Cumberland's daughter, is never made known to the nation during our reign; but from a sense of religious duty, we will that she be acknowledged by the Royal Family after our death, should she survive

170

ourselves, in return for confidential service rendered ourselves by Dr. Wilmot in the year 1759.

Kew Palace,
May 2nd, 1773.
(Signed)   CHATHAM
WARWICK

Indorsed, London,
     June 1815.
Delivered to Mrs. Olive Serres
     by Warwick.
         Witness, EDWARD[2]

Hampstead, July 7th 1768.

Provided I depart this life, I recommend my two sons and my daughter to the kind protection of their Royal Father, my husband, his Majesty George III, bequeathing whatever property I may die possessed of to such dear offspring of my ill-fated marriage. In case of the death of each of my children, I give and bequeath to Olive Wilmot, the daughter of my best friend, Dr. Wilmot, whatever property I am entitled to or possessed of at the time of my death.—Amen.

(Signed) 'HANNAH 'REGINA.

Witnesses—
     J. Dunning.
     William Pitt.

George built a grand secluded house for Hannah at Peckham, England. She lived a very isolated life and waited many times for George to return home after he had completed his work as Prince of Wales. She was very lonely when George was gone because she had been expelled from the Society of Friends, and could not be found afterwards.

Hannah wrote letters to her mother, but would not tell where she lived.

Hannah and George were both very happy when their first child was born. In Hannah's will she stated that they had two boys and one girl.

George had a portrait of Hannah painted in 1755/6, by an outstanding artist of the time –Sir Joshua Reynolds. The portrait is reported to be hanging at Reynolds Gallery, Knole House, Seven Oaks, Kent in England.

There are several versions of the family after the royal family found out about George's past with Hannah Lightfoot. One is that George gave the children the surname of Rex. Another story told is that Hannah Lightfoot

---

[2] This is the signature of the late Duke of Kent.

171

died in England. The most popular story is that the royal family had her and her children sent to South Africa. There she contacted her Quaker relatives in Pennsylvania who sent for her. Her oldest son was named George Rex and has descendants in Pennsylvania to this day.

CHAPTER XIII

THE CHEW, DUNCAN, BARROW, STONE, AND MINOR LINE OF DESCENT

The Chew Family

[1]JOHN CHEW was the ancestor of the Maryland family. He came from Chewton, Somersetshire, England, with three servants in the ship *"Charitite"* in 1622. His wife, SARAH WALKER came the following year in the ship *"Seafloure"*. John Chew was born 1590, Worchestershire, England and died 1668 in Virginia. John[2] and Sarah were living on Hog Island, opposite Jamestown in 1624. Sarah died before 1651. John moved to Ann Arundel County, Maryland, about 1649 and married Mrs. RACHEL CONSTABLE.

John and Sarah Chew had five sons, but only two are documented. SAMUEL CHEW was born about 1630 and died 1676. He married ANN AYERS who was born in 1640 and died in 1695, heiress of WILLIAM AYERS of Nansemond County, Virginia. Samuel and Ann Chew had nine children. Their fifth child Benjamin was our ancestor.

BENJAMIN CHEW was born in 1670 and died 3 March 1700. His estate was Maidstone Plantation. He was married 8 December 1692 to ELIZABETH BENSON born in 1677 the daughter of JOHN and ELIZABETH (SMITH) BENSON. Elizabeth married RICHARD BOND of Calvert after the death of Benjamin Chew and died in 1725. Benjamin and Elizabeth had the following issue: SAMUEL CHEW born 30 October 1693 and died 16 June 1743; ELIZABETH CHEW was born 12 March 1694 and died 9 February 1726/7; ANN CHEW was born 14 October 1696; and MARY CHEW was born in December of 1698.

Mary Chew went to Virginia from Maryland to visit her brother Samuel, Chief Justice of Lower Counties. There she met and married GOODRICH LIGHTFOOT.

---

[1] *Chew Family* by Francis b. Culver – Maryland Historical Magazine.
[2] Hotten's Emigrants, p. 237.

There has been a controversy over the years about Goodrich Lightfoot and his marriage to Mary Chew.

The compiler of this book has found many references to their marriage such as:

Virginia Council Journals – volume 32, page 1,   *Virginia   County Records* – Edited by Crozier, page 126,

Records of St. Mark's Parish, Spotsylvania County – June 5, 1733,

"Mary, Wife of Goodrich Lightfoot, Acknowledged Her Dower, Etc.".

New England Family History. Henry Cole Quimby. Volume IV. Page 647.

Goodrich and Mary Lightfoot had 6 children.

The Duncan Family

Scotland is a treasure house for heraldic history. One can still find customs lingering through the centuries. The name Duncan has become one of the most famous of all Scottish surnames and its history can be traced back to medieval times.

Many titles were held by Duncan ancestors, the most famous of which belonged to Duncan I, King of Scotland in 1040, who was defeated and killed by Macbeth, Mormaor of Moray.

The earliest reference to the name was that of Dunchad, the 11th Abbot of Iona. The original Clan Donnchaidh derived its name from Fat Duncan de Atholia, Chief of the clan in the time of Bruce.

In the 1467 Gaelic genealogical manuscript, the name appeared as Donnchaid and in 1520 the early Celtic form was Duncha and Donnchad.

The generally accepted meaning of Duncan is 'powerful chieftain', from the Gaelic 'dun' meaning a fortress and 'ceann', head or chief. In Wales "fort warriors" were known as Dunocatus.

Captain Nathaniel Duncan who came to Dorchester, Massachusetts in 1630 from England is listed on record as one of the earliest arrivals to America with the Duncan name.

There are 11 coats of arms on record for the Duncan name. The most illustrious of these shows a red shield, silver chevron with three red escutcheons, two silver rosettes and hunting horn of gold and green.

ANDREW DUNCAN was our first documented ancestor, born before 1575 in Scotland[3]. All of the Reverend Andrew's sons were killed in battle and which left him to raised all his grandchildren. His children were: JOHN who was born about 1605; WILLIAM; DAVID; and BESSIE.

JOHN DUNCAN had one child, WILLIAM, born January 7, 1628 in Perth, Scotland and died January 2, 1691/2 at Perth. William married

---

[3] There may be errors, since the Duncan clan had so many children.

SUSAN SARAH HALDANE August 9, 1657, the daughter of RICHARD HALDANE and MARY KENNET. William was a Covenant Presbyterian Minister of Slascoe, Scotland who refused to take a Jacobite Oath and was beheaded by orders of the English Monarch.

The children of William Duncan and Susan Haldane were:

WILLIAM, JR. *was born 1 October 1659 and died 1720 in Alexandria, Virginia.*
CHARLES *was born 6 September 1662.*
HENRY *was born 11 January 1663.*
THOMAS *was born 28 January 1665 and married* SUSAN THOMAS.
MARY *was born 1 February 1667 in Perth, Scotland and died in Northern Neck, Virginia.*
SUSAN
GEORGE
ALEXANDRIA
WILLIAM J. II's *second marriage was to* MARGARET McMURDO *around 1685. Their children were:* JOHN *who was born about 1688;* WILLIAM J. III *was born 19 April 1690 in Prince William County, Virginia and died 24 February 1781 in Culpeper County, Virginia. In 1719 he married* RUTH RALEIGH *in Culpeper County, Virginia.*

CHARLES DUNCAN *was born 6 September 1662 and had:* CHARLES DUNCAN, II; ROBERT; *and* WILLIAM III *who was born in 1692 in Dumfrieshire, Scotland.*

JOHN DUNCAN *and* SINA BROWNING *were married around 1710. Their children were:* WILLIAM MARSHALL DUNCAN; JOHN DUNCAN, JR. *who married* DINAH BRADFORD *and died about 1788; and* ROBERT DUNCAN *was born about 1720 in Stafford, Virginia and died about 1793 in Culpeper Co., Virginia.*

ROBERT DUNCAN *married* ANN GALLOP *in 1740, the daughter of* ROBERT GALLOP. *The information about Robert and Ann Gallop Duncan is documented. Robert Duncan left a will dated 7 June 1788 and proved 21 October 1793, naming his daughter* LAVINA *and her husband* JOHN BARROW LIGHTFOOT *(among others) as beneficiaries.*

Robert and Ann's children were:

PHYLLIS *was born about 1743 and married* JOHN BARBEE *in Stafford County, Virginia. She died 16 March 1826 in Kentucky.*
LAVINA DUNCAN *was born in 1755 in Stafford, Virginia and died in Pendleton, Kentucky.*
ROSEY
ROBERT
JOHN
CHARLES

SAMMY

JOHN

GALLOP

MARY DUNCAN *married* JOSEPH HACKLEY *first and after his death she married* THOMAS GRINNAN

ANN DUNCAN *married* THOMAS POPE.

The Barrow Family

The Surname Barrow means one who lived by a grove or a hill. It is derived from the old English "Bearu" with the dative form "bearwe." and from the old English "beorg" and the Middle English "berwe, Barwe," which became Berrow and Barrow respectively.

Occasionally, the hills, were wooded and were used for pasturing livestock, however, barrow also referred to mounds of stone or earth placed over the remains of the dead, especially in the pre-Christian era. First a fence surrounded the mounds from the past, and later these earthen mounds were encircled with trenches made of rocks placed around the barrows. English barrows usually had one chamber in which were placed the favorite possessions of the deceased.

The surname appears in the earliest English records including in 1192 a listing of a "de Barewe" from Lincolnshire in the Pipe Rolls. A "Del Berwe" from Cambridgeshire is recorded on the Assize Rolls in 1620 and "atte Barwe" is listed in 1237 from Somerset on the Subsidy Rolls.

WILLIAM LIGHTFOOT the youngest son of GOODRICH and MARY (CHEW) LIGHTFOOT of Orange County, Virginia, was probably born about 1729. On 23 November 1744 he came into Court and made choice of Edward Spencer, Gent. as his guardian[4]. Before 1749 he had moved to Richmond County, Virginia and on the 19th or 20th of October of that year he and his wife ELIZABETH (BARROW) LIGHTFOOT sold to Thomas Slaughter 300 acres on the south side of the South West Mountains in Orange (now Culpeper) County[5].

The records of Richmond County show that William Lightfoot, Gentleman and Elizabeth his wife, on 3 June 1751 sold to William Flood, Gentleman of Westmoreland County for £128 a tract of 128 acres on Rappahannock Creek which he had bought from Stuart Minor[6]. No deed of purchase has been found.[7]

---

[4] Orange County, Virginia, Order Book 4, p. 229.

[5] Orange County, Virginia, Deed Book 11, pp. 180-83.

[6] Richmond County, Virginia, Deed Book 11, p. 75.

[7] Since many Richmond County records are not indexed, this deed may eventually be discovered.

This brief sojourn in Richmond County indicated that William Lightfoot's wife Elizabeth might well have been born there, but no record has been found in Richmond County to identify her parentage. There is, however, a record in Westmoreland County of a marriage contract:

5 March 1746. *William Lightfoot of Orange County, Gent. to Nicholas Minor of Westmoreland County, uncle and guardian of Elizabeth Barrow, spinster.*
A marriage is intended shortly to be solemnized between William Lightfoot and Elizabeth Barrow. Elizabeth being possessed of ten slaves, if William dies before Elizabeth without leaving issue, Elizabeth shall have the slaves and also her dower in the lands of William, but if William have children the Negroes shall descend to the child or children. If he have no child at the time of Elizabeth's death, the Negroes shall be vested in John Barrows and Margaret Ransdell.

Wm. Lightfoot
Nich. Minor

Witnesses: William Bayly, Joseph Peirce, William Bruce
26 May 1747. Proved by the witnesses.[8]

Although the father of Elizabeth Barrow is not named in the marriage contract, the fact that if she dies without issue her slaves were to be vested in John Barrow and Margaret Ransdell establishes conclusively that she was the daughter of EDWARD and ELIZABETH (MINOR) BARROW of Richmond County. Her father died leaving a will, which provided:

Will of Edward Barrow of the Parish of North Farnham in the County of Richmond, being sick and weak, dated 19 October 1732.
My Negroes be equally devided between my son John Barrow and my daughters Margaret and Elizabeth Barrow.
All the rest of my estate in Virginia and England be equally devided between John Barrow, Margaret and Elizabeth Barrow.
My beloved friends Nicholas Minor Senr. and Nicholas Minor Junr. executors.

Edward Barrows

Witnesses: Hum. Pope Junr., Wm. Bertrand, Susana (S) Bertrand.
4 June 1733. Proved by Humphrey Pope, Junr., and William Bertrand[9]

Thomas Asbury, Henry Willson and William Moxley made an inventory of the Edward Barrow estate on 22 June 1733[10]. No total valuation was

---

[8] Westmoreland County, Virginia, Wills & Deeds 10, p. 332.
[9] Richmond County, Virginia, Will Book 5, p. 199.

shown but seventeen slaves, valued at £354, were listed. Nicholas Minor and Nicholas Minor, Jr. prepared a supplementary inventory.

The three children of Edward Barrow were all very young at the time of his death. Margaret was probably the eldest, since she married before 3 December 1744 Wharton Ransdell of Westmoreland County.[11] They moved to Fauquier County, Virginia where he died testate in 1786.[12] The birth of John Barrow, son of Edward and Elizabeth Barrow, on 20 February 1729 (1730) is recorded in the North Farnham Parish Register.[13] He married Margaret Ball of Culpeper County and died there testate in 1810, without issue.[14]

Edward Barrow was the son of an earlier Edward Barrow of Richmond County who also left a will:

Will of Edward Barrow of Richmond County, being sick and weak, undated.

Unto my son Edward Barrow all my land and plantation whereon I now live, only reserving to my loving wife Ann the use of the land and plantation during her naturall life.

My executors to sell that tract of land at the mines to raise mony for to pay what mony I owe.

Unto my well beloved daughter Ann Barrow 300 acres at the Deep run comonly called the land at the Marsh in King George County.

Unto my son Edwd. two Negroes Jack and George and one mulattoe boy Will.

Unto my daughter Anne one Negro Will and one mulatoe girl Sarah.

Unto my daughter Margaret one Negro woman Hannah, one malatoe boy Emanll.

All the rest of my Negroes unto my loving wife Anne during her naturall life and after her decease equally devided between my son Edwd. and my daughter Anne and Margaret.

All my estate in England to my son Edward and alsoe my gray horse Robbin.

To my daughter Anne a caske of rum gt. forty eight gall. that stands in the shed.

---

[10] Ibid., pp. 202-3.

[11] Ibid., Order Book 11, p. 424.

[12] Fauquier County, Virginia, Will Book B, pp. 93-95. His daughter Elizabeth married Cadwallader Slaughter, son of William Lightfoot's sister Ann and her husband Francis Slaughter.

[13] *Virginia Magazine of History and Biography*, V. 7, p. 61.

[14] Culpeper County, Virginia, Will Book F, pp. 144-46. His wife was the sister of William Ball (Ibid., Will Book D, pages 385-86) who married Frances Slaughter, another child of Francis and Ann (Lightfoot) Slaughter.

All the rest of my estate to be equally divided between my wife and children Edward, Anne and Margaret Barrow.

Unto my loving friends Captain George Eskridge and Majr. Nicho. Smith each a gold ring of a ginia price, desiring them to be trustees of my estate.

My wife Anne and my son Edward executors.

Edwd. Barrow

Witnesses: Robt. Jones, Jos. Belfield, John Morton.

7 March 1721 (1722). Proved by Joseph Belfield and John Morton.[15]

An inventory of his estate was made 22 March 1721/2. While no total valuation was shown, the three Negroes listed were valued at £60.[16]

The elder EDWARD BARROW was a man of considerable prominence in Richmond County. He was a Justice of the County Court for a number of years and from March 1714/5 until his death was surveyor of the upper part of Richmond County.[17] He held the military rank of captain.[18] His home plantation consisted of 719 acres on Rappahannock Run.[19]

Since both the elder and younger Edward Barrow in their wills referred to an estate in England, it would appear that the elder Edward was an immigrant to Virginia.[20]

The Stone Family

EDWARD BARROW, SR. married ANNE (STONE) METCALFE, widow of Richard Metcalfe who died in 1698,[21] and daughter of COLONEL JOHN STONE who was a justice of Richmond at the time of its formation in 1692 and a man of considerable prominence in the county.

---

[15] Richmond County, Virginia, Will Book 4, p. 200.

[16] Ibid., pp. 201-2.

[17] Ibid., Order Books, Passim; Miscellaneous Records 1699-1724, p. 83A. See Beverley Fleet, *Virginia ColonialAbstracts*, V. 17 (Richmond, 1943), passim, for numerous references to him.

[18] Richmond County, Virginia, Miscellaneous Records 1699-1724, pp. 73A, 78A, 83A.

[19] Ibid, p. 73A.

[20] There were earlier Barrows in the Richmond County area but the name Edward does not appear in that family.

[21] Richmond County, Virginia, Miscellaneous Records 1699-1724, p. 78A.

Colonel John Stone died between 6 August 1696, the last time he sat upon the Bench as a Justice of the County Court,[22] and 1 June 1698 when the following order was entered:

Judgment is granted to Francis Meriwether against the estate of Colo. John Stone, deceased, in the hands of Mr. Richd. Metcalfe as executor...for 558 pounds of tobacco.[23]

Although Richard Metcalfe was then described as Stone's executor, the court proceedings do not indicate that the will was presented for probate until 7 June 1699:

The last will and testament of Colo. John Stone, deceased, being presented to this Court by Mrs. Ann Metcalfe, the same was proved by the oaths of Elias Wilson Senr. and Thomas Lawson witnesses thereto.[24]

No copy of John Stone's will is now of record in Richmond County.

COLONEL JOHN STONE married about 1670 SARAH () FLEET WALKER, widow first of Captain Henry Fleet (circa 1600-1660) and then of Colonel John Walker (died 1668/9).[25]

Since the estate of John Stone had become mixed with that of his son-in-law Richard Metcalfe, the order directing that an inventory be made encompassed both estates:

7 June 1699. Order of administration is granted to Mrs. Ann Metcalf upon the estate of her deceased husband Mr. Richard Metcalf within this county, she giving in security.

Ordered that Mr. Alvin Monjoy, Mr. Samuel Bayly, Mr. Rawleigh Travers, Mr. Charles Barber...do meet at the house of Mr. Richard Metcalf, deceased, and...inventory and appraise...the estate, the said appraisers...having regard to and setting apart all and singular the estate of Colo. John Stone, late deceased, and now intermixt with the estate of the said Richard Metcalf...[26]

---

[22] Richmond County, Virginia, Order Book 2, p. 160.

[23] Ibid., p. 306.

[24] Ibid., p. 405.

[25] Annie Lash Jester and Martha Woodroof Hiden, *Adventurers of Purse and Person, Virginia, 1607-1625.* (Princeton, 1956), pp. 172-4; William M Sweeney, *Wills of Rappahannock County Virginia, 1656-1692* (Lynchburg, 1947), pp. 6-7.

[26] Richmond County, Virginia, Order Book 2, pp. 405-6.

Mrs. Anne (Stone) Metcalfe Barrow was living in 1728 when her son John Metcalfe bequeathed to his "honoured mother Ann Barrow" a Negro woman named Betty and all his cattle and household stuff during her life.[27]

The Minor Family

The shield on which early knights bore their coat of arms was not always militaristic in purpose. It was protective as well as a means of distinguishing the family or lord for whom the knight wages battle but it was also the keynote in many of the jousts and tournaments held in the arenas of Medieval Europe.

These skirmishes offered the knight the practice and training in the art of warfare.

The Miniers of France and the Miners of England engaged on the field of battle and tournament wearing the colors of the family.

The Minier surname began in France in the 11th century developing from the word "mineur", a miner who worked in the pit-mines. From this humble occupation emerged several noble lines including the Miniers of Brittany who brought the name to England after the Conquest in 1066. The English spelling of the name became Minor and Miner and records indicate that the name had taken hold as early as the 12th century when Jordan le Mineur appeared in a Court function in Cumberland in the year 1195. The American line of Miners appear in Charlestown, Massachusetts, in 1632 where they founded the church. They are in direct descent to Henry Miner, a knight under Edward III of England who confirmed the family arms.

ELIZABETH (MINOR) BARROW, wife of EDWARD BARROW, was the daughter of NICHOLAS MINOR of Westmoreland County. Although she is not named in Edward Barrow's will, her father's will establishes that she survived him and married a WHERRET.

Nicholas Minor died leaving a will dated 11 October 1743 which provided:

Nicholas Minor of the parish of Cople in the county of Westmoreland being very sick and weak of body,

Unto my son William Stewart Minor ten young Negroes...when he shall attain to the age of twenty one years. In case William die without any issue to return unto my sons, John, Nicho. and Stewart Minor.

Unto my daughter Elizabeth Wherret 2000 pounds of crop tobacco over and above what I have already given her.

Unto my son William Stewart Minor my largest stil with one dozen large silver spoons at the age of twenty one years.

---

[27] Ibid., Will Book 5, Pp. 121-2.

All the rest of my personal estate unto my loving wife Jemima Minor during her natural life and after her decease my Negroes unto my sons John Minor, Nichs. Minor and Stewart Minor equally, and the rest to my sons John, Nicho., Stewart and William Stewart Minor equally.

Unto my son John Minor 536 acres in the little fork of Rappahannock which I bought of John Edy.

Unto my son Nicho. Minor 496 acres in the county of King George which I bought of John Edy, as also 330 acres in the County of Westmoreland known by the name of the White Marsh.

Unto my son Stewart Minor one tract which I bought of Joseph Scott being in the County of Richmond, as also 100 acres known by the name Watts Quarter, the mill run to be the bounds between the said Stewart Minor and my son William Stewart Minor, being part of the tract whereon I now live. For want of heirs to the male heir of my sons John Minor and Nicholas Minor equally to be divided between them, and to the heirs of my son William.

Unto my son William Stewart Minor my now dwelling house and the remainder of the tract and the mill thereon, as also 150 acres I bought of George Blackmore and for want of issue to the male heirs of my sons John, Nicholas and Stewart Minor equally.

Unto Thomas Templeman fifteen shillings.

My loving wife Jemima, my son Nicholas and my son William Stewart Minor, William Jordan Gent. and John Minor, executors.

Nicholas Minor

Witnesses: Thos. Templeman, Jno. Bridges, William Kirkham.
29 May 1744. Presented by Jemima Waddy his relict. Proved by all the witnesses.[28]

Of the four sons of Nicholas Minor, the eldest was Nicholas Minor, Jr., who was the guardian of Elizabeth (Barrow) Lightfoot. He resided in Westmoreland County for a number of years but then moved to what became Cameron Parish, Loudoun County, where he died testate in 1782.[29] The next son, John Minor, settled in what became Truro Parish, Fairfax County, and died there testate in 1753.[30] Stewart Minor, the next son, also settled in Loudoun County; whether he left descendants has not been determined. The youngest son, and apparently the only child of Nicholas

---

[28] Westmoreland County, Virginia, Wills & Deeds 10, pp. 24-26.
[29] Loudoun County, Virginia, Will Book B, pp. 432-33.
[30] Fairfax County, Virginia, Will Book B, pp. 31-32.

Minor's second marriage, was William Stewart Minor who died in Westmoreland County in 1751.[31]

Since the will of Nicholas Minor left a greater proportion of his estate to his youngest son than to the eldest, the Westmoreland County Court on 27 March 1744 entered the following order:

The last will and testament of Nicholas Minor, deceased, is ordered to be lodged till next Court for the heir at law to inspect the said will.[32]

The heir at law apparently had no objection, however, since the will was admitted to probate two months later without litigation being noted in the Order Book.

Nicholas Minor was the son of JOHN MINOR of Westmoreland County who died in 1699 leaving a will:

John Minor of the Parish of Cople in the County of Westmoreland, being sick in body, dated 30 March 1698.

To my eldest son Nicholas Minor 400 acres out of the tract of land which I now hold, and my said son to have his first choice.

Unto my second son William Minor 300 acres out of the aforementioned tract, and he to have his second choice.

Unto my youngest son John Minor 300 acres out of the said tract.

Unto my eldest daughter Frances Minor 200 acres, to have her first choice after her three brothers.

Unto my youngest daughter Eliza. Minor 200 acres next adjasent to her sister Frances Minor's land.

Unto my loving wife Ellenor Minor all her wearing apparrell. Also one third of my estate both real and personal.

The residue of my land should be sold to pay some part of my debts if occasion required.

William Read should have 100 acres in any part of my tract during his natural life.

My loving wife Ellenor Minor and my eldest son Nicholas Minor executrix and executor.

Morgan Williams should have twenty shillings to buy him a ring.

Morgan Williams and William Read executors in trust.

John Minor

Witnesses: Anthony Carpenter, Catharine Williams, Ester Kampe.

---

[31] Westmoreland County, Virginia, Deeds & Wills 9.

[32] Ibid., Order Book 1743-7. p. 22.

22 February 1698 (1699). Proved by Anthony Carpenter, and Katharine White (lately Katharine Williams), Peter Kempe being dead.[33]

John Minor is mentioned frequently in the Westmoreland County records. He was Deputy Sheriff for several years before his death:

29 November 1693. Mr. John Minor being presented by Capt. Law. Washington, High Sheriff of this County, to bee his Undersheriff in the roome and stead of Mr. Wm. Clark, deceased, was admitted and accordingly sworn.[34]

Jemima, the widow of Nicholas Minor, was married three times. She was JEMIMA WADDY daughter of Thomas Waddy of Northumberland County and married first John Spence and second Lawrence Pope.[35] Her second husband died in 1723 leaving a will that contained, among others, the following bequests:

Larrence Pope of the County of Westmoreland in the Parish of Washington, being sick and weak of body, dated 23 March 1722 (1723).
Unto my Godson John Minor, son of Nicholas Minor, one young mare.
Unto my loving brother Humphrey Pope and my brother Nicholas Minor one piece of gold weighing 33 shillings to make each of them a ring.

Lawr. Pope

24 April 1723. Presented by Jemima his relict and Humphrey his son. Proved by the witnesses.[36]

Our first information concerning the possible background of John Minor was the discovery of mention of a will written by one Lewis Gilbert dated 28 September 1625 and proved in the Prerogative Court of Canterbury 24 May 1628. In his will, Lewis Gilbert left cash legacies to (amongst others) Henry Minors, William Minors, John Minors, widow Anne Minors, Catherine wife of Robert Hadley, Jane Kidwalider wife of John Kidwalider – all of whom had gone to America – and George Minors son of Harry Minors. With the assistance of Sir Humphrey Mynors who still resides in the 15th century castle of Treago, England, we were able to locate the family from which these immigrants came. Absolute proof cannot be established because church birth records for that period are no longer

---

[33] Ibid., Deeds and Wills 2, pp. 182-182a.
[34] Ibid., Order Book 1690-98, p. 112.
[35] *William and Mary Quarterly*, 1st series, V. 13, pp. 280-82.
[36] Westmoreland County, Virginia, Deeds & Wills 7, pp. 189-92.

extant, but Sir Humphrey has assured us that there can be no doubt that the immigrant belonged to the Treago Castle Mynors.

The ancestry of John Minor as given to us by Sir Humphrey Mynors was taken from his family papers. He has provided sources only in the immediate generation preceding the birth of John. The family papers have been carefully preserved and all of this information can safely be accepted as true.

The family descends from GILBERT DE MINERS, who was holding land in County Gloucester given him by the Bishop of Worcester in the last quarter of the 11th century. The surname derives from village Les Minieres in Normandy.

Gilbert de Miners's son GILBERT II also held land in County Gloucester, given him by Miles of Gloucester. ROGER de MINERS succeeded his father Gilbert II and was granted the Manor of Westbury by Henry II.

WILLIAM DE MINERS succeeded his father Roger. This William also occurs circa 1160-70 as tenant of Burghill north of Hereford, under Roger of Hereford who was the eldest son of Miles of Gloucester.

In the first half of the 13th century the family lost both the original land in County Gloucester and at Westbury on Severn but they continued at Burghill. There is evidence of them at Burghill and its immediate neighborhood through the 14th and 15th centuries, but it has not been possible to derive a continuous line. At some time – possibly toward the end of the 14th century – they acquired land at St. Weonards, south of Hereford; the earliest date for them there is 1437.

On the evidence thus far available, a continuous line begins with:

PHILIP MINERS of Treago was born sometime between 1400 and 1415 and married ALICE, daughter of GWILLIM JOHN, son of JENKINS, of Llanfair Kilgoed, County Gwent, with one child.

RICHARD son of Philip and Alice Miners, succeeded his father to ownership of land. He was sometimes Chamberlain and Deputy Justiciar of South Wales under the Earl of Pembroke. Richard married first JOAN, daughter of WILLIAM (who was son of THOMAS) of Gillow in Hentiland, a neighbor. He married second SYBIL, daughter of SIR JAMES BASKERVILLE of Eardisley, County Hereford and kinswoman of the Countess of Pembroke. Richard retired from active service in South Wales in 1484 and, based on circumstantial evidence, is believed to have built the present house at Treago (the name Treago for the land is much older than the house). At Richard's death in March 1528 he was also holding land at Burghill. By his first wife he had five daughters whose descendants are unknown. By his second wife he had three sons. SIR ROGER was for many years Sergeant of Cellar to King Henry VII and knighted in June 1527. He married ALICE daughter of SIR HENRY

MILLS and widow of Nicholas Knyston. Sir Roger died in 1537 without issue. REGINALD was a lawyer and sometimes a Member of Parliament for Hereford but never married.

THOMAS son of Richard Miners and Sybil Baskerville succeeded to ownership because his older brothers both died without issue. He was probably the man of the name who was a Page at the Chamber of the Coronation of King Henry VIII. He married first JOAN VAUGHAN, daughter of WATKINS VAUGHAN of Hergest, County Powys. He married second ELIZABETH de THICK of Newhall, County Derby. Thomas died by his own hand in 1539. He had two children by his first wife, a daughter Sybil and a son Richard.

RICHARD was the son of Thomas Miners and Joan Vaughan. Apparently Richard was not yet of age when his father killed himself and the land must have been sequestered. At any rate, the lineage mentions that Richard had some trouble recovering his father's possessions. Richard married ANNE BURGH, daughter of THOMAS BURGH of Guildford, County Surrey. He died in 1550 when he was not yet 30 years of age leaving four young children. MABEL; RICHARD succeeded to the estate and married CATHERINE VAUGHN; JOHN married MARGARET VAUGHN and secondly MARGARET BARKLEY; and WILLIAM.

WILLIAM son of Richard Miners and Anne Burgh, was born about 1549. As a younger son, he did not inherit Treago. He lived at The Oldfield in Garway, next parish to St. Weonards. He married KATHERINE GILBERT. Katherine was the daughter of THOMAS GILBERT of Dulas and his wife ANNE PRICE and granddaughter of PHILPOTT PRICE. Katherine was a sister of Lewis Gilbert of Orcop who probably inherited the Orcop property of his grandfather Philpott Price. William died in September of 1610, leaving one son Harry.

HARRY apparently the only child of William Miners and Katherine Gilbert. Because the above mentioned William was a younger son who did not inherit Treago, the family papers of the Treago Mynors do not include descendants of Harry. That he was undoubtedly the nephew of the Lewis Gilbert who wrote the aforementioned will, leaving money to the immigrants has been established.[37] The exact relationship of the immigrant John to Harry, son of William, must be a matter of conjecture. Since it is not reasonable to assume that Lewis Gilbert would have lived long enough to leave money to grown and married great, great nieces and nephews. The only reasonable assumption that can be made is that the immigrants were his great nieces and nephews, the children of his only nephew, Harry Miners who predeceased him. This leads us to the inevitable conclusion that Harry Miners married ANNE _____; their children were HARRY,

---

[37] Reference of Book of Baglan compiled by John Williams between 1606 and 1607.

JR. (Henry), WILLIAM, JANE who married JOHN KIDWALIDER, CATHERINE married ROBERT HADLEY, JOHN, and GEORGE. George apparently remained in England; the widow Anne and her other children emigrated to the American colonies. Where Anne and the other children settled has not yet been discovered, but John settled in Westmoreland County, Virginia.

A comparison of the Mynors lineage as provided for us by Sir Humphrey Mynors from the family papers with the lineage as it is shown in Burke's *The Landed Gentry* will show a good many discrepancies.

In the first place, Burke gives the name John de Miners to the member who accompanied William the Conqueror from Normandy to England, rather than Gilbert de Miners as he is shown on family records. There are throughout succeeding generations a number of glaring errors contained in Burke's book, particularly with regard to women who married into the family. He also adds a few generations into the years between William (Roger, Gilbert, Gilbert) and Philip Miners who is shown as the first generation of continuous line. We are inclined to believe that the ancestry as given by Sir Humphrey Mynors is much more nearly correct.

Sir Humphrey Mynors does not know at what time the surname was changed from de Miners to Miners to Minors to Mynors, but he does say that the spelling has been Mynors for at least the last 200 years.

The Coat of Arms as carried by the Mynors of Treago is: Sable (black) an eagle splayed gules (red); on a chief azure (chief means top third of shield: azure is blue) bordered argent (silver) a chevron of the last (meaning last color mentioned – silver) with two crescents in chief (above the chevron) and a rose in base (below the chevron) of the second (crescent and rose are of the second mentioned color – red). Crest: a man's hand holding a bear's paw (representing "main-ours", a typical heraldic pun in French). Motto: Now shown as "Spero ut Fidelis". There is no Motto shown in the Visitation of 1530 and the age and provenance of this Motto is not known. This information was received from Sir Humphrey Mynors.

187

CHAPTER XIV

THE GOODRICH LINE OF DESCENT

The Goodrich surname is from the Anglo-Saxon name Godric, which was "so common as to make Godric and Godiva the Jack and Jill of their day." Godric, which was first used as a personal name, is recorded in the Domesday Book of 1066.

Goodrich means "son of Godric," and was first seen around the 13th century. Godric means "good ruler". The name Ambrosius Filius (son of) Godrige, who lived in Cumberland, England, around 1279 was one of the first in early records.

The first record of the Goodrich spelling is found in 1341, when James Goodrich was listed at Colchester Court. Other spellings included Godriche (1221), Goderich (1388), Gutteridge and Goodritch (1659 and Goodrich (1661).

The name Goodrich was used in other countries, including the Scandinavian countries where the name became Gudrekr.

The coat of arms was granted to the bearer of the Goodrich surname at Seling Grove in County Essex, England. The shield is blue with a gold lion on a background of gold crosses.

It seems that there were two Charles Goodriches living in Virginia at the same time. One was a son of Captain John Goodrich of Isle of Wight and the other one was a son of Colonel Thomas Goodrich of Rappahannock.

Colonel Thomas Goodrich imported himself, Anne his wife, seven Negroes and four other persons to Lower Norfolk County, for whom he received a Certificate from the Court of that county 17 June 1652, for 1250 acres. Seven of these headrights, Goodrich assigned to Peter Sexton, viz., himself, wife Anne and five Negroes. On March 31, 1653, Peter Sexton was granted 350 acres for the transportation of those seven persons, Thomas Goodrich, Anne Goodrich and five Negroes. In 1654 Thomas Goodrich testified in court at Lower Norfolk that he was aged 40. That would place his date of birth in the year 1614. He soon moved to the south side of the Rappahhannock River where on June 10, 1657, as "Major Thomas Goodrich" he patented 600 acres of land. On 16 March 1657/58 he also patented 400 acres in the same place as "Lieutenant Colonel" Thomas Goodrich. He patented 1134 acres and 2000 acres with the same designation, and in the same place on 12 June 1664. He joined Nathaniel Bacon in "Bacon's Rebellion" in 1676 and was appointed by him Lieutenant General in charge of forces along the Rappahannock and Potomac. When the Rebellion collapsed the General was sentenced by a Berkeley Court Martial to be hanged. The timely intervention of influential friends and loyal members, of the House of Burgesses allowed him to go free. With the stipulation that he "with a rope around his neck and on his knees, did beg for his life," from the Governor and Council and upon payment of a fine of 50,000 pounds of tobacco.

Colonel Thomas Goodrich made his will March 15, 1678/9 which was, probated April 3, 1679. He bequeathed "to eldest son Benjamin 300 acres of land on the riverside bought of Clement Thresh. To his son Joseph he bequeathed ½ of the dividend of land called "Matapony" containing 1800 acres. To his son Charles he bequeathed a tract of land containing 400 acres joining upon the dividend I settled on Hoskins Pocoson. To his daughter Ann he bequeathed 900 acres of land being a moiety of dividend called "Matapony". To his son Peter he bequeathed 800 acres part of dividend called Hoskins Pocoson. To his daughter Kathrine he bequeathed 800 acres of part of the dividend of 4000 aforesaid.

Ann Goodrich married Colonel John Lightfoot a Member of the Council and Commander in chief of King and Queen County Militia.

Benjamin Goodrich, the eldest son, of James City County, in 1703 deeded.... Three of Benjamin Goodrich's children are evidently mentioned in a lawsuit. "Robert Goodrich, living in James City, Thomas Ravenscroft, next friend to Anne Goodrich, and Elizabeth Goodrich, infant orphans of Benjamin Goodrich: versus the petition of Phillip Ludwell for an acre of land on Chickerhouse Creek, James City, November 17, 1719.

COLONEL THOMAS GOODRICH *was born 1614 and married* ANNE SHERWOOD. *Their offsprings were* BENJAMIN, JOSEPH, CHARLES, ANN, PETER *and* KATHERINE. *Benjamin had* ROBERT, ANNE *and* ELIZABETH *married* WILLIS WILSON.

Here is a shortened list of the Goodrich lineage to John Lightfoot and Ann Goodrich.

EDWARD GOODRICH *of Kirby, co. Lincoln married* JANE WILLIAMSON *daughter of* JAMES WILLIAMSON, ESQUIRE *in 1465.* HENRY GOODRICH *was born in 1487 and married* MARGARET RAWSON *daughter of* CHRISTOPHER RAWSON *in 1508.*

RICHARD GOODRICH *of Ribston was born in 1510 and married* CLARE NORTON *daughter of* RICHARD NORTON, ESQUIRE *of Norton Conyers.*

RICHARD GOODRICH *of Goodrich Castle, Herfordshire, England, married* MURIEL EVANS *daughter of* SIR WILLIAM EVANS, *Lord of Eure.*

JOHN GOODRICH *married* REBECCA ALLEN.

LIEUTENANT GENERAL THOMAS GOODRICH *was born in 1614 and married* ANNE SHERWOOD.

ANN GOODRICH *was married in 1681 to* COLONEL JOHN LIGHTFOOT *who was born in 1644 the son of* JOHN LIGHTFOOT.

The first civil war of America, the "Bacon's Rebellion of 1676" was caused by the smoldering grievances of Virginia's small planters. The planters and settlers were being attacked indiscriminately by bands of Indians and the Governor was using impractical and ineffective means of stopping the attacks.

Finally under the direction of Nathaniel Bacon, a wealthy gentleman and a member of the Governor's Council, who was sympathetic to their hardships, the planters retaliated and attacked a peace loving tribe on the Carolina border. This was done without the Governor's permission. There were many skirmishes against the Indians and against the Governor's troops, and eventually led to the rule of Virginia by the planters. Bacon had started the war to change Indian policy and found himself in control of the colony.

The fighting got out of hand with the planters and settlers attacking not only the Indians but burning the plantations of loyalists to the Governor, as well. Many of the rebels denounced Bacon and rejoined Berkeley to stop the plundering and burning. Havoc reigned in Virginia.

Bacon continued to manage enough men for another Indian campaign until his sudden death by disease in October of 1676. Along the Rappahannock, a unit of the old northern force under Colonel Thomas Goodrich remained in action.

Warships and troops from England crushed the rebellion in late 1676, but not until after many casualties to settlers of the western Tidewater. The King of England pardoned the rebels, but Governor Berkeley executed them in large numbers anyway. Many like Colonel Thomas Goodrich were lucky to get away with a heavy fine and had to beg on their knees to the Governor and Council for their lives. It was only because they knew the right people in the right places that they survived. John Lightfoot being a hot head was still raising his voice about the Indian trouble. The Indian trouble continued in the colonies. The King did replace Governor Berkeley, and heavy taxes were levied on the settlers because of monies lost during the Rebellion.

The rebels may have lost this war, but the repercussions did start a low flame that was slowly stoked until it became the raging fire of the Revolutionary War.

CHAPTER XV

A PRICELESS HERITAGE-MAGNA CHARTA

To all descendants of Colonel John Lightfoot, Councillor of Virginia (died 1707) and his wife, Ann Goodrich, daughter of Thomas Goodrich, Lieutenant Colonel in Bacon's Rebellion:

KNOW YE THAT:

Seven hundred and eighty-seven years ago, on June 15, 1215, your ancestor Saere de Quincey, Earl of Winchester, a gallant knight, came with a group of other knights as gallant as he to challenge King John, and wrest from him the crushed liberties of his Anglo-Saxon subjects.

In the meadow of Runnymede they assembled, dauntless and determined. The place chosen, had for generations been a favorite meeting place of kings in council, Runnymede – a meadow of council – was, in 1215, already a memorable spot. Under an ancient and venerable oak (whose boughs and branches had looked down on the ceremonies of Druids), at a spot where the valley of the Thames River widens out in quiet beauty. Between Windsor and Staines', the Saxon Kings had been wont to gather their people about them to discuss questions of more than usual importance.

[1]In January it had been arranged that the parties should meet at Northampton on Low Sunday, 26 April. The barons came in arms. The northerners mustered at Stamford in Easter week and then marched south, gathering strength as they went. Before they reached Northampton they were joined by Robert fitz Walter, Geoffrey de Mandeville, and presumably other men from East Anglia. The king did not come; all he did was to issue a safe conduct of 23 April lasting up to 28 May to those who came to speak with him through the mediation of the archbishop. Indeed he spent the second half of Easter week at some of his usual haunts in the southern countries. Not until the 30 April, when he reached Wallingford,

---

[1] Magna Charta, J.C. Holt, pp. 143-144.

was he within reasonable distance of the palace appointed for the negotiations. By then the barons had moved to Brackley, a manor of one of their party, [2]Saere de Quincey, Earl of Winchester, and there they seem to have remained during the course of the negotiations. The king meanwhile moved restlessly between Wallingford, Reading, and London. Hence, the principals never met; the argument was carried on through mediators, usually through the archbishop and William Marshal, Earl of Pembroke.

[3]The fall of London was decisive. If Bouvines brought on a political crisis and Pope Innocent III's intervention, a war, the baronial seizure of London led directly to Runnymede, for it forced the king to go much further in accepting the baronial demands than he had done hitherto. The barons apparently exploited their good fortune by bringing pressure to bear on the waverers, and many only joined the cause against the king at this late stage. Letters of 25 May provided for safe conduct up to the 31st, for Saere de Quincey, Earl of Winchester, to come and speak with the king. Letters of the 27th provided for a similar safe conduct for Stephen Langton and those who came with him to Staines.

[4]The phrases of the letters of safe conduct issued between 25 May and 8 June suggest that the negotiations were now producing something concrete. The letters of the 25th and 27th issued in favor of Saere de Quincey, Langton, and his companions, state that these men were coming "to treat concerning peace".

[5]Hence the last stage of the settlement, the firm peace of 19 June, came only after a period of intensive negotiation and hard committee work. Peace was secured or made "firm" by the renewal of the barons' homage, for by this and this alone was the state of war consequent on the [6]baronial defiance brought to an end. It was a serious and formal act, which must have been carried out by each erstwhile rebel individually, in an atmosphere of due solemnity – the renewal of homage and the restraint of royal agents were the essentials of peace. The king would not grant, nor would the barons accept, a concession of privileges while still at war, for it would offend the majesty of the one and deny legal title to the other. The point is clearly made in royal letters, of 21 June, addressed to Saere de

---

[2] Ancestor's name spelled Quincey, Quincy, Quince and Quenci. Saere de Quincey was born before 1154, and died November 3, 1219, as a Crusader on the way to the Holy Land. He married Margaret Bellemont, daughter of the Earl of Leicester, who died 12 of January 1235/36.

[3] Magna Charta, J.C. Holt, p. 153.

[4] Magna Charta, J.C. Holt, p. 155.

[5] Magna Charta, J.C. Holt, p. 163.

[6] Among the Twenty-five, Roger Bigod, William de Albini, and Saere de Quincey had acted as justices.

Quincey, Earl of Winchester. "We order you to restore the castle of Fotheringay, which we have committed to your custody, to Earl David as soon as he has done homage to us, and if by change he dies before he has done homage then you shall restore the castle to us."

[7]The rebel barons must have been aware of the need to produce a legally watertight agreement. They were not without administrative experience, and they chose their most experienced administrator, [8]Saere de Quincey, Earl of Winchester, to conduct the final negotiations.

[9]An even longer chain of conveyance was revealed in 1220 on the death of Saere de Quincey, Earl of Winchester. It was then reported to the Crown that Robert de Vieuxpont had disseised Saere's son and heir Roger de Quincey, of Liddel and its appurtenances, which Nicholas de Stuteville had assigned to his nephew Eustace de Stuteville until he came of age. The custody of the land had come into the hands of William de Valoines. He bequeathed it on his death to Saere de Quincey and Saere subsequently gave it to Roger. Robert de Vieuxpont was now ordered to restore the custody to Roger.

Cardinal Stephen Langton, Archbishop of Canterbury, and Saere de Quincey had previously met with King John to try to work out the terms of the charter. On the date set for the accepting of the charter, with the Barons came the Marshal of their arms, Robert fitz Walter, and a great concourse of the Nobility of England. With King John came only four and twenty persons of any note, most of who despised him, and were merely his advisors in form.

The Barons embodied their demands in the form of a Royal Grant scrupulously respecting constitutional usage. Stephen Langton (a true English patriot, appointed by a foreign Pope, without consultation of the English Church) read the draft to King John. John swore furiously, the tradition goes, that "they might as well ask the kingdom at once!" However, the only alternative to signing was the loss of his kingdom, so on that great day, and in that great company, the king conceded, confirmed and set his seal to the Magna Charta.

[10]Magna Charta – or Great Charte, a document forming part of the English Constitution and regarded as the Foundation of English liberty. It was extorted from King John by the confederated barons in 1215. Its most

---

[7] Magna Charta, J.C. Holt, p. 196.

[8] Saere was a baron of the Exchequer, named first after the justiciar, Geoffrey fitz Peter, in 1212. He was a member of the bench at Westminster, sitting with Simon of Pattishall and others, in Michaelmas, 1213.

[9] Magna Charta, J.C. Holt, p. 215.

[10] New Practical Reference Library, V. III, Page (Not numbered), Published 1913 – Roach-Fowler Publishing Company.

important articles provided, that no free man shall be taken, or imprisoned, or proceeded against, except by lawful judgement of his peers, or by the law of the land. And that no scutage or aid shall be imposed in the kingdom (except certain feudal dues from tenants of the crown), except by the common council of the kingdom. The remaining and greater part of the charter is directed against abuses of the king's power a feudal superior.

On that little island on the Thames, near Windsor, called Magna Charta Island, and on it where John met the Barons to put his seal on a lump of wax to show that he "signed" and consented to keep the promises set out in the Charter. He was in a furious state of anger all the time. It is said that as soon as the deed was done "he threw himself on the ground, gnashing his teeth, and gnawing sticks and straws in rage".

The charter was confirmed several times during the reigns that succeeded John's, and the form adopted in the reign of Edward I was set down in the statute books. The most accurate and complete copy of the original charter is that preserved in Lincoln Cathedral. The board of commissioners on the public records ordered a facsimile of it to be engraved, and it has been frequently translated into English.

The pope supported John and freed him from his promises, and crowds of foreign soldiers came to help John to burn, and rob, and kill all over the country. It was a troublous time. Louis of France evidently felt he was going to take John's place – you can see amongst the charters a grant from him, giving away the town of Grimsby. Then the end came suddenly.

John had to cross the Wash, that broad inlet between Lincolnshire and Norfolk. When the tide is out, there are miles of sands, and the long train of carts and wagons which were carrying the king's treasures were lost in soft quicksand as the tide came flowing in. Quite lately a handsome cup was washed up near the shore of the Wash, and it is believed to be part of this lost treasure of King John. The grief and worry of it all caused John's death.

[11]Writs of the 19 June, enrolled on the dorse of the Patent roll, provided for the enforcement of the oath to the Twenty-five (barons); for the election of the juries of twelve who were to inquire into evil customs; and for the public reading of the Charter throughout the county. Saere de Quincey, Earl of Winchester, another member of the Twenty-five received the writs for Warwickshire and Leicestershire.

[12]The Twenty-five Barons were: Richard, Earl of Clare; William de Fors, Earl of Aumale; Geoffrey de Mandeville, Earl of Clauceste, Saere de Quincey, Earl of Winchester; Henry de Bohun, Earl of Hereford; Roger Bigod, Earl of Norfolk; Robert de Vere, Earl of Oxford; William Marshal

---

[11] Magna Charta, J.C. Holt, pp. 247-248.
[12] Magna Charta, J.C. Holt, p. 338.

Junior; Robert fitz Walter; Gilbert de Clare; Eustace de Vesci; Hugh Bigod; William de Mowbray; William de Lanvallei; Robert de Ros; John de Lacy, Constable of Chester; Richard de Percy; John fitz Robert; William Malet; Geoffrey de Saye; Roger de Montbegon; William of Huntingfield; Richard de Montfichet; William de Albini of Belvoir; and the Mayor of London.

Listed below is a brief summary of the Magna Charta.

He pledged –
To maintain the Church in its rights…
To relieve the Barons of oppressive obligations as vassals of the crown, and the Barons in their turn pledged themselves to relieve their vassals, the people;
To respect the liberties of London, and all other cities and boroughs;
To protect foreign merchants who came to England;
To imprison no man without a fair trial; and
To sell, delay, nor deny justice to no man.

As the Barons well knew his falseness, they further required as their securities:

That he should send out of his kingdom all his foreign troops,
That for two months they should hold possession of the city of London, and that Stephen Langton hold possession of the Tower of London,
That five and twenty of their body, chosen by themselves, should be a lawful committee to watch the keeping of the charter, and
To make war upon him if he broke it.

King John was obliged to sign it.

The charter was confirmed several times during the reigns that succeeded John's, and the form adopted in the reign of Edward I was set down in the statute books. The most accurate and complete copy of the original charter is that preserved in Lincoln Cathedral. The board of commissioners on the public records ordered a facsimile of it to be engraved, and it has been frequently translated into English. [13] In the British Museum hangs a copy of the Great Charter, often called by its Latin name, Magna Charta. It was forced from King John, with great courage and difficulty, by the barons. In it he had promised certain rights to the people, so that they might live in safety under good government. This Great Charter, which is often called the foundation-stone on which liberty was built, was drawn up from the

---

[13] The Book of Knowledge – V. 5, p. 1571.

charter which Henry I gave to the people when he became king, which, again, was established upon the laws of Edward the Confessor and Alfred. Four hundred years later a charter called the Petition of Rights, based on Magna Charta, was presented to King Charles I for signature.

England's Magna Charta laid the foundation of the present form of habeas corpus in all English-speaking nations. The usefulness of the writ against public officers became firmly established in the days of the Stuarts. It has been a part of English law since that time, and has been carried over into the legal systems of the United States and Canada.

CHAPTER XVI

THE SURETY BARONS

There were twenty-five original Surety Barons. Twenty-two of them were linked either before or after the signing of the Magna Charta by marriage. Intermarriage was what the families did then to keep their properties in the family or to increase their properties or lordships. If any of the twenty-five died or parted from the group then another baron would be picked in his place, so long as there were twenty-five Surety Barons. Of the original twenty-five only one deserted within the first year of the signing of the Magna Charta. Roger de Montbegon deserted and Roger de Mowbray replaced him as a Surety Baron. Neither of them had issue. Sixteen of the first Surety Barons died within 15 years of the signing. Pope Innocent III excommunicated all of them for their part in the rebellion and in the drafting and signing of the Charter of Liberty or the Magna Charta as it is known.

ANCESTRAL ROLL CALL OF HONOR

William d'Albini
Roger Bigod
Hugh Bigod
Henry de Bohum
Richard de Clare[*]
Gilbert de Clare*
John fitz Robert
Robert fitz Walter
William de Huntingfield*
John de Lacie*
William de Lanvallei
William Malet
William de Mowbray*
Saire de Quincey*
Robert de Roos

---

[*] Ancestors proved by Edith Ellen Williams

Geoffrey de Saye
Robert de Vere*
Names of other Barons with no issue living today:
William de Fortibus
William de Hardell
Geoffrey de Mandeville
William Marshall, Jr.
Roger de Montbegon
Richard de Montfichet
Richard de Percy
Eustace de Vesci

William d'Albini
Lord of Belvoir Castle, Leicestershire

The seat of William d'Albini, the Surety, was Belvoir Castle founded in 1088 by Robert de Todeni, or Toni. D'Albini succeeded to the Castle in 1167/8.

Located on the great Northwest Southeast Road built by the Romans and known to later Englishmen as Watling Street is the Castle of Rochester, where William d'Albini had his real struggle with King John.

The King appeared on the scene in person during the siege that continued for seven weeks. William and his men held the Castle against the King and his mercenaries with the outer wall badly damaged. The soldiers had to resort to the keep. When John's soldiers made a breach in the wall and attempted to enter, they were promptly repelled. The siege continued until hunger and thirst forced their surrender. All of d'Albini's men were killed. Their leader was spared, but he had to spend a long time in a medieval prison and was heavily fined.

William was the third Baron of his family. When his father died he was ward to King Henry II and, in 1194, he was in the army of Richard I in Normandy. Already a wealthy man at the time of the accession of John to the throne, he received several additional grants of great value. In 1201, when the Barons refused to follow their Sovereign into France, King John demanded that their castles should be given up to him as security for their allegiance, beginning with William d'Albini, and therewith Belvoir Castle, instead of which d'Albini gave him his son, William, as a hostage.

He appears to have remained faithful longer to King John than most of the other Barons. He did not join the insurgents until he could no longer with safety remain neutral or adhere to the King for, as late as January 1214/5, he was one of King John's commissioners appointed for the safe conduct of such as were traveling to his Court at Northampton.

After he joined the Baron's party, d'Albini looked upon with suspicion by the other Sureties, entered with great spirit to their cause. They were suspicious because he did not attend the grand tournament in Staine's Wood on 29 June 1215, to celebrate the victory. It wasn't until the other Barons had alarmed him that he fortified his Castle and joined the others in London. After the siege of Rochester Castle, King John ordered that all the nobles in the Castle be hanged. But his chief counselors resolutely opposed this sentence and William d'Albini and his son Odonel, with several other Barons, were merely committed to the custody of Peter de Mauley, and sent as prisoners to Corfe and Nottingham Castles.

While d'Albini remained at Corfe, the King marched, on Christmas morning 1216, from Nottingham to Langar near Belvoir Castle, and sent a summons to surrender. Upon this, Nicholas d'Albini, one of the Baron's sons and a Clerk in Orders delivered the keys to the King, asking only that his father should be mercifully treated. The Fortress was then committed to the custody of Geoffrey and Oliver de Buteville. William's liberty was gained by paying to the King a fine of 6,000 marks (more than £4,000) and his wife raised the sum from his own lands. After King John's death, though he submitted himself to King Henry III, William d'Albini was forced to give his wife and son Nicholas as hostages for his allegiance, but in 1217 he was one of the King's commanders at the Battle of Lincoln. He died at Offington 1 May 1236, and his body was buried in Newstead, and *'his heart under the wall opposite the high altar'* at Belvoir Castle.

He married Margaret Umfraville and his daughter Agnes later married William de Mowbray.

Roger Bigod
Earl of Norfolk (and Suffolk)

Bigod is the name associated with Framlingham Castle in Suffolk. It remained in the Bigod family for some generations, then passed into the hands of the Mowbrays.

Roger Bigod, 2nd Earl of Norfolk and Suffolk was born about 1150. He married Isabella Plantagenet; daughter of Hameline Plantagenet, who descended from the Earls of Warren, and had six children, the first one being Hugh Bigod, one of the Sureties' for the Magna Charta.

It is fitting that, after Richard's return to England after his captivity in Germany, Roger Bigod was chosen to be one of the four Earls who carried the silken canopy for the King, as Hugh Bigod had borne the Royal scepter in the Royal procession.

Roger Bigod was appointed in 1189 by King Richard one of the Ambassadors to King Philip of France, to obtain aid for the recovery of the Holy Land. In 1191 he was keeper of Hereford Castle. He was chief judge in the King's Court from 1195 to 1202. In 1202 he was sent by King John as one of his messengers to summon William the Lion, King of Scotland, to do homage to him in the Parliament which was held in Lincoln, and subsequently attended King John into Poitou. On his return he changed sides and became one of the strongest advocates of the Charter of Liberty. He died before August 1221.

Hugh Bigod
The Earl of Norfolk's Heir

Hugh Bigod, 3rd Earl of Norfolk and Suffolk was born before 1195. He took part from the beginning in the Barons' Magna Charta proceedings. He married Maud Marshall, eldest daughter of William Marshall, the Protector and sister to William Marshall, Magna Charta Baron, about 1212. They had four children. Maude died in 1247 and Hugh died in February of 1224/25.

Henry de Bohun
Earl of Hereford

The name of Bohun suggests Hereford. Henry de Bohun, the Surety, was born before 1177. He became the first Earl of Hereford of the family, the title being created by the Charter of King John, dated 28 April 1199. Even though he took the Barons' side against the King, on becoming Earl of Hereford he had promised that he would never make any claim against John or his heirs, on the basis of a Charter given to his great uncle Roger by Henry II. The office of Lord High Constable of England he inherited from his father, but he seems to have played no other active part in John's government. As he took a prominent part with the Barons against King John, his lands were confiscated, but he received them again at the granting of the Magna Charta. After King John died he became one of the commanders of the Army of Louis the Dauphin, at the Battle of Lincoln, and was taken prisoner by William Marshall. After this defeat he joined Saire de Quincey and other Magna Charta Barons in a pilgrimage to the Holy Land in 1220, and died on the passage 1 June 1220. His body was brought home and buried in the chapter house of Llanthony Abbey in Gloucestershire.

He married Maude fitz Geoffrey de Mandeville, Countess of Essex, daughter of Geoffrey fitz Piers, Baron de Mandeville, and his first wife, Beatrix Saye. After his death Maude remarried and died 27 August 1236.

Richard de Clare
Earl of Hertford

The Hertford Castle of the de Clares is one of two Castles; Gilbert de Clare built a Castle at Caerdigan, Pembrokeshire, Wales. A marriage brought it into the hands of William Marshall, who soon controlled the strongest castles on the peninsula. Of all the castles that finally came into William Marshall's possession, this was the most important to the area. Scholars believe there is evidence that it was originally built of wood.

Richard de Clare, 4th Earl of Hertford, like his father and uncle was more generally called the Earl of Clare. He married Amice, Countess of Gloucester, second daughter of William fitz Robert, Earl of Gloucester, and his wife Hawise, daughter of Robert de Bellemont, Earl of Leicester. Richard died sometime between 3 October and 28 November 1217 and Amice died 1 January 1224/5.

He was present at the Coronation of King Richard I at Westminster, 3 September 1189, and of King John, 27 May 1199. He sided with the Barons against King John, and his Castle at Tonbridge was taken. On 9 November 1215 he was one of the commissioners who, on the part of the Barons, was to talk of peace with the King. On 4 March 1215/6 his lands in counties Cambridge, Norfolk, Suffolk, and Essex were granted to Robert de Betun.

Gilbert de Clare
the Earl of Hertford's Heir

Gilbert de Clare, son of Surety Richard de Clare, and himself a Surety, was born about 1180. He married Isabella Marshall, sister of William Marshall the Surety and daughter of William Marshall the Protector, on 9 October 1217. Their daughters were: Agnes (Rose), who became the wife of Roger de Mowbray, grandson of the Surety, William de Mowbray, and Isabel Clare, born 2 November 1226. Isabel married in May 1240 to Robert Bruce, son and heir to Robert Bruce, Lord of Annandale and his wife Isabel, and second daughter of David, Earl of Huntingdon.

In June 1202 he was entrusted with the lands of Harfleur and Mostrevilliers. He was one of the Barons still opposing the arbitrary proceedings of the Crown. He championed Louis the Dauphin, fighting at Lincoln under the Baronial banner, and was taken prisoner by William Marshall, whose daughter he later married. He led an army against the Welsh in 1228 and captured Morgan Gam, who was released the next year. After an engagement in Brittany, he died on his return at Penros in that Duchy 25 October 1230. His body was conveyed to Tewkesbury, where he was buried before the high alter, 10 November 1230. His widow Isabella erected a monument there.

John fitz Robert
Lord of Warkworth Castle, Northumberland

John fitz Robert, the Surety, married Ada Baliol, and in her right became lord of Barnard Castle, whose founder was Barnard Baliol.

This same Surety, fitz Robert, was also lord of the handsome Warkworth Castle in the border country of Northumberland.

When the Barons met at Saint Edmondsbury, John fitz Robert, the Surety was still loyal to King John and was, with John Marshall, joint governor of the Castles of Norwich and Oxford. Subsequently he joined the insurrection, and took such a prominent part that the King seized his lands. He returned allegiance in the next reign, his Castles and vast estates were returned to him, and he was constituted High Sheriff of co. Northumberland and governor of New-Castle-upon-Tyne. He died in 1240, the same year as his father.

Robert fitz Walter
Lord of Dunmow Castle, Essexshire

Robert fitz Walter, the Surety, was third lord Dunmow Castle and leader of the Magna Charta Barons and their Army, styled "Marshal of the Army of God and the Holy Church." The first public act recorded of this subsequently important Baron and standard bearer of the City of London conveys at first a bad impression of him. It is recorded that *"in 5th John 1203 Robert fitz Walter, being trusted, together with Saire de Quincey, also a Surety, to keep the Castle of Ruil in France, delivered it up to the King of that realm as soon as he came before it with an army."* This appears to imply a measure of cowardice rather than disloyalty, but in a short time it was proven to which of these motives the deed was to be ascribed. There was a possibility that fitz Walter and Quincey surrendered the Castle for a false bribe from Philip. It is also likely that the two were involved in a general baronial conspiracy against John, knowing that he would have to be lenient with them. In 1212 John was being unusually careful about the use of the exchequer seal, possibly fearing Baronial plotting for Canons of St. Paul's, intimates of exchequer officials, were known to be involved in fitz Walter's conspiracy. There is also controversy over fitz Walter's later hasty departure for France. Whether it was because of John's alleged seduction of Robert's daughter or his refusal to live under the reign of an excommunicate King, we cannot say.

At the time the Barons, at home and abroad, were preparing to compel King John to keep his promises in the matter of the proposed statutes, several conspiracies to this end were discovered, wherein Robert fitz Walter was materially concerned. On the discovery of his "treasonable practices," fitz Walter, with his wife and children, sought refuge in France; but the following year, 1213, his friends persuaded him to return home, and, with the other Barons, he was reconciled to King John. But this friendship was only of short duration. Soon it was discovered that he was still plotting against the King in the interests of reform in the government; so his residence in London, the Castle of Baynard, was in consequence almost entirely destroyed, and the hatred between King John and fitz Walter became yet more violent. His lands were seized, effectually binding him to discontented Barons and the people. The active spirit of fitz Walter made him a desirable leader for their party, and he was selected as one of the commissioners who hoped to cement the differences of opinion at a meeting at Erith Church, and subsequently was elected their leader.

After the granting of Magna Charta, when King John endeavored to elude his promises, fitz Walter was one of the committee of the baronial party who went to France to invite Dauphin to accept the throne of England. On this Prince's coming, he with William de Mandeville and William de Huntingfield, the Sureties, reduced the counties of Essex and Suffolk to the authority of the Dauphin. Upon the accession of Henry III, fitz Walter, then a prisoner, along with a majority of the rebel Barons, finding the Dauphin a useless political factor, dropped him and sent him back to France. In 1218, although he was a prisoner, fitz Walter was allowed to assume the Cross and join a Crusade. He took part in the famous siege of Damietta, returned home and died a peaceful death in 1234. He was buried before the High Altar of Dunmow Priory.

Notwithstanding his enmity to King John and King Henry III, and the frequent confiscation of his property, fitz Walter died possessed of an extensive estate. His first wife was Gunora, daughter of Robert, second Lord of Valoines, and he married second, Rohese, who survived him. By his first wife, fitz Walter had, with other children, a daughter, Matilda the Fair, called "Maid Marion," said to have been poisoned by King John.

William de Huntingfield
A feudal baron in Suffolk

Dover Castle, the stronghold that William de Huntingfield held in the Barons' War, is a famous one, fulfilling the dream of the grim place of nameless cruelties and horrible prisons.

William de Huntingfield, the Surety, born about 1165, married Isabel Gressinghall, widow of Osmond de Stuteville. He was made constable of Dover Castle in 1204, and delivered up his son and daughter as hostages for his loyalty to the King. The son was to remain with the Earl of Arundel, the daughter with Earl Ferrers.

He was one of five wardens of the Ports of Norfolk and Suffolk from 1210 to 1212, and the following year he was one of the itinerant justices of Lincoln. He was High Sheriff of Norfolk and Suffolk until the end of 1214. He witnessed King John's grant of freedom of election to churches in 1214. He was governor of Sauvey Castle in Leistershire when he joined the cause of the Barons in arms against King John. His lands were then given to Nicholas de Haya. According to the close and patent rolls he was one of the men actively in rebellion against King John before the issuance of the

Magna Charta. Very likely the cause of the Protector's severity toward Huntingfield was that he was one of those who plotted to have the Dauphin come to England and, after the Dauphin's landing, was very active in reducing the Courts of Essex and Suffolk to French authority. He fought at Lincoln 20 May 1217, and was taken prisoner by the King's forces. William had a daughter, Alice Huntingfield, who her father paid the King a fine of "six fair Norway Goshawks," in the 15th of King John, for permission to marry. Alice was the widow of Richard de Solers. William de Huntingfield, the Surety, died 25 January 1220/1 on a Crusade.

John de Lacie
Lord of Halton Castle, Cheshire

The Lacie strongholds on the Welsh border are Beeston, Chester and Halton Castles.

John de Lacie, the Surety, born 1192, seventh Baron of Halton Castle and hereditary constable of Chester, was one of the earliest Barons to take up arms at the time of Magna Charta. He was also appointed to see that the new statutes were properly carried into effect and observed in the counties of York and Nottingham. Upon the accession of King Henry III, he joined a party of noblemen and made a pilgrimage to the Holy Land, rendering valuable service at the Siege of Damietta.

In 1232 Lacie was made Earl of Lincoln and, in 1240, governor of Chester and Beeston Castles. He died 22 July 1240, and was buried in the Cistercian Abbey of Stanlaw in co. Chester. His first wife was Alice, daughter of Gilbert d'Aquila, but by her he had no issue. She died in 1215 and he married second, after his marked gallantry at the Siege of Damietta, Margaret, only daughter and heiress of Robert de Quincey, a fellow Crusader, who died in the Holy Land, eldest son of Saire de Quincey, the Surety. They had three children; Lady Margaret survived him and married second Walter Marshall, Earl of Pembroke.

William de Lanvallei
Lord of Stanway Castle, Essex

William de Lanvallei, the Surety, died 1217. He was governor of Colchester Castle in 1215, when he joined the insurgent Barons. He also had Stanway Castle, which has since crumbled to dust. In 1212 Alan Basset of Wycombe, co. Bucks (father of Philip Basset, Chief Justice of England, who is named in the Magna Charta as one of the King's liegemen) gave the King two hundred marks and "an excellent palfrey." This was so that his daughter Hawise might be married to William de Lanvallei.

William Malet
Lord of Curry-Malet, Somersetshire

William Malet, the Surety, was mentioned as a minor in the year 1194, in connection with an expedition made that year into Normandy. His principal estate was Curry-Malet. From 1210 to 1214 he was sheriff of counties Somerset and Dorset. He then joined the Barons against King John and became one of the Sureties. He had lands in four counties which were confiscated and given to his son-in-law, Hugh de Vivonia and to Thomas Basset, his father-in-law. He was also fined 2,000 marks, but the sum was not paid until after his death, and at that time 1,000 marks were remitted, being found due to him for military service to King John in Poitou. William Malet died about 1217, having married Mabel, also called Alice and Aliva, daughter of Thomas Basset of Headington.

William de Mowbray
Lord of Axholme Castle, Lincolnshire

William de Mowbray, the Surety, came of age in 1194/5. He was early embittered against King John by being compelled to surrender the Barony of Frontboeuf, which Henry I had conferred upon his great grandfather, Sir Nigel d'Aubigny. That, and the aid exacted from his vassals, enraged him. We note in Magna Charta, Article 16, that a lord is forbidden to demand more service than a fief owes. Perhaps William was influential in getting this clause accepted. The debt was probably exacted because Mowbray, upon the accession of King John, was tardy in pledging his allegiance and at length swore fealty only on condition that "the King should render to every man his right." At the breaking out of the Baronial war, he was governor of York Castle, and it is not surprising that he at once sided with the Barons against King John, and was one of the most forward among them.

He was a party to the "Covenant for holding the City and Tower of London." He continued in arms after the death of King John and in the Battle of Lincoln he was taken prisoner. His lands were confiscated and bestowed upon William Marshall, Jr., the Surety, but he was subsequently allowed to redeem them. After this he attached himself to King Henry III. He died in 1223/4 at his Castle in the Isle of Axholme, and was buried in the Abbey of Newburgh in Yorkshire. His wife was Avice d'Albini.

Saire de Quincey
Earl of Winchester

Saire de Quincey, the Surety, born before 1154, was a Baron present at Lincoln when William the Lion of Scotland did homage to the English monarch in October 1200. He obtained large grants and immunities from King John and was created Earl of Winchester, 2 March 1207, having been governor in 1203 of the Castle of Ruil in Normandy. He is created with rewriting Magna Charta from the Charter of King Henry I and the Saxon Code. Because he had opposed the King's concession to the Pope's legate, he was bitterly hated by King John. He was one of the Barons to whom the City and Tower of London were resigned. The other Barons sent him, with Robert fitz Walter, the Surety, to invite the Dauphin of France to assume the Crown of England and even after the death of King John, he kept a strong garrison in Montsorell Castle in behalf of Prince Louis. When the Barons, being greatly outnumbered, were defeated by the troops of King Henry III, Saire de Quincey, with many others, was made prisoner and his estates forfeited. In the following October his immense estates were restored upon his submission. In 1218 the Earl of Winchester went with the Earls of Chester and Arundel to the Holy Land, assisted at the siege of Damietta in 1219, and died 3 November in the same year, on the way to Jerusalem. His wife was Margaret Bellemont, whom he married before 1173.

Robert de Roos
Lord of Hamlake Castle, Yorkshire

The Barons de Roos owned Helmsley or Hamlake Castle. Robert de Roos of Fursan, the Surety, fourth Baron of Hamlake Manor, was born in 1177. When only fifteen years of age he had paid a thousand marks' fine for livery of his lands, and in 1197 when aged twenty years, while with the King of Normandy, he was arrested, though we know nothing of the offense. He was committed to the custody of Hugh de Chaumont. However, de Chaumont trusted his prisoner to William de Spiney, and the latter allowed him to escape out of the Castle Bonville. King Richard thereupon hanged de Spiney and collected a fine of twelve hundred marks, about £800, from Roos' guardian as the price of his continued freedom.

When John became King, he gave young Roos the whole Barony of his great grandmother's father, Walter d'Espec, as conciliation. About the 14th of King John, Robert assumed the habit of a monk, whereupon the custody of all his lands and Castle Werke, were committed to Philip d'Ulcote. But Robert did not long continue as a recluse, as in about a year he was executing the office of High Sheriff of co. Cumberland. At the beginning of the struggle of the Barons for a constitutional government, he at first sided with King John and, in consequence, obtained some valuable grants from the Crown. He was made governor of Carlisle, but was later won over by the Barons. He returned to his allegiance in the reign of Henry III for, in 1217/8, his manors were restored to him, and, although he was a witness to the second Great Charter and the Forest Charter of 1224, he seems to have been in favor with the King.

Roos erected the Castles of Helmsley, or Hamlake, in Yorkshire, and of Werke, in Northumberland. He was a member of the Order of Knights Templar. He died in 1226/7 and was buried "in his proper habit": in the Knights' Church, or the New Temple in London, where his tomb may be seen. Gough describes his effigy, in "Sepulchral Monuments." He married Isabel, daughter of William the Lion, King of Scotland, and widow of Robert Bruce.

Geoffrey de Saye
A feudal baron in Sussex

Geoffrey de Saye, the Surety, was in arms with the other Barons against the King, and consequently his extensive lands and possessions in ten counties were seized. These were given to Peter de Crohim. Six of the counties we can name, Northampton, Cambridge, Essex, Norfolk, Suffolk, and Lincoln, but we cannot be sure of what Castles in those areas were Geoffrey's, or which other four counties he could claim.

While William d'Albini and his companions were holding Rochester Castle, they had been assured that other baronial leaders would relieve them if the Castle were to be besieged by King John. Such a rescue would not have been easy unless the Royal guards were lax in watching the bridge over the Medway. If this bridge were under guard, a march to Rochester from London along the Dover Road would prove impossible, the company then being forced to detour and approach Rochester from Maidstone. Nevertheless, on 26 October, they moved in as far as Dover, where they soon heard that the King was on his way to meet them. They promptly returned to London, leaving the Rochester garrison to do the best it could.

On 9 November King John issued letters of conduct for Richard de Clare, Robert fitz Walter, Geoffrey de Saye and the Mayor of London, to confer with the Royal emissaries: Peter de Roches, Hubert de Burgh and the Earls of Arundel and Warren. There is no certainty that these men ever met. If indeed they did, nothing came of it. We suspect that the meeting was originally planned with the hope that a proposal would be accepted, and it is not unlikely that the proposal would have been a willingness to surrender Rochester Castle to the King if the garrison could go free, but no such move resulted. Yet despite the futility of the meeting, at least we see Geoffrey de Saye connected, if lightly, with Rochester Castle. And this is the only Castle with which we are able to link his name.

Geoffrey de Saye returned to the Royalist party when the civil war was over, and sided with King Henry III, thereby regaining his lost lands after the expulsion of the Dauphin. He died 24 October 1230 leaving a son, William, as his heir, by Alice, daughter of William de Cheney.

Robert de Vere
Earl of Oxford

The principal residence of the de Veres was Castle Headingham. Oxford Castle was the seat of the Earls de Vere. Oxford Castle is thought to be the oldest in all England.

Robert de Vere, the Surety, born after 1164, became heir to his brother, Aubrey de Vere, who died without issue before September of 1214, and who was reputed to be one of the "evil councilors" of King John. Although he was hereditary lord great Chamberlain of the kingdom, Robert pursued a different course in politics from that of his brother. He became one of the principal Barons in arms against King John, a party to that convenant that resigned the custody of the City and Tower of London to the Barons. In the beginning of the reign of King Henry III, after he had made his peace with that young monarch following the Battle of Lincoln, Robert was received into his favor. He was appointed one of the judges in the Court of King's Bench, but he died only a few months afterward, 25 October 1221, and was buried in the Priory of Hatfield, Broad Oak, in Essex. His wife was Isabel, who died 3 February 1245, daughter of Hugh, second Baron de Bolebec in Northumberland.

William de Fortibus
Earl of Albemarle

William de Fortibus, the youngest of the Magna Charta Sureties, came of age in 1214/5, when King John confirmed to him all the lands which accrued to him by inheritance from his mother, and he succeeded in her right as Earl of Albemarle.

Although originally on the side of the Barons, this Surety deserted them and joined King John in that expedition into the North of England so marked by destruction. For his services the King granted him all the lands belonging to his sister Alice, the wife of William Marshall, Jr., the Surety. The King constituted him in 1218, governor of the Castles of Rockingham in Northamptonshire, Sauvey in Leistershire and Botham in Lincolnshire, with strict command to destroy all the houses, parks and possessions of those Barons who were in arms against the King. In the reign of King Henry III this nobleman fought under the Royal banner at the Battle of Lincoln, and shared largely in the spoils of the victory. He was alternately for and against the Charter. Since he was opposed to the King, his submission was accomplished only by excommunication. In 1230 he was one of the commanders of the Royal troops in Normandy. He set out on a pilgrimage to the Holy Land, and died on the Mediterranean Sea 29 March 1241.

Bishop Stubbs has described William as "a feudal adventurer of the worst type." He changed sides as often as suited his policy. Following his election as a Surety he wanted, most of all, to revive the independent power of the feudal Barons, and carried out his plans with Falkes de Breaute and other foreign adventurers whom John had established in the country. He was twice excommunicated, once in John's reign, once in Henry III's. He was never really in the Royal favor until after the death of Falkes de Breaute.

William de Hardell
Mayor of London

William de Hardell, the Surety, was Mayor of the City of London at the time of the insurrection of the Barons. It is highly probable that it was he who induced the citizens to deliver up one of the entrances of the City of the Barons, the one called the Aldgate, through which they passed Sunday morning, 17 May 1215, while the people were at Mass.

There is no evidence that Hardell was a feudal Baron or a Baron by tenure and, since he was a civil officer of so early a period, there is some doubt as to the arms attributed to him. He served as sheriff of the City of London in 1207, and was the first Mayor of the City by popular election in 1215, by consent of King John. It was at his installation that the "Ridings' or Lord Mayor's Shows" were instituted when the candidate was obliged by Royal command to ride in state to Westminster, where the Royal palace was situated and where the judges sat, to be presented for the King's approval.

Geoffrey de Mandeville
Earl of Essex and Gloucester

Geoffrey de Mandeville, the Surety, upon paying King John 20,000 marks, obtained a license in 1214 to marry Avisa or Isabella, daughter of William, Count of Meullent, who had first been King John's wife. But who was repudiated in 1200 because of consanguinity, since both the King and Queen were great grandchildren of King Henry I. Geoffrey died two years after their marriage, and Avisa was promised to Hubert de Burgh, but the marriage never took place, and she died without issue. In right of his wife Geoffrey de Mandeville became Earl of Gloucester, and was placed in full possession of all the liberties belonging to this Earldom and to the lordship of Glamorgan in Wales. He was one of the wealthiest of the Barons opposed to King John. His life was short. He was mortally wounded in a tournament in London in February 1216, and died 23 February, without issue. He was interred in the Priory of the Holy Trinity in the suburbs of the City.

He was succeeded by his brother William de Mandeville, who also took the part of the Barons and maintained it, even after the death of King John, for he had assisted Louis of France in the siege of Berkamstead Castle, which was occupied by the King's forces. William died without issue 8 January 1227, when the Earldom of Essex devolved upon his sister, Maud Bohun, Countess of Hereford. The lands, which he inherited, passed to his half brother, John fitz Geoffrey, whose wife was Isabel Bigod, widow of Gilbert de Lacie and daughter of Hugh Bigod, the Surety.

Geoffrey de Mandeville's Castle at Gloucester is nothing but a city jail, yet once it was a Saxon Castle and later a Norman stronghold.

William Marshall, Jr.
The Earl of Pembroke's Heir

William Marshall, the Surety, was sometimes as strenuous a supporter of the baronial cause as his father was of the Royal interests. When the Dauphin came to London he was one of the prominent men who recognized him as King of England. Upon the death of King John, the Protector procured the consent of the Barons to the coronation of young Henry, requiring the allegiance of the Barons including his own son, William Marshall, Jr. When the rebels were finally conquered, he went back to the King's cause, profiting nicely at the expense of some of his slower former colleagues. In 1223/4 he returned from Ireland and gained a great victory over Prince Llewellyn and the Welsh who in his absence had taken two of his castles. He was made governor of the Castles of Caerdigan and Caermarthen and, in 1230, captain-general of all the King's forces in Bretagne. William Marshall succeeded as second Earl of Pembroke and died 24 April 1231, very wealthy but without issue.

The Marshall country is the tip end of the Welsh Peninsula. One of his finest Castles was Pembroke.

Roger de Montbegon
Lord of Horneby, Lancashire

Roger de Montbegon, the Surety, was the successor of Adam de Monte Begonis, whose principal lands were in Lincolnshire. Roger was apparently the son of this Adam by his wife Maud fitz Swaine. During the imprisonment of Richard I in Germany, Roger de Montbegon seems to have favored Prince John'' designs on the throne, since he was one of those who held the Castle of Nottingham against the Bishop of Durham. When, however, the King on his return advanced to besiege that fortress, he came out and submitted himself without shooting an arrow. He was one of the most adamant in refusing to pay the levy assessed to those who did not supply the King with soldiers, and must have been more mercurial than most of the Barons. Whenever he was in one of his periodic lapses of disgrace, the King would reclaim some of the lands he had previously granted. In the Barons' proceedings to procure the Charter of Liberty from King John, he took a prominent part. He was one of the parties to the covenant for surrendering the City and Tower of London into the hands of the Barons, although several lordships were granted or confirmed to him by King John as late as 1215/6. There is, however, no reason to doubt his original loyalty to the cause of the Barons for when he took up arms against the King, his possessions were seized and given to Oliver d'Albini. Roger de Montbegon had no issue by his wife Olivia, whom he married about 1200, widow of Robert St. John. When he died in 1224/6 his Castle of Horneby in Lancashire was given to John de Warren, Earl of Surrey; but when Henry de Montbegon became heir to Roger, he recovered it. Nevertheless Roger deserted the Barons before Magna Charta was confirmed a year and Roger de Mowbray was substituted for him among the Sureties. He was a younger brother of the Surety William de Mowbray. He did not marry and died in 1217/8, his elder brother William, succeeding to his estate. The armorial ensigns of Roger de Mowbray are extant in the South aisle of Westminster Abbey, as he was one of its benefactors.

Horneby Castle was in Lancashire and Nottingham, the other Castle held by Roger de Montbegon, was once the key to the North. It now is overshadowed by a palatial combination museum and art gallery.

Richard de Montfichet
A feudal baron in Essex

Richard de Montfichet, the Surety, was under age at the time of his father's death, and his wardship was committed to Roger de Lacie, Constable of Chester. He evidently came of age almost within the month of the signing of the Magna Charta. It is notable that so young a man was so soon elected a Surety for the observance of the Magna Charta, and to a position of political responsibility. As he was not of age until the spring of 1215, his first public act appears to have been that of joining the Baronial party in arms against the King. The next year he went with the Surety Robert fitz Walter into France to solicit aid and continued to be one of the most enthusiastic of the Barons, until he was taken prisoner at Lincoln. Even after he was released he attended a tournament at Blithe in the 7th of King Henry III, contrary to the King's prohibition, for which his lands were seized. Later he made peace with the King and was, in 1236/7, constituted Justice of the King's forests or game parks in nineteen counties of England, and in 1241/2 was made of sheriff of Essex and governor of

Hertford Castle. It would appear that he was the last survivor of the Sureties.

Richard de Montfichet died without issue, never having married and after 1258 his lands were divided among his three sisters, one of whom was Aveline, wife of William de Fortibus, the Magna Charta Surety.

Richard de Percy
A feudal baron of Yorkshire

Richard de Percy, the Surety, inherited from his aunt, the "countess of Warwick," who died without issue, her share of the Percy heritage. He was one of the first powerful lords to take up arms against King John in the cause of "a constitutional government." He died without issue about 1244.

Eustace de Vesci
Lord of Alnwick, Northumberland

The Vesci family had control of Alnwick Castle built as a threat to Scotland in Northumberland. The Vesci family came to an end, and the Castle went to the Percys in 1309.

According to the chronicler of Alnwick Abbey, the Barony of Alnwick belonged to Gilbert Tyson prior to the Conquest. His son and heir, William, died at Hastings, leaving no issue. His daughter and estates were granted to Ivo de Vesci. In 1297 William, first Baron Vesci, died without surviving issue, and left the Barony to the Bishop of Durham, who sold it to Sir Henry Percy.

Eustace de Vesci, the Surety, was feudal lord of Alnwick Castle. He came of age in 1190 and, in 1199, was sent by King John as one of the ambassadors to King William the Lion of Scotland. He married one of William's daughters. Soon he became closely connected with the rise and progress of the baronial cause. In 1212 he and Robert fitz Walter, the Surety, were called to give security for faithful allegiance, whereupon they fled to Scotland. De Vesci's English possessions were seized and also his Castle of Alnwick, which was to be destroyed, but the order was never carried out. This order so embittered de Vesci that he became the most persistent of the King's enemies, and a principal leader in the insurrection. He soon was taking a prominent part in all their conventions, endeavoring to revive the laws of Edward the Confessor. He was one of the Barons to whom the City and Town of London were committed, and he was one of those who urged the Dauphin to come to England. While attending his brother-in-law, Alexander, King of Scots, as he welcomed Prince Louis and paid him Scotland's homage in 1216, Eustace de Vesci passed Bernard Castle in Yorkshire and noted that it displayed the Royal banner. He approached the Castle to see if and how it could be captured, and was mortally wounded in the attempt.

CHAPTER XVII

SAIRE de QUINCEY

Saire de Quincey, the Surety, was born before 1154. He was one of the Barons present at Lincoln when William the Lion of Scotland did homage to the English monarch in October of 1200.

At the beginning of John's reign, Saire de Quincey was not a Baron, much less a great one. In the civil war the King had had the advantage over the rebels. Few of the Barons had had much actual military experience. The Barons' contribution to the war was the scutage they paid, a war fund substituted for the contingent of knights owed to the King's service. The money was collected from vassals, and mercenary knights were paid from it. Many of the mercenaries were regulars who served the same Baron from campaign to campaign, but those Barons who are known to have had extensive military experience were only Saire de Quincey, Robert fitz Walter, William de Mawbray, William d'Albini, Roger de Cressi and Robert de Roos.

Saire de Quincey is associated with two stalwart Castles in the South of England: Colchester and Winchester, both with the Latin castrum root, signifying that they were once the sites of Roman forts.

Colchester Castle could not have been built before the early 12th Century, though Roman materials may have been re-used in its construction. The keep, the only portion now surviving, is in complete harmony with other Norman castles.

Colchester must have been a formidable stronghold, and a challenge to Saire de Quincey. The King's men held the Castle against Quincey, the first Earl to attack Colchester. John had given the fortress into the charge of a Fleming whom he thought he could trust. But Quincey took the Castle, and later found holding it more difficult. The fighting was of such a nature that John himself came to Colchester to see just how stubborn Saire de Quincey was. The Earl held the Castle for two months, but lack of food forced him to give up and take flight to France.

Colchester was the largest Norman keep in England. It measures one hundred fifty-two by one hundred seventeen feet, enclosing nearly twice the area of the Tower of London. Its walls vary between eleven and thirty feet in thickness. It was erected either by William the Conqueror or by William II. It is of the quadrangular variety, turreted at the corners. In it and elsewhere herringbone masonry has been noted.

William the Conqueror first erected Winchester Castle. Henry III added later alterations and extra height, about the year 1138. The great Hall has Purbeck columns of 13th Century architecture, supporting a restored roof and containing handsome windows of the same approximate period. Only the keep remains. Thanks to the old builders who made the keep strong and high to withstand time and so difficult to tear down that it escaped the looters of the ages.

Saire de Quincey obtained large grants and immunities from King John and was created Earl of Winchester on 2 March 1207. He had been governor in 1203 of the Castle of Ruil in Normandy, which is what helped him to get the title. He is credited with the rewriting of the Magna Charta from the Charter of King Henry I and the Saxon Code. Because he had opposed the King's concession to the Pope's legate, he was bitterly hated by King John. He is one of the Barons to whom the City and Tower of London were resigned and Saire de Quincey was excommunicated with the other Barons the following year. The other Barons sent Saire de Quincey along with Robert fitz Walter, the Surety, to invite the Dauphin of France to assume the Crown of England. Even after the death of King John, he kept a strong garrison in Montsorell Castle in behalf of Prince Louis. When the Barons, who had been greatly outnumbered, were defeated by the troops of King Henry III, Saire de Quincey, with many others, was made a prisoner and his estates forfeited. In the following October, after his submission, his immense estates were restored upon him. In 1218, along with the Earls of Chester and Arundel, Saire de Quincey traveled to the Holy Land, assisted at the siege of Damietain in 1219, and died 3 November in the same year, on the way to Jerusalem. He was married to Margaret de Bellemont, sometime before 1173. Margaret was born in Hampshire, England about 1154 and died in England 12 January 1234. Margaret had been the daughter of Robert de Bellemont and his wife Petronella Grantmesnil. Petronella Grantmesnil was a descendant of the Emperor Charlemagne.

Saire de Quincey's arms: Or, a fess gules, a label 8 points azure.

Their children were:

HAWISE QUINCEY *was born in Great Britain and married* HUGH *de* VERE, *son of the Surety* ROBERT *de* VERE.

ROBERT *de* QUINCEY *the eldest son, married* HAWISE *the daughter of* HUGH KEVELIOK, *Earl of Chester and died in the Holy Land. He only had a daughter*

MARGARET QUINCEY *married the Surety* JOHN *de* LACIE.

ARABELLA QUINCY *was born and died in England. She married* RICHARD *de* HARCOURT, *of Stanton Harcourt and Ellenhall, and through his marriage with her he acquired the manor of Bosworth. His death occurred in 1258, and they had a son*

WILLIAM *de* HARCOURT's *first wife was* ALICE *the daughter of* ROGER *la* ZOUCHE. *By Alice he had two daughters.*

MARGARET *married* SIR JOHN CANTELUPE *and died without issue*

ARABELLS *married* SIR FULKE PEMBRUGGE.

By his second wife ELEANOR *the daughter of* HENRY, *Lord Hastings and his wife* ADA *of* HUNTINGDON, *he had only one son.*

RICHARD *de* HARCOURT *married* MARGARET *the daughter of* JOHN BEKE, *Lord of Eresby, county Lincoln and died in 1293.*

JOHN *de* HARCOURT *married his first wife* ELEANOR *the daughter of* EUDO *la* ZOUCHE *and was a descendant of Saire de Quincey.*

WILLIAM

John was knighted 22 May 1306 and married his second wife ALICE *the daughter of* PETER CORBETT *of Causcastle, Salop. John died in 1330.*

ROGER QUINCY *was born about 1174 in Winchester, England. He held his father's estates while his brother Robert was absent in the Holy Land, and succeeded as the 2nd Earl of Winchester in 1235. He married* HELEN MacDONAL *the daughter of* ALAN MacDONAL, *Lord of Galloway and his wife* MARGARET *the daughter of* PRINCE DAVID, *a Grandson of* KING DAVID I *of* SCOTLAND. *In 1235 he also by the rights of his wife became the Lord High Constable of Scotland. Roger's arms: gules, 7 mascles or, three, three, and one. He had three daughters by Helen.*

MARGARET *married* WILLIAM *de* FERRERS, *7th Earl of Derby and brought to him the Manor and Barony of Groby. From the time of his youth William suffered greatly with the gout and therefore had to be carried from place to place in a chariot. He lost his life by being thrown, through the heedlessness of his driver, over the bridge of St. Neots, county Huntingdon, in 1254. He was the eldest son of* WILLIAM *de* FERRERS, *6TH Earl of Derby and his wife* AGNES *of* CHESTER. *Margaret was the second wife of William. His first wife was* SIBILLA *one of the daughters of* WILLIAM MARSHALL, *Earl of Pembroke and they had seven daughters. By Margaret, William had four children.*

ROBERT *de* FERRERS *was born about 1239. When the Baron's War broke out in 1263 he seized three of Prince Edward's castles. The following year he captured Worchester and destroyed the town. In the next few months Prince Edward retaliated by wasting his lands* and demolishing Tutbury Castle. On 24 December 1264 he was summoned to Parliament, where he was accused of various trespasses and was sent to the Tower by Earl Simon, his lands being taken into the King's hand. Once again he was fully pardoned and admitted to the King's grace on 5 December 1265. His first wife was MARY the daughter of HUGUES le BRUN. He married his second wife ALIANORE the daughter of HUMPHREY de BOHUN and his wife ALIANORE BRAOS.

ALIANORE married ROBERT fitz WALTER.

JOHN de FERRERS was born at Cardiff in June of 1271. In 1297 he was the principal supporter of the Earls of Hereford and Norfolk in their quarrel with the King. He was unsuccessful in his attempts to regain the lands that had been forfeited by his father's rebellion. John was in Scotland on the King's service in 1298 and in 1303, and was a constable of the army of Scotland in 1306. He was given the custody of Gloucester Castle for a term beginning 24 September 1311. He married HAWISE the daughter of ROBERT de MUCEGROS sometime between 2 February 1297 and 13 September 1300. In August 1312 John died in Gascony of poisoning.

WILLIAM de FERRERS married JOAN DESPENCER the daughter of HUGH DESPENCER. His second wife was ELEANOR the daughter of MATTHEW LOVAINE. He obtained as a gift from his mother the manor at Groby in Leicestershire, whereupon he assumed the arms of the de Quincey family. He died in 1288.

ANNE FERRERS married JOHN, Lord Grey of Wilton.

WILLIAM FERRERS was active in the wars of Scotland during the reigns of Edward I, and Edward II, dying in 1325. He married MARGARET the daughter of JOHN 2nd Lord Segrave.

ANNE FERRERS was EDWARD DESPENCER's first wife. In the 10th of King Edward II he was constituted Justice of North Wales, and Governor of the Castle of Caernarvon. When he died in 1323, Lord John had, among other possessions, the manor of Eston Grey, in Wilts, and the Castle of Ruthyn, in North Wales.

HENRY de GREY was the 3rd Baron Grey. He was abroad when his father died and could not claim his inheritance during the allotted time according to custom. King Edward III, therefore, in the first year of his reign, in consideration of de Grey's imminent services, remitted him a debt he owed to the exchequer. He married ANNE the daughter of RALPH de ROCKLEY. He died in 1342.

REGINALD de GREY, the 4th Baron Grey married MAUDE the daughter JOHN BOTETOURT and died in 1370.

MAUD GREY married SIR JOHN NORVILLE.

220

THOMAS FERRERS

HENRY FERRERS *was the 2ⁿᵈ Baron Ferrers of Groby. He took an active part in the wars of King Edward III in Scotland and in France and in consequence acquired very large territorial possessions, by grants from the crown, in recognition of his services. He married* ISABEL *the fourth daughter of* THEOBALD *de* VERDON *and through her obtained lands in Ireland. Lord Henry died in 1343.*

    WILLIAM FERRERS

    RALPH FERRERS *married* JOAN *the daughter of* RICHARD GREY, *Baron of Codner.*

    PHILIPPA FERRERS *married* GUY *de* BEAUCHAMP *son of* THOMAS.

    ELIZABETH FERRERS *married* DAVID, *Earl of Athol.*

AGNES FERRERS

JOAN FERRERS *was married in 1267 to* THOMAS *de* BERKELEY, *feudal Lord of Berkeley, also called Thomas the Wise. Thomas was born at Berkeley in 1245 and was present at the bloody battle and defeat of the Scots at Falkirk 22 July 1298. In July of 1300 he was at the siege of Carlaverock. Taken prisoner at the Battle of Hannockburn, 24 June 1314, he paid a large sum for his ransom. As a statesman he had important duties, being in June 1292 on the Commission to examine the claims to the Crown of Scotland, and in January 1296 on an Embassy to France, and to Pope Clement V in July 1307. He died 23 July 1321 at Berkeley and Joan died 19 March 1309/10 and is buried at St. Augustine's, Bristol.*

    MARGARET BERKELEY *married* THOMAS *fitz* MORICE *also called the Crooked Heir, was the son of* MORICE *fitz* JOHN *and his wife* MAUD *de* BARRY *on 7 February 1283. Thomas was born about April 1261 and came to England in 1281 where he remained until February 1291. He was summoned for military service from 29 June to 17 May 1291, holding the position of Keeper of Ireland from 19 April to 2 December 1295, and received the salary of Justicar. He died 4 June 1298 at Knockainy, co. Limerick and was buried in the Cominican Friary at Tralee. Their children were:*

    THOMAS *fitz* THOMAS *died young.*

    MORICE *fitz* THOMAS *was admonished in 1325 for refusing to obey the Justicar, and having quarreled with the Earl of Ulster, peace was made between them in a Parliament at Dublin in May of 1345. On 10 July 1344 he was summoned for military service in France. The Earl absented himself from a Parliament held in Dublin, in June 1345, whereupon the Justicar Ralph d'Ufford, seized his lands into the King's hand, and besieged and took his castles. Fitz Thomas escaped and could not be found, and his lands were therefore forfeited. He was excepted from pardon on 12 May 1346, but on 28 June he received a special protection in order that he might come to England to answer to his accusers before the King. On 20 July the Justicar was ordered to send him to England, and he embarked at Younghai with his wife and two sons on 13 September, the King making him an allowance of 20 shillings a day from the time he reached England. For more than a year he remained in custody, and was released on 18 February 1347. Finally on 28 November 1349 he was admitted to the King's grace, pardoned from all treason, but he was required to leave his two sons there as hostages during the King's pleasure. Returning to Ireland about May 1350, he received, on 16 September 1351, a special protection against his enemies there. In May 1355 he was again in England, and on 8 July 1355 he was appointed Justical of Ireland, which office he held until his death. He married his first wife KATHERINE the daughter of RICHARD de BURGH, Earl of Ulster and his wife MARGARET 5 August 1312. She died in Dublin 1 November 1331 and he married his second wife MARGARET the daughter of CONOR O'BRIEN of Thomond. He married his third wife AVELINE the daughter of NICHOLAS fitz MORICE of Kerry. Morice died 25 January 1355 in Dublin Castle.*

MAURICE de BERKELEY, *Lord de Berkeley also called Maurice the Magnanimous was born sometime between April 1271 and 1281. He distinguished himself in the Scottish Wars from 1295 to 1318, and was present at the siege of Carlaverock in July 1300. Within six months of his father's death he was sent prisoner to Wallingford Castle, 20 January 1321, where he died four years later. His first wife, whom he married in 1289 when they were both very young, was EVE, daughter of EUDO la ZOUCHE. She died 5 December 1314 and was buried in Portbury Church, Somerset. His second wife, ISABEL was born 10 March 1262 the daughter of GILBERT de CLARE, Earl of Gloucester and his wife ALICE de BRUN. They were married in 1316. Lord Maurice died 31 May 1326 and was buried firstly at Wallingford and later removed to St. Augustine's, Bristol.*

ISABEL BERKELEY *married* ROBERT de CLIFFORD *a descendant of the Sureties,* RICHARD *and* GILBERT de CLARE *in 1328. Robert was born in 1305 and died 20 May 1344. Her second husband was* THOMAS MUSGRAVE; *one of the commanders in the van of the English army that entirely defeated David, King of Scotland at Durham, in the 20th King Edward III. Later he was made Sheriff of Yorkshire and the governor of the*

Castle of York. The barony was not continued in his descendants, nor were any of them deemed barons of the realm.

THOMAS *de* BERKELEY, *Lord Berkeley also called Thomas the Ritch. On 4 April 1327 he was made Joint Custodian of the deposed King Edward II, whom he "courteously received" the next day at Berkeley Castle. But being commanded to deliver over the government thereof to his fellow custodians he left there to go to Bradley "with heavy cheer perceiving what violence was intended". As an accessory to the murder of the deposed King, he was tried by a jury of 12 Knights in the 4th of King Edward III, but was acquitted. He married his first wife* MARGARET *the daughter of* ROGER MORTIMER, *Earl of Narch and his wife* JOAN GENEVILLE *on 25 July 1320. She died 5 May 1337 and was buried at St. Augustine's Bristol. He married his second wife* KATHARINE *the daughter of* JOHN CLIVEDON *and his wife* EMMA *30 May 1347 at Charfield, co. Gloucester. Lord Thomas died 27 October 1385 and Katharine died 13 March 1385. They are both buried at Berkeley Church.*

ELIZABETH *married* ALEXANDER COMYN, *2nd Earl of Buchan.*

ELA *also called* ELENA, *married* ALAN *4th Baron la Zouche of Ashby, son of* ROGER *and descended from the Earls of Brittany. In the 26th of King Henry III he had a military summons to attend the King into France. He was later made justice itinerant for the counties of Southampton, Buckingham, and Northampton. Arbitration being made between King Henry II and the barons by King Louis of France saw Zouche was one of the Sureties in behalf of the Tower of London, and Governor of the Castle of Northampton. He was violently assaulted and severely wounded at Westminster Hall, in 1268, by John, Earl of Warren and Surry, because of a dispute arising from a question of some landed property. His son Roger, who was with him, was also wounded. A year later Alan la Zouche died. Ela died in 1296.*

ROGER *la* ZOUCHE *married* ELA *the daughter of* STEPHEN LONGESEPEE *and his wife* EMELINE *of Ulster. Stephen was the son of* WILLIAM, *Earl of Salisbury. He died in 1285.*

ALAN *la* ZOUCHE *was born in 1267 and died in 1314. He distinguished himself in the wars of Gascony and Scotland during the reign of King Edward I. In 1311 he was made governor of Rockingham Castle in Northamptonshire, and steward of Rickingham Forest. He married* ELEANOR *the daughter of* NICHOLAS *de* SEAGRAVES.

ELIZABETH ZOUCHE *the youngest became a nun at the order in Brewood, co. Stafford.*

ELLEN ZOUCHE *married first* NICHOLAS ST. MAUR *and second* ALAN *de* CHARLTON.

MAUD ZOUCHE *married* ROBERT *de* HOLAND *of a family of great antiquity in the county of Lancaster. Robert was secretary of Thomas, Earl of Lancaster, to whom he owed his advancement. In the 15ᵗʰ of King Edward II, at the insurrection of Earl Thomas, his former master, Robert promised him all the aid in his power. But he was not able to fulfill his engagement, and Lancaster was forced to escape to the North and was finally taken prisoner at Boroughbridge, whereupon Lord Holand gave himself up to the King at Derby and was taken prisoner to Dover Castle. He was accordingly held in great disfavor by the people, for his duplicity, and when he was again made prisoner, in the year 1328, in a wood near Henley Park, towards Windsor, he was beheaded and his head sent to Henry, Earl of Lancaster.*

    ROBERT *de* HOLAND
    THOMAS *de* HOLAND
    ALAN *de* HOLAND
    OTHO *de* HOLAND
    JANE HOLAND *married* SIR EDMOND TALBOT.
    MARY HOLAND *married* SIR JOHN TEMPEST.
ROBERT *la* ZOUCHE
EUDO *la* ZOUCHE *was living in 1273 and married* MILLICENT *the daughter of* WILLIAM *de* CANTILUPE *and his wife* EVA BRAOS.
    WILLIAM *la* ZOUCHE
      EUDO *la* ZOUCHE
        WILLIAM *la* ZOUCHE
    ELEANOR ZOUCHE *married* JOHN HARCOURT.
    LUCY ZOUCHE *married* THOMAS *de* GREENE.
    EVE ZOUCHE *married* MAURICE *de* BERKELEY.
Roger's second wife was MAUD, *Countess of Pembroke the daughter of* HUMPHREY *de* BOHUN, *Earl of Hereford and Essex. And his third wife was* ALIANORE *the daughter of* WILLIAM *de* FERRERS, *the 6ᵗʰ Earl of Derby, who survived him and became the wife of* ROGER *de* LEYBOURNE. *Upon his death the earldom became extinct, and his possessions devolved upon his daughters.*
ROBERT II, *the* YOUNGER *married* HELEN *the eldest daughter of* LLEWELYN *the* GREAT, *Prince of North Wales, and the widow of* JOHN SCOT, *Earl of Huntingdon. Robert died in 1257 in the tournament at Blie. They had three daughters.*
    ANNE *became a nun.*
    JOANE *married* HUMPHREY *de* BOHUN, *the* YOUNGER.
    MARGARET QUINCEY *was the wife of* BALDWIN WAKE, *feudal lord, who died in 1282.*
      JOHN WAKE *was summoned to Parliament as a Baron 1 October 1295.*

MARGARET QUINCY *married* JOHN *de* LACIE, *the Surety.*

The Lineage of Saire de Quincey.

SAHER *de* QUINCEY
SAIRE *de* QUINCEY, *Lord Bradenham, died about 1157. He married* MAUD *de* ST. LIZ, *the daughter of* SIMON *de* ST. LIZ *and* MATILDA *of* NORTHUMBRIA. *Maud was born about 1094 and died in 1140. Simon de St. Liz, Earl of Huntingdon was born about 1068 in Normandy, France and died in 1111, his father was* RANLPH *the* RICH. *Matilda of Northumbria, Countess of Huntingdon was born in 1072 and died in 1131. Her parents were* WALTHEOF II *and* JUDITH *of* LENS.
ROBERT *de* QUINCEY, *Lord Buckley was born about 1125 in Winchester, Hampshire, England and died in 1192. He married* ORABILIS *de* MAR. *Orabilis died before 30 June 1203 and her father was* RALPH *de* MAR *the son of* WILLIAM.
SAIRE *de* QUINCEY *the Surety, and the first Earl of Winchester, was born before 1154 and died 3 November 1219, a crusader on the way to Jerusalem. His wife* MARGARET BELLEMONT *was born about 1155 in Hampshire, England and died 12 January 1234/5.* ROBERT *de* BELLEMONT, *3rd Earl of Leicester, was born before 1135 and died 31 August 1190 in Durazzo, Greece. He married* PETRONELLA, *daughter of* HUGH *de* GRANTMESNIL.
HAWISE KEVELIOK, *wife of* ROBERT *de* QUINCEY, *was the daughter of* HUGH *de* KEVELIOK, *Earl of Chester, called also* HUGH *de* MESCHINES.

The Lineage of JOHN de LACIE.

JOHN *de* LACIE *married* MARGARET QUINCEY *the granddaughter of* SAIRE *de* QUINCEY.
JOHN *de* LACIE *was descended from* KING MALCOM CANMORE.
ILBERT *de* LACI, *whom King William presented with the castle and town of Brokenbridge, county of York, which he afterwards named "Pontfract". He also possessed other vast territorial grants, at the time of the general survey, having nearly 164 lordships.*
ROBERT *de* LACIE, *also known as Robert de Pontefract. His son,* ILBERT *de* LACIE *married* ALICE, *daughter of* GILBERT *de* GANT. *Having died without issue, he was succeeded by his brother.*
HENRY *de* LACIE's *son* ROBERT *de* LACIE *succeeded him. Robert died without issue in 1193.*
ALBREDA LACIE, *called Aubreye, married* ROBERT *(Eudo), son of* FULK *de* LISOUKS, *and had*

225

ALBREDA LISOURS, *became the wife of* RICHARD *(Robert) fitz* EUSTACE, *Feudal Baron of Halton Castle, and Constable of Chester. She inherited from her first cousin,* ROBERT *de* LACIE, *the Barony of Pontfract, and all his other lands, under pretense of a grant from* HENRY *de* LACIE, *her uncle. Her son* JOHN *fitz* EUSTACE *became heir to the said* ROBERT *de* LACIE, *assuming the surname, and inheriting as:*

JOHN *de* LACIE, *the Baron of Halton and Pontfract was Constable of Chester, and his wife was the daughter of* GEOFFRY *de* MANDEVILLE. LACIE *died in the year 1190, while in the Holy Land, and was succeeded by his eldest son:*

ROGER *de* LACIE, *Constable of Chester, under the banner of Richard the Lionhearted, assisted at the siege of Acon in 1192. He died in 1211, leaving by his wife* MAUD, *daughter of* RICHARD *de* CLARE, *the Surety, his son*

JOHN *de* LACIE, *the Surety, seventh Baron of Halton Castle, and hereditary Constable of Chester, at the time of the accession of King Henry III, joined a part of noblemen, and made a pilgrimage to the Holy Land. In 1232 he was made Earl of Lincoln, and in 1240, Governor of Chester and Beeston Castles. He died 22 July 1240, and was buried in the Cistercian Abbey of Stanlaw, in the county of Chester. His first wife was* ALICE, *daughter of* GILBERT *d'*AQUILA. *By her he had no issue, and he married second* MARGARET QUINCEY, *the only daughter and heir of* ROBERT *de* QUINCEY, *a fellow crusader who died in the Holy Land, eldest son of* SAIRE *de* QUINCEY, *Surety. John, Earl of Lincoln had three children by Lady Margaret, who survived him and married a second time to* WALTER MARSHALL, *Earl of Pembroke. The eldest daughter,* MAUD, *was given in marriage to* RICHARD *de* CLARE, *sixth Earl of Hertford. Both Maud and her sister Idonea were removed to Windsor Castle, there to be educated with King Henry III's own daughters.*

The following persons may claim descent from Baron RICHARD de CLARE, and KING WILLIAM the CONQUEROR.

RICHARD *de* CLARE was also a descendant of CHARLEMAGNE. His arms: Or, three chevrons gules.

RICHARD *fitz* GILBERT, *a lawyer and Chief Justice of England, born before 1035, was the founder of the House of Clare in England. He was the eldest son of* GISLEBERT CRISPIN, *Count of Eu, and Brionne, a descendant of the* EMPEROR CHARLEMAGNE. *He accompanied Duke William into England, and later held one hundred and seventy-six lordships or manors. One of these lordships was that of Clare, in the county of Suffolk which, becoming his chief seat, caused him to be styled Richard de Clare, and his descendants known as the Earls of Clare. He fell in a skirmish with the Welsh in 1090.* He married ROHESE, *daughter of* WALTER GIFFARD *de* BOLEBEC, *and had in addition to* ROBERT *fitz* RICHARD, *and* ALICE, *wife of* WILLIAM *de* PERCIE, *a son:*

GILBERT *de* TONEBRUGE, *Second Earl of Clare, born before 1066. He appears to have joined in the rebellion against King William Rufus, and lost his castle of Tonebruge and, dying shortly afterwards, in 1114 or 1117. A munificent benefactor of the church, he was survived by his widow,* ADELIZA, *daughter of* HUGH, *Count of Clermont, and his wife* MARGUERITA. *Their daughter* ADELIZA, *was wife of* AILBERIC *de* VERE.

RICHARD FITZGILBERT *de* CLARE, *was born before 1105. He invaded Wales with an army and became lord of vast possessions there by the power of his sword, but finally was slain in a skirmish with a few Welsh yeomen, near Abergavenny, 15 April 1136. Richard married* ADELIZA, *daughter of* RANULPH *de* MESCHINES, *Earl of Chester who died in 1128. There were the parents of:*

ROGER *de* CLARE, *born before 1116, who succeeded his brother Gilbert when he died without issue in 1151. In 1164 he assisted with the Constitution of Clarendon. This Earl who, from his munificence to the Church, and his numerous acts of piety, was called the "good Earl of Hertford", died in 1173, leaving by his wife* MAUD, *daughter of* JAMES ST. HILLARY, *a son*

RICHARD *de* CLARE, *the Surety, was Fourth Earl of Hertford, but like his father and uncle was more generally known as Earl of Clare. He was present at the coronation of King Richard I at Westminster, 3 September 1189, and of King John on 27 May 1199. He aided with the Barons against King John, and his castle of Tonbridge was taken. On 9 November 1215, he was one of the commissioners on the part of the Barons to treat of peace with the King. On 4 March 1215/6 his lands in counties Cambridge, Norfolk, Suffolk, and Essex were granted to* ROBERT *de* BETUN; *and he and his sons were among the Barons excommunicated by the Pope in 1215. He died between 3 October and 28 November 1217. He married* AMICE[1], *Countess of Gloucester, second daughter of* WILLIAM *fitz* ROBERT, *Earl of Gloucester, and his wife* HAWISE, *daughter of* ROBERT *de* BELLEMONT, *Earl of Leicester. She died 1 January 1224/5. Among their children was*

MAUD CLARE, *whose first husband was* ROGER, *Baron Lacie, Lord of the Castles of Halton and Pontefract, and they were the parents of* JOHN *de* LACIE, *the Surety. Maud Clare was married a second time to* WILLIAM *de* BROAS, *who was starved to death with his mother at Windsor Castle. He was the son of* WILLIAM *de* BROAS.

---

[1] Also called Amiece Meullent.

EDMUND STAFFORD, *and* MARGARET BASSET *of Drayton had* RALPH, *Lord Stafford, born in 1299, arms: or, chevron gules, married* MARGARET, *daughter of* HUGH AUDLEY *and* MARGARET CLARE. *Ralph, Lord Stafford was a Knight of the Garter.*
His descent from WILLIAM d'AUBIGNY is as follows:

WILLIAM *d'*AUBIGNY, *a Baron at Runnymede, cousin of the Surety* WILLIAM *d'*ALBINI, *married and had*
NICOLE *d'*AUBIGNY *married* ROGER *de* SOMERI, *Baron of Dudley, son of* RALPH *de* SOMERI, *also a baron of Runnymede, but not a surety. They had*
MARGARET SOMERI, *widow of* URIAN *St.* PIERRE, *married* RALPH BASSETT, *Lord of Drayton, county of Stafford, slain in the battle of Evesham, son of* RALPH BASSETT, *also a Baron at Runnymede, but not a surety. Their son*
RALPH BASSETT, *a warrior of renown, died in 1295, married*
HAWISE, *or* JOAN, *daughter of* JOHN *de* GREY, *Justice of Chester, and had*
MARGARET BASSETT, *who married* EDMUND, *Baron of Stafford, fought in the Scottish Wars, and died in 1308, son of* NICHOLAS *de* STAFFORD.
RALPH, *Lord Stafford, married* MARGARET AUDLEY.

EURE

JOHN *de* BURGO, *feudal lord of Tourborough, or Tonsburgh, in Normandy, was commanding general in the army of William the Conqueror. His son*
EUSTACE *de* BURGO, *Lord of Tonsburgh, was the father of*
JOHN MONOCULOUS *de* BURGO, *governor of Bamburgh Castle, married* MAGDALEN *and had*
EUSTACE FITSJOHN *de* BURGO, *or Burgh, Feudal Lord of Knaresborough Castle, one of the wealthiest, most powerful and influential barons, a favorite of King Henry I. He married first* BEATRIX *de* VESCI, *and second* AGNES, *daughter and heiress of* WILLIAM *fitz* NIGEL, *feudal baron of Halton Castle, Constable of Chester. By her he had*
RICHARD (ROBERT) *fitz* EUSTACE *feudal baron of Halton Castle, and Constable of Chester. He married* ALBREDA LISOURS, *daughter of* ROBERT (EUDO) *de* LISOURS *and his wife* ALBREDA, *sister of* HENRY *de* LACIE.
RODGER *fitz* RICHARD *was the third son, granted by King Henry II lordship of Warkworth, in Northumberland. He married* ALICE, *also*

228

called Adelisa, widow of Henry of Essex, Lord of Raleigh, and daughter of ALBERIC *de* VERE, *great High Chamberlain of England, their son* ROBERT *fitz* ROGER *was thrice High Sheriff of the counties of Norfolk, Suffolk, and Northumberland. He married* MARGARET, *daughter of* WILLIAM *de* CHENEY, *Lord of Horsford, Norfolk, and had*

JOHN *fitz* ROBERT, *the Surety, High Sheriff of county Northumberland, and Governor of New-Castle-upon-Tyne, by his wife* ADA BALIOL, *he had*

HUGH *fitz* JOHN, *father of*

JOHN *of* EURE

MILDRED, *daughter of* SIR WILLIAM EURE, *married* RICHARD GOODRICH, *of Goodrich Castle, Herfordshire, England.*

JOHN GOODRICH *married* REBECCA ALLEN.

LIEUTENANT GENERAL THOMAS GOODRICH, *born in 1614 in England, married* ANNE SHERWOOD, *born and married in England, whose daughter* ANN GOODRICH *married* JOHN LIGHTFOOT.

CHAPTER XVIII

THE ROYAL ANCESTRY OF MARGARET BELLEMONT WIFE OF SAIRE de QUINCEY

SAIRE *de* QUINCEY[1], *the Surety, Earl of Winchester, was born before 1154 and died 3 November 1219, a crusader on the way to Jerusalem. His wife* MARGARET BELLEMONT *was descended as follows:*

CHARLEMAGNE, *Emperor of the West, was born in 742 and died in 814. He married* HILDEGARDE *of Suabia, who was born in 757 and died in 782.*

LOUIS I, *the Debonaire, married for his second wife* JUDITH *daughter of* GUELPH III.

LOUIS *of* GERMANY *married* EMMA *of Andech.*

CARLOMAN *died in 880 and married* LITWINDE *of Carinthia.*

ARNULPH, *King of Germany and Emperor in 896, died in 899, and was married to* ODA *of Bavaria.*

EDITH *of* GERMANY *married* OTTO, *Duke of Saxony and died in 912.*

HENRY I, *the Fowler, Emperor of Germany, was born in 876 and died in 936. He married* MATILDA.

HEDWIGE *married* HUGH, *Duke of France and died in 956.*

HUGH CAPET, *King of France was born in 938 and died in 996. He married* ADELA.

ROBERT *the* PIOUS *was born in 971 and married* CONSTANCE.

HENRY I, *King of France, was born about 1005 and died in 1060. His third marriage was to* ANNE *of Russia.*

HUGH MAGNUS, *a leader of the First Crusade, married* ADELHEID.

ISABEL VERMANDOIS's *first marriage was to* ROBERT *de* BELLEMONT, *Earl of Leicester and Meullent.*

ROBERT *de* BELLEMONT *(Beaumont), 3rd Earl of Leicester, died in 1168 and married* PETRONELLA *daughter of* HUGH *de* GRANTMESNIL.

---

[1] Magna Charta, John S. Wurts.

MARGARET BELLEMONT *married* SAIRE *de* QUINCEY.

HAWISE KEVELIOK *the wife of* ROBERT *de* QUINCEY *was the daughter of* HUGH *de* KEVELIOK, *Earl of Chester, called also* HUGH *de* MESCHINES. *She was descended as follows:*

OLAF I, *King of Vestfold died in 710 and had*

HALFDAN I *of Vestfold died in 750. He married* ASA *daughter of* EYSTEIN, *Earl of Throndheim had*

EYSTEIN I *of Vestfold died in 780. He married* HILDA *daughter of* ERIC *and granddaughter of* AGNAR. *Their issue*

HALFDAN II *of Vestfold died in 800 and married* LIFA *daughter of* DAG *of Vestmare and their son*

GUDROD *of Vestfold died in 810 and had*

OLAF II, *King of Jutland and Vestfold, died in 840, leaving a son*

ROGNVALD *of Jutland died in 850 and whose daughter*

ASEDA *of Jutland became the wife of* EYSTEIN, *Earl of More the great grandson of* SVEIDE *the Viking. Their issue*

ROGNVALD, *Earl of More, died in 890. He married* HILDA *daughter of* HROF *(Rollo) and had*

ROLLO, *Duke of Normandy, was born in 846 and died in 931. He married* LADY POPPA, *sister of* BERNARD *of St. Liz and had*

WILLIAM LONGSWORD, *Duke of Normandy, died in 942. He married* ESPRIOTA *(Sporta) daughter of* HUBERT, *Count de Senlis, and had*

RICHARD *the* FEARLESS, *Duke of Normandy, was born in 933 and died in 996. He married* GUNNORA CREPON *who died in 1031. Their issue*

RICHARD II, *Duke of Normandy, died in 1026. He married* JUDITH *of Brittany the daughter of* CONAN I, *Count of Bretagne and his wife* ERMENGARDE *d'*ANJOU. *She died in 1018. Richard's and Judith's son*

RICHARD III, *Duke of Normandy, died in 1028 and had*

ALICE *of* NORMANDY *was the wife of* RANULPH, *Count of Bayeux and they had*

RANULPH *de* MESCHINES, *Viscount de Bayeux, who married* MARGARET *d'*AVRANCHES *the daughter of* RICHARD GOZ *and his wife* EMMA *who was the daughter of* HERLOUIN *de* CONTESVILLE *and his wife* HERLEVE *of Falaise, and had*

RANULPH *de* MESCHINES, *1ˢᵗ Earl of Chester, died in 1129 and married* LUCIA TAILBOIS. *She was descended as follows:*

ALFRED *the* GREAT, *the ablest king who ever sat upon the English throne. As a child he was a comely person with a sweet disposition, and was the favorite of his father* ETHELWULF. *He was sent to Rome at an early age to be anointed by the Pope. He ascended to the throne at the age of 23. He launched his people upon a great advance in civilization, and showed a horde of untaught countrymen that there were other and* worthier pursuits than war, or eating. He was born in 849 and died in 901. In 869 he married LADY ALSWITHA the daughter of ETHELRED, Earl of Gainas of Mercia, and his wife EDBURGA who died in 904. Their issue

LADY ETHELFELDA died 15 June 919 and was the wife of ETHELRED, Earl of Mercia in 895, who died in 912 and was the son of HUGH the GREAT, Earl of Mercia. Their issue

LADY ELFWINA was the wife of EDULF, son of ORDGAR, Earl of Devon and had

LEOFWINE, Earl of Mercia in 1005, married LADY ALWARD daughter of ATHELSTAN, the Danish Duke of East Angles and had.

LEOFRIC III, the GREAT, Earl of Mercia in 1016, died 31 August 1057. He married LADY GODIVA of Coventrytown who died in 1080 and was the daughter of EARL of LINCOLN. Their issue

ALFGAR III's, Earl of Mercia, second wife was ELFGIFU daughter of KING ETHELRED II and wife ELFIED. Their daughter LUCIA married IVO de TAILBOIS and their daughter LUCIA TAILBOIS married RANULPH de MESCHINES, First Earl of Chester.

The Goodrich, Lightfoot, Quincey and Charlemagne Connection.[2]

BELI (Heli) the GREAT died B.C. 72 leaving 2 sons, CASWALLON and LUD.

LUD died B.C. 62 and was the father of

TENUANTIUS described as "a gentle ruler", had

CYNVELIN (Cymbeline), King of Britain was educated in Rome by Augustus Caesar and later forestalled the third invasion of the island. His eleventh son

ARVIRAGUS, King of Britain, lived in Avalon. The renowned enemy of Rome and called cousin of King Caradoc, married VENISSA and had

MERIC (Marius), King of Britain, married the daughter of BOADICEA (Victoria). They had a daughter EURGEN and a son COEL, who became King of Britain in 125. OLD KING COLE[3] was a "merry old soul" and was educated in Rome. He built Colchester (Coel-Castra) and died A.D. 170.

EURGEN was the mother of

GLADYS who became the wife of

LLEUVER MAWR (Lucius the Great) a great grandson of CARADOC. He was baptized at Winchester by his father's first cousin St. Timothy, who suffered martyrdom at the age of 90, on 22 August A.D. 39. When in A.D. 170 Lucius succeeded to the throne of Britain he became the first Christian

---

[2] Magna Charta, John S. Wurts, V. 1-2, Chapter 27, p. 162.

[3] Magna Charta, John S. Wurts, V. 1-2, chapter 30.

King in the world. He founded the first church at Llandaff, and changed the established religion of Britain from Druidism to Christianity. He died in 181, leaving an only recorded child, a daughter

GLADYS *became the wife of* CADVAN *of* CAMBRIA, PRINCE *of* WALES. *Their daughter*

STRADA *"the Fair" married* COEL, *a later king of Colchester, living in A.D. 232, whose parentage is not stated. They were the parents of*

HELEN *"of the Cross", was born in 248. The arms of Colchester were "a cross with three crowns." She became the wife of* CONSTANTINE I *afterward Emperor of Rome and, in right of his wife, King of Britain. He was born in 242 and died in 306. Their son* CONSTANTINE *the* GREAT *was born in 265 and died in 336. Of British birth and education, he is known as "the first Christian Emperor". With a British army he set out to put down the persecution of Christians forever. The greatest of all Roman Emperors, he annexed Britain to the Roman Empire, and founded Constantinople.*

In 325 he assembled the Council, which he attended in person, at Nicea, in Bithnia, Asia Minor, which formulated the Nicene Creed. The following edict of Constantine, clearing sets forth the standards of his life. "We call God to witness, the Savior of all men, that in assuming the government we are influenced solely by these two considerations – the uniting of the empire in one faith, and the restoration of peace to a world rent in pieces by the insanity of religious persecution." He married FAUSTA, *and had three sons,* CONSTANTINE II, CONSTANTIUS II, *and* CONSTANS I.

His eldest son, CONSTANTINE II *was the father of* UTHER PENDRAGON, *who became King of Britain in 498. The latter's son,* KING ARTHUR, *one of the Nine Worthies, succeeded his father in the year 516 at the age of 15, repulsed the invading Saxons, and died 21 May 542. He is most popularly known in connection with his fabulous Knights of the Round Table. In a sumptuous tomb at Glastonbury, he rests beside his wife* GUINEVERE.

CONSTANTINE II, *was second son of* CONSTANTINE *the* GREAT, *married* FAUSTA *and died in 360. Their son*

CONSTANTIUS III *married* PLACIDA *and died in 421.*

VALENTINIAN III *died in 455 and whose line of descendants continues as follows:*

EUDOXIA *became the wife of* HUNNERIC *who died in 480*
HILDERIC *was King of the Vandals in 525*
HILDA *the wife of* FRODE VII *died in 548*
HALFDAN, *King of Denmark*
IVAR VIDFADMA, *was King of Denmark and Sweden in 660*
RORIC SLINGEBAND, *King of Denmark and Sweden in 700*
HARALD HILDESTAND, *King of Denmark and Sweden in 725*

SIGURD RING *living in 750*

RAYNER LODBROK[4], *King of Denmark and Sweden, died in 794 and married* ASLANGA

SIGURD SNODOYE, *King of Denmark and Sweden, died in 830*

HORDA KNUT, *King of Denmark, died in 850*

FROTHO, *King of Denmark, died in 875*

GORM ENSKE *married* SIDA *and died in 890*

HAROLD PARCUS, *King of Denmark, married* ELGIVA *daughter of* ETHELRED I, *King of England and a brother of* KING ALFRED *the* GREAT

GORM *del* GAMMEL, *King of Denmark, died in 931 and married* THYRA

HARALD BLAATAND, *King of Denmark, died in 931*

LADY GUNNORA, *wife of* RICHARD I, *Third Duke of Normandy, was born in 933 and died in 996. They had (beside their son* RICHARD II*) a son*

ROBERT *d'*EVEREUX[5], *the Archbishop died in 1087.*

RICHARD, *Count d'Evereux died in 1067.*

AGNES EVEREUX *became the wife of* SIMON I *de* MONTFORT

BERTRADE MONTFORT, *wife of* FULK IV, *Count D'Anjou, was born in 1043 and died in 1109. Faulk's descent from Old King Cole is as follows:*

The Frankish Kings[6]

OLD KING COLE, *son of* MARIUS, *was the father of*

ATHILDIS *was the wife of* MARCOMIR IV, *King of Franconia, who died in 149 and had*

CLODOMIR IV, *King of the Franks, died in 166. His wife was* HASILDA *daughter of the* KING *of the* RUGIJ. *The lineal descent as follows:*

KING FARABERT *died in 186*

KING SUNNO *died in 213*

KING HILDERIC *died in 253*

KING BARTHEUS *died in 272*

KING CLODIUS III *died in 298*

KING WALTER *died in 306*

KING DAGOBERT *died in 317*

GENEBALD I, *Duke of the East Franks, died in 350*

KING DAGOBERT *died in 379*

---

[4] Magna Charta, John S. Wurts, V. 1-2, chapter 27, pp. 164-165.

[5] Magna Charta, John S. Wurts, V. 1-2, chapter 27, p. 194.

[6] Magna Charta, John S. Wurts, V. 1-2, chapter 27, pp. 162 & 190.

KING CLODIUS I *died in 389*
KING MARCOMIR *died in 404*
KING PHARAMOND *married* ARGOTTA *daughter of* GENEBALD
KING CLODIO, *married* BASINA *de* THURINGIA *and died in 455*
SIGERMERUS I *married the daughter of* FERREOLUS TONATIUS
FERREOLUS *married* DEUTERIA, *a Roman lady*
AUSBERT *died in 570. He married* BLITHILDES *the daughter of* CLOTHAIRE I *the King of France and his wife* INGONDE. *The granddaughter of* CLOVIS *the* GREAT, *King of France, who was born in 466, baptized in 496 at Rheims, and died in 511, and his wife* ST. CLOTHILDE *of* BURGUNDY, *"the Girl of the French Vineyards". It was she who led him to embrace Christianity, and 3,000 of his followers were baptized in a single day. When Clovis first listened to the story of Christ's crucifixion, he was so moved that he cried, "If I had been there with my valiant Franks I would have avenged Him."*
Ausbert and Blithildes were the parents of
ARNOUL, *Bishop of Metz, died in 601. He married* ODA *of* SAVOY *and had*
ST. ARNOLPH, *Bishop of Metz, died in 641. He married* LADY DODO *and had*
ANCHISES *married* BEGGA *of* BRABANT, *who died in 698. They had*
PEPIN *d'*HERISTAL, *Mayor of the Palace, died in 714 and married* ALPAIS.

Magister Palatii

The royal successors of Clovis were woefully inefficient. They left the rule of the kingdom to their Mayors of the Palace, and only showed themselves to the people once a year, at the March Parliament, when, adorned with crowns and their fair hair flowing loose to their waists, they rode in a cart drawn by oxen. As they did little but eat and drink and enjoy themselves, they went by the name of the sluggard kings, all power being in the hands of the Mayors of the Palace. Among these mayors, Pepin of Heristal made himself conspicuous. His home was near Spa, in the pretty woodland country about Liege. He made the office hereditary in his family. His heroic son

CHARLES MARTEL, *the Hammer, Mayor of the Palace, King of France, was still more famous because, in the decisive Battle of Tours in 732 he utterly routed the Arabs who had conquered Spain and the south of France. Charles Martel married* ROTRUDE *and died in 741.*
PEPIN *the* SHORT *and* KARLOMANN, *succeeded him, but Karlomann resigned his authority unto his brother's hands and tired of fighting, entered a monastery. Pepin had much to do:*

The Saxons, Bavarians and Arabs were all menacing or revolting, and he had to rush from one part of the kingdom to another, defending its frontiers, and getting no help from the stupid sluggard king, at Paris. At last, impatient of the farce, he sent this question to the Pope: "Who is king, he who governs, or he who wears the crown?" "He who governs, of course." answered the Pope. "That is myself", said the little man with a great will; "so the sluggards shall go to sleep forever", and he sent the last of them Childeric III, into a monastery. Then his nobles put their shields together, and the little man was seated on a chair, on their shields, and with him thus, shouting and raising their shields as high as they could. They marched three times around the parliament, and then, by St. Boniface, he was anointed Archbishop of Metz, A.D. 752. Pepin did not forget that he owed a debt of gratitude to the Pope for the answer he had given to his question. And when, shortly after, the Pope sent to complain of the trouble occasioned by the Lombards, Pepin crossed the Alps, punished the Lombards, took from them all their territory about Rome, and gave it to the Pope "to belong to him and the bishops of Rome forever". That was the beginning of the Papal sovereignty. The States of the Church, as they were called, remained under the sovereignty of the Popes until 1871.

PEPIN *le* BREF, *King of France, died in 768, leaving by his wife* BERTHA *of* LAON, *two sons,* CHARLEMAGNE *and* CARLOMANN. *The latter died a few years later, and then with the consent of the great nobles,* CHARLEMAGNE, CHARLES *the* GREAT, *became king.*

CHARLEMAGNE, *the greatest figure of the Middle Ages, by his wife* HILDEGARDE *of* SUABIA *born in 757 and died 30 April 782, had a son* LOUIS I, *the Debonaire, by his wife* JUDITH, *daughter of* GUELPH, *Count of Andech and Bavaria and his wife* EDITH *of* SAXONY *was father of* GISELA, *grandmother of* DUKE BURKHART, *who died in 911, from whom descended* ULRICH *von* UERIKON, *Swiss Knight, born in 1259. Gisela was also the ancestress of* HUGH CAPET, *King of France and of* AMICIA, *wife of* RICHARD *de* CLARE, *the Surety.* LOUIS I *by his first wife* EMENGARDE, *who in 818, daughter of* INGAM, *Count of Hasbania, was father of*

LOTHAIRE, *Earl of Germany, married* ERMENGARDE *of* ALSACE *and had*

ERMENGARDS *was wife of* GISLEBERT

GISLEBERT, *Duke of Lorraine, married* GERBERGA *and died in 930*

ALBREDA, *of Lorraine, wife of* RENAUD, *Count de Roucy died in 973*

ERMENTRUDE ROUCY, *wife of* ALBERIC II, *Count de Macon, died in 975*

BEATRICE MACON *was the wife of* GEOFFREY I *de Gastinois*

GEOFFREY II *de* GASTINOIS *married* ERMENGARDE *d'ANJOU*

FULK IV, *Count d'Anjou, born in 1043 and died in 1109, married*
BERTRADE *de* MONTFORT, *and had*
FULK V, *Count d'Anjou, born in 1092 and died in 1144. He married*
ERMENGARDE *du* MAINE *who died in 1126. They were the parents of*
GEOFFREY PLANTAGENET *was born in 1113 and died in 1151. He*
married MATILDA *of* ENGLAND, *born in 1103 and died in 1167, a*
great, great, great granddaughter of RICHARD I, *Duke of Normandy (and*
his wife LADY GUNNORA) *as follows. Richard I's son*
RICHARD II, *Duke of Normandy, died in 1026 and married* JUDITH *de*
BRETAGNE, *who died in 1018*
ROBERT *of* NORMANDY *who by* HERLEVE *de* FALAISE *had*
WILLIAM *the* CONQUEROR, *born in 1027 and died in 1086. He married*
MAUD *of* FLANDERS, *who died in 1083 and had*
HENRY I, *King of England, born in 1070 and died in 1135, whose wife,*
MATILDA *of* SCOTLAND, *was born in 1082, and died in 1118. She was*
the daughter of MALCOLM III CANMORE. *Henry and Matilda had*
MATILDA *of* ENGLAND *was the wife of* GEOFFREY PLANTAGENET
and had
HENRY II, *King of England, married* ELEANOR *of* ACQUITAINE
JOHN, *King of England, married* ISABEL *de* TAOLLEFER
HENRY III, *King of England, married* ELEANOR *of* PROVENCE
EDWARD I, *King of England, married* ELEANOR *of* CASTILE

The Lineage of Eleanor of Castile

WILLIAM I, *Count of Montreuil, died in 965. He was eighth in descent*
from CHARLEMAGNE *and the father of*
HILDUIN *living in 981 and had*
HUGUES I, *Count of Ponthieu, married* GISELE *the daughter of* HUGH
CAPET *and his wife* ADELA
ENGUERAND I, *Count of Ponthieu, died in 1046, having married*
ADELE, *daughter of* ARNULPH, *Count of Holland, and wife*
LUITGARDE *of* CLEVES.
HUGUES II, *Count of Ponthieu, died in 1052 and married* BERTHA
daughter of GUERINFROI, *Signor d'Aumale and had*
GUY I, *Count of Ponthieu, died in 1101 and left by his wife* ADA, AGNES
PONTHIEU *married* ROBERT II, *d'Alencon. He died in 1119. They had*
WILLIAM III, *Count of Alencon and Ponthieu died in 1172. He married*
ALICE *daughter of* EUDES I, *Count of Bourgogne, whose wife* MAUD
daughter of WILLIAM I, *Count de Bourgogne, and* STEPHANIE, *was a*
first cousin once removed of WILLIAM *the* CONQUEROR. *Alice was*
great granddaughter of RICHARD II, *Duke of Normandy and his wife*
JUDITH BRETAGNE, *who were the grandparents of the Conqueror.*
William III and his wife Alice were the parents of

GUY II, *Count of Ponthieu, died in 1147. He and his wife* IDA *had*
JEAN I, *Count of Ponthieu, whose wife was* BEATRICE *daughter of*
ANSELME, *Count de St. Pol. He died in 1191, leaving a son*
WILLIAM III, *Count of Ponthieu, born in 1179 and died in 1221. He
married in 1195,* ALICE *the daughter of* LOUIS VII, *King of France, and
his wife* CONSTANCE, *daughter of* ALPHONSO VII, *of Castile and*
BERENGUELA *his wife. The daughter of* WILLIAM III *and* ALICE *was*
MARIE, *Countess of Ponthieu, died in 1251. In 1208 she became the wife
of* SIMON *de* DAMMARTIN, *Count of Aumale, who died in 1239 and
they had*
JOANNA DAMMARTIN *was the second wife of* FERDINAND III, *King
of Castile and Leon. They had*
ELEANOR *of* CASTILE *and* LEON *was the wife of* EDWARD I, *King of
England. Their daughter*
JOAN *of* ACRE, *wife of* GILBERT *de* CLARE, *was born in 1272, in the
Holy Land where her mother had insisted on going with her husband, King
Edward I, of England, on a Crusade.*

The Plantagenets

A surname given to Geoffrey, Count of Anjou, and said to have
originated from his wearing a branch of broom (plantagenesta) in his cap.
This name was borne by 14 Kings, from Henry II, great grandfather of
Edward I, through Richard III. They were distinguished for their light
golden hair, blue eyes and striking appearance. Geoffrey was the
handsomest of the Plantagenets, possessor of a figure of elegant symmetry,
and a man of most winning manner. He was quick in understanding, and
an excellent scholar, with an inherent sense of honor.

Edward I was of Kingly appearance, called Edward of the Flaxen Hair, and
later, because of his height, Edward Longshanks. He was said to be a
handsome, blond giant, with an expression full of fire and sweetness. At
the age of 15 he was married to Eleanor of Castile, who was 10 years old at
the time, although they did not live together until many years thereafter,
this was the beginning of one of the truly great romances of history.
Edward I, King of England, and Dona Eleanora of Castile became devoted
to each other, and would remain so until death separated them.

The Druids

Before the days of Abraham

Druidism was introduced into England more than two thousand years
before Christ by Hu Gadarn, the Mighty, the first colonizer of Britain, and
for many generations Boadicea's people had been Druids. The whole

population of southern England, including the eastern coast inhabited by the Lceni was under the control of Druidical priesthood consisting of three orders:

The Druids, the guardians and interpreters of the laws, and the religious guides and instructors of the youth, and the judges of the people.

The Eubates, were the working clergy who performed all the rites.

The Bards, whose duty it was to preserve in verse the memory of any remarkable event, to celebrate the triumph of their heroes, and by their exhortation and songs, excite the chiefs and people to deeds of courage and daring on the day of battle.

Notwithstanding its many errors, its terrible idolatry, superstition and cruel practices, Druidism had some points in its favor. For example, it made immortality of the soul the basis of all its teachings, holding it to be the principal incentive for a righteous life. The defense of one's country in a just war was a high virtue in its system. Yet for a people of such remarkable civilization and culture, their conduct was barbarous and cruel. Druidism declined and at last disappeared because although it taught forgiveness and love, it lacked the power to perform these virtues. Christianity supplied this power and Druidism vanished. Not however, until it had accomplished its special mission, the preservation in Western Europe of the idea of the unity and trinity of God, and in extension of this principle, it employed the triads, of trinities of life and worship, of which many hundreds were taught.

There is touching beauty in many of these ancient Druidic and later Welsh triads, for example:

There are three obligations of every man: Justice, love, and humility.

There are three rights of every man: Life, freedom, and achievement.

There are three duties of every man: Worship God; Be just to all men; Die for your country.

Believe in God who made thee; Love god who saved thee; Fear God who will judge thee.

Three persons have claims of brothers and sisters: The widow; the orphan; and the stranger.

A Twenty Years College Course

There were in ancient Britain no less than forty Druidic universities, which were also the capitals of the forty tribes, the originals of the modern counties, which preserve for the most part the ancient tribal limits. In these universities was a total enrollment of sixty thousand souls, among whom were included the young nobility of Britain. It required twenty years' attendance at college to master the circle of Druidic knowledge, for they taught all that was known concerning natural philosophy, astronomy,

240

arithmetic, botany, geometry, law, medicine, poetry, oratory, and natural theology. Well informed on all the known subjects were the graduates of a Druid university.

Caesar records in his commentaries that they instructed their pupils in the movements of the heavenly bodies, and the grandeur of the universe. Their knowledge of mathematics must have been considerable, since they applied it to the measurement of the earth and the stars. In mechanics they were usually advanced, judging from the huge monuments which remain.

Present day Druids hold their summer solstice rites at Stonehenge[7], as they have for hundreds of years. According to modern archeologists, Stonehenge existed many years before the time of the Druids.

In clan times, the preservation of a pedigree was necessary to maintain all that was valuable in blood, station, and property. Without a pedigree a man was an outlaw; he had no clan, consequently, he had no legal rights, nor standing. Genealogies were guarded with extreme jealousy and recorded with painful exactitude by the herald-bards of each clan. On the public reception into the clan of a child at the age of fifteen, his family genealogy was proclaimed, and all challengers of it commanded to come forward. By the common law every Briton held as his birthright ten acres of land.[8]

The Order of Druids

No one could be a candidate for the Order who could not prove his descent from nine successive generations of free forefathers. No slave could be a Druid; becoming one, he forfeited his Order and privileges.

Clad in white and wearing ornaments of gold, they celebrated their mystic rites in the depths of the forest. The Druids held the mistletoe in deepest veneration, and when found growing upon an oak it represented man, a creature entirely dependent on God for support, and yet with an individual existence and will of its own. Marriage to one woman was early established among the Britons.

Caesar's First Invasion

Caesar found the people in a very primitive state, depending for support on their farms, flocks, and herds. Their houses were rudely built, formed of wicker, plastered with mud. They were a handsome, athletic race wearing their hair long, and the moustache long and flowing. Julius Caesar's invasion occurred on August 4, 55 B.C. After campaigning 55

---

[7] National Geographic, June, 1960.
[8] I am indebted to Dr. G. Campbell Morgan and Dr. R. Wynn Morgan for the above, and much that follows.

days, he failed to advance more than 7 miles from the coast. Caesar fled by night, taking hostages with him.

Queen Boadicea

45 Generations to King Edward III

Rule Britannia! Britannia rules the waves! Britons never shall be slaves! Thus sang James Thompson two hundred years ago.

Sad indeed is the lament of the Ancient Briton: "We dwelt in a goodly land. We were peaceful and happy. By and by the Romans came and brought us new laws and a strange religion. Then the Romans went and the Saxons came, and the Danes came, and all manners of strange and fierce people landed on the eastern shores of Britain. With beguiling words they entered our homes and with loving protestations they married our daughters. But soon, alas so soon! They trampled out our hearth fires and despoiled our altars; and they set up kingdoms and kingships amongst us and now the shepherd and the husbandman of the Cymry and the great and Sovereign Lords of the Cymry are gone. Even the speech of our fathers has passed from us and the songs of our childhood are forgotten. Once happy Britain has become the home of strangers!"

Knowledge of noble ancestry should be an incentive to noble living.[9]

Boadicea, in Latin "Victoria," is described in the records as "cousin" of Caradoc and his sister Gladys.

One of her daughters, whose name has not been preserved, became the wife of Meric, whom the Romans called Marius. He was son of Arviragus, King of Britain, and his wife Venissa Julia, daughter of Tiberius Claudius Caesar, Emperor of Rome, who was grandson of Mark Anthony.

Marius died A.D. 125. His remarkably long ancestry has been preserved in the ancient Welsh records.

King Caradoc's birth-book or pedigree register records his own as well as others' descent from "clari majores" illustrious ancestors, through thirty-six generations from Aedd Mawr and runs as follows:

AEDD MAWR, *King Edward the Great, who appears to have lived about 1300 B.C., the time of Boaz and Ruth, had a son*
BRYDAIN *who settled in the island at an early date and being a great legislator as well as a warrior, according to tradition gave his name to the entire island, which has since been corrupted into Britain. His son*
ANNYN TRO *was father of*
SELYS HEN
BRWT

---

[9] Diary, 18 June 1897.

CYMRYW
ITHON
GWEYRYDD
PEREDUR
LLYFEINYDD
TEUGED
LLARIAN *lived during the days when London was a considerable town, having been founded 1020 B.C., or earlier as some hold, at least 270 years before the founding of Rome.*
ITHEL
ENIR FARDD
CALCHWYNYDD
LLYWARCH
IDWAL
RHUN
BLEDDYN
MORGAN
BERWYN
CERAINT FEDDW, *an irreclaimable drunkard, deposed by his subjects for setting fire just before harvest to the cornfields of Siluria, now Monmouthshire.*
BRYWLAIS
ALAFON
ANYN
DINGAD
GREIDIOL
CERAINT
MEIRION
ARCH
CAID, *had*
CERI
BARAN
CASWALLON *was king at the time of the first invasion. The antagonist of Caesar, he successfully repulsed the armies of the ablest general of antiquity, the conquerors of Europe, Asia and Africa. He continued to reign after the invasion seven years.*
LLYR *(King Lear) was educated in Rome by Augustus Caesar. Among the "wise sayings" recorded by the Bards we find this attributed to Llyr: "No folly but ends in misery." He was the father of*
BRAN, *King of Siluria, and was commander of the British fleet. In the year 36 A.D. he resigned the crown to his son Caradoc and became Arch-Druid of the college of Siluria, where he remained some years until called upon to be a hostage for his son. During his seven years in Rome he became* the first *royal convert to Christianity, and was baptized by the*

243

Apostle Paul, as was his son Caradoc and the latter's two sons, Cyllinus and Cynon. Henceforth he is known as Bran the Blessed Sovereign. "He was the first to bring the faith of Christ to the Cymry." His recorded proverb is: "There is no good apart from God." He introduced the use of vellum into Britain. His son

CARADOC *(Caractacus) was King of Siluria (Monmouthshire, etc.), where he died. He was born at Trevan, Llanilid, in Glamorganshire. His valiant services to his country have been told in connection with the attempted invasions of the island. The Bards record his wise saying: "Oppression persisted in brings on death." He had three sons, CYLLIN (Cyllinus), LLEYN (Linus) and CYNON, and two daughters, EURGAIN and GLADYS (Claudia).*

ST. CYLLIN, *King of Siluria, and the son of Caradoc, was sainted by the early Church of Britain. "He first of the Cymry gave infants names, for before names were not given except to adults, and then from something characteristic in their bodies, minds or manners." His brother Linus the Martyr, his sister Claudia and her husband Rufus Pudens aided the Apostle Paul in the Christian Church in Rome, as recorded in II Timothy 4:21 and Romans 16:13.*

PRINCE COEL, *son of Cyllin, was living A.D. 120. Prince Coel was the father of*

KING LLEUVER MAWR, *of whom later, the second Blessed Sovereign (Cadwallader was the third).*

Contemporaneous Events

AUGUSTUS OCTAVIUS CAESAR, the first Roman Emperor was the successor and grandnephew of Julius Caesar. During his reign and at a moment of universal peace when "no war or battle sound was heard the world around," there was born in Bethlehem among the hills of Judea. One whose influence on the future of the world, was destined to outshine the influence of all the warriors and emperors the world has ever seen. JESUS was born among the lowly, and the rushing, seething Roman world knew nothing of the event. But the time was coming when all history would be reckoned by so many years before or after the birth of Christ. "He came unto His own things and His own people received Him not." Said they, "We will not have this Man to reign over us," and He was put to death under a pretense of religious and civil law. His disciples bore witness to the fact that HE rose from the dead and they eagerly devoted their lives, even unto death, to proclaiming the Good News. No wonder, that, thousands of converts soon joined them. Nor was the new way to succeed by force, but by persuasion and conviction. Saint Paul, a Roman citizen, became the chief instrument in carrying the new religion to the Roman dominions, near and far. It was not long before the converts were made to suffer terrible persecutions. The first of these was in the time of Nero, who to divert suspicion from himself accused the Christians of setting fire to the City of Rome. Nero was one of the wickedest men who ever sat upon a throne and instead of trying to stop the fire is said to have fiddled and danced while Rome burned. Tacitus tells us that a great many Christians were put to death. Some were crucified, and others devoured by wild beasts. And some were covered with pitch and set on fire to light the public places at night. "Yet, they were stoned, they were sawn asunder, were slain with the sword; they wandered about in sheepskins and goatskins; in deserts, and in mountains, and in dens and caves of the earth." With the universal decline of private virtue, the mighty Roman Empire inevitably decayed, but Christianity survived all the terrific persecutions and within three centuries became the religion fostered and promoted by the State.

No civilization has ever survived a moral breakdown.

Pedigree of the Descent of Her Majesty Queen Elizabeth[10]

Through 73 generations and 20 centuries and showing kinship with some Virginia Families.

BOADECIA, *in Latin "Victoria", British Queen, died 62 A.D., whose daughter, name unknown married* MARIUS *son of* ARVIRAGUS, *King of Britain, and his wife* VENISSA JULIA *the daughter of* TIBERIUS CLAUDIUS CAESAR, *Emperor of Rome, son of* ANTONIA, *daughter of* MARK ANTHONY, *born 83 B.C. Their son*

OLD KING COLE, *King of Britain, 125 A.D., built Coel-Castra (Colchester) whose daughter*

ATHILDIS *married* MARCOMIR IV, *King of Franconia and died in 149*

CLODOMIR, *King of the Franks, died in 166 and married* HASILDA. *From them the line continues*

KING FARABERT *died in 186.*

KING SUNNO *died in 213.*

KING HILDERIC *died in 253.*

KING BARTHERUS *died in 272.*

KING CLODIUS III *died in 298.*

KING WALTER *died in 306.*

KING DAGOBERT *died in 317.*

KING GENEBALD I, *Duke of the East Franks, died in 350.*

KING DAGOBERT *died in 379.*

KING CLODIUS I *died in 389.*

KING MARCOMIR *died in 404.*

PHARAMOND, *King of Westphalia, married* ARGOTTA.

---

[10] Magna Charta, John S. Wurts.

CLODIO, *the Long Haired, King of Westphalia married* BASINA.

MEROVEE, *King of France, died in 458 and married* VERICA.

CHILDERIC I, *King of France, was born in 436 and died in 481. He married* BASINA *of* THURINGIA.

CLOVIS *the* GREAT *was born in 465 and died in 511. He was the King of France and married* ST. CLOTHILDE.

CLOTHAIRE I *was born in 497 and died in 561. He was the King of France and married* INGONDE.

BLITHILDES *died in 570 and married* AUBERT *of* MOSELLE.

ARNOUL, *Bishop of Metz, died in 601 and married* ODA *de* SAVOY.

ST ARNOLPH, *Bishop of Metz, died in 641 and married* LADY DODO *of* SAXONY.

ANCHISES, *died in 685 and married* BEGGA *of* BRABANT, *who died in 698.*

PEPIN *de* HERISTAL, *Mayor of the Palace, died in 714 and married* ALPAIS.

CHARLES MARTEL, *born in 689 and died in 741. He was the King of France and married* ROTRUDE, *who died in 724.*

PEPIN *the* SHORT, *born in 714 and died in 768 He was the King of France and married* BERTHA *of* LAON, *who died in 783.*

CHARLEMAGNE *was born in 742 and died in 814. He was the Emperor of the West and married* HILDEGARDE, *who was born 757 and died in 782.*

PEPIN, *born in 778 and died in 810. He was the King of Italy and married* BERTHA *of* TOULOUSE.

BERNHARD, *King of Lombardy, died in 812 and married* CUNEGONDE.

PEPIN, *Lay Abbott in 840 married and had*

HERBERT I, *Count of Vermandois, died in 902, married and had*

HERBERT II, *Count of Vermandois, died in 943 and married* HILDEBRAND.

ROBERT, *Count of Vermandois, died in 968 and married* ADELAIDE *de* CHALONS.

ADELAIDE, *Countess of Chalons, died in 976 and married* GEOFFREY, *Count d'Anjou.*

FULK III, *Count d'Anjou, died in 1040 and married* HILDEGARDE.

ERMENGARDE *d'*ANJOU *married* GEOFFREY II, *de Gastinois.* FULK IV *was born in 1043 and died in 1109. The Count of Anjou married* BERTRADE *de* MONTFORT.

FULK V *was born in 1092 and died in 1144. The Count of Anjou married* ERMENGARDE *de* MAINE, *who died in 1126.*

GEOFFREY PLANTAGENET *was born in 1113 and died in 1151. He married* MATILDA *of* ENGLAND *granddaughter of* WILLIAM *the* CONQUEROR.

HENRY II *born in 1133 and died in 1189 was King of England. He married* ELEANOR *of* ACQUITAINE.

ELEANOR *of* ENGLAND *married* ALPHONSO IX, *King of Castile and died in 1214.*

BERENGARIS *of* CASTILE *died in 1244 and married* ALPHONSO X, *King of Leon.*

FERDINAND III *born in 1191 and died in 1252 was King of Castile. He married in 1237,* JOAN *de* DAMMARTIN.

ELEANOR *of* CASTILE *died in 1290. She was married in 1254 to* EDWARD I, *King of England.*

EDWARD II, *King of England, married* ISABEL *of* FRANCE *and died in 1358.*

EDWARD III, *King of England, married* PHILIPPA *of* HAINAULT, *born in 1333 and died in 1369.*

LIONEL *born in 1338 and died in 1368 was the Duke of Clarence, Knight of the Garter, and married to* ELIZABETH BURGH.

PHILLIPA PLANTAGENET *married* EDMUND *de* MORTIMER, *Earl of March.*

ELIZABETH MORTIMER *married* HENRY *de* PERCY, *Knight of the Garter, called "Hotsput".*

HENRY *de* PERCY, K.G., *the Earl of Northumberland married* ELEANOR NEVILL.

HENRY *de* PERCY, *Earl of Northumberland, married* ELEANOR POININGS.

MARGARET PERCY *married* WILLIAM GASCOIGNE *who died in 1486, was Lord of Bentley Manor, county of Yorkshire.*

ELIZABETH GASCOIGNE *married* GEORGE *de* TAILBOIS, *Lord of Kyme Manor, county of Yorkshire.*

ANNE TAILBOIS *married* EDWARD DYMOKE, *Lord of Scrivelsby Manor, county of Lincoln.*

FRANCES DYMOKE *married* THOMAS WINDEBANK, *Lord of the Manor Haines Hall, county of Berkshire, Knighted by King James I, 25 July 1603.*

MILDRED WINDEBANK *born in 1584 and died in 1630 was married in 1600 to* ROBERT READE *of Linkenholt Parish, Hants, who died in 1626.*

COLONEL GEORGE READE *was born in England, 25 October 1608, came to America in 1637, was Acting Governor of Virginia in 1638 and died October 1674. He married* ELIZABETH MARTIAN.

MILDRED READ, *Great Grandmother of George Washington, married* COLONEL AUGUSTINE WARNER *and was born in 1643 and died in 1681.*

MARY WARNER *married in 1680* COLONEL JOHN SMITH *of Purton.*

247

MILDRED SMITH *was born in 1682 and married in 1700* ROBERT PORTEUS *of Newbottle, Virginia, who was born in 1679 and died in 1758.*

REVEREND ROBERT PORTEUS *was born in 1705 and died in 1754. He was Rector of Cockayne Hatley, county of Bedford. He married in 1736* JUDITH COCKAYNE, *who was born in 1702 and died in 1789.*

MILDRED PORTEUS, *born in 1744, married* ROBERT HODGSON *of Congleton, county of Chester, who was born in 1740.*

REVEREND ROBERT HODGSON, *Dean of Carlisle, married in 1804* MARY TUCKER.

HENRIETTA MILDRED HODGSON *married in 1824* OSWALD SMITH, *of Blendon Hall, county of Kent, who was born in 1794 and died in 1863.*

FRANCES DORA SMITH *died in 1922 and married in 1853* CLAUDE LYON BOWES, *later Bowes-Lyon, 13th Earl of Strathmore, who was born in 1824 and died in 1904.*

CLAUDE GEORGE BOWES-LYON, *14th Earl of Strathmore, K.G.K.T was born in 1855 and married in 1881* NINA CECELIA CAVENDISH-BENTINCK, *who died in 1938.*

ELIZABETH ANGELA MARGUERITE *born in 1900, married in 1923* HIS MAJESTY KING GEORGE VI, *born in 1895, succeeded to the throne in 1936 and died in 1952.*

QUEEN ELIZABETH II, *born 21 April 1926, married* PHILIP MOUNTBATTEN, *son of Prince Andrew of Greece, great, great grandson of Queen Victoria. Her coronation was 2 June 1953.*

CHAPTER XIX

LIGHTFOOT TIDBITS

John Lightfoot, the naturalist, was born in New Kent, Glouchestershire 9 December 1735. Stephen Lightfoot his father was a yeoman and John attended the Crypt school, Gloucester. In 1753 he entered Pembroke College, Oxford as an exhibitioner and graduated B.A. in 1756. The Dowager-Duchess of Portland appointed him as her librarian and chaplain at a stipend of £100 a year. There was a common interest shared by him and the Dowager-Duchess in botany and conchology. He worked for her until her death in 1785 and died himself after a brief illness in 1788. He married the only daughter and heiress of William Burton Raynes in 1780 and had five children.

John wrote the book "Flora Scotica" that was published in 1778. It contains thirty botanical and five zoological plates arranged on the Linnean system, with descriptions in English, Scottish, and Gaelic of the names of the plants.

John Lightfoot the biblical critic was born at the rectory-house of Stoke-upon-Trent in 1602. He was the second son of Thomas Lightfoot, curate of Stoke and later rector of Uttoxeter until his death in 1658. His mother was Elizabeth Bagnall from a well-known family at Newcastle-under-Lyme. John entered Christ's College, Cambridge in 1617 under the tutorship of Dr. William Chappel. He distinguished himself in classical scholarship and showed great promise as an orator. After taking holy orders he was appointed to the curacy of Norton-in-Hales, Shropshire. He studied Hebrew and other cognate languages. He wrote his first work, "Erubhim, or Miscellanies, Christian and Judaical" in 1629 and after that his pen never stayed still. Lightfoot's first wife was Joyce the daughter of William Compton of Stone Park and his second wife was Anne the widow of Austin Brograve, Esquire.

This chapter is where we thought it would be best to put all the little extras, the items we're not sure of exactly where to place in the book. It will be typed exactly the way we have it without any revisions and there will be no footnotes. Unfortunately we have a family that stuck to certain names with no variations. Because of that there could be 7 John Lightfoots living at the same time and place. What we have put in the other chapters were research till there was no doubt or there was proof of where they belonged. We have also decided it would be easier to put the lists of our ancestors with their ranks, positions and where they fought in the various wars that have sprang up in our nations history or courthouse records in their original forms.

Ship Passenger Lists:

The South (1538 – 1825) by Carl Boyer, 1979
a.   Lists of the Living and the Dead in Virginia, February 16, 1623.
     At James Citie and within the Corporation thereof:
     John Lightfoote
b.   Names of Inhabitants at Jamestown in 1624: John Lightfoote
c.   John Lightfoote, ship Seaventure, 1623.
Cavaliers & Pioneers, introduction page xxx is mentioned among the "Ancient Planters," (these include those who are known to have come to Virginia before the close of the year 1616, survived the massacre, appear in the Muster of 1624/5 as then living in Virginia and to most of whom the term "Ancient Planter," may be applied "a Justification") John Lytefoote, of James City, Yeoman, "who came in the Sea Venture with Sir Thomas Gates," patent 14 August 1614, page 5. He left his estate to William Spencer by a nuncupative will. See Journal of the Council & General Courts.
21 January 1628/9 Patent Book #1, Part 2, Page 3:

John Lytefoote, 12 acres, August 14, 1624, page 10. An old planter who came over in the Sea Venture with Sir Thomas Gates, "and hath abode hitherto in this country."
Within the island of James City, toward Goose Hill, near the land of Wm. Spencer being part of his first devident of 100 acs. measured by Wm. Clayborne.
Fee rent 3 pence.
Just above this, I find
William Spencer, yeoman & ancient planter, 12 acs. James City, 14 August 1624. Part of his first devident within the island towards Goose Hill, near land of Sir Thomas Dale and John Lytefoote.
Due for his personal adv. land measured by Wm. Clayborne. Fee rent 3 pence.
Marginal note: "which is to be abated out of his devident at Spencers."
Page 9
Patent Book #3 Page 314

Thomas Hancks, 100 acs. Gloucester Co., 16 February 1653, p. 369 N.E. side of the head of Arakiaco Swamp upon SE side of Mattapony River & SW upon Hanckes br. of said swamp Transport of 2 persons: Joane Lightfoot, John Range.

These are articles that were found in the Virginia County Records:

P.84 MARRIAGE LICENSES – SPOTSYLVANIA COUNTY, VA.

From "An Account of Ye Governor's Dues" Order Book 1
1729 June 3, Francis Slaughter and Ann Lightfoot
£1000 Joel Johnson, admr. of Richard Johnson, decd., with John Grayson & G. Lightfoot, sec. Nov. 1726

P.55 ADMINISTRATION BONDS

£100 Robert Green, admr. of Henry Henderson, decd., with Goodrich Lightfoot, sec., May 2, 1727
£200 John Grame, admr. of John Samm, decd., with Goodrich Lightfoot & Robert Spotswood, sec. May 2, 1727
P.104
Feb. 4, 1728 Augustine Smith of Caroline County, Gent. to Thomas Slaughter of the same County, Gent., £100 ster., 300 a. of land in Spots. Co. in the fork of Rappk. River;
Witness: Jo. Taliaferro, G. Lightfoot, Abraham Field,
Rec. Feb. 4, 1728-9
P.105
February 3, 1728 Thomas Slaughter of Caroline County, Francis and Robert Slaughter of Spotsylvania County, to Augustine Smith of Caroline County. £100 ster. 288 a. in Spots Co., on both sides of Black Walnut Run – granted to Robert Slaughter, father of the same. Thomas, Francis and Robert Slaughter, by patent June 30, 1726.
Witnesses: Jo. Taliaferro, G. Lightfoot, Abraham Field,
Rec. Feb. 4, 1728-9
P.106
May 7, 1729 Henry Willis of King & Queen County, Gent. to Goodrich Lightfoot of Spotsylvania County on South side of the South West Mountains.
Witnesses: Wm. Johnson, Ambr. Grayson, Wm. Hackney.
Rec. May 6, 1729
P.121
April 4, 1732 Goodrich Lightfoot of Spotsylvania Co., Gent, to John Lightfoot of same county, Gent. £100 ster. 300 a. in Spots. Co., Thomas Chew, Wm. Bledsoe, April 4, 1732

P.129

March 2, 1733 Goodrich Lightfoot of St. Mark's Par., Spts. Co., to Richard Wright of same parish and county. £4 curr. 50 a. in St. Mark's Par., Spts. Co., xx part of a tract granted said Lightfoot by patent June 26, 1731.

Jane X Teele, Anthony Soulthorpe, W. Russell

March 5, 1733

P.512 Sheriffs of Spotsylvania County

Deed Book 1 1722-1729

Wm. Bledsoe, Gent. Com. dated July 9, 1722. Took the oath of office at the first court held for Spotsylvania County, August 1722 (page 16.)

Will book A 1722-1729

Thomas Chew, Gent. Com. dated April 30, 1724 (p. 6)
Thomas Chew, Gent. Com. dated April 5, 1725 (p.31)
Goodrich Lightfoot, Gent. Com. dated April 25, 1726 (p.32)
Goodrich Lightfoot, Gent. Com. dated April 1, 1727 (p. 48)
Larkin Chew, Gent. Com. dated April 27, 1728 (p.69)
Edwin Hickman, Gent. Com. dated Mar. 24, 1728/29 (p.92)
Edwin Hickman, Gent. Com. dated Apr. 7, 1730 (p.113)
William Johnson, Gent. Com. dated May 5, 1731 (p.134)
Joseph Brook, Gent. Com. dated April 25, 1733 (p.186)
Joseph Thomas, Gent. Com. dated April 21, 1735 (p.253)
John Chew, Gent. Com. dated May 5, 1737 (p.303)
John Taliaferro, Gent. Com. dated July 15, 1741 (p.326)
John Minor, Gent. Com. dated July 12, 1743 (p.366)
John Waller, Jr., Gent. Com. dated July 14, 1746 (p.440)
Richard Tutt, Gent. Com. dated Aug. 31, 1748 (p.474)

Will Book B. 1749-1759

John Thornton	Gent. Com. dated Sept. 1, 1750 (p.52)		
John Thornton	"	"	Aug. 13, 1751 (p.76)
John Chew	"	"	July 15, 1752 (p.130)
Larkin Chew	"	"	July 17, 1754 (p.214)
Rice Curtis	"	"	July 11, 1756 (p.298)
William Carr	"	"	July 12, 1758 (p.379)
Robert Jackson	"	"	Aug. 25, 1760 (p.489)

Will Book D 1761-1772

Charles Dick	Gent. Com. dated Aug. 10, 1762 (p.32)		
Beverley Winslow	"	"	Oct. 15, 1764 (p.158)
Joseph Brock	"	"	Oct. 18, 1766 (p.263)

John Carter	"	"	Oct. 12, 1768 (p.348)
Robert Goodloe	"	"	Nov. 2, 1779 (p.448)
John Crane	"	"	Oct. 26, 1772 (p.25)
William Smith	"	"	Oct. 25, 1774 (p.83)
Charles Yates	"	"	Nov. 6, 1776 (p.164)
Edward Herndon	"	"	Oct. 13, 1778 (p.244)
John Lewis	"	"	Nov. 8, 1780 (p.370)
George Stubblefield	"	"	Oct. 19, 1782 (p.498)

P.125

April 3, 1733

Thomas Chew, (the elder son and heir of Larkin Chew, Gent. decd) of Spts. Co., to Rice Curtis (the assignee of Wm. Hansford, Gent. the assignee of Samuel Short) of the same county, £20 ster. 611 a. in St. Georges Parish, Spts. Co., Part of patent granted Larkin Chew, June 4, 1722.

Anthony Thornton, G. Lightfoot, John Minor, April 3, 1733.

P. 126

April 3, 1733

Goodrich Lightfoot of St. Mark's Par., Spts. Co., to Charles Morgan of same par. County, £12 curr. 86 a. in St. Mark's Par. Spts. Co., R. Progens, Elisha Perkins, June 5, 1733. Mary, wife of Goodrich Lightfoot, acknowledged her dower, etc.

P.351

Dec. 31, 1779

Col. Fielding Lewis and Betty, his wife, of Spts. Co., to Charles Yates of Fredksbg. £600 Lots 126 & 128 in town of Fredksbg.

George Lewis, Hay Battaile, Phillip Lightfoot, John Taliaferro, Feb. 17, 1782

P.1

Roberts, John, St. George's Parish, d. Sept. 10, 1724, p. Nov. 3, 1724

Wit. G. Lightfoot, John Brown, Matthew Bailey

Ex son-in-law Francis Kirkley, son John Roberts.

Leg. son John, land on Flatt Run joining Hack Norman; son Benjamin, land joining Roger Abbott; son George; dau. Mary Paten.

Here is a list of the Virginia Colonial Militia found in the Virginia County Records.

Joseph Bradberry, soldier under Captain John Lightfoot in Colonel Byrd's regiment, in 1670. Henry County, May 25, 1780. Page 13.

George Vaughan, soldier under Captain John Lightfoot, in a regular corps raised in the state in 1758 against Fort DuQuesne. Halifax County, March 16, 1780. Page 14.

Thomas Sanders, soldier in the 2nd Virginia Regiment, under command of Captain John Lightfoot in the last French & Indian War, New Kent County, March 9, 1780. Page 32.

Francis Lightfoot, Sargent in last war between Great Britain and France, Colonel Mercer's Company, 2nd Virginia Regiment, Mecklenberg County, May 8, 1780. Page 49.

Cumberland County, Virginia, September 1758 --- William Lightfoot Page 70.

Fauquier County, Roster of William Edmond's Company of Virginia Troops in the French & Indian War 1761.

John Duncan, Junior. Page 97.

List of officers in King & Queen County, June 12, 1707

Colonel John Lightfoot. Page 97.

Military Officers in Virginia, 1680.

Gloucester County

Lieutenant Colonel Philip Lightfoot. Page 104.

The history of Prince Edward County, Virginia had an interesting article on page 104.

Prince Edward played a leading part in the counterfeit money disturbance of 1773. Robert Carter Nicholas, treasurer of the colony, published a warning "against dangerous and ingenious forgeries of five-pound bills emitted in November 1769 and July 1771" and pointed out the differences between the genuine and the counterfeit. As soon as the situation became known the Governor, Lord Dunmore, on the advice of the Council, summoned the Assembly to meet. He felt it necessary to do this because the credit of the paper currency of the two emissions had been destroyed by the counterfeiting.

After the Assembly had been summoned, a person from "one of the most remote counties" who had been associated with the counterfeiters informed the Governor of those involved in the counterfeiting and advised that if they were not apprehended shortly they would either assemble such a force of friends that they could with difficulty be taken or that they would escape into the neighboring province of North Carolina. The Governor then called into consultation Speaker Peyton Randolph of the House of Burgesses, Attorney General John Randolph and Treasurer Robert Nichols. On their advice John Lightfoot was sent to Pittsylvania County to round up the counterfeiters. Lightfoot had a dangerous, though successful trip. He returned to Williamsburg with the engineer, the papermaker, the printer of the paper money, and the coiner of pistoles and dollars, with their plates, tools, and implements and a considerable quantity of paper money ready for circulation. The accuseds were committed to the Publick Goal to await trial.

When the House of Burgesses met early in March, it took several actions relating to the Counterfeiting. First, it adopted resolutions drawing up by the committee of the whole; the resolutions thanked the Governor for his vigorous efforts; called attention to the practice that an examining court for the accused be held in the county where the arrest was made or the crime committed (evidently Lightfoot had brought the accused to Williamsburg without going through with that formality); voted Lightfoot a reward of £200 over and above his expenses because of his diligence and the risks he took; agreed that persons who assisted Lightfoot should be rewarded by the Colony. To the proposed rewards the Council agreed and the Governor signed the acts, "for better securing the publick Credit of the Colony" (which provided for a new emission of money to take the place of two which had been counterfeit) and to prevent counterfeiting of paper money. Among those who received payment for assisting Lightfoot in his undertaking was Daniel Stone, a tavern keeper in Prince Edward, who was voted the sum of £5:5:8.

Culpeper County Courthouse in Culpeper, Virginia had these wills in their archives. There were no wills for the Fry family until 1928.

Lightfoot, Goodrich, will 4/24/1778 #3 P.337, Book B Page 257 (mentions wife, Susanna, dtrs. Elizabeth James, Ann Grasty, Mary Hubbard, Fanny (Frances) Hackley, Susanna Brooks, Prissilla, Martha, sons, John, Philip & Goodrich.

	Book	Page	Date
Lightfoot, Goodrich, Inventory	B	272	5/19/1783
Lightfoot, Goodrich Exors. Acct.	E	24	9/20/1803
Lightfoot, Thomas W., Inv. & App. (missing)			
Lightfoot, Thomas W. Acct. Sales (Missing)			
Lightfoot, Thomas W. Adm'rs Acct. (Missing)			
Lightfoot, Thomas	N	220	12/15/1834

Grantor	Grantee	Book	Page	Date
Fry, James	Geo. Noe	L	316	5/19/1783
Fry, James	Geo. Noe	M	278	10/18/1784
Fry, Reuben, et al	John Grinnan	R	93	7/16/1792
Fry, Reuben, et al	Robt. Scott	S	347	10/19/1795
Fry, John	Thos. Jennings	W	59	4/21/1801
Lightfoot, Goodrich & wf Thos Jones		A	93	1/18/1748
Lightfoot, Goodrich & wf Thos. Jones		A	95	1/18/1748
Lightfoot, Goodrich & wf Jacob Kendrick		A	184	6/21/1750
Lightfoot, Goodrich & wf Mrs. Humphrey Wallin		B	111	5/17/1754
Lightfoot, Goodrich & wf John Wright		F	139	9/17/1770
Lightfoot, William & wf John Strother		F	247	4/16/1772
Lightfoot, William & wf John Strother		L	110	6/17/1783

Lightfoot, Philip & John	John Price	M	330	2/21/1785
Lightfoot, John	Philip Lightfoot	O	139	9/17/1787
Lightfoot, William	Goodrich Lightfoot	P	168	9/21/1789
Lightfoot, John & wf	David Henderson	P	194	9/21/1789
Lightfoot, John & wf	Jeremiah Rosson	P	198	8/21/1789
Lightfoot, John & wf	Philip & Robert Slaughter	P	280	1/18/1790

The Marriage Records found were listed by the female's name first.

Nancy Fry	William Bradford	1	21	2/6/1806
Lucy Ellen Fry	Robert Anderson	2	92	4/26/1870
Amanda Fry	Chas. Collins	2	100	5/27/1871
Eliza Fry	Thos. Puter	2	110	10/13/1872
Amanda Fry	Washington Smith	2	113	1/4/1873
Judy Fry	John H. Jackson	2	132	5/14/1875
Julia Fry	Philip Hart	2	152	5/21/1877
Julia Fry	George Hart	2	161	5/20/1878
Martha Fry	Bailor Parker	3	20	5/15/1880
Louisa Fry	Lewis Braxton	3	41	11/17/1884
Margie Fry	James C. Johnson	3	57	2/29/1888
Bella Fry	Horace Smith	3	64	2/23/1890
Lizzie Fry	Stanton, Jno W.	3	66	4/27/1890
Mary Fry	John Ross	4	30	9/20/1903
Ann Lightfoot	Henry Gateshill	1	78	12/2/1784
Martha Lightfoot	Wm. Edzer	1	52	12/30/1785
Frances T. Lightfoot	Chas. T. Crittendon	2	34	11/23/1858
Mary C. Lightfoot	James C. Herndon	2	50	2/1/1865
Kitty L. Lightfoot	Sandy Bill	2	60	11/30/1866
Elisha Lightfoot	David Taylor	2	82	3/20/1869
Clementine Lightfoot	George Hudon	2	82	3/17/1869
Celia Lightfoot	Henry Roberts	2	88	12/23/1869
Amanda Lightfoot	Frank Waters	2	103	11/17/1871

These Lightfoot family records are from the old Kentucky entries and deeds.

Page 345 – Philip Lightfoot – 200 acres. Warrant 878
      3 years corporal Virginia Line – 6/26/1783
      (Military Warrant)
Page 427 – Francis Lightfoot Lee – deed dated 11/19/1810,
      3,400 acres. Book N. Page 477 – Green R&M Licking.
      (Court of Appeals Deeds Grantees)
Page 506 – Francis Lightfoot Lee – Alexandria – 7/23/1804, Book
      H, Page 504 Virginia – 6/23/1810, Book N, Page 488

(Court of Appeals Deeds Grantors)
Page 564 – Old Kentucky Entries and Deeds
    Philip Lightfoot – Residence Deed Date Book Page
    Port Royal 3/6/1817 R 448 – Contract
    (Court of Appeals Deeds – Attorneys)

Fayette Entries

	Acres	Book	Page	Date	Watercourse
William Lightfoot	4569	1	286	12/26/1782	None Surv.
Jefferson Entries					
Mildred Lightfoot	9431	A	309	11/25/1783	18 Mile Crk
Philip Lightfoot	1581	A	298	10/25/1783	Rolling Fork

Grants in County Court Orders

Lightfoots	Acres	Book	Page	Date of Survey	County	Watercourse
Robert	40	23	25	1847	Simpson	Barren Fork
Francis D.	19	30	391	1/8/1850	Pendleton	Blanket Cr
William D.	6	42	163	5/6/1854	Warren	Drakes Cr
Robert	8	47	418	1856	Simpson	None
Sherry & Moore Co	10	53	326	5/14/1858	Allen	Drakes Cr
William D.	4 ½	69	232	4/3/1886	Warren	Drakes Cr
William D.	4 ½	69	233	4/3/1886	Warren	Drakes Cr
William D.	4 ½	69	333	4/3/1886	Warren	Drakes Cr
William G.	½	93	308	1/10/1873	Allen	None
John	1000	6	158	4/8/1783	Jefferson	Hardins Cr
John	1000	6	160	4/12/1783	Jefferson	Hardins Cr
Philip	1500	7	2	3/26/1783	Jefferson	Rolling Frk
Goodrich	500	7	351	6/29/1784	Jefferson	Rolling Frk

The Kentucky Society of Colonial Wars had the following information:

Warrant #250 John Lightfoot, Lieutenant, 2000 acres, July 12, 1775; by Jno. Floyd, Fincastle Co., on Elk Horn Creek, Ass'd to David Bell and to John and James Bell, his devisees. Page 75.

Roll of Members
Fifth from Captain John Smith
Fourth from Colonel Daniel Smith
Seventh from Colonel John Lightfoot
Sixth from Major Goodrich Lightfoot
Seventh from Lieutenant Colonel Cadwalader Jones
Fourth from Captain John Van Bibber
Fifth from Colonel Francis Slaughter

Eighth from Captain Francis Slaughter
Fifth from Captain Daniel Harrison
Eighth from Lieutenant General Thomas Goodrich
Mr. Rogers Morris Smith – St. Matthews, Kentucky. Page 33

Lightfoot, Major Goodrich --------Virginia
Died Orange County, Virginia, 1738
Major Colonial Militia September 5, 1729;
Sheriff April 25, 1726; Justice Spotsylvania County, October 2, 1722.
Mr. Rogers Morris Smith. Page 50.

Lightfoot, Colonel John -------- Virginia
Born Northamptonshire, England, died New Kent County, Virginia, 28
May 1707. Auditor-General of Virginia 1670; Member of Council 1692-
1707; County Lieutenant of King & Queen County; Collector of County
Between James and York Rivers; Commander-in-Chief of King and Queen
County, Virginia.
Mr. Rogers Morris Smith. Page 50.

Goodrich, Lieutenant-General, Thomas ----------- Virginia
Born England; died Rappahannock, Virginia, 10 April 1679;
Lieutenant General in Bacon's Army in Northern Virginia 1676. After the
downfall of the Rebellion the Council decreed that with a rope around his
neck and on his knees, he beg his life of the Governor.
Mr. Rogers Morris Smith
Mr. William Overton Harris-Louisville. Page 45.

These are the records found in the ABS Tracts of Culpeper County Court
Minute Book 1763-1764.
P. 338 20 May 1763
Sarah and William Montgomery of London versus Thomas Rucker, admr.
of William Pierce, decd. Dismissed agreed.
P. 386 22 July 1763
Ann Strother Appt's admx of her husband Benjamin Strother, decd, and
Goodrich Lightfoot, Richard Young, James Turner and John Rossen,
apptd. appraisers.
P. 281 18 March 1763
Joseph Stevens versus William Lightfoot, contd.
P. 292 19 March 1763
Roger Dixon versus William Lightfoot, Judgmt for plaintiff
P. 301 18 March 1763
Will of James Wider, exhibited by his widow Peggy Wilder, proved by
William Green, Robert Green, and Robert Slaughter; and William
Lightfoot, James Green and Joseph Norman apptd. appraisers

P. 337 19 May 1763
Joseph Stevens versus William Lightfoot, contd.
P. 344 19 May 1763
James Buchanon versus William Lightfoot, contd.
P. 383 22 July 1763
James Stevens versus William Lightfoot, contd.
P. 415 19 August 1763
Joseph Stevens versus William Lightfoot, contd.
P. 453 20 October 1763
10 Tithables of William Lightfoot added to list of Henry Field
P. 449 15 September 1763
Bernard Platt versus William Lightfoot

The will of John Lightfoot was found in the Brunswick County, Virginia
Will Book 7, on pages. 204-5.

In the Name of GOD, Amen, I, John Lightfoot of Brunswick County, being
sick and weak of body, but of sound mind and desiring to make and this
my last Will & Testament in manner and form following:
Viz: Imprimis, it is my will & desire that all my just debts & funeral
expenses be first paid out of my estate.
Item: I give & bequeath unto my beloved daughter, Naly Lightfoot one
negro woman name Betsey during her natural life and at her death to be
valued by three whom my two sons may choose and one half of the
valuation money to be paid unto my son Claiborne Lightfoot and my son
John Lightfoot to have the said Negro woman Betsey to him and his heirs
forever.
Item: I give and bequeath to my beloved daughter Naly Lightfoot feather
bed and furniture which she now has and at her death to be sold and the
money equally divided between my said two sons to them and their heirs
forever.
Item: I give & bequeath unto my beloved daughter Naly Lightfoot my
home and one third part of my land, whereon I now live during her natural
life and at her death to be equally divided between my two sons John
Lightfoot and Claiborne Lightfoot to them and their heirs forever.
Item: I give and bequeath the residue of my land unto my two sons
Claiborne Lightfoot and John Lightfoot, equally to them and their heirs
forever.
Item: My will & desire is that my two sons John, Claiborne and Naly, the
residue of my estate equally during her life and at her death to be equally
divided between my said two sons to them and their heirs forever.
Lastly, I constitute and appoint my two sons Claiborne Lightfoot and John
Lightfoot executors of this my last Will & Testament revoking all other

wills whatsoever. Signed, sealed and delivered by the testator to be his last Will & Testament this 2nd day of October 1806.

Signed John Lightfoot (Seal)

Witnesses
James Powell
Alex Williams
Beverly Foster

The following articles are from the Virginia Gazette:

17 September 1736
Williamsburg, September 17, next Monday night will be perform'd, the Drummers; or the Haunted House, by the Young Gentlemen of the College.
Ships, etc., Clear'd in the Upper District of James River.
Aug. 19 Ship Scipio, John Clark, for Glasgow.
    11 Ship Christian, George Phillpot, for London.
    14 Ship Mercury, William Clark, for London.
    16 Ship Union, Richard Shelton, for White Haven.
    20 Brig. Owner's Endeavor, Richard Williamson, for White Haven.
    25 Brig. Pretty Betsy, John Boyse, for London.
    25 Ship Stannage, Thomas Hill, for Liverpool.
    26 Ship Daniel and Anne, G. Norwood, for London.
    27 Ship Lively, Joseph Littledale, for White Haven.
    28 Ship Amey, Jonas Newham, for London.
    30 Ship Plymouth, William Cole, for Plymouth.
Sept. 3 Ship Sophia, Samuel Bowman, for Glasgow.
    6 Ship Harrison, Thomas Bolling, for London.
    6 Ship Virginia Planter, Tho. Underdown, for London.
    8 Ship Glasgow, Andrew Gray, for Glasgow.

Enter'd at the Port of York Lines:
Sept. 3 Ship Priscilla of Virginia, Richard Williams, from Barbadoes.
Clear'd out at the Port of York Lines:
Aug. 27 Ship Lightfoot, of London, Thomas Harwood, for London.
    28 Ship Burwell, of London, Constantine Cant, for London.
Sept. 1 Nelson, of White Haven, William Taylor, for London.
    2 Braxton, of London, Thomas Dancie, for London.
    3 Martin Galley, of Bristol, William Beal, for Bristol.
    3 Gooch, of London, William Whitesides, for London.

3 Hatley, of London, Ralph Barres, for London.
11 Buchanan, of Glasgow, Robert Rae, for London.

25 February 1737
Williamsburg – February 25 – The Ship arrived since our last, bringing us a confirmation of His Majesties' safe arrival in England, to the great joy of his Subjects, after a very bad passage, in which His Majesty was in great danger. The Princess Louisa Man of War lost, and some others much damaged.
We hear from Gloucester County that Miss Betty Washington, Daughter of Major John Washington of that County, a young Gentlewoman of great Merit and Beauty, died there lately, very much lamented.
Entered in York River, Since Our Last,
Ship Humphrey, James Lane, from London.
Ship Hatley, Ralph Barres, from London.
Ship Gooch, William Harding, from London.
Ship Whitaker, Robert Whiting, from London.
The Ship Dolphin, John Smith, from London, enter'd here the 3rd Instant, but went to Piankotank.
The Ship Lightfoot, Capt. Robinson, and
The Ship Cesar, Capt. Long, both from London, are arrived in Rappahannock.
Entered in the Upper District of James River since the 11th. Instant,
Sloop Mary, of Bermuda, Joseph Hinson, Master, from Antigua.
Ship Duke of Cumberland, of Bristol, Joseph Barnes, Master, from Bristol.
Ship Anne Gally, of London, George Wigg, Master, from London.
Ship Rappahannock, of London, John Wilcox, Master, from London.
Sloop Anne, of Bermuda, John Joell, Master, for Bermuda.
Sloop Mary, of Bermuda, John Dickinson, Master, for Bermuda.

16 September 1737
William Keith of the City of Williamsburg, having lately got ingenious workmen in the Taylor's Trade, does hereby give Notice to any Gentlemen, and others, that they may have their work done readily, and as well as it can be done in Virginia, either Gold, Silver, or Lac'd cloathes.
Also Buckskin Breeches, for theirselves or Servants. And they may depend upon being honestly dealt with, by, WILLIAM KEITH
This is to give notice, That Col. Richard Randolph will attend at Williamsburg, for the Business of the Treasurer, from the 20th of October next, to the Last Day of the General Court.
30 December 1737
Williamsburg, January 6, We are informed, That Mr. Carter Burwell, was married yesterday to Miss Lucy Grymes, a Daughter of the Hon. John

Grymes, Esq., one of His Majestys Council, of this Colony, a very agreeable Young Lady, of great Merit and Fortune.

Williamsburg, December 30, 1737, Yesterday was Se'nnight, Mr. Beverly Randolph, eldest son of the Honorable William Randolph, Esq., one of His Majesty's Council of this Colony, was married to Miss Betty Lightfoot, Niece of the Hon. Philip Lightfoot, Esq., an agreeable Young Lady with a fortune of upwards of £5000.

Pendleton County formed in 1798 and named in honor of Edmund Pendleton of Virginia. It was the 28th County in the State and formed out of portions of Bracken and Campbell Counties, but in 1820, it gave the West one-half of its territory to form Grant County. It is bounded North by Kenton and Campbell Counties, Northeast for five miles by the Ohio River, east by Bracken, south by Harrison and West by Grant Counties. It is situated in the northern part of the state, nearly square in shape and embraces about 300 square miles.

Falmouth, the county seat, was established in 1793 by Virginians and was named after Falmouth, Virginia. In 1846 it was the only town in Pendleton County and its population was only 250. Other towns include: Boston, Butler, Calaway, Demossville, Levingood, Meridan, Morgan, Bachelor's Rest, Elizabethville, Knoxville, Gardnersville, Dividing Ridge, Montier, Ash Run, Huntsville and Salem.

The Pendleton County, Kentucky, Marriage Records 1700-1843 by Robert D. Craig contained this information:

Applegate, Jas. T.	Mary Ann Katherine Colvin	10 Nov. 1841
Chaffin, Wm	Jane Colvin	7 Feb. 1811
Colvin, Charles B.	Peggy Mountjoy	21 July 1808
Colvin, Henry	Margaret Sharp	28 Mar. 1811
Colvin, Josiah	Mary Jane Wright	2 Nov. 1840
Colvin, Nimrod	Melinda Minor	29 May 1821
Colvin, Robert F.	Sarah W. Wright	6 Nov. 1834
	(Father Lewis Wright)	
Duncan, Ambrose	Cynthia Colvin	1 Feb. 1836
Duncan, Willis	Frances Colvin	10 Apr. 1800
Fields, John	Elizabeth Lightfoot	30 May 1820
(Father dead)	(Father left her mother)	
Hamilton, Elijah	Nancy West	15 Aug. 1831
Homes, Sam'l G.	Judith Applegate	18 Aug. 1835
	(Stepfather John Ginn)	
Keith, John D.	Marann Thomas	11 Dec. 1834
Lightfoot, Geo. C.	Malinda B. Holton	10 June 1830
Lightfoot, James	Milley Delaney	2 Oct. 1810
Lightfoot, Francis D.	Louisa Duncan	30 Mar. 1834

Lightfoot, Edw.	Susannah Colvin	18 Sept. 1806
Lightfoot, Philip	Susannah Smith	29 Dec. 1803
Lightfoot, Deeston	Jean Steele	9 Nov. 1802
Lightfoot, Goodridge	Catherine Colvin	19 Feb. 1801
	(Mother Margaret Colvin)	
Lightfoot, John C.	Polly Shawhan	5 Aug. 1824
Lightfoot, De Estang	Sarah Kendall	14 July 1824
Lightfoot, Elkin	Ann L. Willett	11 Mar. 1839
Lightfoot, Wm. B.	Elizabeth Colvin	4 Sept. 1823
	(Proof Mason Colvin)	
Lightfoot, Wm.	Letty Blasingame	21 Nov. 1832
McKindley, Jos. M.	Matilda Webster	21
	(Proof Daniel Webster)	
Riddell, Geo.	Margaret Colvin	16 June 1808
Riddle, Robert	Nancy Lightfoot	25 July 1802
	(Father John Lightfoot)	
Routt, Riley	Nancy B. Colvin	3 Jan. 1842
Rush, William P.	Sarah W. Minor	22 July 1818
Sterne, David TW	Harriett Minor	16 Aug. 1830
	(Widow of Richard J.)	
Turner, Thomas	Elizabeth Lightfoot	22 Mar. 1804
Wells, Thomas	Susannah Lightfoot (w)	16 Feb. 1815

Many years ago Ellen Williams and her sisters spent their summer vacations driving to Virginia, Kentucky and any other place they might find genealogy material on our Lightfoot ancestors. They went to courthouses, libraries and cemeteries researching Lightfoots. As you can tell from this book they found plenty of material over a period of 50 years or more.

At one small town in Virginia they stopped at a library, asking about Lightfoots. The librarian told them about a very elderly Lightfoot man who lived at the edge of the village. They went out to see him. While they were talking he noticed Ellen looking at his mantle. There was a rather large (seven pounds) brick in the middle of his mantle. He told her a story about the brick.

It had been handed down to him to pass on down the line – not necessarily to a close relative, but to one who had the most interest in the Lightfoot family. He had no one who showed any interest in the brick.

He gave the brick to Ellen telling her that it had been used as ballast in John and Philip's ship "Lightfoot". She kept it for many years, and a few months before her death she told me she wanted me to have it. Two days before she died she gave it to me. It now sits on my mantle, and I will probably hand it down to my cousin Leslie Oakes of Virginia, who is a

Lightfoot descendant and has contributed so much help in my writing this book.

Mary Morton

(This brick was used as ballast on the ship "Lightfoot".)

CHAPTER XX

A TRIBUTE TO EDITH ELLEN WILLIAMS

Edith Ellen Williams the daughter of John R. and George Anna (Lightfoot) Lewis was born on 25 January 1906 at Weatherford, Texas. Ellen came from a very close and loving family and lost her mother in 1919 and her father in 1922. She attended Brantley Draughon College from 1923 through 1924 and Methodist University in 1951. On 23 January 1932 she married Stanley Albert Williams who was born in 1905. He served in World War II and returned a severely injured Veteran. Ellen took care of her husband until his death in 1971. She died in December of 1998 in Dallas, Texas and is buried at Weatherford, Texas.

She spent her life thinking of her family and friends in good health and in bad and of those who were less fortunate than she was. Her motto had always been "Others", and that is the way she lived.

Ellen was without a doubt, the most knowledgeable genealogist of the Lightfoot family. She spent more than 50 years researching and documenting the Lightfoot family plus additions to each generation. She and her sisters spent many years of their vacation time going to Virginia, Kentucky and other states visiting courthouses, libraries and church records looking for Lightfoots and related families. She helped countless numbers of Lightfoot descendants to trace their ancestries.

Ellen Williams was a very intelligent lady with a remarkable memory for people, dates and events. She was a humanitarian and inspiration to all that knew her.

She[1] was the most amazing person I have ever known and certainly the most caring. She loved people and always had time to listen and encourage or help others to reach their goals no matter what the circumstances were.

Ellen had lived during many changes in our world but always adapted to new ideals.

---

[1] Cathy Thompson wrote this letter to me about Ellen Williams.

(Edith Ellen Williams – 50 years old)

She loved her family and had great pride in her ancestors and never tired of researching her beloved Lightfoots.

Ellen was also a business executive. She worked as an Office Secretary/Accountant for A. Stemmons, Jr., of Real Estate Investments from 1941 to 1973. She was the Treasurer/Assistant Secretary, for L.A. Stemmons, Jr., President of Merco Manufacturing, Inc. from 1962 to 1973. And was employed as Treasurer for L.A. Stemmons, Jr., President of Survey Analysis Corp. from 1965 to 1973. She retired in 1973.

She joined the Grace Presbyterian Church of Weatherford, Texas in 1912 and after living in Dallas for many years transferred to the Wynnewood Presbyterian Church of Dallas, Texas. In 1974 after she and her sister Hazel retired they moved their membership back to the Grace Presbyterian Church of Weatherford but moved back to Dallas in 1975 due to Hazel's ill health.

Ellen served as a Volunteer Teacher for the Little Sisters' Club, George Loving Center and W. Dallas Social Center from 1952 to 1976. She was the Representative of Realtors' Secretaries of Dallas and was the recipient of the 10 Years Service Citation in 1962. From 1949 to 1975 she was a

266

member of the Realtors' of Dallas until it was disbanded in 1975 and served as president from 1966-67. From 1957 through 1998 she served in the Dallas local History & Genealogical Society and was Vice-President of communications. From 1955 through 1998 she was with the Fort Worth Genealogical Society.

Ellen was the President and Editor for the Lightfoot Family Association Newsletter from 1978 through 1985.

She researched and compiled several books: Lineage and Revolutionary Service, Book I (1959), Book II (1961), Book III (1963) and Book IV (1965); Bible Records and Other Genealogical Materials, Book I (1958) and Book II (1961); and Genealogical Records & Manuscripts, "The Lanham Family" (1963) and "The Beckham Family and The Cowgill Family" (1965).

Ellen was a member of the Mount Auburn Chapter of the Order of the Eastern Star. She was a Past Worthy Matron and received her 50-year membership in November of 1988. She received the Grand Cross-of-Colors from the International Order of Rainbow For Girls for all her unselfish help and contributions for the girls of this organization.

She was a charter member and officer from 1948 till her death in 1998 for the Daughters of the Nile (Shrine ladies).

Ellen served as treasurer, Chaplain, vice-regent in 1966-1967 and Regent from 1967 through 1969 in the General Levi Casey Chapter in Dallas of the National Society Daughters of the American Revolution. She was inducted 12 June 1957 by virtue of descent from a patriot who with unfailing loyalty rendered material aid to the cause of American Independence during the Revolutionary.

She served as Past Correspondence Secretary and Past Treasurer of the Colonel Cole Digges Chapter of Dallas of the National Society Colonial Dames 17th Century. She was inducted 3 February 1958 for Lineal descendants of persons who lived in one of the British Colonies in the United States before 1701 as a colonist, or descendant of one, and who rendered various civil or military services.

On 30 August 1965 she became a member of the National Society Magna Charta Dames. This organization was to perpetuate the memory of the men who extorted the Magna Charta "The Great Charter" from King John in 1215, the original 25 Barons.

On 10 August 1971 she became a member of the Colonial Order of the Crown. This was her right as an accredited lineal descendant of Emperor Charlemagne.

Due to her descent from John Lightfoot, emigrant from England in 1670, who rendered loyal services in the Colony of Virginia thereby furthering the establishment of the great Commonwealth of the United States she became a member of the National Society Daughters of American Colonists 9 April 1973.

Cathy Thompson, one of the many young ladies that Ellen helped sent this brief note that Ellen had written to her:

> Dear Cathy,
> Be good, sweet girl
> And let, who will, be clever.
> Do noble things,
> Not dream them all day long.
> And so, make life, death
> And that vast forever,
> One grand sweet song.
>
> Love,
> Ellen

BIBLIOGRAPHY

Magna Charta – John S. Wurts. Pages 32, 33, and 290. Vol. I, II.
This sketch has been presented as a contribution toward the seven hundred and eighty-seventh anniversary observance of the granting of the Magna Charta. In its preparation the compiler has made a special use of the following books and articles, and would here like to acknowledge her indebtedness to them:

The Great Charter. William Blackstone, 1759 &c.
Observations Upon the Statutes. Daines Barrington, 1766.
Historical Treatise on the Federal Law. Francis S. Sullivan, 1772.
Historical Essay on the Magna Charta. Richard Thomson, 1829.
Chartes de Libertes Anglaise. Charles Bemont, 1892.
The Magna Charta. Boyd C. Barrington, 1900.
Second Institute. Edward Coke, 1641 &c.
Magna Charta. A commentary. William S. McKenzie, 1905, 1914.
Magna Charta made in 9 Henry III. Edward Coke, 1684.
England Under Angevin Kings. Kate Norgate.
John Lackland. Kate Norgate.
The Angevin Empire. James Henry Ramsay.
The Foundations of England. James Henry Ramsay.
The Constitutional History of England. Henry Stubbs.
Henry III and the Church. Abbot Gasquet.
History of Procedure in England. Melville M. Bigelow.
Feudal England. John H. Round.
Progress of the English Constitution. Edward Creasy.
History of the English Constitution. Rudolf Gneist.
English Constitutional History. Thomas P. Taswell Langmead.
Chronica. Florence of Worcester.
Chronica. Henry of Huntingdon.
Sketches from English History. Arthur m. Wheeler, 1886.
A Child's History of England. Charles Dickens, 1868.
A Short History of the English People. John Richard Green, 1879.
History of England. Charles McLean Andrews, 1921.
A Student's History of England. Samuel R. Gardiner, 1898.
Magna Charta (1215-1915). Nicholas Murray Butler.
Notes of Blackstone's Commentaries. Christian.
Coke Upon Littleton. Edward Coke, 1644.
Commentaries Upon the Laws of England. William Blackstone,

1765.

Magna Charta Barons. Charles Henry Browning, 1898, 1915.
The Day We Celebrate. Henry Corneau Diller, 1915.
Magna Charta Defined. Elihu Root, 1915.
History of England. Cassel.
Statutes of the Realm. British Record Commission, 1810.
Select Statutes. George W. Prothero.
Chronica Majora. Matthew Paris. British Rolls Series.
Chronicum Anglicanum *(1235-1273).* British Rolls Series.
Chronica (to 1201). Roger de Hovenden. British Rolls Series.
Chronica Sive Flores Historarium (to 1235). Roger of Wendover.
  Rolls Series.
Annals of Dunstable. Rolls Series.
Annals of Waverly. Rolls Series.
Memoriale. Walter of Coventry. Rolls Series.
Gesta Regum Anglorum. William of Malmesbury. Rolls Series.
Chronicon de Gesta Regum Angliae. Walter of Hemingburgh.
  English Historical Society.
Gesta Regis Henry II. Rolls Series.
Select Charters. William Stubbs.
Chronica de Rebus Gestis Samsonis. Jocelyn of Brakelond. Camden
  Society.
Memorials of St. Dunston. Rolls Series.
The Red Book of the Exchequer. Rolls Series.
Testa de Neville. Record Commission Publication, 1807.
Foedera, Conventiones, etc. Thomas Rymer, Record Commission
  Publications.
Ancient Charters. Pipe Roll Society. Vol. X.
Great Roll of the Pipe, Temp. 12 Henry II. Pipe Roll Society, Vol.
  IX.
History and Antiquities of the Exchequer. Thomas Madox.
Firma Burgi. Thomas Madox.
Baronia Anglica. Thomas Madox.
De Legibus. Henry de Bracton. Rolls Series.
Political History of England. George B. Adams.
History of John, King of England. W. Prynne.
History of the Reign of John, King of England J. Berington.
John, King of England. John Chadwick.
England, 1066 to 1215. George B. Adams.
England Under Normans and Angevins. H.W.C. Davis.
Simon de Montfort. Charles Bemont.
Geoffrey de Mandeville. John H. Round.
History of the Norman Conquest. E.A. Freeman, Vols. I and II.
William the Conqueror and His Companions. Planche.

Historical Works of Gervais de Canterbury. Rolls Series.
Gesta Stephani Chronicals Temp. Henry II. Rolls Series.
Archaelogia Cambrensis. 3rd Series, Vol. VIII.
Annals of Bury St. Edmund's Harl. MS. 447. (Lieberman).
Annales Monastici. Rolls Series.
de Antiquis Legibus Liber. Camden Society Publications.
Calendar of English Documents in France to 1206. London, 1899.
Calendar of Charter Rolls, 1226-1257. London, 1903. Vol. I.
Calendar of Patent Rolls, 1232-1247. London, 1906, Vol. I.
Close Rolls. 1227-1237. London, L902-5-8, Vols. I, II, III.
Flores Historiarum. Matthew of Westminster (to 1307). Rolls Series.
Calendar of Inq. P.M., Temp. Henry III. London, 1904, Vol. I.
Royal, and Other Letters, Temp. Henry III. London, 1904, Vol. I.
Monastican Anglicanum. Sir William Dugdale.
Chronicle of Robert of Gloucester. Rolls Series.
Political History of England. Longman.
Epochs of Modern History. Longman.
Mediaeval England. Mary Bates.
The Making of England. John R. Green.
Royal Castles of England. H.C. Shelley.
Orderici Vitalis Historis Ecclesiastica. Paris, 1838-1855.
L'Art de Verifier les Dates des Faits Histoiques.
Calendar of Papal Registers, 1198-1304. London, 1893, Vol. I.
Rotuli Chartarum in Turri Londinensi Asservati, 1199-1216. Rolls Series.
Rotuli Litterarum Clausarum in Turri Londinensi Asservati. 1204-24.
Excerpta e Rotulis Finium, 1216-46. Vol. I. Record Commission.
Rotuli Litterarum Patentium in Turri Londinensi Asservati. 1201-1216. Vol. I, British Record Commission, London, 1835.
Rotuli de Liberate ac de Misis et Praestitis Regnante Johanne. London, 1835.
History of English Law. W.S. Holdsworth.
A Constitutional History of the House of Lords. L.O. Pike.
The History of English Law. F. Pollock and F.W. Maitland.
A History of English Law. W.S. Holdsworth.
Two Principles of Magna Charta. G. Campbell Morgan, 1931.
Genealogical Tables. Hereford B. George, 1930.
Royal Genealogies. James Anderson, D.D., 1736.
Genealogy of the Most Illustrious Houses of all the World. Venice. 1743.
The Plantagenet Ancestry. W.H. Turton. 1928.
The Genealogists' Magazine. 1938-1939.
The Genealogical Quarterly. 1934-1935.

Yorkshire County Magazine. 1892, 1893, 1894.

Histories of the Counties of England.

The Royal Houses of Europe. Illuminated Genealogical Chart, 1854.

Americans of Royal Descent. Charles Henry Browning. 9 Volumes.

New Complete Peerage. Vicary Gibbs. 8 Volumes.

Peerage and Baronetage. Sir Bernard Burke, 1929, 1937.

Dormant and Extinct Peerage. Sir Edmund Burke, 1883.

Landed Gentry. Sir Bernard Burke, 1939.

General Armory. Sir Bernard Burke, 1878.

Irish Pedigrees. John O'Hart, 1892.

Dictionary of National Biography.

Memorials of the Order of the Garter. George Frederick Belts, 1841.

The Register of the Order of the Garter. "The Black Book." John
　　Anstis, 1724.

Garter Stall Plates (1348-1485). W.H. St. John Hope, 1901.

45 GENERATIONS to KING EDWARD III *242*

A BRIEF SUMMARY of the MAGNA CHARTA *197*

A MEMORIAL CONCERNING the AUDITOR'S PLACE of VIRGINIA *42*

A MEMORIAL on GOVERNOR NICHOLSON'S MALADMINISTRATION *46*

A TWENTY YEARS COLLEGE COURSE *240*

ABBOTT, *Roger 253*

ABS TRACTS of CULPEPER COUNTY COURT MINUTE BOOK 1763-1764 *258-259*

ADA *238*

ADELA *231, 238*

ADELAIDE, Countess of Chalons *246*

ADELE *238*

ADELHEID *231*

ADMINISTRATION ACT BOOKS *1*

ADMINISTRATION BONDS *251-252*

AEDD MAWR (King Edward the Great) *242*

AGNAR *231*

AGNEW
  Eugene V. *66*
  Willie Reid *66*

ALAFON *243*

ALBERIC II, Count de Macon *237*

ALBREDA of Lorraine *237*

ALDREDGE, *E.T. 151*

ALDRICH, *George 37*

ALEXANDER
  Georgina Lightfoot *135*
  James *135*

ALEXANDER, King of the Scots *214*

ALFGAR III, Earl of Mercia *233*

ALFORD
  Goodrich *79*
  Julius *79*
  Lodwick *79*

ALFRED the GREAT King of England *198, 232, 235*

ALICE *238-239*

ALICE of Normandy *232*

ALLAFRYE, *William 35*

ALLEGREE
  Eliza Lightfoot *117*
  Robert D. *117*

ALLEN
  ? *157*
  Clara Walker *102*
  David *65*
  John *102*
  Joseph *102*
  Mary *95*
  Mary Lightfoot *102*
  Nancy McConnell *65*
  Patsy *102*
  Sarah Katherine Lightfoot *157*
  Thomas, Sir *35*
  William *95, 102*

ALPAIS *236, 246*

ALPHONSO VII, of Castile *239*

ALPHONSO IX, King of Castile *247*

ANCHISES *236, 246*

ANCIENT COAT of ARMS *20*

ANDERSON
  Lucy Ellen Fry *256*
  Mr. *10*
  Robert *256*

ANDROS, *Edmund, Sir 45*

ANNE of Russia *231*

ANNYN TRO *242*

APOSTLE PAUL *244*

APPLEGATE
  James T. 262
  Mary Ann Katherine Colvin 262
ARCH 243
ARCHBISHP of CANTERBURY 27
ARGOTTA 236, 245
ARMISTEAD
  ? 102
  Ann Allen 102
  Ann Lee 96
  William 96
ARNOUL, Bishop of Metz 236, 246
ARNULPH, Count of Holland 238
ARNULPH, King of Germany 231
ARVIRAGUS, King of Britain 233, 242, 245
ASA 232, 238
ASBIE
  Jane Lightfoot 26-27, 35
  William 26-27
ASBURY, Thomas 177
ASEDA 232
ASHCRAFT
  Emma Lightfoot 149
  George 149
ASKE, Robert, Esq. 31
ATHELSTAN, Danish Duke of East Angles 233
ATHILDIS 235, 245
ATKINSON, William 79
ATTEBERRY
  Erma Eileen Parks 156
  Fern 156
  Frances Jean 156
  Frances Luvena Snodgrass 156
  John Andrew 156
  Larry Dean 156
  Sharon Ann 156
AUBERT of Moselle 246
AUDLEY
  Hugh 228
  Margaret Clare 228
AUSBERT 236
AXFORD, Isaac 170
AYERS, William 173
AYLETT, William 43

BACON, Nathaniel 41, 89, 190-191
BACON'S REBELLION of 1676 41, 190-191, 193
BAGNALL, Elizabeth 249
BAHR
  Alice Ray Dickson 57
  William Augustus 57
BAILEY
  Charles E. 146
  Matthew 253
  Susan Anne Lightfoot 146
BAKER
  Asa Blaine 152
  Barbara Jean 152
  Forest Leonard 152
  Ina Eleanor 152
  Jeraldean Ruth 152
  Leona Jane Stigall 152
  Orville Wayne 152
  Steven Gale 152
  Viola Mae Brown 152
BALIOL, Barnard 203
BALL
  Anna Catherine Tayloe 110
  Frances Slaughter 110
  Margaret 178
  Mary 110
  Samuel 107, 110
  William 110
BALTHIS
  Eliza M. Maury 133
  W. 133
BANKHEAD
  Charles 99
  John 99
  William 99
BANNISTER
  John 43
  Mr. 11
BARAN 243
BARBEE
  John 175
  Phyllis Duncan 175
BARBER
  Charles 180
  James 126
BARBOUR, James 107

BARNES, *Joseph 261*
BARRES, *Ralph 261*
BARRON, *William 106*
BARROW
  Anne 178-179
  Anne Morehead Dameron 73
  Anne Stone Metcalfe 179, 181
  Beulah 54
  Edward 125, 177-179, 181
  Elizabeth Minor 125, 177-179, 181
  Jane Stone 125
  John 177
  Lewis 73
  Margaret 177-179
  Margaret Ball 178
  Sarah M. Dameron 73
  Thomas H. 73
BASINA of Thuringia *236, 245*
BASKERVILLE, *James, Sir 185*
BASS
  John Henry 147
  Laura Holton Lightfoot 147
BASSETT
  Alan 206
  Colonel 12
  Hawise Grey 228
  Margaret Someri St. Pierre 228
  Philip 206
  Ralph 228
  Thomas 207
  William 47, 78-79
BASYE
  Edmond 148
  Elizabeth Taylor 148
BATCHELDER, *Joseph Frederick 135*
BATTAILE, *Hay 253*
BAYLY
  Samuel 180
  William 177
BEAL, *William 261*
BEALL, *Walter 110*
BEATRICE, *Macon 237, 239*
BEAUCHAMP, *Philippa Ferrers 221*

BECKHAM
  Griffis 7
  James 7
  John Lewis 27
  Robert 7
  William 7
BEESON
  Curtis Grubb 61
  James H. 61
  Jasper N. 61
  John F.M. 61
  Laura M. 61
  Louisa J. 61
  Martha A. 61
  Martha Clark 61
  Senia S. 61
BEFORE the DAYS of ABRAHAM *239*
BEGGA of Brabant *236, 245*
BEKE, *John 219*
BELFIELD, *Joseph 179*
BELI (Heli) the Great *233*
BELKNAP
  Hazel Lightfoot 123
  Wilber 123
BELL
  David 257
  James 257
  John 257
BELLEMONT
  Isabel Vermandois 231
  Petronella Grantmesnil 218, 231
BENSON
  Elizabeth Smith 173
  John 173
BENTLY, *Efford B. 99*
BERENGARIS of Castile *247*
BERENGUELA *239*
BERKELEY
  Eve Zouche 222, 224
  Governor 41, 191
  Isabel Clare 222
  Joan Ferrers 221
  Katharine Clivedon 223
  Margaret Mortimer 223
BERNARD
  Fanny Hopkins 99
  Sarah Savin/Savigne 99

BERNARD (Continued)
William 99
BERNHARD, King of Lombardy
246
BERTHA *238*
BERTHA of Laon *237, 246*
BERTHA of Toulouse *246*
BERTRAND
Susana 177
William 177
BERWYN *243*
BIBLE
Christopher Columbus 160
Elizabeth Hall 160
BIGOD
Hugh 197, 199, 201-202, 212
Isabella Plantagenet 201
Maud Marshall 202
Roger 196-197, 199, 201
BILL
Kitty L. Lightfoot 256
Sandy 256
BING, *Edward 35*
BINNEY
Henrietta Lightfoot 67
Melvin 67
BIRK
Carl 110
Martha Sue Sublette 110
BISHOP of GLOUCESTER *27*
BLACKMORE, *George 182*
BLAIR, *James 44-45, 47*
BLAKELEY
George 98
Mary Elizabeth Bolling Lightfoot
98
BLAND
? 102
Martha Allen 102
BLEDDYN *243*
BLEDSOE, *William 251-252*
BLEDSOR, *William 107*
BLITHILDES *236, 246*
BLOOD
Lorraine Kathryn Watson 160
Robert H. 160
BOADICEA (Victoria) *233, 239,*
245

BOAZ *242*
BOHON
Elijah 113
John 113
John L. 113
Lucy Gilmore Lightfoot 113
Martha Fry Lightfoot 113
Mary Ann Threlkeld 113
Mary Vanarsdell 113
Reuben L. 113
Richard Henry 113
Sarah Hedrick 113
Verlinda Hutchinson 113
William Fry 113
BOHUN
Alianore Braos 220
Joane Zouche 225
Maud 212
Maude fitz Geoffrey de Mandeville
202
BOLLING
Robert 97
Sarah Melville Minge 97
Thomas 260
BOND
Elizabeth Benson Chew 173
Richard 173
BOONE, *Danl' 127*
BOSWELL, *William 31*
BOTETOURT, *John 220*
BOWES, *Claude Lyon 248*
BOWES-LYON, *Claude George*
248
BOWMAN, *Samuel 260*
BOYD
Frank Lander 118
Luella Bruce Newsom 118
BOYSE, *John 260*
BRADBERRY, *Joseph 253*
BRADFORD
Nancy Fry 256
William 256
BRADLEY
Lillie Gordon Lightfoot 71
Sterling Price 7
BRAN, King of Siluria *243*

BRAXTON
Lewis 256
Louisa Fry 256
BRIDGES, Jno 182
BROCE
L. Gale 98
Marjorie Jordan 98
BROCK, Joseph 252
BROGRAVE, Austin 249
BROOK, Joseph 252
BROOKE
Francis E. 101
Harriett Lightfoot 101
Lightfoot 101
Philip Howell 101
BROOKER, Stephen 79
BROOKS
Isola May Lightfoot 150
James 114
Larry Theodore 150
Mary Lightfoot 114
Susanna Lightfoot 107, 114, 255
Wesley 48
William 114
BROWDER
Angelina Dameron 73
John 73
BROWN
? 153
Barbara Anne 154
Bellphena Ellen Mizener 152
Beverly Jean 154
Carlton Leroy 154
Charles Elbert 154
Daisy Bennet 152
Doris Skates 154
Earl Leon 152
Edith Edimston 154
Edna Grace Brown 153
Elbert Granet 154
Eldon Geathen 154
Fred 153
Gary Eldon 154
James Alva 152
John 253
Lowrence 153
Mary ? 154
Orville Ray 152

Peggy Bartholemew 154
Rosalie Brown Bartley 154
Sarah Ruth 154
Shirly Joan 154
Stella Bartley 154
Vera Helen Stinson 153
Verda Graves 154
Vernon Harley 154
Wanda Grace 153
Warren Adam Wilson 154
BRUCE
Isabel 203, 209
Robert 203, 209
William 177
BRWT 242
BRYAN
Joseph 63
Sarah ? 63
BRYDAIN 242
BRYWLAIS 243
BUCHANON, James 259
BUIE
Colonel ? 131
Malissa Thompson 131
BULGER
George Ann Lightfoot 149
M.L. 149
BULLOCK, William 48-49
BURDEN, Benjamin 108
BURGE
Mary Lightfoot 63
Rufus 63
BURGH
Elizabeth 247
Margaret 222
Thomas 186
BURGO
Agnes fitz Nigel 228
Beatrix Vesci 228
Magdalen 228
BURNETT, Jeff 51
BURNS, Robert 49
BURWELL
Anne 95
Carter 261
James 95
Lewis 95
Lucy Grymes 261

BURWELL (Continued)
 Mary Willis 103
BYRD
 Lucy Parke 80
 William 8, 44, 48-49, 79-80, 105,
 253
BYRNE, Lorena J. 152
CADVAN of Cambria, Prince of
Wales 234
CAESAR
 Augustus 243-244
 Julius 241, 244
 Tiberius Claudius 242, 245
CAESAR'S FIRST INVASION
241
CAID 243
CALCHWYNYDD 243
CALDWELL
 Andrew 144
 Elizabeth Farris 144
CALLERMAN
 John L., Jr. 112
 Susan M. Lightfoot 112
CAMPBELL
 John 157
 Malinda Lightfoot 157
 William Mead 60
CANT, Constantine 260
CANTELUPE
 John, Sir 219
 Margaret Harcourt 219
CANTILUPE, Eva Braos 224
CARADOC (Caractacus) King of
Siluria 233, 242-244
CARLOMAN 231, 237
CARMICHAEL
 Malcolm M. 56
 Nancy Oswalt 56
CARPENTER, Anthony 183-184
CARR, William 252
CARTER
 Charles 94
 John 3, 253
 Robert 45-46
 William 3
CASWALLON 233, 243
CATE
 ? 159

Josephine Sterchi 159
CATESBY, Mr. 11, 106
CATLETT
 George 3
 Lawrence 3
CAVALIERS & PIONEERS 250
CAVE, Benjamin 107
CAVENDISH-BENTINCK, Nina
Cecelia 248
CERAINT 243
CERAINT FEDDW 243
CERI 243
CHAFFIN
 Jane Colvin 262
 William 262
CHAMBERLAYNE, Colonel 79,
82
CHAPMAN
 Anne 4
 Boyd 159
 Richard 94
 Viola Lightfoot 159
CHAPPEL, William, Dr. 249
CHARLES
 James Wesley 156
 Lauretta Parks 156
CHARLES II of England 26, 35
CHARLES MARTELL, King of
France 236, 246
CHARLOTTE, Mecklenburg-
Stralitz 167
CHEDESTER
 James B. 114
 Stephen 114
 Susanna Brooks 114
CHEW
 Ann 173
 Ann Ayers 173
 Benjamin 173
 Elizabeth 173
 Elizabeth Benson 173
 John 173, 252
 Larkin 252-253
 Rachel Constable 173
 Samuel 173
 Sarah Walker 173
 Thomas 107, 251-253

CHILDERIC I, King of France
246
CHILDERIC III *237*
CHRISTOPHERS, *John 106*
CLACK
  James 103
  Mary ? 103
CLAIBORNE, *William 47, 250*
CLARE
  Adeliza Meschines 227
  Alice Brun 222
  Amice fitz Robert 203, 227
  Amicia 237
  Isabella Marshall 203
  Maud Marshall 226
  Maud St. Hillary 227
CLARK
  ? 69
  Abner "Abraham" 69
  Elizabeth Stone 69
  George 130
  Henry 61
  John 260
  Margaret Lightfoot Cook 61
  MaryLightfoot 69
  William 184, 260
CLAUDIA *244*
CLAY, *E.F. 144*
CLAYTON, *Philip 3*
CLENDENIN
  Elizabeth Glasgow 137
  Isabella Rippey Kerr 137
  John E. 137
  William Austin 137
CLENDININ
  Eliza Barrow Lightfoot 137
  James Moores 137
CLERMONT, *Marguerita 227*
CLIFFORD, *Isabel Berkeley 222*
CLIVEDON
  Emma 223
  John 223
CLODOMIR IV, King of the
Franks *235*
CLODOMIR, King of the Franks
245
CLOPTON, *John 3*

CLOTHAIRE I, King of France
236, 246
CLOVIS the GREAT, King of
France *236, 246*
COAT of ARMS of JOHN &
PHILIP LIGHTFOOT *18*
COAT of ARMS of RICHARD
LIGHTFOOT *17*
COCKAYNE, *Judith 248*
COCKE, *Mr. 49*
COCKSTINT, *John 35*
CODY
  Barnet 71
  Sinai McCormick 71
COEL (Old King Cole), King of
Britain *233-235, 244-245*
COGAN, *? 146*
COLDWELL, *Tobie 24*
COLE, *William 260*
COLEMAN
  Mr. 136
  Robert 109, 130-131
  Sarah Ann Saunders 131
COLES
  Catherine Thompson 103
  Elizabeth 95
  Elizabeth Lightfoot 102
  Isaac 102-103
  Jacob T. 103
  John 102-103
  Lightfoot 103
  Lightfoot Carrington 103
  Mary Winston 102-103
  Mildred 95
  Mildred Lightfoot 102
  Walter 102
COLGIN, *John 3, 98*
COLLINS
  Amanda Fry 256
  Catherine Elsie Ronco 159
  Charles 256
  Clifton William 159
  Douglas Stewart 159
  James 159
  Lowell Clifford 159
  Mollie Glass 159
  Ollie Lightfoot 159

COLVIN
  Alexander Robert, M.D. *100*
  Benjamin *6*
  Catherine Williams *147*
  Charles B. *262*
  Daniel *6*
  Elkin *6*
  George *6*
  Henry *6, 147, 262*
  James *6*
  Jeremiah *6*
  John *146, 158*
  Josiah *262*
  Margaret *158, 263*
  Margaret Sharp *262*
  Mary Jane Wright *262*
  Mason *6, 263*
  Melinda Minor *262*
  Nimrod *262*
  Peggy Mountjoy *262*
  Robert F. *262*
  Sarah Lightfoot Tarleton *100*
  Sarah W. Wright *262*
  William *6*
COMPTON, *William* *249*
COMYN
  Alexander *223*
  Elizabeth *223*
CONAN I, Count of Bretagne *232*
CONSTANCE *231, 239*
CONSTANS I *234*
CONSTANTINE II *234*
CONSTANTINE the GREAT
234
CONSTANTINE, King of Britain
234
CONSTANTIUS II *234*
CONSTANTIUS III *234*
**CONTEMPORANEOUS
EVENTS** *244*
COOK
  Frank *134*
  Henry *60*
  James *134*
  Joel *84*
  John *61*
  John Henry *134*
  Margaret Susannah Lightfoot *60*

  Mary *134*
  Mary Irwin *61*
  Mary Irwin *61*
  Peggy Rush *61*
  Philip *61*
  Susannah H.M. Lightfoot *134*
  Virginia *134*
COOKENDORFER
  Copley *95*
  E.O. *149*
COPPAGE
  Albert L. *148*
  B. Lawrence *148*
  Baldwin *148*
  Baldwin Fielding *148*
  Catherine *149*
  Catherine Maria Keith *148*
  Dorman *149*
  Eleanor O'Farrell *148*
  Elizabeth *149*
  Ella Flowers *149*
  Estelle Howell *148*
  Ferdinand *149*
  Florence *148*
  Francis Elkin *149*
  Fred Fries *148*
  George Allen *148*
  Hannah Waller *148*
  Homer *149*
  James *149*
  John *149*
  Keith *148*
  Laura *149*
  Lela Perry *148*
  Margaret Lightfoot *148*
  Maria Madden *149*
  Mary *149*
  Milton *149*
  Nina *148*
  Sallie Reed *149*
  Sarah *149*
  Thomas F. *148*
  Virginia Bondurant *148*
  William *149*
  William Fielding *148*
COPPEDGE
  Elizabeth Basye *148*
  Elizabeth Dameron *148*

COPPEDGE (Continued)
John 148
William 148
CORBETT, Peter 219
CORBIN
Alice Eltonhead 89
Henry, Honorable 89
CORDWINER, Thomas Gutteridge
24
**COUNCIL JOURNALS for 10
MAY 1699** 44
COX
Arch 160
Bell Lightfoot 160
Betsy Ann Grady 111
Brian Curtis 152
Charles Lee 111
Charley S. 156
Gregory Christopher 152
Iva Florence Parks 156
Louise Irene Roper 152
Robert 152
Teresa Lynn 152
CRAIG
Joseph 111
Robert 111
Susan Peachy Grady 111
CRANDALL
Kimberly Irene 154
Lyle Wayne 153
Marcia Adell Walker 153
Robert Lester 153
Robin Lea Ann 153
CRANE, John 253
CRAWFORD
Elizabeth Lightfoot 60
John 60
CREPON, Gunnora 232
CRISPIN
Brionne 226
Gislebert 226
CRITTENDEN
Charles T., Colonel 136, 256
Frances Thornton Lightfoot
136, 256
CROSYER
? 36-37
John 36

CROW, Warner, Judge 120
CRUMP
Charles, Captain 82
William W., Judge 101
**CULPEPER COUNTY
COURTHOUSE MARRIAGE
RECORDS** 256
**CULPEPER COUNTY
COURTHOUSE WILLS** 255
CUNEGONDE 246
CUNNINGHAM, David 48
CURTIS, Rice 252-253
CUSTIS
Charles 108
Daniel Parke 79-82
Fanny 80
Frances Parke 80-81
George Washington Parke 83-84
Jackie 84
John, Colonel 79-81
John Parke 81-82
Martha 81
Martha Dandridge 81-82
Patsy 82
CYLLIN (Cylinus) 244
CYLLINUS 244
CYMRYW 243
CYNON 244
CYNVELIN (Cymbeline), King of
Britain 233
d'ALBINI
Margaret Umfraville 201
Nicholas 201
Odonel 201
Oliver 213
William 197, 199-201, 217, 228
d'ANJOU, Ermengarde 232, 237,
246
d'AQUILA, Gilbert 206, 226
d'AUBIGNY
Nigel, Sir 207
William 228
d'AVRANCHES, Margaret 232
d'ESPEC, Walter 208
d'EVEREUX, Robert 235
d'ULCOTE, Philip 208
DAG if Vestnare 232
DALE, Thomas, Sir 250

DAMERON
  Alexander 73
  James 73
  John H. 73
  Julia Mangum 73
  Rebecca Lightfoot 73
  William Henry 73
DANCIE, *Thomas 260*
DANDRIDGE
  John, Colonel 79, 81
  Martha 79, 81
  Nancy 81
DANIEL
  Maria ? 115
  Nancy Hunt 115
  Nat 115
  Peter 115
  Philip T. 115
  Rosa 115
  Rosina Lightfoot 115
  Travis 115
DARE
  Anne Phillips 35-36
  Leonard 27, 35-36
  Rose Lightfoot 27
DAVID, Earl of Athol *195, 221*
DAVID, King of Scotland *219, 222*
DAVIS
  B.B. 120
  Elvin 156
  Estel Arlene Parks 156
  Tim 120
DAY, *George 37*
DAYES, *Joseph 26*
de BEAUCHAMP
  Guy 221
  Thomas 221
de BELLEMONT, *Robert 203, 218, 225, 227, 231*
de BERKELEY
  Maurice 222, 224
  Thomas 221, 223
de BETUN, *Robert 203, 227*
de BOHUN
  Henry 196, 199, 202
  Humphrey 220, 224
  Roger 202

de BOLEBEC
  Hugh 210
  Walter Giffard 227
de BREAUTE, *Falkes 211*
de BROAS, *William 227*
de BURGH
  Hubert 209, 211
  Richard 222
de BURGO
  Eustace 228
  Eustice fits John 228
  John 228
  John Monoculous 228
de BUTEVILLE
  Geoffrey 201
  Oliver 201
de CANTILUPE, *William 224*
de CHARLTON, *Alan 223*
de CHAUMONT, *Hugh 208*
de CHENEY, *William 210, 229*
de CLARE
  Gilbert 197, 199, 202-203, 222, 239
  Richard 196, 199, 202-203, 209, 222, 226-227, 237
  Richard fitz Gilbert 227
  Roger 227
de CLERMONT, *Hugh 227*
de CLIFFORD, *Robert 222*
de CONTESVILLE, *Herlouin 232*
de CRESSI, *Roger 217*
de CROHIM, *Peter 209*
de DAMMARTIN, *Simon 239*
de FERRERS
  John 220
  Robert 219
  William 219-220, 224
de FORTIBUS, *William 196, 200, 210-211, 214*
de GANT, *Gilbert 225*
de GRANTMESNIL, *Hugh 225, 231*
de GREENE, *Thomas 224*
de GREY
  Henry 220
  John 228
  Reginald 220

de HARCOURT
  John 219
  Richard 219
  William 219
de HARDELL, William 200, 211
de HAYA, Nicholas 205
de HOLLAND
  Alan 224
  Otho 224
  Robert 224
  Thomas 224
de HUNTINGFIELD
  David 203
  William 197, 199, 205-206
de KEVELIOK, Hugh 218, 225, 232
de LACI, Ilbert 225
de LACIE
  Gilbert 212
  Henry 225-226, 228
  John 197, 199, 206, 218, 225-227
  Robert 225-226
  Roger 213, 226-227
de LANVALLEI, William 197, 199, 206
de LEYBOURNE, Roger 224
de LISOURS
  Fulk 225
  Robert 225, 228
de MANDEVILLE
  Geoffrey 193, 196, 200, 211-212, 226
  William 205, 212
de MAR
  Ralph 225
  William 225
de MAULEY, Peter 201
de MESCHINES
  Hugh 225, 232
  Ranulph 227, 232-233
de MEULLENT, William 211
de MINERS
  Gilbert 185, 187
  John 187
  Roger 185
  William 185
de MONTBEGON

Henry 213
Roger 197, 199-200, 212-213
de MONTE BEGONIS, Adam 212
de MONTFICHET, Richard 197, 200, 213-214
de MONTFORT, Simon I 235
de MORTIMER, Edmund 247
de MOWBRAY
  Agnes d'Albini 201, 203
  Roger 199, 203, 213
  William 197, 199, 201, 203, 207, 213, 217
de MUCEGROS, Robert 220
de PERCIE, William 227
de PERCY
  Henry 247
  Richard 197, 200, 214
de QUINCEY
  Robert 206, 218-219, 225-226, 232
  Saher 225
  Saire 193-196, 199, 202, 204, 206-208, 217-219, 225-226, 231-232
de QUINCY, Roger 195
de ROCHES, Peter 209
de ROCKLEY, Ralph 220
de ROOS, Robert 197, 199, 208-209, 217
de SAYE
  Geoffrey 197, 200, 209
  William 210
de SEAGRAVES, Nicholas 223
de SOLERS, Richard 206
de SOMERI
  Ralph 228
  Roger 228
de SPINEY, William 208
de ST. LIZ, Simon 225
de STAFFORD, Nicholas 228
de STUTEVILLE
  Eustace 195
  Nicholas 195
  Osmond 205
de TAILBOIS
  George 247
  Ivo 233

de **TODENI,** *Robert 200*
de **TONEBRUGE,** *Gilbert 227*
de **VALOINES**
  Robert 205
  William 195
de **VERDON,** *Theobald 221*
de **VERE**
  Ailberic 227
  Aubrey 210
  Hugh 218
  Robert 197, 200, 210, 218
de **VESCI**
  Eustace 197, 200, 214
  Ivo 214
  William 214
de **VIEUXPONT,** *Robert 195*
de **VIVONIA,** *Hugh 207*
de **WARREN,** *John 213*
DEAL
  Arthur David 64
  Arthur Ray 64
  Vivian Renee 64
  Vivian Ruth Lightfoot 64
DEAN
  Margaret Fry Bohon 113
  Thomas 113
DECLARATION of
EJECTMENT *141-142*
DEERING
  Edward 146
  Levina Lightfoot 146
DESCANDANTS from BARON
RICHARD de CLARE &
WILLIAM the CONQUEROR
226
DESPENCER
  Anne Ferrers 220
  Edward 220
  Hugh 220
DEUTERIA *236*
DICK, *Charles 252*
DICKINSON, *John 261*
DIDDLE
  James 111
  Mildred Hughes 111
DIGGES
  Cole 49
  Edward 42-43

  Martha Walker 49
DINGAD *243*
DINWIDDIE, *Robert 125-126*
DIXON, *Roger 258*
DOBBINS
  Jane 156
  Levi 156
DOCUMENTS PRINTED in
"THE APPEAL FOR
ROYALTY" *170-171*
DONNELL
  Hartwell Weaver 150
  Mary Paralee Bass 150
DOOLITTLE
  George 58
  Mary Webster 57
  Susan Webster 58
  William 57
DORSEY
  Clara Virginia Wynkoop 135
  James Owen, Reverend 135
DOWDEN
  Adeline Lightfoot 116
  George 116
DRUMMOND
  Elizabeth Stone 100
  Greene/Grieve 100
du **MAINE,** *Ermengarde 238*
DUKE
  Margaret Webster 58
  Walter 58
DUKE BURKHART *237*
DUNCAN
  Alexandria 175
  Ambrose 262
  Andrew 174
  Ann Gallop 139, 175
  Archibald 6
  Benjamin 6
  Bessie 174
  Charles 6, 175
  Christopher 6
  Claiborne 6
  Cynthia Colvin 262
  David 6-7, 174
  Dinah Bradford 175
  Edward 7
  Frances Colvin 262

DUNCAN (Continued)
Gabriel 7
George 7, 175
Gollop 176
Henry 175
James 7
John 7, 174-176, 254
Jonah 7
Joseph 7
Luke 7
Margaret McMurdo 175
Mary 175
Nathaniel 174
Nimrod 7
Robert 7, 139, 175
Rosey 175
Ruth Raleigh 175
Sammy 176
Samuel 7
Sina Browning 175
Susan 175
Susan Sarah Haldane 175
Susan Thomas 175
Thomas 175
William 174-175
William J. 175
William Marshall 175
Willis 262
DUNCAN I 174
DUNHAM
Amos 162-163
Anna E. Bolton 163
Barbara Ellen Dye 162
Benjamin Armistead 162
Elijah Collivar 162
Elizabeth Jane Swank 163
Elwilda Pugh 162
George Washington 162
James Guilford 162
John Thompson 162
Joseph Eldridge 163
Leandus Logan 163
Levina Lightfoot 162
Loretta Marquess 162
M.J. Chaning 162
Mary Ann Moore 162
Quintin Parker 162
Samuel Arthur 163

Sarah Colliver 162-163
William Henry 162
DUNKLEY, Elizabeth 26
DUNLAP
George H. 100
George Hamilton 100
Sallie Savigne Lightfoot 100
DUNMORE, Lord 254
DUNN
John James 58
Mrs. 9
Smythe Mardissa Webster 58
DUNNING, J. 171
DYMOKE
Edward 247
Frances 247
EARL OF LINCOLN 233
EASTHAM, Robert 107
EDBURGA 233
EDITH of Germany 231
EDITH of Saxony 237
EDULF 233
EDWARD III 220-223, 247
EDWARD the Confessor 198, 214
EDY, John 182
EDZARD
James 110
Martha Lightfoot 110, 256
William 110, 256
ELEANOR of Acquitaine 238, 247
ELEANOR of Castile & Leon 238-239, 247
ELEANOR of England 247
ELEANOR of Provence 238
ELFGIFU 233
ELFIED 233
ELGIVA 235
ELLIOTT
? 123
Alexander 111, 114
Ann Campbell 114
Evalina Lightfoot 123
George Campbell 111
Lucinda Thomas 110
Susan Nelson 111
William, Dr. 110

ELLYSON
 Anne Clopton 3
 Gerard 3
 Robert 3
 Robert Gerard 3
 Sarah Clopton 3
ELTON
 Anthony Malcolm 61
 Eleanor McElvany 61
EMENGARDE 237
EMMA of Andech 231
EMPEROR CHARLEMAGNE
(Charles the Great) 218, 226, 231,
237-238, 246
ENGUERAND I, (Count of
Ponthieu) 238
ENIR FARDD 243
EPPS, Colonel 9
ERIC 232
ERMENGARDE of Alsace 237
ERMENGARDE 237, 246
ESKRIDGE, George 179
ESPRIOTA (Sporta) 232
ETHELRED, Earl of Gainas 233-
234
ETHELRED, Earl of Mercia 233
ETHELWULF 232
EUDES I, Count of Bourgogne
238
EUDOXIA 234
EURE 228
EURE
 John 229
 William, Sir 229
EURGAIN 244
EURGEN 233
EVANS
 Clenice 123
 Mary Lightfoot 123
 W. Vaughn 123
 William 123, 191
EVERETT
 Grace Lightfoot 98
 Wilbur McLauren 98
EWING
 John O. 67
 Sarah Ann Lightfoot 67
EYSTEIN I 232

EYSTEIN, Earl of More 232
EYSTEIN, Earl of Throndheim
232
FAGAN
 John F. 112
 Mary E. Lightfoot 112
FARMER
 Alvin Morris 150
 Charles Larry 150
 Gladys Pauline Lightfoot 150
 James David 150
 Jimmy ? 150
 Joyce Griffith 150
 Maxine ? 150
 Quanita 150
FARTHING (Lightfoot)
 James 50
 Susan Lightfoot 50
FAUSTA 234
FERDINAND III, King of Castile
& Leon 239, 247
FERRANTE
 Helen Ann Lightfoot 161
 Jack 161
FERREOLUS 236
FERRERS
 Agnes 221
 Agnes Chester 219
 Alianore Bohun 220
 Eleanor Lovaine 220
 Elizabeth 221
 Hawise Mucegros 220
 Henry 221
 Isabel Verdon 221
 Joan Despencer 220
 Joan Grey 221
 Margaret Seagraves 220
 Margaret Quincey 219
 Mary Brun 220
 Ralph 221
 Sibilla Marshall 219
 Thomas 221
 William 220-221
FIELD
 Abraham 107, 137, 251
 Anne Lightfoot 137
 Elizabeth 137
 Henry 3, 137, 259

FIELD (Continued)
John   126
FIELDS
Elizabeth Lightfoot   262
John   262
FINLASON, *John   107*
FINNELL
John   113
Martha Divers Bohon   113
FISHER
Delila Lightfoot   115
Ezekial   115
fitz EUSTACE
Albreda Lisours   226, 228
John   226
Richard   226, 228
fitz GEOFFREY
Isabel Bigod Lacie   212
John   212
fitz GILBERT
Richard   226
Rohese Bolebec   227
fitz JOHN
Hugh   229
Maud Barry   221
Morice   221
fitz MORICE
Margaret Berkeley   221
Nicholas   222
Thomas   221
fitz NIGEL, *William   228*
fitz PIERS
Beatrix Saye   202
Geoffrey   202
fitz RICHARD
Alice Vere   228
Robert   227
Rodger   228
fitz ROGER
Margaret Cheney   229
Robert   229
fitz THOMAS
Aveline   222
Katherine Burgh   222
Margaret O'Brien   22
Morice   221-222
Thomas   221
fitz WALTER

Alianore Ferrers   220
Gunora Valoines   205
Matilda   205
Robert   193, 195, 197, 199, 204-205, 208-209, 213-214, 217, 220
Rohese   205
FLEET, *Henry   180*
FLOOD, *William   176*
FLOYD, *Jno   257*
FORBES, *General   49*
FORD
S. Hassel   59
Virginia Frances Grey   59
Virginia Frances   59
FORTIBUS, *Aveline Montifichet 214*
FORTNER
Mary Belle Lightfoot
Richard   51
FOSTER
Beverly   260
Joseph, Colonel   5, 47
FOWLER
Elizabeth Lightfoot   168
Stephen   168
FOX
Arthur   132
Frances Lightfoot   132
FREELOVE
Charles   151
Louise Lightfoot   151
FRODE VII   234
FROST
Ann Webster   58
William   58
FROTHO, King of Denmark   235
FRY
Benjamin   8
Gabriel   8
George   8
Henry, Reverend   111, 130, 133
Jacob   8
James   255
John   8, 255
Joseph   5
Joshua   8
Nathan   8
Reuben   255

FRY (Continued)
Samuel 8
Susannah Walker 111, 133
Thomas 8
William 8
FRYE
Elizabeth Lucy Lightfoot 169
James Henry 169
FULK III, Count d'Anjou 246
FULK IV, Count d'Anjou 235,
238, 246
FULK V, Count d'Anjou 238, 246
FURR
Edward 146
Elizabeth Lightfoot 146
GABBERT
C.W., Dr. 115
Mary Ella Lightfoot 115
GALLOP, Robert 139, 175
GAM, Morgan 203
GARDNER
Martha Lightfoot 5
William 5
GARREN
Charles 132
Cora Fidelia Hill 132
GARVEY
Alice 118
Allice Kay Belle 119
Amelia 118
Amelia Lightfoot 118
Ben A. 119
Ben Pendleton 119
Cary 119
Clarence 119
Clayton Hamilton 119
Clifford Pendleton 119
Edgar 120
Edgar Lawrence 119
Harry P. 119
Hazel 119
James 118
James Pendleton 119
James Russell 119
James Stanley 119
Jane Dickey 119
Jane Thomsy 118
John 118

John Frederick, Dr. 118
John Lightfoot 118
John S. 119
Katherine 119
Katherine ? 119
Katherine McBrayer 119
Luella Rhodes 119
Marion 119
Mary Hamilton 119
Mary Lutie Hays 119
Myrtle 118
Nancy Reed 118
Nell 119
Phillip G. 119
Phillip Lawrence, Dr. 118
Robert A. 118
Robert Piper 120
Rosa Franks 119
Roy 119
Ruby 119
Ruth 119
Samuel Thomas 118
Susannah 120
Virginia 119
Virginia ? 119
Wallace G. 119
Will 119
William S. 119
William Sanford 119
GASCOIGNE
Elizabeth 247
William 247
GATES, Thomas, Sir 250
GATESHILL
Ann Lightfoot 256
Henry 256
GEER
Bertha Lightfoot 159
Marion 159
GENEBALD I, Duke of the East
Franks 235-236, 245
GENSENLUTER, Eddie John
162
GEOFFREY I, de Gastinois 237
GEOFFREY II, de Gastinois 237,
246
GEOFFREY, Count d'Anjou 239,
246

GEORGE II *167*
GEORGE III *167, 169-171*
GEORGE, *Judith* *37*
GERBERGA *237*
GILBERT
  Anne Price *186*
  Lewis *184, 186*
  Thomas *186*
GINN, *John* *262*
GISELA *237-238*
GISLEBERT, Duke of Lorraine *237*
GIST
  John *123*
  Susannah Lightfoot *123*
GIVINS
  David Andrew *153*
  Dixie Lea Walker *153*
  Lance David *153*
  Paige Lea *153*
  Staci Lynn *153*
GLADYS *233-234, 242*
GLADYS (Claudia) *244*
GODBEE
  H.D. *62*
  Mary Jane Lightfoot *62*
GOHAGAN
  ? *123*
  Lucille Gist *123*
GOODLOE, *Robert* *253*
GOODRICH
  Anne *190*
  Anne Sherwood *41-42, 189-191, 229*
  Benjamin *42-43, 190*
  Charles *42, 190*
  Clare Norton *191*
  Danby *43*
  Edward *190*
  Elizabeth *190*
  Henry *190*
  Jane Williamson *190*
  John *41, 189, 191, 229*
  Joseph *42-43, 190*
  Kathrine *190*
  Margaret Rawson *190*
  Mildred Eure *229*
  Peter *42, 190*

  Rebecca Allen *191, 229*
  Richard *191, 229*
  Robert *190*
  Thomas, Lt. Col. *41-43, 189-191, 193, 229, 258*
GOODRICH, LIGHTFOOT, QUINCEY & CHARLEMAGNE CONNECTION *233*
GOODRICHES, *Charles* *189*
GOODWIN, *Theodore A.* *72*
GORDON
  A.C., General *71*
  Charles Henry Allen *137*
  Evelyn Hudspeth *71*
  Zella Kate Porter *137*
GORE
  Dean Franklin *63*
  Edna Bell *63*
GORM del GAMMEL, King of Denmark *235*
GORM ENSKE *235*
GORNTO
  David *60*
  Eliza Allen *60*
  Everett *74-75*
  Frances H. Lightfoot *74*
  Talula Lightfoot *75*
GOVERNOR DINWIDDIE'S LETTERS of the CULPEPER MILITIA *126*
GOZ
  Emma Contesville *232*
  Richard *232*
GRADY
  Lincefield *111*
  Mildred Thornton Lightfoot *111*
  William Fry *111*
GRAEME, *Mr.* *8-9*
GRAME, *John* *251*
GRANT
  Johnny *150*
  Martha Cora Farmer *150*
GRANTMESNIL, *Petronella* *225*
GRASTY
  Ann Lightfoot *107, 114, 255*
  George *114*
  Goodrich L. *114*

GRAY
Agnes Audine Brown   154
Andrew   260
Barbara   154
Benny Paul   154
Bonnie Lou Atteberry   156
Clara Nella   60
Dean   154
Donald   60
Eddie   154
Emily Lightfoot   62
Emma Dunn   59
George Dabney   132
James   62
James A.   59
Jerry   156
Jesse Lightfoot   59
Lillian Elizabeth   60
Patricia Sue   154
Rosemary   154
Roy Dean   154
Ruby   154
Sarah Frances S. Lightfoot   59
Susan Cornelia Lightfoot   60
Willis   154
GRAYSON
Ambrose   251
John   251
GREEN
James   259
John   3, 126
Robert   3, 107, 126, 251, 259
William   3, 48, 126, 259
GREENE
Lucy Zouche   224
Nathaniel   49
GREIDIOL   243
GREY
Anne Rockley   220
Maude Botetourt   220
Richard   221
GRICE, John   89
GRIFFIN
John Tayloe   103
Larkin   48
Mary Lightfoot   95, 103

GRINNAN
Daniel   107
Jane J.   107
John   107, 255
Thomas   176
GRYMES
Anne Burwell Lightfoot   103
John   103, 261-262
GUDROD   232
GUELPH III   231
GUELPH, Count of Andech   237
GUERINFROI, Signor d'Aumale
238
GUINEVERE   234
GUSTAFSON, William Gores   161
GUY I, Count of Ponthieu   238
GUY II, Count of Ponthieu   239
GWEYRYDD   243
HACKLEY
Fanny Lightfoot   107
Frances Lightfoot   114, 255
Francis   114
Joseph   176
Mary Duncan   176
HACKNEY, William   251
HADLEY
Catherine Miners   184, 187
Robert   184, 187
HAIDS, Elizabeth   37
HAIRE
Aaron Mancy   64
Eunice Nadine Chapman   64
Jeffrey Steven   64
Leron Mancy   64
Steven Mancy   64
Wande Berneice Lightfoot   64
HALDANE
Mary Kennet   175
Richard   175
HALFDAN I   232, 234
HALFDAN II   232
HAMBLETON, James   115
HAMILTON
Elijah   262
Nancy West   262
HAMMOND
James   115
Manwarring   77, 79

HAMMOND (Continued)
Nancy Lightfoot   70
William   70
HANCKS, *Thomas   251*
HANCOCK
Daniel L.   59
Louisa Cornelia Sheppard   59
HANKINS
David P.   50
Mary C. Lightfoot   50
HANSFORD, *William   253*
HARALD BLAATAND, King of
Denmark   *234*
HARCOURT
Alice Corbett   219
Alice Zouche   219
Arabella Quincey   219
Eleanor Hastings   219
Eleanor Zouche   219, 224
John   224
Margaret Beke   219
HARDING, *William   261*
HARE
A.A.   161
Katy Mae Lightfoot   161
HARFIELD, *Michael   79*
HARMAN, *William   4*
HARMON
Albert   52
Audrey Naomi Lightfoot   52
Jude   5
Robert   4-5
Will   5
HARN
Elijah   145
Margaret Jane Lightfoot   145
HAROLD PARCUS, King of
Denmark   *235*
HARRINGTON, *Robert, Esq.   35-
36*
HARRIS, *William Overton   258*
HARRISON
Benjamin   45, 96
Daniel, Captain   258
Major   9, 11
Mrs.   9-11
William H.   97

HART
George   256
John T.   65
Julia Fry   256
Philip   256
HARTWELL
Harrison   52
Henry   44
Rebecca Lightfoot   52
HARWOOD, *Thomas   260*
HASBROOK
?   132
Frances Thompson Lightfoot   132
HASILDA   *235, 245*
HASTINGS, *Henry   219*
HAWKINS
Betty Maxwell   121
John   110
Joseph   107
Matthew   121
HEDWIGE   *231*
HEIDELBERG
J. Oscar   60
Virginia Gray   60
HELEN   *224, 234*
HENDERSON
David   256
Henry   251
HENDREN
Sarah Catherine Dunham   163
Zachary T.   163
HENDRICKS
Mary Jane Lightfoot   164
Stephen Smith   164
HENLEY
?   50
Catherine Norvell Lightfoot   50
HENNING, *Samuel   3*
HENRY of Essex   *229*
HENRY I   *198, 207-208, 211, 218,
228, 231, 238*
HENRY II   *185, 200, 202, 223,
228, 238-239, 247*
HENRY III   *201, 205-211, 213,
218, 223, 226, 238*
HERBERT
Margaret Sawyer   35
Thomas   35

HERBERT I, Count of Vermandois *246*

HERBERT II, Count of Vermandois *246*

HERLEVE of Falaise *232, 238*

HERNDON
Edward *253*
James Cloud *135, 256*
Mary Catlett Lightfoot *135, 256*

HEWITT
Elizabeth *95*
Richard *95*

HICKERSON
Lou Ella Gray *60*
Luella Francis *60*
R.F. *60*

HICKMAN, *Edwin 252*

HILDA *232, 234*

HILDEBRAND *246*

HILDEGARDE of Suabia *231, 237, 246*

HILDERIC, King of the Vandals *234-235, 245*

HILDUIN *238*

HILL
Betty *10*
Colonel *9-10, 42, 44*
Francis A. *132*
Lydia Elizabeth *132*
Martha Alice *132*
May Lucy *132*
Quintella Cinderella Lightfoot *132*
Sarah Ann Rebecca *132*
Thomas *260*

HINSON
Joseph *261*
Minnie Estha Lightfoot *54*
Rowan Thomas *54*

HISTORICAL REGISTER of VIRGINIANS in the REVOLUTION *5-8*

HITE, *Joist 108*

HOBSON, *George 108*

HODGSON
Henrietta Midlred *248*
Robert *248*

HOLAND, *Maud Zouche 224*

HOLLOWAY
Amey *139*
Charles *139*

HOLMES
Joseph *168*
Ruth Lightfoot *168*

HOLTON, *Elijah 147*

HOME, George *107*

HOMES
Judith Applegate *262*
Samuel G. *262*

HONEYWOOD, *Philip, Esq., Col. 78-79*

HOPKINS
Fanny Pratt *99*
John *99*

HORDA KNUT, King of Denmark *235*

HOUGHTON, *Thomas 26, 34*

HOUSE
Gwen Johnson *164*
Harvey H. *164*

HOWELL
John, Sir *95*
Mrs. *95*

HOWISON
Elizabeth Lightfoot *130*
Thomas *130*

HROF (Rollo) *232*

HU GADARN, the Mighty *239*

HUBBARD
Ephraim *114*
MaryLightfoot *107, 114, 255*

HUBERT, Count de Senlis *232*

HUDON
Clementine Lightfoot *256*
George *256*

HUDSON
Nancy Lightfoot *114*
Robert *114*

HUFF
? *62*
Mary Lou Lightfoot *62*

HUFFMAN
Arthur B. *150*
Hilda M. Lightfoot *150*

HUGH CAPET, King of France *231, 237-238*

HUGH MAGNUS *231*
HUGH the GREAT, Earl of Mercia
233
HUGH, Duke of France *231*
HUGHES
George *111*
Margaret Thornton Grady *111*
HUGUES I, Count of Ponthieu
238
HUGHES II, Count of Ponthieu
238
HUME
Elizabeth Lightfoot *133*
Ellen *133*
Emma *133*
Joseph *133*
HUNNERIC *234*
HUNT
Helm *157*
Martha Lee Lightfoot *157*
HUNTINGDON, Ada *219*
HUNTINGFIELD
Alice *206*
Isabel Gressinghall *205*
HURST
? *123*
Clell *123*
Horase *123*
Susan Gist *123*
HUTTON
Elizabeth McCullough *145*
John *144-145*
IDA *239*
IDWAL *243*
INGAM, Count of Hasbania *237*
INGONDE *236, 246*
INGRAM, John *103*
INNES
Edward *169*
Jane Josepha Lightfoot *169*
IRWIN
? *61*
Rachel Cook *61*
ISABEL of France *247*
ISHAM
Ed *148*
Frank N. *148*
Georgia A. Coppage *148*

Lena C. *148*
ITHEL *243*
ITHON *243*
IVAR VIDFADMA, King of
Denmark *234*
JACKSON
Alfred Bell *155*
Amanda F. Lightfoot *146*
Eli K. *155*
George C. *146*
George H. *155*
John *24*
John H. *256*
Judy Fry *256*
Laura Bell *155*
Mary L. *155*
Robert *252*
Tabitha Ann Parks *155*
JAMES
? *114*
Elizabeth Lightfoot *107, 114, 255*
JAMES II *35*
JARRELL
Catharine S. Lightfoot *72*
Elisha P. *72*
Nancy *71*
JEAN I, Count of Ponthieu *239*
JENINGS, Edmund *44*
JENKINS *185*
JENNINGS
Colonel *45*
Thomas *255*
JERDONE, Francis *94*
JERNEW, Mr. *78*
JOAN DAMMARTIN *239, 247*
JOAN of Acre *239*
JOELL, John *261*
JOHN, Gwillim *185*
JOHNES, Bruentta Lightfoot *48*
JOHNSON
? *164*
Anna M. Thompson *145*
Anthony Lightfoot *48*
Charles *69*
Daniel *145*
Elizabeth Lightfoot *48*
Frankey *48*
George *48*

JOHNSON (Continued)
  Gladys Angeline Leer 164
  James C. 256
  Joel 251
  John 48
  Margie Fry 256
  Martha Lightfoot 69
  Richard 44, 251
  Susannah Lightfoot 48-49
  Susannah M. 48
  William 251-252
JONES
  ? 63
  Ben 58
  Cadwalader, Colonel 257
  Francis 31
  Hendley 70
  Henry 72
  Henry Lightfoot 72
  Howell 57
  John 35
  John Hollinger 73
  Josephine Lightfoot 63
  Lurana Stewart 73
  Martha 31
  Mary Baker 70
  Mary Elizabeth Marcus 72
  Mary Hogan 72
  Mathew 68
  Nellie Payne 72
  Priscilla Aske 31
  Rebecca Westbrook 73
  Robert 179
  Sarah Lightfoot 72
  Sarah Elizabeth Webster 57
  Sally Webster 58
  Thomas 25, 31, 35, 73, 106, 255
  William 31, 72
  William Henry 73
  Willie Winston 84
  Winnie Elder 72
JORDAN
  Almira Caroline Lightfoot 98
  George 110-111
  Joseph P. 98
  Levi 69
  Sarah Stone 69
  William 182

JOUETT/JEWETT
  Narcissa ? 66
  Thomas 66
JUDGE
  ? Burge 63
  L.J. 63
JUDITH 237
JUDITH of Brittany 232, 238
JUDITH of Lens 225
KAMPE
  Ester 183
  Peter 183
KARLOMANN 236
KAVANAUGH, Philimon 106
KEELING, George 47
KEITH
  Calvin S. 157
  John D. 262
  Marann Thomas 262
  Mary Ellen Lightfoot 157
  William 261
KELLY
  John Joseph 59
  Martha Ann Elizabeth Sheppard 59
KENDALL
  Harold Harris 121
  Maud Ethel Lightfoot 121
KENDRICK, Jacob 255
KENNON
  Laurence James, Jr. 52
  Pamela Ann Lightfoot 52
**KENTUCKY SOCIETY of
COLONIAL WARS** 257
KIDWALIDER
  Jane Miners 184, 187
  John 184, 187
KILVENTON
  Daniel 168
  Dorothy Lightfoot 168
KIMBER, Edward 93
KING
  Eveline Roberta Lightfoot 120
  Frank 120
KING ARTHUR 234
KING BARTHEUS 235, 245
KING CHARLES I 198
KING CLODIO 236, 246

KING CLODIUS I *236, 245*
KING CLODIUS III *235, 245*
KING DAGOBERT *235, 245*
KING EDWARD I *196-197, 220,*
223, 238-239, 247
KING EDWARD II *220, 223-*
224, 247
KING ETHELRED II *233*
KING FARABERT *235, 245*
KING GEORGE VI *248*
KING JOHN *193, 195-197, 200-*
214, 217-218, 227, 238
KING MALCOLM CANMORE
225, 238
KING of the RUGIJ *235*
KING SUNNO *235, 245*
KING WALTER *235, 245*
KING WILLIAM *225*
KING WILLIAM RUFUS *227*
KINGSTONE
  Robert 25, 27, 35
  Sarah Lightfoot 25, 27
  William 24
KIRKHAM, *William 182*
KIRKLEY
  Frances 126
  Francis 253
  William 126
KIRKLY, *Francis 107*
KNIGHT
  James 53
  Mary An Rio Lightfoot 53
KNOTT
  ? 63
  Grace Williamson 63
KNYSTON, *Nicholas 186*
KOLSTAD
  Donna Darlene Parks 157
  Robert 157
la ZOUCHE
  Alan 223
  Eudo 219, 222, 224
  Robert 224
  Roger 219, 223
  William 224
LACEY, *John, Capt. 47*

LACIE
  Alice Aquila 206, 226
  Alice Gant 225
  Margaret Quincy 206, 218, 225-
  226
  Maud Clare 226-227
LADY ALSWITHA *233*
LADY ALWARD *233*
LADY DODO of Saxony *236, 246*
LADY ELFWINA *233*
LADY ETHELFELDA *233*
LADY GODIVA *233*
LADY GUNNORA *235, 238*
LADY POPPA *232*
LAKE
  Ann Virginia Lightfoot 136
  Robert P. 136
LAMPTON
  Mark 114
  Susannah H. Lightfoot 114
LANDER
  Mary 115
  Nathaniel 115
LANE
  ?, Professor 98
  James 261
  Mary E. Lightfoot 98
LANGTON, *Stephen 194-195,*
197
LANTERMAN
  Dolly Ashby Lightfoot 112
  Peter 112
LANVALLEI, *Hawise Basset 206*
LAWRENCE
  Samuel 119
  Tabby Eliza Garvey 119
LAWSON, *Thomas 180*
le BRUN, *Hugues 220*
LEBER
  Maude Mae Lightfoot 97
  Robert Wesley 97
LEE
  Francis Lightfoot 256
  George Bolling 85-86
  Mary Custis 84, 86
  Richard 44
  Robert E. 84-85, 95, 136
  William H.F. 84

LEER
Mary Jane McKinley 164
William 164
LEIGH
Edward, Esq. 36
Francis, Capt. 89
LEITCH
John Clyde 116
Sarah Johnne Lightfoot 116
LELY, Peter, Sir 95
LEOFRIC III, the GREAT 233
LEOFWINE, Earl of Mercia 233
LeSEUER
Henrietta Frances Lightfoot 98
Littleberry 98
LETTER from JOHN B.
LIGHTFOOT to PHILIP
LIGHTFOOT 140
LEWIS
Anne Cocke Lightfoot 98
Betty 253
Charles 99
David H. 62
Elizabeth J. Lightfoot 112
Fielding 253
George 253
George Anna Lightfoot 157, 265
Georgia V. Lightfoot 62
Hugh H. 149
John 253
John R. 157, 265
Lucy Taliaferro 99
Margaret Coppage 149
Richard T. 112
William 98
LIFA 232
LIGHTFOOT MEMORIAL 29
LIGHTFOOT
? 101
? Carlson 123
? Coke 169
? Scott 37
Ada Woodard 51
Adah Lander 115
Addie Bell Whittington 64
Alberta Taylor 162
Alexander 53
Alfred 168

Alfred C. 147
Alfred W. 147
Alice 4, 75, 79
Alice B. 112
Alice Corbin 89-90, 96
Alice Hurt 97
Alice Jean Bahr 57
Alice Springer 145
Allen 55, 70
Allen A. 52
Allen B. 53
Alma 117
Alvah Haney 161
Amalie ? 159
Amelia Eldridge 131
Amelia Jane 116, 118
Amos 163
Anderson J. 72
Andrew Jackson 121
Angela Leann 65
Ann 251
Ann E. 158
Anne E. Nuckolls 58
Ann Goodrich 4, 41-43, 47, 105,
190-191, 193, 229
Ann Isabelle Drummond 100
Ann L. Willet 150, 263
Ann T. Newman 115
Anna 31
Anna Lancaster 72
Anna M. Flatt 164
Anne 4, 34, 36, 68, 95, 109-110
Anne Bennett 168
Anne Brograve 249
Anne Burwell 103
Anne Cocke 96
Anne Clopton Ellyson 98
Annie Eliza Bryan 63
Annie Mudd 151
Anona ? 159
Archibald 51
Archibald McKissack 67
Armistead 50, 95, 103
Armistead C. 147, 158
Armistead Norvell 50
Arria Moseley 120
Asenath Reynolds 72
Bathsheba Elton 61

xxxvi

LIGHTFOOT (Continued)

Baxter Davis   120
Bee R.   51
Belle Drummond   100
Benjamin   53, 163
Benjamin Franklin   121
Berl   62
Bernice ?   64
Bertha Barthena   54
Bertha Bird   158
Bessie A. Randberg   145
Bessie May   54
Betty Farmer   71
Beverley Ann ?   51
Billie Dzuris   145
Billy Mac   51
Bythel J.   52
Calvin Tom   64
Caroline A. Hill   72
Caroline Crow   120
Caroline Cynthia   120
Caroline Matilda Guerrant   97
Caroline Rebecca   57
Caroline Wolfe   56
Carolus   62
Carrie ?   121
Carrie Hamilton   116
Carrie May   151
Carter   98
Catalina ?   168
Catharine   163
Catherine   159, 169
Catherine Bryan   72
Catherine Colvin   157, 263
Catherine Delia Reed   66
Catherine Donaldson Cody   71
Catherine Elizabeth   70, 72
Catherine Maury   134
Catherine Norvell   49
Charles   34, 36, 51
Charles E.   130
Charles Earl   54
Charles Edward   116, 135
Charles Hartwell   150
Charles Henry   54
Charles Leslie   150
Charles Ross   116
Charles W.   112

Cheat   114
Chris   160
Christopher C.   164
Clackston   52
Claiborne   259-260
Clara Augusta   157
Clara Lyons   123
Clara P. Winn   52
Clarence   75, 159
Claria B.   75
Cleon Dee   164
Clyde Aubrey   97
Collen A., Colonel   72
Cora Edward Donnell   150
Cora Paralee Pearl Ellen   150
Cornelius   74
Cynthia Anna Watson   150
D'Estang   143, 263
Daniel   6
Daniel Jackson   63
David   53
David S.   146
Deila Clark   115
Delilah Korns   121
DeLores Absher   97
Diana   165
Don Phillip   63
Dora   67
Dora Ann   120
Dora Bell Maxey   67
Doris June   147
Druscilla Carpenter   62
E.D.   64
Earnest   64
Ed   65
Edgar Vivien   101
Edith L. Hutchinson   55
Edmund   2, 34, 36
Edna   65
Edna Gertrude Gore   63
Edna P.C. ?   51
Edward   6, 52, 127, 130-132, 143,
157, 263
Edward Barrow   54
Edward Taylor   132
Edward Morris   150
Edwin B.   71
Edwin Drummond   100

LIGHTFOOT (Continued)

Eldred Walker 117
Eleanor Ross 143
Eli B. 164
Elisha 61
Eliza J. Brizedine 164
Elizabeth 4, 36, 62, 68, 123, 127, 143, 165, 169
Elizabeth ? 96
Elizabeth A. Johnson 53
Elizabeth Annette 64
Elizabeth Babcock Pomeroy 161
Elizabeth Barrow 123, 125, 127, 130, 139, 176-177, 182
Elizabeth Benton 147
Elizabeth C. Simmons 65
Elizabeth Caldwell 143
Elizabeth Carter 168-169
Elizabeth Colvin 147, 263
Elizabeth Conner 130, 136
Elizabeth Dyer 121
Elizabeth Jones 163
Elizabeth Morrell 151
Elizabeth Perry 59
Elizabeth Phillips 26-27, 30, 34-36, 39-40, 90
Elizabeth Rhodes 70
Elizabeth Russell 158
Elizabeth Smoot 163
Elizabeth Stone 68
Elizabeth Tailor 34, 39-41, 90
Elizabeth Virginia Nicholas 97
Elizabeth W. Anderson 100
Elizabeth Walker 134
Elizabeth Wilson 55
Elkin 150, 263
Elkin D. 149
Ella 97
Ella I. 117
Ellen Ross 74
Elmira 69
Elton 52
Emerine 122
Emily 143, 149
Emily Hill Mitchell 74
Emma 65, 117
Emma A. ? 117
Emma Batcheller 145

Emma Caroline 57
Emma Pate 116
Emmie Crump 101
Erma Dobbs 52
Etta Wooten 67
Eunice Thames 54
Eva 117
Eva Parkhurst 122
Evelyn Rae 164
Ewing 117
Fannie F. Kelly 112
Fannie Pyle 97
Flora McCrady 147
Flora Belle Marietta 121
Florence 65
Florence S. 65
Floyd Henry 121
Forrest Lee 116
Frances 4-6, 8-11, 68, 127, 133, 146, 151, 165
Frances Ann 51
Frances Funnerll 121
Francis 4, 11, 34, 36, 48, 90-91, 96-97, 103, 158, 254
Francis D. 257, 262
Francis Day 149
Francis Marion 121
Francis Thornton 135
Frank 117, 130
Frank Alfred 147
Frank D. 117
Frank Korns 121
Frank Leslie 151
Frank W. 54
Frayser 69
Frayzer 4-5
Frederick 51
Gabriel 112
Gabriel M. 113
George 34, 36, 101
George A. 97
George Benskin 50
George C. 262
George Chapin 135
George Colvin 139, 146-147
George Jordan 121
George Nicholas 148
George P. 117

LIGHTFOOT (Continued)

George W. *164*
George Washington *163*
Georgia Ann Wallace *62*
Georgia Chapin *135*
Georgiana Chapin *135*
Geraldine Guielmus Jackson
  Fielder *130, 135*
Gertrude Babcock *162*
Goodrich *3-4, 11, 48, 79, 105-
  110, 113, 120, 125, 127, 130, 132-
  133, 173-174, 176, 251-253, 255-
  258*
Goodrich E. *112, 131*
Goodridge *263*
Grace *144*
Green Jackson *63*
Gross, Dr. *144*
Gussie Elton *63*
Guthrie Goodrich *157*
Guy Donald *151*
Hannah *167-171*
Hannah Gornto *60*
Hannibal *158*
Harriet Collins *74*
Harriet Rachel *62*
Harriett Brown *100*
Harriett Field *101*
Harrison *50*
Harry John *145*
Harry Owens *117*
Harvey Monroe *122*
Hattie Bell Mallory *67*
Helen Josephine Rockwell *161*
Helen P. *117*
Henrietta *51, 66*
Henry *4, 69, 103, 110, 159, 169*
Henry Benskin *48-49*
Henry Byrd *159*
Henry C. *75*
Henry Cole *65-66*
Henry Davis *158*
Henry E. *117*
Henry F. *112*
Henry Fauster *118*
Henry Harrison *121*
Henry McKinnon *75*
Henry Pendleton *117*

Henry W. *112*
Henry Wadsworth *120*
Henry Wesley *53*
Henry William *67*
Hollie L. *117*
Howard *101*
Hugh H. *160*
Hugh Kyle *122*
Ida *144*
Idell Turner *51*
Irene *118*
Irvin *53*
Irving Washington *121*
Isabel *164*
Isabel R. Hitch *149*
Iva Thrailkill *164*
Jacqueline *55*
James *50, 146, 165, 168, 262*
James A. Halligan *63*
James Anderson *97-98*
James Archibald *61-62*
James Augustus *151*
James Cosby *97*
James Earl *52*
James Edward *54, 144*
James F. *122*
James Henry *55*
James Herndon *135*
James M. *67*
James Madison *122*
James Newell *71*
James Pendleton *120*
James Philip *57*
James R. *66, 112*
James Sharp *72*
James Steele *143*
James/John Thomas *161*
James Tindell *161*
James Wesley *53*
Jane *24-27, 30-31, 33-36*
Jane Caroline Simonton *70*
Jane Eliza Mitchell *98*
Jane Martin *131*
Jane Phinney *121*
Janet ? *151*
Janice Young *150*
Jean Steele *143, 263*
Jeannetta Hamilton K. Caskey *157*

LIGHTFOOT (Continued)

Jeannette Laird Finch 120
Jesse 54-55, 62, 68
Jesse Faulton 63
Jesse Hobbye 63
Jim Frank 65
Jim Garrett 62
Jo Ann Wilson 63
Joane 251
Joanna Dulany 143
Joel 143, 165
Joel Franklin 134
John 2, 4, 6, 11, 34, 36, 48-50, 55, 65, 68, 92, 97, 103, 107, 110, 114-115, 130, 136, 143, 146, 158, 164-165, 167-169, 249-251, 254-257, 259-260, 263
John, Captain 2, 25, 34, 36, 39-41, 90
John, Esquire 2, 24-27, 30, 33-35, 39-40, 90
John, the Immigrant 2, 4-5, 11-12, 16, 36, 40-47, 78-79, 83, 89-90, 105, 190-191, 193, 229, 254, 258, 263, 267
John A. 70
John Ashby 112
John B. 62, 123, 127, 130
John Barrow 131, 139, 143, 175
John Bernard 101
John C. 75, 263
John Colvin 146
John Daniel 145
John E. 149
John Elton 62
John Foster 116
John Francis 97-98
John Frazier 66-67
John Goodrich 115, 122
John H. 121
John Henry 120
John James 134
John Jones 113
John L. 50, 112
John Lee 48-49
John Luther 97
John McKissack 66
John Pinkston 57

John Slaughter 115
John Smith 158, 160
John Steele 56
John W. 53, 70, 72, 146
John Warner Crow 120
John Wesley 134
John William 54
John William Bell 145
John William Thomas 147
Johnnie 70
Joseph Greenberry 53
Joshua 55
Joshua Pendleton 120
Joyce Compton 249
Judith L. 112
Judith M. Hanes 97
Julia 72
Julia Ann 112
Julia Ann Aminda 53
Julia Hardin 54
Julia Ophelia Wilson 55
Julia R. Plunkett 112
Julia Steele 57
Julia Weber 145
June Cumbus 64
Kate 65, 75
Kate Gallagher 134
Katherine 143
Katherine Enders 145
Katie Alverson 160
Kezia Ann Yancey 136
Lacie Rosettie Bass 62
Laura Coffrin 121
Lavina 54, 165
Lavina Duncan 131, 139, 143, 175
Lawrence Gordon 71
Leannah Colvin 146
Lee 158
Lee Gano 67
Lee Roy 64
Lemuel Ethelbert 145
Lena Sterchi 158
Leon Lamar 65
Leonard 117
Leonora 169
Letty Blasingame 263
Levi Butler 164

LIGHTFOOT (Continued)
Lewis H. 101
Lillie Madora Shelton 75
Linda Lee 161
Lizzie Ann 163
Lloyd H. 120
Loretta Sue Tyler 52
Louis Berrien 62
Louisa C. 98
Louisa Duncan 149, 262
Louisa F. ? 50
Louisa F. Hayes 117
Louisiana ? 113
Louvester Jefferson Weaver 53
Love 158
Lowell Daniel 145
Lucinda Leona 147
Lucreatia ? 74
Lucy 67
Lucy ? 164
Lucy Ann 158
Lucy Armistead Digges 49-50
Lucy Brown 169
Lucy H. 66
Lucy McBride 158
Lucy T. Marshall 115
Luther Francis 97
Lydia Ann Reynolds 65
Major 53
Major Gustavos 52
Maleana 67
Maleana Jones McKissack 66
Malinda B. Holton 147, 262
Malissa 54
Mamie Ross Pinkston 57
Marcus Orville 67
Margaret 143, 163
Margaret ? 1, 122
Margaret Ann Smith 147
Margaret Bodine 122
Margaret Cornelia Sigler 112
Margaret Dunham 163
Margaret Eveline Newman 117
Margaret Leanna 157
Margaret Mildred Fry 111
Margaret Pendleton Slaughter 120
Margaret S. Lightfoot 112

Margaret Thomas McGowan 58
Margaret Wilson Bragg 50
Maria Frances 134
Maria Matthews 146
Maria Pauline Ryan 74
Marietta Daniels 63
Marilyn Virginia 63
Marquis de La Fayette 121
Marshall 120
Marshall Lynn 65
Martha 27, 48, 107, 132, 255
Martha ? 56
Martha A. 151
Martha A. Barnett 113
Martha Ann 56
Martha Anne 134
Martha D. Sneed 52
Martha Eldridge 131
Martha Fry 133
Martha Frances 120
Martha Jane Hutton 144
Martha Steele 57
Martha Wiggins 62
Martin Percival 150
Mary 4, 34, 36, 50, 64-65, 67, 72, 75, 94, 120, 123, 143-144
Mary ? 48, 50, 69, 163
Mary A. 112, 122
Mary A. Nevill 121
Mary Ann Jones 70
Mary Ann Vaughn 50, 98
Mary Anne 168
Mary Anne ? 168
Mary Armistead Burwell 96
Mary Atkinson 62
Mary Ballou 97
Mary Belle 117
Mary C. Davis 120
Mary Catherine Bible 160
Mary Chew 48, 106, 109, 125, 173-174, 176, 253
Mary Clack 103
Mary D. 62
Mary E. Hurst 58
Mary E. Miller 116
Mary Elizabeth Bennett 161
Mary Ella 97
Mary Ella Snider 55

LIGHTFOOT (Continued)

Mary Frances Barnes 122
Mary Frasee 121
Mary Gordon McAlister 71
Mary Hawkins 121
Mary Hedger 122
Mary J. 70, 164
Mary Jane 57
Mary Lee Carney 51
Mary Louisa Colvin 149
Mary Lou Hobby 63
Mary M.C. 134
Mary Maxey 67
Mary Mayberry 55
Mary Munford 48
Mary Nell Bailey 63
Mary Shawan 146
Mary Stone 53
Mary Turner Jones 111
Mary Virginia Smith 99
Mary Warner Lewis 99
Mary Washington Minor 101
Mary Wheeler 168-169
Mary Williams 52
Matilda Coston 53
Matilda Elizabeth van Nuss 122
Matthew 167-169
Matthias 55
Mattie Claire Gano 66
Mattie Tweedy 66
Maxey Bell 67
Maxie J. ? 62
McCall 143
Merlin Lee Roy 64
Milburn 52
Mildred 95, 257
Mildred Delany 146, 165
Mildred Howell 95-96
Mildred McGill 51
Milley Delaney 262
Minerva Audrey 157
Minerva Tuberville 74
Minnie 75
Minnie E. 57
Mittiebelle Ross 151
Mittie Vashtie Hatley 53
Millie ? 160
Montgomery 143

Morgan C. 51
Mort 145
Moses Edward 64
Naly 259
Nancy 49
Nancy B. Callarman 112
Nancy E. 122, 164
Nancy Elizabeth Woodside 158
Nancy Guerrant 98
Nancy Jane 163
Nancy W. Henderson 134
Nannie Rose 160
Nannie Snoddy 97
Nannie Tallulah 57
Nathaniel Lander 116
Nellie Hamilton 74
Nellie Smith 158
Newt 160
Nicholas 49, 55-56
Nimrod C. 151
Nomie Ellender Stephens 64
Nora Alston 51
Nora Edith 150
Ola Mae Batcheller 145
Opal L. ? 120
Osa T. Smith 164
P. Augustus 151
Patricia Alene Hagin 64
Patsy Rhodes 70
Paulina Ann 146
Pearce 144
Pendleton Goodrich 120
Penelope Holton 61
Peterson B. 70
Philip 6, 11, 34, 36, 49, 56, 60-
61, 69, 89-90, 92-96, 99-100, 103,
107, 111, 115, 127, 130-131, 163-
164, 253-257, 263
Philip, the Immigrant 12, 16, 40-
41, 43, 89-90, 96, 262-263
Philip Benjamin 62
Philip C. 52
Philip F. 112
Philip H. 58, 113
Philip John 98
Philip Lewis, M.D. 99-100
Philip Malcolm, M.D. 57
Philip T. 116

LIGHTFOOT (Continued)

Philip W. 98
Phoebe Butler 164
Polly Shawhan 263
Prescilla 54
Presley G. 151
Priscilla 107, 255
Priscilla Margaret 111
Rachel Atkinson 61
Rachel Cena Pearson 121
Rebecca 34, 36
Rebecca Ellen Carmichael 56
Rebecca Hunt 151
Rebecca Reynolds 116
Reed Norvel 64
Ressie Shrewsbury 116
Reuben 112-113
Reuben Edward 136
Rhetta Whitson 51
Richard 24-25, 27, 33-37, 39, 56,
58, 62, 143, 165, 167
Richard, Reverend 2, 12, 16, 23-
27, 30-31, 33, 90
Richard Earl 52
Richard Lee 164
Richard Neal 57
Richard P. 117
Richard Pendleton 118
Richard T. 117
Richard William 58
Rita Daniel 160
Robert 26, 34, 36, 143, 257
Robert Andrew, Dr. 144
Robert Armistead 98
Robert D. 59
Robert Duncan 66
Robert Harrison 121
Robert Hunter 151
Robert James 74
Robert L. 75, 159
Robert Malcolm, M.D. 57
Robert Ray 145
Robert Scott 162
Robert Slaughter 113
Robert W. 66, 122
Robert Walton 56
Roberta Beverly 100
Rosa 158

Rosalie B. 100
Rose 24, 27, 35
Roy 63-64, 117
Roy Faulton 63
Ruth Newman 168
Salina Wesley Crew 53
Sallie 57, 144
Sallie B. 66
Sallie Lee 67
Sallie M. ? 149
Sallie Martena Johnson 145
Sallie Stuart 53
Sally Ballou 97
Samuel 27, 160, 168-169
Samuel Arthur 163
Saphrona E. 151
Sara Elizabeth Adams 54
Sara Elizabeth Barrow 54
Sara Jane Guthrie 53
Sarah 24, 30, 52, 99, 101, 168-
169
Sarah ? 2, 168
Sarah A. ? 158
Sarah Allen 65
Sarah Ann Hobson Mathews 150
Sarah Ann Jouett 66
Sarah Bee Ross 100
Sarah Catherine 158
Sarah E. 164
Sarah E. Harshberger 62
Sarah E. Pate 117
Sarah E. Stockwell 144
Sarah Kendall 143, 263
Sarah M. 70
Sarah Savin Bernard 99
Sarah Short Steward 96
Sarah Snider 55
Sherod 65
Sherry 257
Sherwood 4-5, 11, 48-49, 55-56,
62, 64, 79, 105
Shirley Ann 54
Sid 119
Sophronia Jenny Mims Snider 55
Sophronia Miller 116
Stephen 249
Sue 65
Sue M.E. Turner 130, 136

LIGHTFOOT (Continued)

Susan 67, 136
Susan Ann ? 121
Susan Ann H.M. Franklin 134
Susan D. Hopper 146
Susan J. Jones 112
Susan L. 151
Susan M. 66, 112
Susan M. Elliott 113
Susan M. Lowe 53
Susanna 107, 164, 255
Susannah Colvin 157, 255
Susannah Elizabeth Slaughter
110, 127
Susannah Hurley 103
Susannah Smith 163, 263
Synathia 164
T.W. 151
Tabitha Slaughter 114
Tarpley 6
Temperance Jordan McKinnon
74
Teressa 158
Terry Ellen Myers 161
Theodore 149
Theodore N. 149
Thomas 2, 4-6, 66, 68, 73, 79,
149, 165, 167-168, 249, 255
Thomas A. 65
Thomas Benjamin 64
Thomas Benton 147
Thomas Chenoweth 67
Thomas Eldridge 66, 131
Thomas H. 70
Thomas James 62
Thomas Jefferson 74
Thomas M. 51
Thomas O. 75
Thomas Reese 71
Thomas W. 255
Thomas Walker 138
Thornton 122
Tommis 54
Vader T. 51
Viola Armitta Landes 51
Viola Mae 158
Violette McBryde 63
Virgil Ira 51

Virginia 130
Virginia Dorsey 135
Walker 130
Wallace Lucius 74
Waller 117
Walter 52
Warren 64
Washington Marion 163
Wesley 55
Whiting Pomeroy 161
Whiting Rockwell 161
Wilford Ungles 157
William 1, 3, 5-6, 13, 26, 34, 36,
39-40, 50-51, 60, 62, 64, 70, 92,
95-98, 122-123, 125-127, 130,
139, 143, 146, 151, 158, 164, 176-
177, 254-259, 263
William Allen 97
William B. 101, 263
William Bennett 147
William Bernard 100
William C. 72
William Claxton 50
William D. 60, 257
William Edwin 71
William Eldridge 131
William Estr 53
William Everett 62
William Fry 114
William G. 121, 257
William Goodrich 120
William H.F. 134
William Harrison 122
William Henry 67, 145
William Henry F. 134
William Homer 151
William Howell 96
William J. 74
William L. 146
William Logan 163
William M. 65, 122
William Marston 49-50
William O. 75
William Pendleton 117
William Philip 62-63
William S. 70, 164
William Stowers 157
William T. 53, 70

LIGHTFOOT (Continued)
William Talley 57
William Thomas 74
William Wallis 118
Willie Pearl Richardson 54
Winifred 161
Worth 151
LIGHTFOOTE
Anne 1
Francis 1
John 250
LIGHTFOT, *William 1*
LIGHTFOTE, *William* 1
LIKES, *William* 144
**LINE of DESCENT of RALPH,
LORD STAFFORD** 228
LINEAGE of JOHN de LACIE
225
LINUS, the Martyr 244
LIONEL, Duke of Clarance 247
LISOURS, *Albreada Lacie* 225,
228
LITHFOT, *Henry 1*
**LITTLE FORK CHURCH in
CULPEPER COUNTY** 108
LITTLEDALE, *Joseph* 260
LITTLEPAGE, *Captain 11-12,
106*
LITWINDE of Carinthia 231
LLARIAN 243
LLEUVER MAWR (Lucius the
Great) 233, 244
LLEWELYN the GREAT 224
LLEYN (Linus) 244
LLYFEINYDD 243
LLYR (King Lear) 243
LLYWARCH 243
LOCK
Amelia Ross Lightfoot 100
Leonard Evans, M.D. 100
LOCKETT
Basil L. 151
Elkin Lightfoot 151
LOCKWOOD, *Frank* 122
LOGAN
James D. 150
Theodosia M. Lightfoot 150
LONG, *Captain* 261

LONGESEPEE
Emeline 223
Stephen 223
William 223
LONGSWORD, *William* 232
LOOMAN
Joanna Marie Lightfoot 145
Reason 145
LOTHAIRE, Earl of Germany
237
LOUDER
Daisy Lightfoot 51
Harry 51
LOUIS I, the Debonaire 231, 237
LOUIS of France 196, 208, 212,
223, 239
LOUIS of Germany 231
LOUIS the Dauphin 202-203, 206-
206, 208, 210, 214, 218
LOVAINE, *Matthew* 220
LOWE, *William* 53
LUD 233
LUDWELL
Colonel 11
Philip 45, 190
LUITGARDE of Cleves 238
LUNCEFORD
Lillian Lightfoot 51
Wyath 51
LYTEFOOTE, *John* 250
MacDONAL
Alan 219
Margaret 219
MacLEAN
Fitzhugh 135
Virginia Dorsey Lightfoot 135
MACHAM, *Mr.* 26
MACON
Sarah Woodson 68
William 68
MADDOX
Frances Jane Garvey 120
John 120
MAGISTER PALATII 236
MALET
Mabel Basset 207
William 197, 199, 207
MALONE, *Roy W.* 162

MANDEVILLE, *Avisa Meullent*
211
MANN
  Alice Irene 122
  Arthur E. 122
  Beverly Fae Whipple 122
  Earl E. 122
  George Walter 122
  Hannah Tremlin 122
  Harrison H. 122
  Ira 122
  Judy Fae 122
  Mary Ellen Lightfoot 122
  Ralph Edward 122
  Sarah Lightfoot 122
  Walter Goodrich 122
MANOR
  ? 62
  Sarah E. Lightfoot 62
MARCOMIR IV, King of
Franconia 235-236, 245
MARCUS
  Daniel 72
  Mary 72
MARGUERITE, *Elizabeth Angela*
248
MARIE, Countess of Ponthieu 239
MARIUS (Meric) King of Britain
233, 235, 242, 245
MARRABLE, *John* 89
MARRIAGE CONTRACT of
WILLIAM LIGHTFOOT &
ELIZABETH BARROW 177
MARSHALL
  Alice Fortibus 210
  Roger, Capt. 77-78
  Walter 206, 226
  William 194, 197, 200, 202-203,
  207, 210, 212, 219, 226
MARSHE, *Thomas* 25
MARTIAN, *Elizabeth* 247
MARTIN
  John G. 132
  Mr. 86
MARY LIGHTFOOT by JOHN
WOLLASTON 102

MASE
  Catherine W. Lightfoot 133
  John 133
MASON
  Hugh, Dr. 101
  John 139
  Rosalie Virginia Lightfoot 101
MATILDA of England 231, 238,
246
MATILDA of Northumbria 225
MATILDA of Scotland 238
MAUD of Flanders 238
MAULDIN, *Richard* 107
MAURY
  ? Amon 133
  ? Buckerstowe 133
  Benjamin 133
  E. Grant 133
  James, Reverend 133
  John S. 133
  Mary Ann Fontaine 133
  Mary Walker 133-134
  Matthew 133
  Matthew W. 133
  Reuben Edward 133
  Susan Frances 133
  Susan Lightfoot 133
  Thomas Walker 133
  William A. Wirt 133
MAXEY, *S.B., General* 67
MAY
  Anne Lightfoot 169
  Henry 169
McAFEE
  Mildred Grady Bohon 113
  William C. 113
McBRIDE
  John 158
  Mary McCarty 158
McCALLISTER
  John 48
  Mary Lightfoot 48
McCAULEY
  Aneta Marguerite Lightfoot 121
  Kenneth Irwin 121
McCLAY
  Alice Louise Lightfoot 121
  Robert James 121

McCOY
Emmie Elesiff Lightfoot 63
Frances Ann 63
Francis Steger 63
Timothy Charles 63
McCRADY
Catherine 147
John 147
McCULLY
Andrew 155
Hazel Alberta Nicodemus 155
McCURDY
Billy Robert 155
Jack Richard 155
Walter Raymond 155
McDOWELL
John G. 73
Martha Ann Jones 73
McELHANEY
Frances Lightfoot 162
Robert LaFayette 162
McFARLAND, John Porter 73
McGAVOCK
Ada 116
Ann 116
Anna 116
Cloyd 116
Emma 116
Gordon 116
Lander 116
Mary Lightfoot 116
Robert 116
Rosina 116
Thomas C. 116
McGEE
Janice Leona Lightfoot 64
Janice Michele 64
Ki Alane 64
Larry Wayne 64
McGILL
Cora Alice Townsend 51
Ernest H. 51
McGOWAN
Mary Louise Cunningham 58
Thomas F. 58
McKELLAR
? 62
Annie Belle Lightfoot 62

McKINDLEY
Joseph M. 263
Matilda Webster 263
McKINLEY
Nancy Lightfoot 164
William 164
McKINNON
Neill 74
Sarah Raines Mitchell 74
McKISSACK
Archibald 66
Susan Harrison 66
McNEELY, J.W. 58
MEADOWS
Ann Kathryn 155
James Manton 155
Jeffrey Manton 155
Jon Mac 155
Jon Patrick 155
Marilee McCurdy 155
Marsha Mosley 155
Myrna Ruth Parnell 155
Susan Elizabeth 155
MEIRION 243
**MEMORIAE of RICHARD
LIGHTFOOT** 23
MERIWETHER, Francis 180
MERRIWEATHER, Mr. 12
MEROVEE, King of France 246
MESCHINES, Lucia Tailbois
232-233
MESSENGER
Asa 68
Nancy Ann Lightfoot 68
METCALFE
Ann 180
John 181
Richard 179-180
METROULAS
Basil 161
Dorothy Fay Myers Lightfoot
161
MIDDLETON, Arthur 158
MILLER
Annette Victoria Lightfoot 116
John 68
Nancy Jane Stillman 116
Narcissa W. Lightfoot 68

MILLER (Continued)
Peter S. 116
Roy 153
William 116
MILLS, Henry, Sir 185-186
MILTENBERGER
Charles Eliot 137
Delores Shepherd 137
Dorothy Zelle Gordon 137
Ellen Clendenin 137
George Kerr 137
George Kerr Gordon 137
Henry Bryan 137
Lynn Barbara Kreuter 137
MINERS
Alice John 185
Alice Mills 185
Anne ? 186
Anne Burgh 186
Catherine Vaughn 186
Elizabeth Thick 186
George 187
Gilbert 187
Harry 186
Joan 185
Joan Vaughan 186
John 186-187
Katherine Gilbert 186
Mabel 186
Margaret Barkley 186
Margaret Vaughn 186
Philip 185, 187
Reginald 186
Richard 185-186
Roger 185-187
Sybil 186
Sybil Baskerville 185-186
Thomas 186
William 186-187
MINGE
John 96-97
Sarah Harrison 96-97
MINOR
Elizabeth 183
Ellenor 183
Frances 183
Jamima Waddy 182, 184
John 181-185, 252-253

Nicholas 125, 177-178, 181-184
Richard J. 263
Stewart 182
Stuart 176
William 183
William Stewart 181-183
MINORS
Anne 184
George 184
Harry 184
Henry 184
John 184
William 184
MISAJON
Carolyn Eugenia Lightfoot 63
Frederick 63
Jasmine Kalani 63
MITCHELL
Harvey 113
Judy Fry Bohon 113
Nathaniel Raines 74
Temperance Jordan 74
MIZENER
Adam Clark 152
Paulina Louisa Parks 152
MONJOY, Alvin 180
MONROE, President 99
MONTBEGON, Olivia 213
MONTE BEGONIS, Maud fitz
Swaine 212
MONTFORT
Agnes Evereux 235
Bertrade 235, 238, 246
MONTGOMERY
Sarah 258
William 258
MONUMENTAL
INSCRIPTIONS of ST. MARY
31
MOORE
Benjamin Wickham, Dr. 60
Clyde Charles 153
Keith 153
Kenneth 154
Louisa Winford Lightfoot 60
Maxine Louise 153
MORCE, David 93
MORGAN 243

MORGAN
Charles 108, 253
G.W. 67
Mattie Lightfoot 67
MORRIS
? 159
Joshua, Reverend 120
Sarah Sterchi 159
MORTIMER
Elizabeth 247
Joan Geneville 223
Roger 223
MORTON
Elwyn W. 160
John 179
Mary Edd Watson 160, 264
MORYSON, Francis 42
MOSBY
? 151
Sallie Lightfoot 151
MOSSOM, David, Rev. Mr. 83
MOUCHETTE
Jacob 61
Susanna Cook 61
MOUNTBATTEN, Philip 248
MOWBRAY
Agnes Clare 203
Avice Albini 207
Isabel Clare 203
MOXLEY, William 177
MUDD, Austin 151
MUNFORD
Ann Stanhope 48
Mr. 9, 49
MUSGRAVE
Isabel Berkeley 222
Thomas 222
MYNORS, Humphrey, Sir 184-185, 187
NABB
Charles 136
Mildred Lightfoot 127, 130, 136
NAPIER
Leroy 75
Mary Lightfoot 75
NELSON
Henry 111
James Josiah 111

Joseph O'Bannion 111
Pamelia T. Creel 111
Philip 111
Susannah Fry Lightfoot 111
Thomas 93-94
Wade 111
NERO 245
NETHERLAND
Anne Williamson 68
Frances 68
John 68
Mary Lightfoot 68
Sarah ? 68
Wade 68
NEVILL, Eleanor 247
NEWHAM, Jonas 260
NEWMAN
Mary S. McQuiddy 115
Thomas V. 115
NEWSOM
Alfred Lander 118
Annastacia Lightfoot 118
Ina Belle 118
Leila May 118
Mary Frances 118
Percy Lee 118
Robert Louis 118
Travis Lightfoot 118
William Waverly 118
NICHOLAS
John, Col. 97
Louisa Carter 97
Robert Carter 254
NICHOLS
J.L. 53
Prusilla Lightfoot 53
Robert 254
NICHOLSON
Elizabeth Lightfoot 2
Francis, Governor 45-46
NICODEMUS
Albert W. 155
Alice Leora Mizener 154
Harry Leroy 155
William Burton 154-155
NOE, George 255

xlix

NORMAN
  Hack   253
  Joseph   259
NORTH, Lord   167
NORTON, Richard   191
NORVELL, William   49
NORVILLE
  John, Sir   220
  Maud Grey   220
NORWOOD
  G.   260
  Henry, Col.   78-79
O'BRIEN, Conor   222
OAKES
  Arlene Heitman   159
  James   159
  Larry James   159
  Leslie Christine Collins   159, 263
ODA of Bavaria   231
ODA of Savoy   236, 246
OLAF I, King of Vestfold   232
OLAF II, King of Jutland   232
OLD KENTUCKY ENTRIES & DEEDS   256
OLDHAM
  E.W.   149
  Theodosia Lightfoot   149
OLIVER
  Eliza Jane Hudson   114
  Rice W.   114
ORDGAR, Earl of Devon   233
ORIGINAL FOUNDATION of the ORIGINAL WHITE HOUSE MANSION   87
ORIGINAL LAND GRANT   129
ORIGINAL SURVEY DONE BY DANIEL BOONE   128
ORRICK
  Edna   148
  Edward C.   148
  Georgia   148
  Mary E. Coppage   148
OSMENT
  Florence Lightfoot   54
  J.E.   54
OTTO, Duke of Saxony   231
PAGE, Matthew   45

PAISLEY, William   79
PARKE
  Daniel   44, 80
  Jane Ludlow   80
PARKER
  Bailor   256
  Martha Fry   256
PARKS
  Derald Dean   156
  Edgel Otis   156
  Evelyn Mae Walling   157
  Evelyn Miranda   156
  Evert J.   156
  Elijah M.P.   151
  Elva Lauvenia Williams   156
  Francis Lee   156
  Ida Lois Brown   156
  Ivan Evert   156
  Lyle Elburn   156
  Mary L. Lightfoot   151
  Minnie Dungy   156
  Normadean Moody   156
  Sarah Jane Dobbins   155
  Wilford T.   155
  William Alfred   155
PARSLEY
  Alonzo   157
  Ed   157
  Jeannette Kirk Lightfoot   157
  Laura May Lightfoot   157
PATE, Minor E.   116
PATEN, Mary   253
PATTERSON
  Margaret F. Lightfoot   134
  T., Dr.   134
PAYTON, William   35, 107
PEACOCK
  ?   53
  Lucinda Lightfoot   53
PEAY
  Austin   137
  Austin Lightfoot   137
  John   137
  Mildred Turner   137
  Peachy Walker Speed   137
PEDIGREE of HANNAH LIGHTFOOT   167

1

PEDIGREE of the DESCENT of
HER MAJESTY QUEEN
ELIZABETH 245
PEDIGREE of the PHILLIPS
FAMILY 26
PEEPLES
  ? 61
  Mary Cook 61
PEIRCO, Joseph 177
PEMBRUGGE
  Arabella Harcourt 219
  Fulke, Sir 219
PENDLETON
  Edmund 262
  James 3
  John L. 99
PENDLETON COUNTY
KENTUCKY MARRIAGE
RECORDS 1700-1843 262
PENQUITE
  Helen Marie Hack 134
  Joseph 134
  Minerva Vandervort 134
  Robert 134
  Stella May Wood 134
  Walter 134
PEPIN 236-237, 246
PEPIN le BREF, King of France
237
PEPIN the SHORT 236, 246
PEPIN, Lay Abbott 246
PERCIE, Alice fitz Gilbert 227
PERCY
  Henry 214
  Margaret 247
PEREDUR 243
PERKINS, Elisha 253
PETITION BY COLONEL
THOMAS SLAUGHTER 126
PETITION of the
INHABITANTS of the NORTH
WEST SIDE of the BLUE RIDGE
MOUNTAINS 107
PETITIONS AGAINST
IMPOSTS, 1668 5
PETLOW, James 107

PETTYJOHN
  Geraldine Lightfoot 135
  Joseph C. 135
PHARAMOND, King of
Westphalia 236, 245
PHELPS
  ? 62
  Eliza Ammandy Lightfoot 62
PHILIP of France 201, 204
PHILIPPA of Hainault 247
PHILLIPS
  Augustine 35
  Francis, Esq. 26, 30, 34, 36
  George 35
  Jane 35
  Joane Houghton 26, 34
  John 35-36
  Mary 35
  Olive Sawyer 26, 34-35
  Philip 35
  Stephen 35
  William 26, 34
PHILIPOT, George 260
PICTURE of EDITH ELLEN
LEWIS WILLIAMS 266
PIERCE, William 258
PINKSTON
  Capitola Haden 57
  William F. 57
PIPPIN
  Audrey Alice Lightfoot 51
  Basil 51
PITT, Younger William 167, 170-
171
PLACIDA 234
PLANTAGENET
  Geoffrey 238, 246
  Hameline 201
  Phillipa 247
PLATT, Bernard 259
PLOWMAN, Richard 26
POINDEXTER
  Armistead 56
  Christian 109
  Edwin 55
  Frances 56
  Frances Lightfoot 55
  George 55

POINDEXTER (Continued)
George Benskin 55
James 55
John 109
Lightfoot 55
Parke 56
Robert 55
Sarah Parke 55
Susanna Marston 55
Susannah 56
POININGS, *Eleanor* 247
POLLARD, *Robert* 130, 136
POMEROY
Olive Celesta Babcock 161
Whiting Griswold 161
POND, *Samuel* 89
PONTHIEU, *Agnes* 238
POPE
Ann Duncan 176
Humphrey 177, 184
Lawrence 184
Thomas 176
POPE CLEMENT V 221
POPE INNOCENT III 199
PORTEUS
Mildred 248
Robert 248
POTTER
T. 133
Martha Maury 133
POWELL
Ambrose 126
James 260
POWER
James 81
Molly 81
POYE
Billye 150
Brenda Lee 150
Leo 150
Patricia Ann 150
PRICE
John 256
Philpott 186
Sterling 66
PRINCE ANDREW of Greece
248
PRINCE DAVID 219

PRINCE LLEWELLYN 212
PROGENS, *R.* 253
PUDENS, *Rufus* 244
PURDIE & DIXON'S GAZETTE
3
PUTER
Eliza Fry 256
Thomas 256
PUTNELL, *Peter* 69
QUEEN BOADICEA 242
QUEEN CATHERINE of
Bragariza 26
QUEEN ELIZABETH II 248
QUINCEY
Hawise Keveliok 218, 225, 232
Helen MacDonal 219
Margaret Bellemont 208, 218,
225, 231-232
Maud St. Liz 225
QUINCY
Orabilis Mar 225
Roger 219
RAE, *Robert* 261
RAMBO
Jincy Stone 69
Lawrence 69
RANDOLPH
Betty Lightfoot 262
Beverley 92, 96, 262
Elizabeth Beverley 96
Elizabeth Lightfoot 92, 96
John 254
Peyton 254
Richard, Colonel 261
Tom 9-10
William, Colonel 96, 262
RANGE, *John* 251
RANSDELL
Margaret Barrow 177-178
Wharton 178
RANULPH the RICH 225
RANULPH, Count of Bayeux 232
RAVENSCROFT, *Thomas* 190
RAWSON, *Christopher* 190
RAY
Eliza Lightfoot 123
John 123

RAYNER LODBROK, King of Denmark *235*
RAYNES, *William Burton* *249*
READ
  Benjamin 93-94
  Gwyn 94
  James 66
  Jane Norvell 66
  Mildred 247
READE
  George, Colonel 247
  Robert 247
  William 183
REAGAN
  Chester H. 148
  Helen Orrick 148
REDDING, *Paul 156*
REED
  Frank 65
  Henry 66
  Kate 66
  Mary 65
  S. Emma Reid 65
  Sylvanus 65-66
REEVES
  Caroline Donaldson Lightfoot 71
  Edwin Lightfoot 71
  Frank Clyde 71
  John Richard 71
  Margaret Caroline 71
  R.L., Dr. 71
REID
  Ann 66
  B. 65
  Felix Calloway 71
  James M., Dr. 65
  Mary Belle King 71
  Mary Katherine 71
  Ruth 66
  Sarah Ann Lightfoot 65
  Sarah Lightfoot 71
  T. 65
  William S. 66
RENAUD, Count de Roucy *237*
REPITON, *Joseph 50*
REX, *George 172*

REYNOLDS
  Berneice Sanderson 65
  Cenoria Lightfoot 100
  J.F. 65
  John 116
  Joshua, Sir 95, 171
  Mariah Brooks 116
  William 100
  William, Mrs. 95
RHUN *243*
RICHARD I, Duke of Normandy
200-201, 203, 208, 212, 227, 232, 235, 238
RICHARD II, Duke of Normandy
232, 235, 238
RICHARD III, Duke of Normandy
232, 239
RICHARD LIGHTFOOT LINEAGE CHART *14-15*
RICHARD, Count d'Evereux *235*
RICHEY
  Tilitha Lightfoot 114
  James H. 114
RIDDELL
  George 263
  Margaret Colvin 263
RIDDLE
  Ann M. Lightfoot 157
  Nancy Lightfoot 263
  Robert 157, 263
RIDLEY, *Francis 35*
RILEY
  Craddock 73
  Henry 35-36
ROBB
  Ada Randolph 101
  Augusta Turner 101
  Fannie Bernard Lightfoot 101
  Robert 101
  Robert Gilchrist, Capt. 101
  Turner 101
ROBERT II *224, 238*
ROBERT of Normandy *238*
ROBERT the PIOUS *231*
ROBERT, Count of Vermandois
246

ROBERTS
Benjamin 3, 126, 253
Celia Lightfoot 256
Charles 98
George 253
Henry 256
John 130, 136, 253
Virginia Nicholas Lightfoot 98
ROBINSON, Captain 261
ROGERS, Mr. 10
ROGERTS, John 105
ROGNVALD 232
ROLLO, Duke of Normandy 232
RONCO
Atillio 159
Mary Garofani 159
ROOS, Isabel Bruce 209
ROPER
Edward V. 152
Esther Irene Baker 152
RORIC SLINGEBAND, King of
Denmark 234
ROSCOW, Jimmy 10
ROSEWELL
Philippa Phillips 36
William, Esq. 36
ROSS
John 256
Mary Fry 256
Richard 79
ROSSEN, John 258
ROSSON, Jeremiah 256
ROTRUDE 236, 246
ROUCY, Ermentrude 237
ROUTT
Nancy B. Colvin 263
Riley 263
ROWLAND
James T. 113
Mary Hannah Bohon 113
ROYESTON
Caroline E.B. Lightfoot 135
Mary Lightfoot 135
Mildred Martin 135
Richard Cary, Col. 135
**RUBBING of RICHARD
LIGHTFOOT MEMORIAL** 22

RUBRECHT
Amelia Emily Lightfoot 157
Jacob 157
RUCKER, Thomas 258
RUFFIN, Robert 103
RUFING
Jo Anne Byrne 152
John Joseph 152
Norman 152
RUNIONS, Robert 86
RUSH
Sarah W. Minor 263
William P. 263
RUSSELL
Mrs. 11
Nancy Middleton 158
W. 252
RUTH 242
SAINT PAUL 244
SAMM, John 251
SAMUELS
Frances Lightfoot 48
Nathaniel 48
SANDERS, Thomas 253
SAWYER
Edmund, Sir 26, 34
George 26, 34-35
Robert, Sir 34
SAYE, Alice Cheney 210
SCARBURGH, Charles 44
SCOTT
John 107, 224
Joseph 182
Robert 255
SCRUGGS
? 98
Virginia Carter Nicholas Lightfoot
98
SEAGRAVES, John 220
SELF
Annie Garland 97
Frank 97
SELYS HEN 242
SENTERFIT
? 75
Ella E. Lightfoot 75
SEXTON, Peter 189
SHACKELFORD, John, Dr. 144

SHARP
Alf   149
Mary Lightfoot   149
SHELTON
Mattie A.   75
Richard   260
SHEPPARD
Charles Richard Wilton   59
David   59
David Wingfield Jackson   59
Lovey R. Edge   59
Melissa Temperance   59
Philip Hutson   59
Sarah Jane Edge   59
Sophronia V.R. White   59
Temperance Lightfoot   59
Wiley Parks   59
William F.   59
SHERWOOD, Philip   41
SHIP PASSENGER LISTS   250
SHORT
Griffin   73
Martha Dameron   73
Samuel   253
SHUCK
Annie Lightfoot   113
Elizabeth M. Lightfoot   113
Henry   113
SHURTZ
Carol Ann Walker   154
Jarrod Wayne   154
Olivia Ann   154
Ronnie Lewis   154
SIBERT
? Wilmore   60
David   60
Elizabeth Cook   60
John David, Reverend   60
SIGERMERUS I   236
SIGURD RING   235
SIGURD SNODOYE, King of
Denmark   235
SIMON, Earl   220
SISCO
Arlie Louis   64
Carolyn Ann   64
Margaret Jeraldine Lightfoot   64
Stephen Dale   64

SLAUGHTER
Anne Lightfoot   109
Betty Poindexter   109
Cadwallader   110
Elizabeth Suggett   109
Frances Anne Jones   109
Francis   3, 108-110, 126, 251,
258
James   126
John   109, 126
Lucy Slaughter   110
Margaret Ransdell   110
Mary Smith   110
Mildred Coleman   109
Philip   256
Reuben   109
Robert   3, 107, 109-110, 120,
251, 256, 259
Sarah Coleman   109
Thomas   126-127, 176, 251
SMITH
Alice   159
Amanda Fry   256
Annie Lightfoot   159
Arthur   159
Augustine   107, 251
Bella Fry   256
Daniel, Colonel   257
Delia ?   99
Elizabeth Lightfoot   72
Frances Dora   248
George   99
Horace   256
John   24, 89, 108, 159, 247, 257,
261
Julian Eldridge   97
Mildred   248
Morton   67
Nathaniel   72
Nicholas   179
Oswald   248
Robbie   159
Rogers Morris   257-258
Sallie   159
Sallie Blanche Lightfoot   97
Washington   256
William   253
Winifred   159

SMITH (Continued)
Wooten Lightfoot 67
SOMERI, Nicole Aubigny   228
SOULTHORPE, Anthony   252
SPEER
Cecil 154
Joe 154
Pearl Gladys Brown 154
Robert Eugene 154
SPEERS
Henry 122
Nancy Jane Lightfoot 122
SPENCE
? 133
John 184
Maria Lightfoot 133
SPENCER
Edward 176
William 250
SPOTSWOOD, Robert 251
ST. ARNOLPH. Bishop of Metz
236, 246
ST. CLOTHILDE of Burgundy
236, 246
ST. CYLLIN, King Siluria 244
ST. HILLARY, James 227
ST. JOHN, Robert 213
**ST. LAWRENCE PARISH
RECORD** 30
ST. LIZ, Bernard 232
ST. MAUR
Ellen Zouche 223
Nicholas 223
**ST. PETER'S PARISH VESTRY
& REGISTER** 42, 45
ST PIERRE, Urian 228
ST. TIMOTHY 233
STAFFORD
Edmund 228
Margaret Audley 228
Margaret Bassett 228
Ralph 228
STANHOPE, Captain 12
STANTON
Jno. W. 256
Lizzie Fry 256
William 126

STEGALL
A.S. 71
Daisy Lightfoot 71
STEPHANIE 238
STEPHENS
Minnie C. Lightfoot 53
Newell 53
William Marcus Jasper 64
Zenomie Brown 64
STERCHI
Carrie Lightfoot 159
Eugene 159
Fred 159
Fred S. 159
Robin 159
Roy N. 159
Willard 159
STERNE
David T.W. 263
Harriett Minor 263
STEVENS
James 259
Joseph 258-259
STINSON
Alice Evalyn Brown 153
Alvin 153
Clifford Alvin 153
Edward Warren 153
James Monroe 153
STITH
John 43
William 96
STOCKWELL,, John 144
STOKE BRUERNE CHURCH
28
STONE
Abigail Jordan 69
Abner 69
Daniel 255
David 69
Emily Moore Hill 69
Frances Fowler 69
Harriett ? 69.
Henry 69
Jesse 69
John 179-180
Martha Frazier 69
Martha Johnson 69

STONE (Continued)
Phebe Price 69
Sarah ? Fleet Walker 180
Sarah Wallace 69
Susannah 69
Susannah Lightfoot 69
Thomas 69
STRADA the FAIR 234
STRAYER
Joseph S. 135
Laura Catlett Lightfoot 135
STROTHER
Ann 258
Benjamin 258
John 255
STUART, *Richard, Col.* 101
STUBBLEFIELD, *George* 253
STUBBS, *Bishop* 211
SUBLETTE
Ann Martha Ringo 110
Harry Ringo 110
James 110
John C. 110
Mary Lou Davis 110
Susan Edzard 110
SUGGETT, *Edgecomb* 109
SULLY
Barbara May Brooks 150
William H. 150
SUTTON
? 118
Tabitha Frances Lightfoot 118
SVEIDE the VIKING 232
SWANN
Fleming Lightfoot 68
Nancy Neill Wisely 68
Sallie Woodson Macon 68
Thomas Thompson 68
TABOR
Harold Irving 161
Olive Kilburn Lightfoot 161
TACITUS 245
TAILBOIS
Anne 247
Lucia 233
TAILOR, *John* 39

TALBOT
Edmond, Sir 224
Jane Holland 224
TALIAFERRO, *John* 107, 252-
253
TAOLLEFER, *Isabel* 238
TAPPAN
David Howard 152
Jerome 152
Maryln Jean Byrne 152
TARLETON
Polly Bernard Lightfoot 100
Robert 100
TARPLEY
Blanche Lightfoot 160
Joe 160
TAYLOR
? 132
Anne 170
David 256
Edward 35
Elisha Lightfoot 256
Elizabeth Digges Lightfoot 50
Frances Thompson Lightfoot 132
Francis 137-138
Francis Henry 132
George 68
John 148
Joseph 161
Judith Field 137
Lightfoot 50
Martha Ann Lightfoot 132
Sharon Kay Myers Lightfoot 161
William 260
William B. 50
Zachary 108
TEELE, *Jane* 252
TEMPEST
John, Sir 224
Mary Holland 224
TEMPLEMAN, *Thomas* 182
TENUANTIUS 233
TEUGED 243
THACKER, *Chichley Corbin, Rev.*
Mr. 80-81
THARP
Evelyn Irene Parks 156
Ira LeRoy 156

THE BARROW FAMILY *176*
THE BRICK *264*
THE CHEW FAMILY *173*
THE DRUIDS *239*
THE DUNCAN FAMILY *174*
THE FRANKISH KINGS *235*
THE LIGHTFOOT HOUSE *91*
THE LINEAGE OF ELEANOR
of CASTILE *238*
THE MINOR FAMILY *181*
THE ORDER or DRUIDS *241*
THE PARSONAGE *29*
THE PLANTAGENETS *239*
THE SECOND "WHITE
HOUSE" *85*
THE SECRET DIARY of
WILLIAM BYRD *8-12*
THE STONE FAMILY *179*
THE WHITE HOUSE MANSION
87
THE WHITE HOUSE MANSION
SPRING HOUSE *86*
THE WILL of EDWARD
BARROW *178-179*
THE WILL of ELIZABETH
PHILLIPS LIGHTFOOT *36-37*
THE WILL of JANE JONES
LIGHTFOOT *25-26*
THE WILL of JOHN
LIGHTFOOT *259*
THE WILL of JOHN
LIGHTFOOT, ESQUIRE *35-36*
THE WILL of JOHN MINOR
183
THE WILL of NICHOLAS
MINOR *181-182*
THE WILL of REVEREND
RICHARD LIGHTFOOT *24-25*
THE WILL of ROBERT
LIGHTFOOTE *1*
THOMAS
 Anne Slaughter 110
 Edward, Jr. 110
 Edwin C. 70
 Joseph 252
 Susannah Beall 110
THOMPSON
 ? Thurston 131

 Camilla 131
 Caroline 131
 Cathy 268
 Elizabeth 131
 Elizabeth Howison 131
 *Elizabeth Marshall Tompkins
 131*
 Elizabeth Massie 131
 Frances Thornton 131
 Francis 131
 John 131
 Mildred 131
 Philip Rootes 131
 Sarah Wigglesworth 131
 Thomas Howison 131
 William 131
 William Lightfoot 131
THORNTON
 Anthony 253
 John 252
THRAILKILL
 Charity Adams 164
 David 164
THYRA *235*
TOMPKINS
 George F. 59
 Nancy Ann Sheppard 59
TONATIUS, *Ferreolus 236*
TONEBRUGE, *Adeliza Clermont*
227
TRAVERS
 Daniel 118
 Rawleigh 180
 Roberta Lightfoot 118
TRIPLETT, *Thomas 126*
TUCK, *Edward 7*
TUCKER
 ? 74
 Ernest A. 54
 Gracie Irene Lightfoot 54
 Mary 248
 Rosa Lee Lightfoot 74
TURNER
 *ElizabethLightfoot 34, 37, 165,
 263*
 James 258
 John 34, 37
 Thomas 165, 263

TUTT, *Richard 252*
TYSON
  Gilbert 214
  William 214
ULRICH von EURIKON *237*
UNDERDOWN, *Thomas 260*
UTHER PENDRAGON, King of
England *234*
VAIL
  ? 101
  Mary Lewis Lightfoot 101
VALENTINIAN III *234*
van BIBBER, *John, Captain 257*
VARNON
  Dorothy Lightfoot 54
  E.M. 54
VAUGHAN
  George 253
  Watkins 186
VAUGHN
  ? 52
  Sarah Lightfoot 52
VENABLE, *? 54*
VENISSA *233*
VENISSA JULIA *242, 245*
VERE
  Adeliza Tonebruge 227
  Hawise Quincey 218
  Isabel Bolebec 210
VERICA *246*
VESTRY & REGISTER from
CULPEPER COUNTY *3*
VINCENT, *William 37*
VIRGINIA COLONIAL
MILITIA *253*
VIRGINIA GAZETTE
ARTICLES *260*
VOLKMAR *95*
WADDY, *Thomas 184*
WADKINS
  Garland 145
  John Wesley 145
  Julia C. Lightfoot 145
  Serene Pruitt 145
WAKE
  Baldwin 224
  John 224
  Margaret Quincey 224

WALKE, *John, Esq. 24*
WALKER
  Brandi Lynn 153
  Clinton Bruce 153
  Dickie Gene 153
  Eddie Dean 153
  Elizabeth Minerva Lightfoot 157
  James 157
  John 55, 180
  Larry Dean 153
  Lydia Kay Donlay 153
  Mary 37
  Mary, Dr. 144
  Tabitha Lightfoot 55
  Thomas, Dr. 133
  Viola Nadine Moore 153
WALLACE
  Nancy Stone 69
  Robert 69
WALLER
  Ann Durrett 115
  Edmund, Reverend 114
  Elizabeth Lightfoot 114
  John 252
  Martha Webster 57
  William 57
WALLIN, *Humphrey, Mrs. 255*
WALTHEOF II *225*
WARD
  James 55
  Martha Lightfoot 55
WARNER
  Augustine, Colonel 247
  Mary 247
WARWICK, *Chatham 171*
WASHINGTON
  Betty 261
  George 49, 60, 82-84, 103, 110,
  126, 247
  John, Major 261
  Lawrence 184
  Martha Dandridge Custis 83-84
WATERS
  Amanda Lightfoot 256
  Frank 256
WATSON
  Bertha Lightfoot 160
  Brinthe Elizabeth Thompson 160

lix

WATSON (Continued)
Henry 160
Hugh Aaron 160
James Ralph 161
Kay Wainscott 160
Larry 160
Lyman Bayard 160
Madison Franklin 160
Ney Franklin 160
Patsy Hensley 160
Ruby Waller 160
Wayman Raleigh 160
Winnie Bess Clark 160
WATTS
Mary Elizabeth Jones 73
William Barnett 73
WEATHERALL, George 126
WEBB, ? 36
WEBER
Daniel 145
Lazetta Strausenback 145
WEBSTER
Amanda 58
Daniel 263
Delia Wood 58
Hannah Forbes 58
James 58
John 58
Lou Jones 58
Mary Jones 58
Nancy Lightfoot 57
Richard Daniel 58
Robert 58
Sally Duke 58
Vienna Tapley 58
William 57
WELLS
Susannah Lightfoot 164, 263
Thomas 164, 263
WESTMORELAND
? 52
Mary Lightfoot 52
WHALEN
Almirah Lightfoot 123
Ann Mariah Lightfoot 123
Bartholomew 123
Patrick 123
WHEELER, Henry 169

WHERCETT, Mr. 125, 181
WHITESIDE
Mary Abby Roberta Lightfoot 162
Richard M. 162
William 261
WHITING, Robert 261
WHITMAN
Clara Eldridge 131
John B. 131
Laura Alice 131
WHITTON
Francis 1
Lucy Lightfoote 1
WICKENS
Richard 24
Robert 24-25
William 24
WIGG, George 261
WILCOX
Ed 96
Frances Kathryn Lightfoot 54
John 261
John W. 54
Murray Wesley 54
WILDER
James 259
Peggy 259
WILKES
Sarah Lightfoot Jones 73
William Usher 73
WILLIAM I, Count de Bourgogne 238
WILLIAM I, Count of Montreuil 238
WILLIAM II 218
WILLIAM III, Count of Alencon 238
WILLIAM III, Count of Ponthieu 239
WILLIAM the CONQUEROR 187, 218, 226, 228, 238, 246
WILLIAM the LION, King of Scotland 201, 207, 209, 214, 217
WILLIAMS
Alex 260
Catharine 183-184
Edith Ellen Lewis 263, 265-268

lx

WILLIAMS (Continued)
James   107
James Lazarus   156
Louisa Daniel Jones   72
Lucy L. Bohon   113
Lula Maude Donham   156
Mary Jane Sheppard   59
Merrill   113
Morgan   183
Paul   43
Stanley Albert   265
Thomas   72
William   3
William F.   59
WILLIAMSON
Charlie   63
Ellen   63
James   190
Johnnie   63
Richard   260
WILLIKEN
Sarah Lightfoot   163
Thomas   163
WILLIS, Henry   251
WILMOT
J., Dr.   170-171
Olive   170
WILSON
?   50
Alice Lucile Mann   122
Elias   180
Elizabeth Goodrich   190
Henry   177
John F.   120
Laura Lightfoot   149
Russel   149
Willis   190
WILTON
Anne Ferrers   220
John   220
WINCHESTER
Margaret Tarleton   100
Marshall   100
WINDEBANK
Mildred   247
Thomas   247
WINEBRENNER
Dunsten   123

Lola Lightfoot   123
Trulalee   123
WINSLOW, Beverley   252
WINTERBORNE, John   25
WOLFE
Jacob   56
Margarite Stoudtenmire   56
WOLLASTON, John   102
WOOD
Albion   134
Clifton   134
Elizabeth Snell   134
Jesse   58
Matilda Lightfoot   134
WOODSON
Mary Lightfoot   68
Tarleton   68
Tucker   68
Wade   68
WOODWARD, C.L.   86
WOOTEN
Henrietta Goodall   67
Thomas, Dr.   67
WORMELEY
Christopher   44
Ralph   44
WORMLEY
Carter, Dr.   101
Ellen Bankhead Lightfoot   101
WRIGHT
John   255
Lewis   262
Richard   252
WYATT
Elwin W.   159
Laura Lightfoot   159
YANCEY
Sarah Mitchell   136
Thomas   136
YATES
?   58
Charles   253
Christianna Webster   58
Viola   58
YORKE, William   24
YONGE, Richard, Sir   31
YOUNG
Bunyan   73

YOUNG (Continued)
 Doyle Earl *153*
 Earl L. *153*
 Emily Jane Jones *73*
 Ethel Hope Brown *153*
 Lois Mildred *153*
 Marcella Juanita *153*
 Richard *258*
ZOUCHE
 Alianore Ferrers *224*
 Anne *224*
 Ela *223*
 Ela Longesepee *223*
 Eleanor Seagraves *223*
 Elizabeth *223*
 Maud Bohun *224*
 Millicent Cantilupe *224*

MARY EDD MORTON was born in Whitney, Texas as the seventh of seven children born to Henry and Bertha Lightfoot Watson. She lives at Lubbock, Texas with her husband Elwyn Morton. They have one daughter Dee Ann who lives at Golden, Colorado with her husband Sandy and small son Jacob.

Mary graduated from Midwestern University at Wichita Falls, Texas with a Major in Voice and Minor in Piano. She also received her Masters Degree in the same field at the University of North Texas in Denton, Texas. She is an American College of Musicians faculty member and a member of the Daughters of the American Revolution.

Mary owes all of her music education to her aunt and uncle, Mr. and Mrs. J.T. Rundell of Wichita Falls, Texas, who took her at the age of 17 and put her through college.

She taught public school music in Wichita Falls and Lubbock, Texas for many years and gave private lessons until her recent retirement, to locals in Hillsboro, Texas.

Ellen Williams, a distant cousin, taught her for several years by telephone about her book, *The Lightfoot Family History*. Just before Ellen's death at age 92, she asked Mary to finish her book. It has taken four years to compile all her notes and get them ready for printing.

1593085